AF677452

International Series on Public Policy

Series Editors
B. Guy Peters
Pittsburgh University
Pittsburgh, PA, USA

Philippe Zittoun
Research Professor of Political Science
LET-ENTPE, University of Lyon
Lyon, France

"Based on high-level theory and research, *Public Policy in the 'Asian Century'* is essential reading for everyone interested in the implications of the contemporary rise of China and modernization of other Asian nations for public policy, governance, globalization, and western approaches to political, economic, and social organization. The editors and contributors have fashioned an outstanding volume that provides a deep understanding of what the 'Asian Century' might be and why it potentially may open a new chapter in human civilization. If one had the opportunity to read only a single book on how China and Asia more generally might change the world by mid-century, this would be an excellent choice."

—David H. Rosenbloom, *Distinguished Professor of Public Administration, American University, USA*

"If we view the globe as a planetary palimpsest, we see the traces of deep-rooted, ancient and atavistic systems nudge through both the historic detritus and more recent approaches to governance that overwrite them. As this book explains, the concept of an Asian Century is not so much a reflection of the impending reality, as a completion of the circle; before the rise of the oceanic empires, China remained re-eminent for millennia. And in order to understand that, alongside the rise of other Asian powers, the book skilfully juxtaposes the impact of history, ideology and culture together with the technical and economic innovations harnessed by the huge Asian markets whilst the world tilts eastwards. Asia is disparate, compare China and India to The Maldives and Myanmar to understand the

The International Series on Public Policy - the official series of the International Public Policy Association, which organizes the International Conference on Public Policy - identifies major contributions to the field of public policy, dealing with analytical and substantive policy and governance issues across a variety of academic disciplines. A comparative and interdisciplinary venture, it examines questions of policy process and analysis, policymaking and implementation, policy instruments, policy change and reforms, politics and policy, encompassing a range of approaches, theoretical, methodological, and/or empirical. Relevant across the various fields of political science, sociology, anthropology, geography, history, and economics, this cutting edge series welcomes contributions from academics from across disciplines and career stages, and constitutes a unique resource for public policy scholars and those teaching public policy worldwide.

More information about this series at
http://www.springer.com/series/15096

differences, but this book is an excellent guide to the way in which Asian powers are asserting themselves and what this may mean for understanding public policy in the Asian Century."

—Andrew Massey, *Professor of Politics, University of Exeter, UK*

"This book provides an important and distinctive contribution to the study of public policy and public administration. It does so in multiple ways. First, by effectively combining both Asian and 'Western' intellectual lenses in studying policy and administration in Asia, hence speaking to diverse audiences in a most effective way. Second, by examining in an integrated way policy and administration, as any in-depth knowledge and understanding of one presupposes the other. Third, by looking both to the past, in search of the long-term explanations of distinctive reform trajectories, and to the future, putting in context the 'Asian Century' argument. A must read."

—Edoardo Ongaro, *Professor of Public Management, The Open University, UK*

Sara Bice · Avery Poole · Helen Sullivan
Editors

Public Policy in the 'Asian Century'

Concepts, Cases and Futures

palgrave
macmillan

Editors
Sara Bice
Melbourne School of Government
University of Melbourne
Melbourne, VIC, Australia

Helen Sullivan
Crawford School of Public Policy
Australian National University
Canberra, ACT, Australia

Avery Poole
Melbourne School of Government
University of Melbourne
Melbourne, VIC, Australia

International Series on Public Policy
ISBN 978-1-137-60251-0 ISBN 978-1-137-60252-7 (eBook)
https://doi.org/10.1057/978-1-137-60252-7

Library of Congress Control Number: 2017948252

Cover illustration: Olena Bogadereva/Alamy Stock Vector

Printed on acid-free paper

This Palgrave Macmillan imprint is published by Springer Nature
The registered company is Macmillan Publishers Ltd.
The registered company address is: The Campus, 4 Crinan Street, London, N1 9XW, United Kingdom

Acknowledgements

The editors wish to thank the many MSoG MPPM students and executive education participants who have enthusiastically and intelligently shared their ideas throughout our courses together. Their thinking has greatly influenced our work.

We wish to thank our research assistants, who have provided support at various stages of this book's development, and without whom the volume would be another three years in the making: Ms. Ruby Bell, Ms. Joanna Hanley, Dr. Margherita Matera, Ms. Angela Merriam and Ms. Susan Wright.

Thank you to the team at Palgrave Macmillan for their support, guidance and patience as we brought together far-flung contributors.

The editors thank their loved ones for providing the support, coffee and acceptance that makes any writing task possible.

About this Book

This volume began as an initiative of the Melbourne School of Government (MSoG), The University of Melbourne, Australia, through the School's support of its Public Policy in the Asian Century (PPAC) program. PPAC formed a cornerstone of MSoG Foundation Director Professor Helen Sullivan's vision for the new school when it was launched in June 2013. Since that time MSoG hosted an international conference on PPAC (December 2013), bringing together over 150 experts from around the global to discuss, debate and tease out the critical considerations for how globalisation is transforming the ways we think about, design and implement public policy. The School has also championed discussion of the ideas contained within this volume at other international scholarly forums, especially the International Conference on Public Policy (Grenoble, France, 2013; Milan, Italy, 2015; and Hong Kong, 2016). Professor Sullivan and Dr. Sara Bice developed curriculum on the topic, creating a new course on PPAC for MSoG's Master of Public Policy and Management (MPPM), which has now seen hundreds of future public administrators consider the opportunities and challenges the Asian Century will pose for their roles. PPAC has also been the topic of a range of executive education activities, engaging public servants from countries including Thailand, Australia and Indonesia. The program continues to thrive through research, teaching and knowledge sharing, and this volume marks an important milestone in its development.

Contents

Editors and Contributors

About the Editors

Sara Bice Ph.D. is Co-Director, Research Translation, at the Melbourne School of Government, The University of Melbourne, Australia, where she coordinates the Public Policy in the Asian Century research program. She is President-Elect of the International Association for Impact Assessment. In 2016, Sara was named one of four inaugural Westpac Bicentennial Foundation Research Fellows. Her most recent book, *Responsible Mining*, is available from Routledge.

Avery Poole is Assistant Director of the Melbourne School of Government at The University of Melbourne. Her research explores institutional change in regional organisations, particularly ASEAN; conceptualisations of democracy in Australia and Southeast Asian states; and Australian engagement with Southeast Asia and the Indo-Pacific region. She has a Ph.D. from The University of British Columbia.

Helen Sullivan is Professor and Director of the Crawford School of Public Policy at the Australian National University. Her research and teaching explores the changing nature of state-society relationships including the theory and practice of governance and collaboration, new forms of democratic participation and public policy and service reform.

Contributors

Chad Anderson is Assistant Professor of Public Administration at Incheon National University, Incheon, Korea. He researches urban administration, cultural administration, education and human and labour relations, and has published in Korean and international books and journals. He has a Ph.D. from Incheon National University.

Wolfgang Drechsler is Professor of Governance at Tallinn University of Technology's Ragnar Nurkse Department and currently Visiting Professor at the Lee Kuan Yew School of Public Policy, National University of Singapore. He has a Ph.D. from the University of Marburg and an Honorary Doctorate from Corvinus University Budapest.

Nicholas Farrelly Ph.D., is Deputy Director (Impact and Engagement) at the Coral Bell School of Asia Pacific Affairs, Australian National University and Director of the ANU Myanmar Research Centre. He studies Southeast Asian politics, with an emphasis on Myanmar and Thailand. He is the founder of New Mandala and has undertaken significant field research in Myanmar over the past 15 years.

Marianna Fotaki is Professor of Business Ethics at Warwick Business School. She has published many articles on the marketisation of public services, health inequalities, gender and otherness in organisations and business in society in leading international journals. She has a Ph.D. from the London School of Economics and Political Science.

M. Shamsul Haque is Professor of Political Science at the National University of Singapore. He has published several books and numerous articles in leading international journals. He is the Editor of *Asian Journal of Political Science* and *International Review of Administrative Sciences*. He received Fred Riggs Award for Lifetime Scholarly Achievement in Comparative and International Administration.

Paul H. Jensen is Professor and Deputy Dean of the Faculty of Business and Economics at The University of Melbourne. He is an industrial economist who specialises in the economics of innovation, science and technology policy, and has published in prestigious international journals.

Rutaichanok Jingjit is a government official (trade officer) at the Department of Trade Negotiations, Ministry of Commerce, Thailand.

She has a Ph.D. in Business and Management from Manchester Business School, University of Manchester. Her thesis focused on the issues of organisational change and culture in the context of Thai public organisations undergoing a major reform.

Adrian Kay is Senior Professor in the Institute of Policy Studies, Universiti Brunei Darussalam. Previously, he was Professor of Government at the Crawford School of Public Policy, Australian National University. His major research interests lie at the intersection of international and comparative public policy, with a particular focus on transnational health policy.

Jong Youl Lee is Professor of Public Administration and Dean of Law, Commerce and Public Affairs at Incheon National University, Incheon, Korea. He researches urban administration, policy studies, cultural administration, risk management and is author of numerous texts and articles in Korean and English. He has a Ph.D. from The City University of New York.

Kim Moloney is a senior lecturer in Comparative Public Administration and Public Policy at Murdoch University, Australia. Her research focuses on the intersection of public administration and development administration, and the administrative life of international organizations. She holds a Ph.D. in Public Administration from American University and a MPA from the Maxwell School at Syracuse University.

Lauren A. Palmer is the Policy and Projects Manager at the Australian Council of Learned Academies Secretariat, and an inaugural participant in the EU-Australia Emerging Leaders' Forum. She manages major research and policy projects in areas of strategic importance to Australia. She has a Ph.D. from The University of Melbourne.

Jon Pierre is Research Professor in the Department of Political Science, University of Gothenburg, Sweden and Professor of Public Governance at the Melbourne School of Government, University of Melbourne, Australia. His research focuses on contemporary governance, both in developing governance theory and in empirical research on the changing role of political institutions.

Jill L. Tao is the first international Professor of Public Administration at Incheon National University, Republic of Korea. Her research examines the behaviour of subnational governments, especially as innovators in political and economic behaviour, in addressing issues such as poverty, intergenerational sustainability and resource depletion. She received her Ph.D. in Public Administration from the Florida State University Askew School.

Mark Turner is Honorary Professor at UNSW Canberra and Emeritus Professor at the University of Canberra where he was previously Professor of Development Policy and Management. Mark has undertaken research and consultancy on public sector management, policy and politics in over 20 countries of Asia and the Pacific over a period of 40 years.

Bo Wang is a Lecturer in Public Administration at Guangxi University for Nationalities, Nanning, China. She has published research on Chinese urban development for Korean, Chinese and international journals. She has a Ph.D. from Incheon National University.

Chit Win is a doctoral candidate at the Australian National University. His research focuses on autonomy and transitional legitimacy in Myanmar's legislature. He has written a number of papers in the *Journal of Contemporary Asia*, *East Asia Forum*, *New Mandala* and *Nikkei Asian Review* on the experience of Myanmar's transition.

List of Figures

List of Tables

CHAPTER 1

Introduction

Sara Bice, Avery Poole and Helen Sullivan

The rise of Asia will be a defining feature of the twenty-first century. For certain countries, most notably China, this ascendance will confirm the re-emergence of a dormant global power. For others, like Indonesia, the twenty-first century will mark their entry onto the global stage as influential actors. Over the coming decades the policy and governance decisions taken by non-Western nations will have greater impact and influence beyond their borders. Likewise, Western policy decisions will have unprecedented reach into other nations and cultures. These developments are facilitated by increasingly joined-up transnational governance networks, tightly linked economic markets and progressively fluid cultural exchanges. Cross-border, cross-cultural and cross-political policy

S. Bice (✉) · A. Poole
Melbourne School of Government, The University of Melbourne,
Melbourne, Australia
e-mail: sara.bice@unimelb.edu.au

A. Poole
e-mail: avery.poole@unimelb.edu.au

H. Sullivan
Crawford School of Public Policy, Australian National University,
Canberra, Australia
e-mail: helen.sullivan@anu.edu.au

S. Bice et al. (eds.), *Public Policy in the 'Asian Century'*, International Series on Public Policy, https://doi.org/10.1057/978-1-137-60252-7_1

pollination will also occur through international efforts to address globally relevant 'wicked problems', including climate change, international market regulation, migration, food and energy security, and health epidemics. This dynamic situation prompts this book to ask: What are the defining features, critical approaches, challenges and opportunities for public policy in the Asian Century?

Public Policy for a Rapidly Changing World

By 2050 China is likely to achieve a global economic dominance reflective of its world status more than 300 years ago (Asian Development Bank 2011). In that same year, India is tipped to become the world's fifth largest consumer economy (Ablett et al. 2007). Indonesia's stock exchange has more than doubled in value since 2008, making it the third largest in Southeast Asia (Department of Foreign Affairs and Trade 2012). An estimated 60 per cent of the global population now resides in 'Asia', geographically defined here as the region bounded by Mongolia in the north, Indonesia in the south, Korea in the east, and Afghanistan in the west (following the definition of the *Journal of Asian Public Policy*). By 2030, 66 per cent of the global middle class will live in this Asian region, accounting for 59 per cent of total global consumption, up from 28 per cent and 23 per cent, respectively, since 2009 (Pezzini 2012). Not only will consumption increase, so too will levels of human development and mobility and access to healthcare, social services and education. In China, for instance, five percent of 18–22 year-olds had access to higher education as of 1995. By 2007, that figure had almost quintupled to 23 percent (Mahbubani 2013). These figures clearly signal a global shift in economic, political and even socio-cultural power that suggests the twenty-first century may very well be the 'Asian Century'.

This book reflects on how we define public policy, administration, and governance; what public policy entails; and how it is managed, analysed and implemented, in light of the ascendance of Asia. Through it we explore new concepts, cases and potential futures for public policy, administration and governance. Our contributors initiate a much-needed dialogue about the changing nature of the creation, administration and analysis of public policy. We encourage our readers to reflect on the unconscious biases that may shape their approaches to public policy and emphasise an attitude that questions taken-for-granted concepts and models. It follows that the chapters in this volume aim to unsettle and, in some instances, reset the way we think about what public policy is, how it is made and the ways it is enacted. Our contributors have been encouraged to consider a range of organising questions:

Why have Western models of public policy and administration dominated scholarship and practice, even where non-Western countries may have much lengthier bureaucratic histories? What do we really mean by 'Western/non-Western'? And is it possible to define an 'Asian' approach to public policy and administration? If so, what would such an approach look like? Where are the exemplary cases and how might those working or studying outside of Asian countries better acquaint themselves with others' values and approaches? How can consideration of non-Western values, approaches and cases improve understanding of others while also opening opportunities for improvement of Western principles and practices, and vice versa? How will public policy in the Asian Century change the roles, nature and remit of public administrators? To what extent does globalisation offer an opportunity for novel, shared approaches to public policy concerns? And what might a future of globalised public policy look like?

Limited Engagement, Limited Understanding

This book is motivated in large part by our concern that public policy scholarship has either historically ignored non-Western policy and administration or engaged it primarily as a means of suggesting how Western policy values, ideas or models might be applied in a non-Western context. Within this, we understand public policy to be government sponsored or sanctioned action designed to re-imagine the (social, economic, environmental, political and/or cultural) future by shaping and being shaped by the institutions, agents, resources and conventions of the present.

Our understanding of public administration is similarly broad and adopts a global focus. It is informed by Nilima Gulrajani and Kim Moloney's (2012, p. 78) call for 'public administration with a global perspective', an idea which aims to bridge 'particularism with universalism', making public administration 'a globally inclusive endeavour'. Such global public administration fosters collaborative research organised around geographies, units of analysis, instruments, methodologies or substantive issues transcending vested disciplinary and national interests resulting in a 'rigorous administrative science' (Gulrajani and Moloney 2012, p. 85).

Although there is an increasing amount of comparative public policy scholarship focused on Asia, much of this work remains solely empirically based and focused on single or two-to-three country case studies. Moreover, Western scholars have yet to tap a growing and substantial corpus of public policy, public management and governance literature being produced by Asian colleagues (Su et al. 2013). A recent literature review that we undertook of five leading mainstream public policy journals published between January 2000 and January 2013, found that only 49 of over 2,000 research articles considered issues pertinent to non-Western public policy (Bice and Merriam 2016; Bice and Sullivan 2014). A further 242 articles from the leading comparative public policy journals discussed non-Western public policy. While perhaps an unsurprising result, given the very nature of comparative policy studies, this finding alone suggests a dearth of attention to the existing and growing challenges that globalisation poses for public policy. These findings further suggest a general lack of interest or familiarity concerning Asian nations' policy practices, challenges, opportunities and achievements, at least among many Western policy scholars.

At the same time that Western policy scholars pay scant attention to non-Western policy developments, public policy scholarship is on the rise in Asian countries. In China, for example, public administration is a rapidly growing field, both in size and importance. In the decade between 1998 and 2008, the top six Chinese public administration journals published close to 3,000 articles, more than the combined total of the top eight European journals during the same period (Wu et al. 2013). This represents a massive field of literature and pool of knowledge; one to which few in the West have access. These findings underline the importance of knowledge sharing, translation, and comparative policy studies between Asian nations and the West. It also reminds us that we have a long way to go in reorienting approaches to public policy scholarship and practice. This volume represents a first step in that direction.

So, Is This the Asian Century?

Before any of our opening questions can be addressed, it is important to follow our own advice and question what the terms 'Asia' and 'Asian Century' mean. It is also important to acknowledge that the 'other' we engage through this volume is purposefully an 'Asian', non-Western other. Yet there are many differences and dichotomies we could discuss in an equally fruitful manner. For instance, there is a strong argument to be made for juxtaposition of Western public policy approaches alongside those of the BRIC (Brazil, Russia, India, China) nations. Certainly, there is much to be learned by exploring what public policy in a non-democratic century might look like, privileging the approaches of China and Russia. Questions of how ideological underpinnings of communist thinking might bring together the economic and the normative in different ways are important and we will return to them in our conclusion.

Here, however, we concentrate on 'Asia', while simultaneously acknowledging it as a problematic concept. As an anecdotal example, we regularly facilitate sessions with postgraduate public policy students and public administrators in which we provide participants with a large world map and ask them to shade in the countries they believe constitute 'Asia'. In five years of the exercise and hundreds of maps, the diversity of regions shaded and variety of criteria for why countries are included as 'Asia' are sundry and fascinating. Participants have shaded countries according to their location along the historic Silk Route, based on particular religions or shared cultural values, dependent upon membership in particular international governance organisations or by dint of trade partnerships or governmental affinities. It is not unusual to see the United States, Russia, islands in the Pacific or Australia shaded as part of Asia in these maps. Perhaps Michael Cox sums up the difficulty of defining Asia best when he admits, "We are nowhere near arriving at an Asian Century, in part because the entity we call Asia hardly exists as a collective actor" (Cox 2016).

For our purposes, we explore Asia and the Asian Century as a productive means of encouraging active deliberation about the implications of globalisation for public policy. We also believe these concepts are helpful for bringing together key traditions and ideas about public policy and administration that have informed thinking and practice well beyond Asian borders. This ranges from Weber's use of Chinese traditions for public administration through to particular practices and values common in political economy. Regardless of one's definition of Asia, the concept brings together a variety of systems of governance that foreground the diverse range of options for future public policy and administration, a vision we will turn to in detail in Part III of the book, 'Futures'.

In terms of the 'Asian Century', specifically, it is an idea that first appeared in the late 1980s and is now almost ubiquitous in public analysis of the future balance of global hard and soft power. Perhaps this was most obviously visible in the United States' Obama era focus on a 'pivot to Asia'. Further afield in Australia, a major government white paper attempted to strategically locate the island continent at the centre of an Asian Century (Australian Government 2012). Current Australian government policies prioritise sending young Australians into Asia as a means of building international ties. In the UK, post-Global Financial Crisis austerity measures fuelled public criticism about the apparent lack of attention and alternative analysis concerning the failure of economics. Critics argued that an expanded consideration of options and debates beyond Europe's own temporal and spatial boundaries could have resulted in better connections being made between the crisis and longer standing crises occurring elsewhere (Geddes 2014). Presumably, such broader considerations would have resulted in important lessons that could, perhaps, have achieved happier results for European nations.

Clearly, politicians, public administrators, scholars and others feel that there is merit to considering the implications of an Asian region that is more geo-politically central. But does this mean that the twenty-first century is the Asian Century? Perhaps surprisingly, and despite the title of this volume, we have come to the conclusion that this quibbling over nomenclature does not particularly matter. This is a position we do not take lightly. It is based on our having spent the past several years studying, thinking about, teaching and discussing the possibility of an Asian Century with academic colleagues, public servants, industry representatives, students and civil society, all around the world. From Melbourne to Milan, Hong Kong to Birmingham, we have asked, "Is this the Asian Century? And does it matter?".

First, we have found that asking others, especially those from Western countries, to consider whether this is the Asian Century results in an important reflection upon their own position in the global environment. Like Said's (1978) Orientalist 'other' the very suggestion of juxtaposition against a context different to one's own opens a door to critical consideration. When we ask this question, our audiences typically turn to discuss globalisation and related arguments concerning global divergence and convergence (Beck 1999). Often, these conversations raise difficult considerations about whether globalisation is driving cultural homogeneity or encouraging heterogeneity (Mahbubani 2013). Is globalisation a powerful force for 'good', in terms of greater contact with and affinity for those different to oneself? Or, as the recent rise in nationalist populism in countries including the United States and the UK would suggest, is globalisation the harbinger of the death of the nation-state and with it individual cultures and values?

Globalisation scholars, such as Ulrich Beck (1999), Manuel Castells (2000), Joseph Nye (2002), Thomas Friedman (2005), Martin Wolfe (2004) and Jagdish Bagwhati (2004), each put forward disparate theories about the drivers behind globalisation and its implications. While there is much disagreement among globalisation scholars, there are several core tenets that are agreed upon. First, the importance of science and technology in compressing time and space presents the necessary platform for globalisation. Secondly, most scholars agree that the spread of knowledge and resources made possible by this compression consequently increases the availability and quality of education, furthering human development. Thirdly, globalisation supports a capacity to bridge more diverse spaces and places than ever before. For example, scholars regularly cite the flow of technology to the developing world and the decreasing digital divide. Finally, most globalisation scholars agree that as societies are increasingly networked they are forming more meaningful and influential ties with one-another, a shift described through the analogy of moving from islands to archipelagos (Castells 2000). Each of these core aspects of globalisation holds implications for public policy, ranging from how we define what issues should be addressed by policy through to the daily performance of public administration.

Secondly, asking whether this is the Asian Century forces those concerned about public policy to consider the historical nature of the task at hand. The history of public policy shapes it as much as the current compression of time and space experienced through globalisation. It is important that we acknowledge public policy not as an ahistorical construct but instead as one that has been moulded over time by the values, principles and leaders responsible for its conceptualisation and delivery. What role has history to play in the construct, conduct, implementation and governance of policy and its administration? And how might this encourage us to attend to culture, religion, social mores and norms? In other words, to what extent is public policy temporally, geographically or culturally specific, and does this matter?

Finally, raising the idea of the Asian Century in relation to public policy encourages us to consider the ways in which what we mean by 'public policy' is changing. In our minds, this questioning is inseparable from the growing concern for addressing 'wicked problems'.

References to 'wicked problems' are ubiquitous amongst public policy makers to the extent that the term is at risk of becoming meaningless, or at least disconnected from the precise formulation of its originators (Rittel and Webber 1973). That original formulation describes a special kind of policy problem, one that confounds mainstream public policy analyses and transcends established boundaries of public policy making. Importantly, Rittel and Webber's identification of this new form of policy problem occurred at the same time that globalisation was gathering pace. Rittel and Webber outline 10 primary characteristics of 'wicked problems' (see, Fig. 1).

The pre-eminent qualities of 'wicked problems'—their complexity, uncertainty and divergence—means that attempting to address them requires policy analysts to go beyond the mainstream 'rational-technical' approaches to policy problems to include deliberation and debate amongst a range of actors, not just established experts. This is all the more challenging in a globalised world in which interdependency is undeniable but our institutional architecture is inadequate to the task. Add to this mix the diversity and difference promised by the 'Asian Century', and the need for and difficulty of developing and applying new understandings of how to make and implement policy are obvious.

Today's dominant 'wicked problem' is arguably climate change. Concerns about global warming and the necessity of global action have led political and policy debates for decades. Globalisation, however, has spawned other 'wicked problems' that now vie for policy makers' attention, including responding to the many crises of 'security' (e.g. resources, food, energy and human) and meeting the challenges of large scale migration.

Globalisation also brings with it debates about the existence and application of 'hypernorms'. Defined as 'consistent universal standards', hypernorms are visible through documents like the United Nations Declaration of Human Rights or the OECD Guidelines for Multinational Enterprises. As globalisation scholar Donna Wood (2006) explains, hypernorms play an important role in expanding the responsibilities governments and corporations take on, with clear implications for policy makers. "As this process of identification with common standards continues, it seems inevitable that those 'stretch goals', such as environmental protection, ethical conduct and human rights, will become expectations," Wood writes (2006: 224). For public policy in the Asian Century, hypernorms illustrate our interconnectedness while reminding

1. There is no definitive formulation of a wicked problem: The nature and scope of the problem including its root cause/s is ambiguous and contested.

2. Wicked problems have no stopping rule: Because of interdependencies [endless causal chains] and the absence of a definitive formulation, there is no clear point at which the problem-solver can recognise that his job is done.

3. Solutions to wicked problems are not true-or-false, but good-or-bad: The presence of multiple parties with diverse interests and values means assessments of proposed solutions are normative (good-bad) rather than definitive (true-false).

4. There is no immediate and no ultimate test of a solution to a wicked problem: Because of interdependencies solutions will 'generate waves of consequences' over an extended period of time, the repercussions of which are impossible to accurately calculate.

5. Every solution to a wicked problem is a "one-shot operation": Solutions leave traces that cannot be undone due to the dynamism introduced by interdependencies. As a result, trial and error problem-solving techniques are not possible as the consequences of any action cannot be reversed to re-introduce the original context.

6. Wicked problems do not have an enumerable (or an exhaustively describable) set of potential solutions, nor is there a well-described set of

Fig. 1.1 The multiple dimensions of wicked problems. *Source* Alexander et al. 2015

permissible operations that may be incorporated into the plan: The absence of definitive problem formulations and the dynamic nature of wicked problems militate against the development of a clear and finite list of solutions.

7. Every wicked problem is essentially unique: Despite apparent similarities, '…there are no classes of wicked problems in the sense that principles of solution can be developed to fit all members of a class'. The specific constellation of problem-features and context ensures 'every situation is likely to be one-of-a-kind'.

8. Every wicked problem can be considered to be a symptom of another problem: According to Rittel and Webber successful attempts to resolve one element of a wicked problem invariably lead to the emergence of higher level problem, of which the initial problem was just a symptom.

9. The existence of a discrepancy representing a wicked problem can be explained in numerous ways. The choice of explanation determines the nature of the problem's resolution: Wicked problems are ambiguous and there is no rule to determine the "correct" explanation or combination of explanations. Nevertheless, problem framing is crucial in determining which solutions to employ.

10. The planner has no right to be wrong: Problem-solvers 'are liable for the consequences of the actions they generate' which usually have significant impacts on citizens. Being 'wrong' therefore has significant real-world consequences.

Fig. 1.1 (continued)

us that any application of universal principles remains fraught with concerns about cultural imperialism and protection of national sovereignty.

After much reflection, we have reached the more nuanced conclusion that, whether it comes to fruition or not, the very notion of the Asian Century is important because it forces us to consider three issues critical to contemporary public policy:

- First, how can we better understand what public policy is, and what it means to create, implement and analyse public policy, in light of diverse global values, approaches and models? This question is concerned with establishing what it is possible for public policy to be about in any given context. It is a question that is not often asked about public policy, as it is usually assumed that we all know what we mean, but it is likely that the potential and limits of public policy will vary depending on a variety of factors, meaning that definitions or descriptions of public policy will likewise vary and are worth interrogating.
- Second, in light of increasingly fluid borders and fuzzy boundaries of responsibility around critical issues, such as climate change, how is the conduct of public policy changing? What are the roles of policy co-creation and collaboration? How can improved understanding of the conduct of public policy in other spaces and places improve policy translation, transfer and knowledge sharing?
- Third, what does the contemporary and future conduct of public policy look like in a globalised environment? How can we open a stronger, meaningful dialogue between policy scholars and administrators from diverse contexts to lead public administrative practice?

Exploring Public Policy in the Asian Century

This book is an attempt to question embedded assumptions, explore alternative perspectives and imagine possible implications. In the pages that follow, we present concepts (Part I), cases (Part II) and futures (Part III) that interrogate what it means to develop, implement and analyse public policy in the globalised context of what may well be the Asian Century. While each part of the book is organised around a particular theme, attentive readers will find that each part speaks to the others, with ideas from the discussion of concepts reflected in empirical reports from cases. The concepts introduced in Part I also inform the potential futures explored in Part III. We can also see glimpses of these futures emerging in the cases of Part II. While we have worked to offer a volume whose whole offers integrated thinking about our central concerns, it is also possible to approach the book as separate essays, dipping into the reader's particular interests or country-specific focus. The following sections offer an overview of the book's contents to assist readers' journey through the book.

Part I: Concepts

Part I of the book focuses on the foundational concepts and intellectual queries we believe to be critical to any study of public policy in the Asian Century. Here, our contributors turn their attention to the values, cultures and theories that shape contemporary public policy. Wolfgang Drechsler leads our intellectual journey in Chap. 2 by forcing us to question our inherent position, in relation to 'the other' and our associated cultural assumptions. Drechsler questions whether traditional claims to global 'best practice' public policy and administration are not more accurately understood as Western? He outlines a non-Western public administration through a close examination of Confucian systems of public administration. While Drechsler's core focus is mainland China, other Confucian systems are considered, including Taiwan, Singapore, South Korea, Vietnam and the somewhat problematic case of Japan. Chapter 2 suggests that recognising non-Western public administration provides an important foundation to define a best practice that is truly global in nature.

Shamsul Haque progresses the consideration of non-Western public policy and administration through his focus on public governance in Chap. 3. Here, Haque demonstrates how comparative studies on the distinction between Western and Asian societies have contributed to a gradual, cumulative production of cross-regional (cross-civilisational) literature on the unique patterns of Asian politics, economy, and culture. He looks to the current surge in Asian studies as symbolic of the recent, unprecedented rise of Asian nations in the global economy, politics, and technology. The chapter engages the 'Asian values' debate to question certain normative claims, while countering this with an argument that current discourse on the Asian Century provides a more evidence-based starting point for consideration of implications for public governance. Ultimately, Chap. 3 argues that a grand discourse on the Asian Century challenges us to rearticulate public policy and public administration based on the narratives and imperatives of the Asian success story. But it remains crucial to consider the limits and hazards of such an Asian model with regard to its inherent authenticity, structural validity, and consequential desirability.

In Chap. 4 Jill Tao engages in a deep exploration of the influence of Weber and Confucius in China and Korea. Through her conceptual study Tao weaves Confucian concepts around Weber's bureaucracy in present day public administration in China and Korea. Chapter 4 reminds us of a long but often ignored tradition of theoretical and values-exchanges between Western and non-Western societies, with the Weberian example revealing an instance in which a non-Western to Western flow is visible. Tao's assertion that "there is far less distance between Confucius and Weber than one might think" is a theme that can be extrapolated across the volume's chapters.

Part II: Cases

Nicholas Farrelly and Chit Win open Part II: Cases with an intimate portrayal of Myanmar's first *Hluttaw* (democratic legislature) assembly. Following the assembly's proceedings and members closely, the authors offer a sympathetic and remarkable record of this historic meeting. Their careful sociological observations capture the essence of a new democracy in action, showing how a Myanmar style of discipline informed the functioning of the country's first *Hluttaw*.

Chapter 6 takes the reader beyond a country-specific case to explore the implications of the Asian Century for science and technology policy. Paul Jensen and Lauren Palmer argue that there is growing understanding that a vibrant innovation ecosystem is an important element of a healthy and prosperous nation. What is less known is what the role of Government is in nurturing this ecosystem. Chapter 6 explores recent experiences in Australia and Asia with science and technology policy to consider how university-industry collaboration occurs across different nations and its effect on the diffusion of technology. Ultimately, the authors suggest that science and technology policy offers an important testing grounds for the tensions between knowledge-sharing for global benefit and local competitiveness.

Mariana Fotaki and Rutaichanok Jingjit question whether there is such a thing as humanistic bureaucracy in Chap. 7, drawing upon an in-depth study in Thailand's public administration. The chapter explores the implications of New Public Management reforms, introduced at the turn of the century, into diverse public organisations. The chapter explores whether and to what extent the introduction of a market-based system of public administration altered cultural values. In so doing, it demonstrates the failure of Western models to be influential within systems where values of seniority and relationship-based norms dominate.

In Chap. 8, Jong Youl Lee, Chad Anderson and Bo Wang explore the ways in which traditional measures of urban development may mask urbanisation and human development in contemporary China. Their study meticulously unpacks standard international measures of urban development such as GDP, population density, and average income, to ask whether these measures provide a relevant and true picture of urban development in the Chinese case. Their study demonstrates that even statistical practice may be culturally biased, with the Chapter demonstrating that the high population densities measurable in many Chinese cities today are not necessarily reconcilable with what one might consider urban development.

Part III: Futures

Part III of the book looks to the future of public policy, public administration and governance in the Asian Century. Mark Turner begins the discussion with an examination of public sector reform in East and Southeast Asia. Chapter 9 pays special attention to three areas of public sector reform—policy transfer, anti-corruption measures and decentralisation—to interrogate commonalities and divergences. The chapter demonstrates a complex, historically embedded pattern of reform activities in East and Southeast Asia, showing the prevalence of importation, adaptation and innovation in contributing to sustained development.

Chapter 10 considers the growth and adaptations necessary to support the daily work of public administrators within a globalised policy environment. Sara Bice draws upon global business leadership and cultural intelligence literatures and research with Australia's public service to suggest the skills, knowledge, capabilities and experiences necessary to support successful public administrative work in this joined-up future. The Chapter offers a global capabilities framework and discusses the ways in which certain skills, including relationship building, have the potential to be taught and cultivated within forward-thinking work environments.

Kim Moloney explores conceptualisations of public administration scholarship and related impediments to an Asian century of public administration. As Chap. 11 looks to the future, Moloney questions whether the recent rise in Asian influence in global politics and markets is reflected in the study and practice of public administration. Her exploration of 'how we know what we know' provides both insights into current limitations of public administration scholarship as well as a pathway to opening the types of research dialogues that would facilitate a setting aside of assumptions and embrace of alternative perspectives.

In Chap. 12 Adrian Kay invokes recent public health epidemics to demonstrate the ways in which the future of international governance is one that will require and support greater coordination between governments. Through its careful exploration of particular non-communicable diseases the chapter shows that Asian nations are already showing stronger international policy coordination capacity than is usually assumed. The chapter demonstrates that a lack of strong formal, supranational institutions in Asia is regularly read as a weakness, but instead shows how informal institutions are bolstering international policy coordination in Asia.

Jon Pierre concludes Part III with a vision that takes the future of governance beyond an East-West dichotomy. Drawing on comparative cases from Japan and Europe, Chap. 13 argues that it is unlikely that European or Anglo-American governments will shift towards Asian institutional structures, even in light of shifting power regimes. Instead, Pierre asserts, policymaking and administration in central Europe share many features similar to those of certain Asian nations. Building on these examples Chap. 13 demonstrates how processes of institutional diffusion and learning and functional requirements supported such similarities to occur, suggesting the basis for future environments in which similarities might flourish.

Chapter 14 completes the volume by distilling five central themes that emerge from the collective work of the contributors. First, the role of histories, values and cultures in policy making and public administration are considered. Secondly, the chapter argues that these individual tenets of identity are increasingly overshadowed but nevertheless critical within an environment in which transnational governance is growing in importance. Thirdly, the role of individual cases in advancing our understanding of public policy is explored, as is the notion that cases often deserve consideration on their own merit without the application of a comparative lens. In certain instances, such cases demonstrate the fourth theme which reveals links between policy work, innovation and national progress. Finally, the editors suggest that all of these considerations must be viewed within the very real changing nature of the daily work of those who ideate, design and implement public policy.

References

Alexander, D., Pierre, J., Sullivan, H., & Lewis, J. (2015). *The AIME of governance: Tackling wicked governance challenges through a multi-dimensional approach.* Paper presented to the second annual meeting of the International Conference on Public Policy, Milan.

Ablett, J., Baijal, A., Beinhocker, E., Bose, A., Farrell, D., Gersch, U., et al. (2007). *The 'bird of gold': The rise of India's consumer market.* McKinsey Global Institute.

Bhagwati, J. (2004). *In defense of globalization: With a new afterword.* Oxford: Oxford University Press.

Beck, U. (1999). *World risk society.* Cambridge: Polity.

Bice, S., & Merriam, A. (2016). Defining Asia capabilities for Australia's public service. *Australian Journal of Public Administration, 75*(3), 263–279.

Bice, S., & Sullivan, H. (2014). Public policy studies and the "Asian Century": New orientations, challenges, and opportunities. *Governance, 27*(4), 539–544.

Castells, M. (2000). *The rise of the network society* (2nd ed.). Malden: Blackwell.

Cox, M. (2016). Asian Century—Western decline: Critical reflections. In D. Walton & E. Kavalski (Eds.), *Power transition in Asia.* Abingdon: Routledge.

(Department of Foreign Affairs and Trade) DFAT. (2012). *Australia in the Asian Century: White paper.* Canberra, ACT: Australian Commonwealth Government.

Friedman, T. (2005). *The world is flat: A brief history of the globalized world in the 21st century* (pp. 393–395). London: Allen Lane.

Geddes, M. (2014). Neoliberalism and local governance: Radical developments in Latin America. *Urban Studies, 51*(15), 3147–3163.

Gulrajani, N., & Moloney, K. (2012). Globalizing public administration: Today's research and tomorrow's agenda. *Public Administration Review, 72*(1), 78–86.

Mahbubani, K. (2013). *The great convergence: Asia, The West, and the logic of one world.* New York: PublicAffairs.

Nye, J. (2002). Globalism versus globalization. *The Globalist, 15.*

Pezzini, M. (2012). An emerging middle class. *OECD Observer, 288,* 64.

Rittel, H. W., & Webber, M. M. (1973). Dilemmas in a general theory of planning. *Policy Sciences, 4*(2), 155–169.

Said, E. (1978). *Orientalism*. New York: Pantheon.

Su, T.-T., Walker, R., & Xue, L. (2013). Reform and transition in public administration theory and practice in greater China. *Public Administration, 91*(2), 253–260.

Wolf, M. (2004). *Why globalization works*. New Haven: Yale University Press.

Wood, D. J., Logsdon, J. M., Lewellyn, P. G., & Davenport, K. (2006). *Global business citizenship: A transformative framework for ethics and sustainable capitalism*. New York City: ME Sharpe.

Wu, X., He, Y.-L., & Sun, M. T.-W. (2013). Public administration research in mainland China and Taiwan: An assessment of journal publications, 1998–2008. *Public Administration, 91*(2), 261–280.

CHAPTER 2

Beyond the Western Paradigm: Confucian Public Administration

Wolfgang Drechsler

Non-Western Public Administration

If there are different paradigms of governance and especially public administration (PA), rather than one global best (practice of) PA (Drechsler 2015, 2013), then what we refer to as "global" PA is actually Western PA. And while "the West" includes Europe, the United States and Canada, Australia and New Zealand (CANZ), with their Greco-Christian-Enlightenment-Scientism legacy plus both production and consumer Capitalism, in PA today, "Western" means to a large extent Anglo-American PA, including the CANZ states (see Pollitt 2015; Cheung 2012; Raadschelders 2013). If PA has two dimensions—following, if informally and without citation, Geert Bouckaert (cf. also Rose-Ackerman 2017)—ethics (goals) and performance (delivery), linked though they may often be, "good PA" means both well-working and ethical by its own standards. Paradigms refer not only to real-existing, but also to potential, historical or theoretical forms of what we can call

W. Drechsler (✉)
Ragnar Nurkse Department of Innovation and Governance,
Tallinn University of Technology, Tallinn, Estonia
e-mail: wolfgang.drechsler@ttu.ee

S. Bice et al. (eds.), *Public Policy in the 'Asian Century'*, International Series on Public Policy, https://doi.org/10.1057/978-1-137-60252-7_2

Non-Western PA (NWPA; on a very similar concept in International Relations theory, see Acharya and Buzan 2007).

But in PA, it is generally, if tacitly, assumed that there is one good PA, and that this is global-Western; it is certainly so in scholarship (see only *Public Administration Review* 2010), but even more so in PA reform (cf. Andrews 2013). In other words, countries and places that do not adhere to or at least move towards the global-Western standard are seen as somehow remiss; they do not provide optimal PA and thus governance. The only excuse they may have is that they are laggards, that they are in transition, but they are expected to eventually arrive at the global-Western goal (see Pierre 2013; cf. also Pierre in this volume).

Contrary to this, I have suggested that, while there are indeed PA solutions to problems that arise from the nature of PA itself, which in turn is based on the fact that more human beings live in society than can be coordinated personally and directly, we can assume that:

A. In different contexts, there are also solutions to common problems that are different but not worse; very likely at least some of them even better;
B. There are adequate, good, indeed excellent solutions that completely depend on context, which is neither necessarily worse than the one for which Western PA is made, nor moving into the latter's direction; and
C. The debate about whether, for all human beings in time and space, there is or should be one set of ethics, is not really closed and in fact the elephant in the room, and much depends on the answer, also for PA.

The two most obvious potential partners, or challengers, of global-Western PA, as largely independent paradigms, are first Chinese and second Islamic PA (Drechsler 2015; on the latter, 2014, 2017); a third one—which strongly catches the imagination when brought up because of its appeal among Western intellectuals, including PA scholars—is Buddhist PA (Drechsler 2016). For the few people dealing with this issue, it is contentious whether there may be more paradigms, and what the other paradigms might be, but I would single out the first two for now because they, and I think only they, share a few significant advantages for such a comparison:

- A large body of theoretical literature
- Centuries of practice
- Strong relevance today
- A convincing carrier country
- A largely non-derivative system.

This is most clearly the case with *classical* Chinese, i.e. largely Confucian, and *classical* Islamic PA. Because of the "classical" part, we will have to look more at history than is usual in PA—not just because of notions of legacy ideas and structures (Yesilkagit 2010) or context (Painter and Peters 2010, pp. 3–16, 237), but because our concern, as indicated, partially has to be potentiality rather than current realisation and recognition in contemporary scholarship. The argument is, basically, about an honest basis for a convincing narrative, or convincing narratives; regarding contemporary empirics, it is somewhat more of an agenda. And even the most fervent advocates of diverse PA will admit that, while global-Western PA *theory* is on a (soft) downswing by now, the *practical* PA world is still in the process of mainstreaming.

But why would all of that be interesting to begin with? The equation global = Western = good can also be extended by the addition of "modern", i.e. global = Western = good = modern. Thus, modernisation equals Westernisation, which is a "good" thing. But, first, the suggestion that modernisation, i.e. any improvement, automatically means Westernisation actually delegitimises the former in those contexts in which Westernisation is at least an ambiguous concept. To show that the improvement of PA does not automatically mean Westernisation, in other words, that modernisation is not necessarily Westernisation, would therefore be a major accomplishment. It may then easily be that countries which do not follow the global-Western model are not laggards but rather pursue their own path towards good PA—perhaps by some criteria even better PA than what one has in the West. In that case, policy recommendations (often linked to financial incentives) to move towards Western PA benchmarks might not only be misguided, but they may even turn out to be highly counterproductive (see Bouckaert 2017).

This brings us to the second point: If the large-scale global effort to improve the world by improving governance and PA was an overwhelming success, one might just as well go with that. However, as

Matt Andrews has rightly argued, there is "mounting evidence that institutional reforms in developing countries do not work. Case studies and multi-country analyses show that many governments in developing nations are not becoming more functional, even after decades and hundreds of millions of dollars of externally sponsored reforms" (2013, p. xi; see 2017, p. 4). One of the reasons, he claims, is that even if the shape of an institution is copied, that says very little about its actual functionality ("isomorphic mimicry"; 2017, p. 31).

Interest vested in the global-Western paradigm is nonetheless very substantial, both in policy and in scholarship, and always has been (see *Public Administration Review* 2010, notwithstanding the sophistication of some contributions; Gulrajani and Moloney 2012; Welch and Wong 1998). However, during the last half decade or so, two phenomena have weakened the assuredness in and of the West that its solutions are the global ones wherever one goes, and this has slowly reached PA, as well. One is the global financial crisis, which has called the Western system into question both in regard to setup and performance, including PA (see Drechsler 2011). Another is the awareness, in West and East, of the (re-) emergence of the largely Confucian Southeast and East Asian "tiger states", about which more infra (see Bice and Sullivan 2014).

Specifically for PA, third, all this occurs at a time in which it is difficult to offer a cohesive (Western-global) PA paradigm, because there really is none anymore. After the demise of the NPM as the ruling one (see Drechsler and Kattel 2009), what we are facing is a post-NPM *Unübersichtlichkeit* with several "paradigmettes", such as the old NPM and the new one (a response to the global financial crisis), traditional Weberianism, NPM-plus concepts, such as New Public Governance and its varied permutations as well as Public Value, and Weberian-plus ones, such as the Neo-Weberian State (see Pollitt and Bouckaert 2011). Some beliefs that were held to be true very recently have become highly volatile—privatisation, say—and some others very questionable—transparency as a goal comes to mind (see Han 2012). So, what is it that the West can responsibly sell?

But even if there is such a thing as NWPA, and even if this can be good, i.e. well-working and ethical, PA, there seems to also be a core of good PA that all systems share, and there are plenty of grey zones in between (see points A. and B. supra). But first, *primarily*, "good" in PA means "fulfilling its purpose in a given context"—PA is good when it does what it is supposed to do; like the market in an economy, it does not come prima facie with values attached. (Certain forms of PA have certain effects that from certain perspectives have normative connotations, but not more than that).

How can we metaphorise good, i.e. primarily well-working, PA in context? Let us say that all paradigms as proposed contribute to solutions that can be said to form "good PA" in the sense that it does do its job in a decent, and primarily then in an effective and secondarily in a contextually ethical way, that it does fulfil its standard purpose on any possible level, including institutions, people and concepts, but that in general, these are adapted to context. That means that there may be:

(a) a small nucleus of PA that almost always works, tiny because it must match all performance and all ethics—and this is a purely empirical, not a normative concept; then
(b) a larger one in which such generally valid principles are adapted to the context and thus work; and
(c) a third level where solutions work well within a given paradigm but not (necessarily) in any other:

Now, (a) is what is generally assumed to be good PA, and the contextualised second nucleus (b) is what the more sophisticated PA research supports today, but our focus is on (c), the postulated spheres of good PA with(in) a certain paradigm each that does not work well, nor does it have to, in any other (cf. Cheung 2012, p. 214). If this is even partially true, then this does mean indeed that one should not judge, and try to improve, PA on the basis of and towards, the outer nucleus (b), let alone the inner one (a), but just ask whether under the given circumstances, PA does its job, or is or can be moving thither.

So much for the concept; how does it play out in practice? The focus of the present volume is Asia, especially Southeast and East Asia, and all four paradigms mentioned in the beginning are well-represented here, prima facie:

- Confucian: (Mainland) China, Hong Kong, (South) Korea, Japan, Macao, Singapore, Taiwan and Vietnam;
- Islamic: Brunei, Malaysia and Indonesia;
- Buddhist: Myanmar, Cambodia, Laos and Thailand; one could also add Mongolia here if one counts it as East Asian;
- Western: Philippines and Timor Leste (which are Catholic).

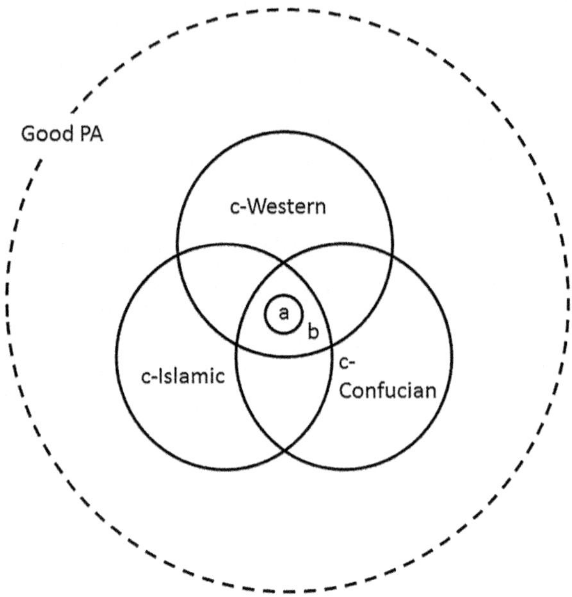

Fig. 2.1 'Good Public Administration': the Non-Western model

Of all NWPA systems, Confucian PA is the most powerful, most complex, most sophisticated and most influential one. It is therefore, from today's perspective, the ultimate challenge to the global-Western system (Drechsler 2015; see Pollitt 2015; Frederickson 2002). Thus, as the potentially most convincing case study, we will look at Confucian PA now—both to see whether the notion of NWPA is tenable and because the PA of the Confucian countries is so relevant in the Asian context, given their relative domination, economically as well as politically, in the region.

Confucianism

In order to do this, a few general considerations regarding Confucianism, and Confucian PA, are necessary. Confucian PA (Hood 1998, 76; Frederickson 2002) can be, prima facie, considered to be the PA of Confucian countries (or areas), i.e. of countries that either have a somewhat Confucian state doctrine or where (public) values etc. might be informed by Confucianism. Naturally, Confucian PA today is a classic "ideal type" in that any PA system in the 21st century is likely to be heavily global-Westernised (see Pollitt 2015).

There is the large-scale periodisation of Confucianism of which we need to be aware:

- **Confucianism** as such, enshrined in the writings by, or attributed to, Confucius (551–479 B.C.) and his immediate disciples, including detailed referrals to earlier predecessors;
- **Neo-Confucianism** (ca. 800–1905 A.D.), largely a concrete state doctrine with a distinct PA element; the time between before 1000 and after 1750 is the *plateau* of classical Imperial Chinese PA (the term Neo-Confucianism covers Buddhist and Taoist, but also Legalist and some other, elements and is, even though originally a purifying reform movement, an amalgam; Tan 2011; Drechsler 2015); and
- **New Confucianism** (since 1905); the intellectual worldview that makes Confucianism applicable, and applies it, to Chinese individual life, society and state today, and it entails a response to the West, with the idea that learning should go both ways (Tan 2008, pp. 141–153; see Bell 2010).

Institutional Confucian PA is largely Neo-Confucian, as there are no original or New Confucian institutions.

Another usual differentiation is that between the official (state) Confucianism, an intellectual/scholarly one, and/or a popular version, which may be either fully realised (Confucius worship) or implicit (living Confucian traditions without calling them that or knowing this) (see McHale 2008, p. 67 *et passim*; Daiber 2010; Murray 2009). This means that, for the specific purpose of PA, and for governance generally, we can talk—following Yesilkagit (2010)—about Confucian legacies both in ideas and in structures, of which structures are more clearly visible and more interesting. But PA can also be based on Confucian beliefs or positions, or react to them in one way or another. The current chapter will focus on institutions, not on "Confucian values" among civil servants and/or citizens, which is its own, quite thriving area of scholarship. (If we take Confucianism merely as a general label for "Asian" inclination towards family and hierarchy, as e.g. Jingjit and Fotaki (2011) do, we lose the specific meaning and the tradition of Confucian PA altogether).

For today's world, we also need to add another aspect, because it concerns the most prominent public and ubiquitously visible form of Confucianism, yet it is distinct from general folk or religious beliefs. This is something that I will label with a Japanese term: Confucius as *kami*, as one of the spirits, saints or gods in *shintō* which are not so much worshiped in a temple or shrine than asked for support (Ono 1962). In most Confucius temples in Asia, the extent of devotion is to beg Confucius—because of his connection with learning, but also with statecraft—for good results in exams or admission tests, often with respective plaques hung by students or, as often, parents near the sanctuary. As important as this is, it is actually not an indication of vibrant Confucianism as such. But to the extent that this stretches to civil-service entrance exams, it is somewhat of a legacy of Confucian PA, as well.

As we saw already, China and Confucianism are not identical. There are six to nine systems today with a PA that one can call Confucian: Mainland China, Hong Kong, Taiwan, Singapore, South Korea, Vietnam; historically also Japan; Macao and North Korea are in the same sphere traditionally as well (Cheung 2010, pp. 40–43; Painter and Peters 2010, p. 26). Most of them are among the success stories of the recent decade or two (Drechsler and Karo 2017).

Nonetheless, Confucianism is intimately intertwined with the history of Imperial China. Sometimes one wonders whether "Confucianism" is only a label for "Chinese characteristics" in general (if in one's discourse national characteristics are a legitimate concept); or is anything Chinese deep down just Confucian? The battle over what Confucianism means has therefore been—and still is—intense, and that within a culture that encompasses more people, and therefore opinions, than any other. Thus, there is almost no conceivable point on anything Confucius-related that has not been made.

Confucian Public Administration in China

If we look for the Confucian PA system "in itself", we find the ideal type in the Imperial Chinese variant. We can say that the modern state itself started in China and not in the West (Fukuyama 2011, p. 18); that this is a state understood very differently from the Western one (Jacques 2011) makes it even more interesting.

> China alone created a modern state in the terms defined by Max Weber. That is, China succeeded in developing a centralised, uniform system of bureaucratic administration that was capable of governing a huge population and territory ... China had already invented a system of impersonal, merit-based bureaucratic recruitment that was far more systematic than Roman public administration. (Fukuyama 2011, p. 21)

One has to acknowledge that there was an unusually large overlap of PA and government however that has occasionally led observers to say that there was no real independent PA (e.g., Bell 2015, 224–225, N61). Yet one also could argue that almost the opposite was the case: It was the bureaucracy, under the ruler and the court, which largely governed.

And this state was enormously successful—so successful that its organisation was not challenged until the mid-19th century (2011, p. 93). "It is safe to say that the Chinese invented modern bureaucracy, that is, a permanent administrative cadre selected on the basis of ability rather than kinship or patrimonial connection" (2011, p. 113).

Some of the most striking features or concepts of Confucian PA include

- the Imperial Civil Service Exam, which solves the problem of how to get the best and brightest of a country to work in PA (which is the core and carrier of government; there is no "political" equivalent), combats nepotism without negating its existence and creates transparency at an unheard-of level (briefly Drechsler 2015, pp. 114–115);
- a perpetually reforming and adapting PA system that is often geared towards, or already explicitly against, modern managerial developments, such as performance pay and managerial autonomy (Drechsler 2013); and
- the concept of the Mandate of Heaven, which creates a strong performance legitimisation of government and bureaucracy—and even potentially a business-innovation-friendly hierarchical system (Drechsler and Karo 2017).

What is visible even from this short list is that Confucian PA arrived at key features of contemporary global-Western PA a millennium earlier; much of this, it appears, was a homologous development, and there was no borrowing either way.

What is hard to fathom even for someone with a Weberian or French-style *étatiste* background is the importance the state and thus PA had in the people's mind and understanding—something that is, if in weaker form, still present in all Confucian countries today; "the world-ordering bureaucrat" is the protagonist of the entire system (Weber 2008, p. 77). And that even pertains to creativity in the wider sense—MacGregor, in the context of describing the creation of a Han Dynasty lacquer cup, even speaks of Chinese Imperial "bureaucracy as a guarantee of beauty" (2011, p. 219). Over time, the bureaucracy even shared the power of the land with the Emperor and the court (Cheung 2010, pp. 38–40; Fukuyama 2012, p. 19), and ministerial councils established themselves and bureaucratised decision-making (Bartlett 1991, esp. pp. 270–278).

As the Qianlong Emperor used to say, and as we now again realise, "There is no governing by laws; there is only governing by people" (Elliott 2009, p. 152). This is a Confucian point: "In Confucian political philosophy, it is more important to have virtuous people in government than to have a good system of laws" (Tan 2011, p. 470; see *passim*). This is the big difference to Legalism, which is based on hierarchy and coercion: Confucians believe in people doing the right thing because they know what the right thing is and therefore want to do it (this is a definition of virtue), not because they have been cajoled to do it. The task therefore is to educate and select or promote virtuous people (see Frederickson 2002).

Mainland China is what gives contemporary Confucianism its global eminence, not only its historical one. But how important is Confucianism really today in China? After the fall of the Qing, the question was whether Confucianism was to blame for the underachievement of China, especially techno-economically. For many intellectuals, it became one of the main culprits that had stood in the way of Modernisation and Westernisation, and that was taken up later with a vengeance (Louie 1980). Under Communism, Confucianism was the enemy, as it symbolised precisely what was wrong, and strong, in ancient China. This gained momentum during the Cultural Revolution, first via a campaign against the "Four Olds" (Old Customs, Old Culture, Old Habits and Old Ideas) from the mid-1960s on (Mittler 2013); the late Mao and the Gang of Four propagated "progressive" Legalism over "reactionary" Confucianism (Guo et al. 2015, 20; cf. Ma et al. 2015). Then, towards the end of Mao's life, the persecution of his then most important inner-party antagonist broke loose in 1974 under the slogan

"Down with Lin Biao, down with Confucius", continuing to Mao's death in 1976 (Louie 1980; Guo et al. 2015, pp. 79–82).

But since Deng Xiaoping's reforms, Confucianism has come back and is now completely established again; there is both a popular and an intellectual Confucian revival (Rosemont 2013, p. 3). In that sense, it may be the most convincing alternative to the "consumerist patriotism" (Zarrow 2008, p. 44) that is more or less the quasi-official line of Chinese development today. On the truly official level, Confucianism has been publicly embraced by the Chinese government more than ever in the last and this century, with President Xi at the forefront (Johnson 2016; *Economist* 2015; Daiber 2014, pp. 106–108).

On the PA level, however, there is still little as far as institutions are concerned. China has more or less tapped into global-Western main stream PA, if not always very successfully, and recent empirical comparisons of civil servants' attitudes (see e.g. Podger and Yan 2013) show some convergence with some Western PA. But, for instance, in today's Mainland Chinese civil-service exam, as well as in a general merit-based competitive civil-service selection and promotion within and without the Party, the continuing Confucian tradition is noteworthy (Xiao and Li 2013, pp. 348–352). Zhang's recent argument (2017) that contemporary Chinese leadership both in government and PA is in fact based on Confucian meritocracy (within and through the Party) and that the selection mechanism is an adaptation of the civil service exam is not insignificant either.

Confucian PA as a scholarly topic is facing opposition in Mainland China from several factions. As usual in NWPA, leading local scholars usually have Anglo-American PhD degrees and promote Western PA, as this is their own Unique Selling Proposition (USP) (Pollitt 2015). For them, even the existence of Confucian PA creates a legitimacy problem. Second, there are structural scholarly reasons as well: In PA, the old Modernist-Maoist suspicion against Confucianism is still paired with an approach that questions whether one really can call Imperial Chinese PA "Neo-Confucian" because of the many other aspects of Chinese intellectual history (Xu et al. 2014; Ma et al. 2015). Since Confucian PA is especially promoted both by practitioners and by younger scholars (and students), time might easily be on its side once again, as so often during the past millennia.

Other Confucian Systems

Institutionally, it is **Taiwan** that carries the Confucian legacy of the Chinese Empire in the most direct way (see Berman 2010; Jan 2010), although it was the Kuomintang government that originally abolished Confucianism on the Mainland. This includes, as proposed by Sun Yat-sen, the organisation of the government in *yuans* and a civil-service exam with a functionality similar to the original one, administered by the Examination Yuan. Of course, at the same time, Taiwan also has very global-Western PA institutions (see So 2015; Jan 2010). In Taiwan, there has been Confucianism on all levels: state, popular and intellectual (see Huang 2009, 7–8).

Ironically, however, the Confucian nature of some Taiwanese PA institutions might be their undoing, as interviews in Taipei in March 2017 showed: The Examination Yuan, for instance, seems under threat of being abolished by the current Democratic Progressive Party government, in power since 2016, which stresses Taiwanese specificity and arguably pursues a course of "soft de-Sinization", not least in cultural and institutional matters. The Examination Yuan is seen as Confucian-Chinese and (therefore) as not in line with mainstream global-Western PA principles and thus, in spite of its great success in performance (Drechsler and Karo 2017, but see So 2015) and a lack of promising alternatives, as somewhat of an anachronism that may be discontinued.

Hong Kong was a haven for New Confucian thinking and never experienced the Cultural Revolution, but its scholarly PA outlook has always been decidedly global-Western (Lo 2014, pp. 40–42). Hong Kong's administration was British-Colonial from the beginning (Lee 2011, p. 240, who, however, confuses that with Weberianism), but it is often described as nonetheless strongly based on Confucian values and attitudes towards PA even today that are at the basis not so much of the PA institutions themselves, but of their adaption to the local context (Burns 2011, esp. pp. 319–320).

In **Macao**, not even this seems to be the case—if anything, it might have a future of Confucian PA, but no legacy except the kind of Confucian values that one commonly attributes to a Chinese population. As a Portuguese colony (whose PA legacy is usually disparaged in a wholesale way by the standard literature; see Bolong 2011, pp. 463–465) which was taken over by Mainland China only in the 1960s, it seems to neither have had nor have Confucian institutions of any kind (the standard section in Berman 2011, pp. 463–560, never mentions Confucianism at all).

Confucianism was part of the state ideology only in Togukawa **Japan**. But in regard to PA, even then, while there were Confucius temples and academies, there was no Confucian bureaucracy. The civil-service exam there only lasted briefly and was abolished a millennium ago (Liu 2007, p. 494). Confucian scholars were almost free-floating intellectuals; they were not bureaucrats or involved formally in the conduct of the state (Hiroshi 2012, pp. 85–88). Just as Confucianism had been against Legalism in China, it was seen as too ethics-based, compassionate and benevolent from a samurai perspective (2012, pp. 96–98).

The question is whether Confucianism has had any significance since the Meiji Revolution/Restoration (see Hiroshi 2012, pp. 9, 362, 435; Yao 2001, pp. 136–137). It has been argued that it certainly helped to bring this change of systems about, as the supreme rule of the Emperor, and the role of the Shogun as a delegate, was the crucial concept here, an idea with consequences that could be traced to Confucian thinking (Hiroshi 2012, pp. 359–362). Today, I would say that there is no state Confucianism left in Japan (what seems to be that is actually Weberian Meiji Prussianism—but this needs further study), except the co-optation of Confucius as *kami*, but even for that, the Confucian statesman, poet and calligrapher Sugarawara no Michizane (Tenjin *kami*) seems much more powerful than the Master (Borgen 1994, pp. 307–337). This means that Japan may be the only place where Confucianism has more of a historical dimension—perhaps because it was imported with a purpose, rather than arising from the national context. (Interviews with senior civil servants and academics in Tokyo in March–April 2015 unanimously stressed the complete absence of any Confucianism whatsoever in Japanese PA today.)

Vietnam's pre-Colonial PA and governance was Confucian (McHale 2008, pp. 72–73); it closely resembled the Chinese system on the level of PA, with a very similar examination and position system that operated from 1075 to 1919, i.e. even a decade and a half longer than in China (Nguyen 2008, pp. 100–102). The Confucian legacy and indeed presence in Vietnam is well-documented and fully discussed in local scholarship but less so elsewhere (e.g. *Confucianism* 2002; Daiber 2010, pp. 28–139). Its centre, the Van Mieu in Hanoi, today's Temple of Literature, has survived more or less intact with the steles commemorating the civil-service-exam graduates (Nguyen 2008).

Post-French Communism partially overturned Confucianism but not fully, because Ho Chi Minh was to a large extent also a Confucian (Daiber 2010, pp. 137–139). Today, Confucianism is quite appreciated even officially by Party and State, so that there is a "Confucian Renaissance" of sorts (McHale 2008, pp. 173, 182). Yet, we know very little about its influence in contemporary PA; in fact, key publications on Vietnamese PA reform do not even mention the Confucian legacy (Acuña-Alfaro 2009; but see Painter 2003). Altogether, Confucianism seems to be important in the North of Vietnam, but not in the South; in Hanoi, PA scholars and practitioners, as well as students, generally acknowledge a Confucian element even in PA (interviews).

Korea's Confucian legacy is very strong (Im et al. 2013; Yao 2001, pp. 115–125), with a very Chinese form of Confucianism as a "state religion" during the Joseon Dynasty up to 1894 and then fading until its expiration one and a half decades later (Daiber 2010, pp. 217–231). Korea had a completely Confucian civil-service system including a Confucian academy and civil-service exam (Daiber 2014, pp. 97–99). (The latter was abolished in 1895: Daiber 2010, p. 234.)

Today, **South Korea** is dominated by global-Westernised PA academics who read the Confucian legacy from a largely Western perspective and who are quite critical towards the Confucian legacy. They even discourage investigation into Korean specificity and a "return" to Confucianism (Kim 2012, pp. 231, 228). In Korea, however, one also has a "modern" discourse on Confucian PA (see only Chung 2007; Kim 2012; Im et al. 2013), which is relatively rare even in those countries where Confucianism is more prominent. In regard to institutions, Daiber's observation that "South Korea is the one country which shows in an unbroken way the strongest Confucian imprint and thus co-shapens contemporary Korean identity" (2014, p. 101; see pp. 108–109) goes too far, however, at least from the PA perspective.

It is fair to say that we know nothing about the PA of **North Korea**, let alone about putative Confucian legacies of any sort; the studies that we do have (such as Jordan and Ip 2013) are only based on the country's Constitution, which is not likely to be indicative of anything.

Last but not least, the poster boy of contemporary Confucian PA is often **Singapore**, where "the debates over political meritocracy were revived" (Bell 2015, p. 3). Singapore is sometimes described as voluntarily Western and thus strong enough to take its own path, rather than obeying Western advice and fashion (Andrews 2013, pp. 190–191), also in PA. However, institutionally, Singaporean PA, like Hong Kong's, is based on British Colonial legacy (strongly along these lines Quah 2010, esp. pp. 18–19; Haque 2009). There never was Chinese government in Singapore before independence, and the Chinese elite was mercantile. Nonetheless, this elite—the basis of today's—often did espouse a Confucian habitus (The Scholar as Gentleman 2017). It is questionable whether the "founding father" of Singapore, Lee Kuan Yew, was a Confucian (Lord 2003, pp. 101–105; Suleski 2008, pp. 272–275) rather than someone who used Confucianism as a "communication tool" (interviews). The Administrative Service's policy-*making* role, indeed the concept of a country run with a long-term perspective, primarily by a meritocratic bureaucracy, and several institutional elements as well (if no civil service exam; Lim and Lim 2015, pp. 59–142), make it possible, however, to ascribe fundamental characteristics of Confucian PA to Singapore.

Singapore is, for instance, able to pay its civil servants—including the elected ones—rates competitive with the private sector (also including downward adjustments, however), something that makes eminent sense but is difficult to pull off elsewhere. However, even here this had to be modified for political reasons in 2011 (Bell 2015, pp. 121–122). This opportunity-cost argument is Confucian, coming right out of the eminent Neo-Confucian PA thinker, the Song Dynasty Chancellor Wang Anshi's 1058 *Memorandum of a Myriad Words*, according to which the salary for civil servants must be "sufficient to make up for what they had lost in farming by being called upon for public work" (Wang 1935, p. 55). Nonetheless, whether Wang or Confucian PA generally really were the source for this measure must, for now, remain an open question.

Coda: Back to Non-Western Public Administration

The cases discussed above show that even for a well-meaning NWPA protagonist, global-Western PA is extremely powerful and that there is not that much *institutional* Confucian PA left. And yet, I would argue that there is sufficient cause to talk about a challenging paradigm, not only potentiality, especially if one looks at the dynamics of Confucianism in Mainland China. In PA, the Confucian legacy sharpens the question of whether there is only one "good" PA or whether there are several—whether, indeed, there is NWPA to begin with. That Confucian PA is one of the two or three main systems within human history is hardly contested; to look at how well it worked, for how long, and with what civilisational impact still means to marvel. It seems to be unique altogether that within Imperial China PA moved to the centre of the stage, even into the driver's seat, determining significantly how other spheres of life were structured, including religion and art. Of all the systems from which global-Western PA can and perhaps has to learn, Confucian PA is the most obvious one.

This is all the more important if we look at the context of development, as the Western countries no doubt were until very recently the more successful ones, and that means that the non-Western ones were, and to a good extent are, less successful. The fact that administrative capacity, institutionally as well as personally, is a *condition sine qua non* for development is clear (Nurkse 1952, 1964; see Drechsler 2009). That too many developing countries do not have it, yet need it—indeed that this could even define the euphemism of "developing" (whatever that means, and whither), is likewise obvious (cf. the UNPAN website).

Now, one could see it either way: Developing countries do not have sufficient administrative capacity and thus need to be motivated or forced to move towards global-Western PA, or—either for now or in general—seeing that this ostensibly does not work (in many places at least) or that it may not even be necessary or desirable, they need to develop optimal capacity according to their own governance system and general context. And what speaks for the latter even if one believes in common goals is that the track record of globalising Westernisation, in PA and otherwise, has not exactly been universally excellent. As pointed out supra, in PA today, this is all the more so because the goals of global-Western PA are currently in flux.

Altogether, what speaks for going beyond the Western Paradigm of PA includes both the success of Confucian PA and of its carrier countries, but also the interest of and in global-Western PA itself—both for self-reflection and to discuss whether and in which way it is really global, rather than just Western. The Asian Century is pushing these questions to the forefront, and rightly so, for potential benefit not only for Asia, nor only for the West, but globally.

Acknowledgements This chapter further develops two sections from Drechsler 2015, and thus, several passages have been adapted from there; a few others are based on my parts in Drechsler and Karo 2017. Funding for facilities used in this research was provided by the core infrastructure support IUT (19–13) of the Estonian Ministry of Education and Research.

Interviews

Information regarding contemporary and traditional Confucianism in PA is also based on fieldwork, normally including interviews with senior civil servants as well as academics, in all putative Confucian countries except North Korea: Mainland China (Beijing, September–November 2013 and March 2015), Hong Kong and Macao (April 2016, no interviews), Japan (Tokyo, March–April 2015), Singapore (January–April 2017), South Korea (Seoul, September 2013), Taiwan (October 2012, November 2013, April 2015 and March and May 2017) and Vietnam (Hanoi February 2014, Saigon March 2015).

References

Pure web-based information is not repeated here; all hyperlinks are valid as of July 2017.

Acharya, A., & Buzan, B. (2007). Why is there no non-Western international relations theory? An introduction. *International Relations of the Asia-Pacific, 7*(3), 287–312.

Acuña-Alfaro, J. (Ed.). (2009). *Reforming public administration in Viet Nam: Current situation and recommendations (Reference book).* Hanoi: UNDP Viet Nam/National Political Publishing House.

Andrews, M. (2013). *The limits of institutional reform in development: Changing rules for realistic solutions.* Cambridge: Cambridge University Press.

Andrews, M., et al. (2017). *Building state capability: Evidence, analysis, action.* Oxford: Oxford University Press.

Bartlett, B. S. (1991). *Monarchs and ministers: The grand council in Mid-Ch'ing China* (pp. 1723–1820). Berkeley, CA: University of California Publishing.

Bell, D. A. (2010). *China's new Confucianism: Politics and everyday life in a changing society* (4th pr.). Princeton, NJ: Princeton University Press.

Bell, D. A. (2015). *The China model: Political meritocracy and the limits of democracy.* Princeton, NJ: Princeton University Press.

Berman, E. M. (2010). Public administration in East Asia: Common roots, ways and tasks. In E. M. Berman et al. (Eds.), *Public administration in East Asia: Mainland China, Japan, South Korea, Taiwan* (pp. 2–32). Boca Raton, FL: CRC Press.

Berman, E. M. (Ed.). (2011). *Public administration in Southeast Asia: Thailand, Philippines, Malaysia, Hong Kong and Macao.* Boca Raton, FL: CRC Press.

Bice, S., & Sullivan, H. (2014). Public policy studies and the "Asian Century": New orientations, challenges, and opportunities. *Governance, 27*(4), 539–544.

Bolong, L. (2011). History and context of public administration in Macao. In E. M. Berman (Ed.), *Public administration in SouthEast Asia, Thailand, Philippines, Malaysia, Hong Kong, and Macao* (pp. 463–473). Boca Raton, FL: CRC Press.

Borgen, R. (1994). *Sugawara no Michizane and the early Heian Court.* Honolulu: University of Hawaii Press.

Bouckaert, G. (2017). Taking stock of "governance": A predominantly European perspective. *Governance, 30*(1), 45–57.

Burns, J. P. (2011). Civil service system in Hong Kong. In E. M. Berman (Ed.), *Public administration in Southeast Asia, Thailand, Philippines, Malaysia, Hong Kong, and Macao* (pp. 315–330). Boca Raton, FL: CRC Press.

Cheung, A. B. L. (2010). Checks and balances in China's administrative traditions: A preliminary assessment. In M. Painter & B. G. Peters (Eds.), *Tradition and public administration* (pp. 31–43). London: Palgrave Macmillan.

Cheung, A. B. L. (2012). Public administration in East Asia: Legacies, trajectories and lessons. *International Review of Administrative Sciences, 78*(2), 209–216.

Chung, S. H. (2007). Reading Korean public administration: An application of Lacanian four discourses. *International Journal of Public Administration, 30,* 1343–1369.

Confucianism in Vietnam. (2002). Ho Chi Minh City: Vietnam National University/Ho Chi Minh City Publishing House.

Daiber, K.-F. (2010). *Konfuzianische Transformationen: Eine religiöse Tradition in der Moderne Indonesiens, der Philippinen, Vietnams und Südkoreas.* Münster: Lit.

Daiber, K.-F. (2014). *Religion in multikulturellen und multireligiösen Staaten Ostasiens: Drei Studien.* Frankfurt/Main: Peter Lang.

Drechsler, W. (2009). Towards the law & economics of development: Ragnar Nurkse (1907–1959). *European Journal of Law and Economics, 28*(1), 19–37.

Drechsler, W. (2011). Public administration in times of crisis. In R. Kattel et al. (Eds.), *Public administration in times of crisis* (pp. 15–25). Bratislava: NISPAcee Press.

Drechsler, W. (2013). Wang Anshi and the origins of modern public management in Song Dynasty China. *Public Money and Management, 33*(5), 353–360. Repr. in B. G. Peters & J. Pierre (Eds.). (2015). *Public administration,* 1: *Fundamental issues in public administration* (pp. 81–94). Los Angeles: Sage.

Drechsler, W. (2014). What is and why do we study Islamic public administration in the former second world? *Administrative Culture, 14*(2), 123–142.

Drechsler, W. (2015). Paradigms of non-Western PA and governance. In A. Massey & K. Johnston Miller (Eds.), *The international handbook of public administration and governance* (pp. 104–131). Cheltenham: Elgar.

Drechsler, W. (2016). Public administration within the sufficiency economy. *Thai Journal of Public Administration, 14*(1), 9–37.

Drechsler, W. (2017). Islamic public administration in Europe. In E. Ongaro & S. van Thiel (Eds.), *The Palgrave handbook of public administration and management in Europe*. Basingstoke: Palgrave Macmillan (in press).

Drechsler, W., & Karo, E. (2017). Explaining the Confucian paradox. In W. Drechsler et al. *Innovation bureaucracy* (Chap. 6). New Haven: Yale University Press (forthcoming).

Drechsler, W., & Kattel, R. (2009). Conclusion: Towards the Neo-Weberian State? Perhaps, but certainly adieu, NPM! *The NISPAcee Journal of Public Administration and Policy, 1*(2), 95–99.

Economist (2015, July 25) = Confucius says, Xi does. The communist party turns to ancient philosophy for support. *The Economist*. Retrieved from http://www.economist.com/news/china/21659753-communist party-turns-ancient-philosophy-support-confucius-says-xi-does.

Elliott, M. (2009). *Emperor Qianlong: Son of heaven, man of the world*. New York: Longman.

Frederickson, H. G. (2002). Confucius and the moral basis of bureaucracy. *Administration & Society, 33*(4), 610–628.

Fukuyama, F. (2011). *The origins of political order: From prehuman times to the French Revolution*. New York: Farrar, Straus and Giroux.

Fukuyama, F. (2012). The patterns of history. *Journal of Democracy, 23*(1), 14–26.

Gulrajani, N., & Moloney, K. (2012). Globalizing public administration: Today's research and tomorrow's agenda. *Public Administration Review, 72*(1), 78–86.

Guo, J., Song, Y., & Zhou, Y. (Eds.). (2015). *Historical dictionary of the Chinese cultural revolution*. Lanham, MD: Rowan & Littlefield.

Han, B.-C. (2012). *Transparenzgesellschaft*. Berlin: Matthes & Seitz.

Haque, M. S. (2009). Public administration and public governance in Singapore. In P. S. Kim (Ed.), *Public administration and public governance in ASEAN member countries and Korea* (pp. 246–271). Seoul: Daeyoung Moonhwasa.

Hiroshi, W. (2012). *A history of Japanese political thought, 1600–1901*. Tokyo: International House of Japan.

Hood, C. (1998). *The art of the state: Culture, rhetoric and public management*. Oxford: Clarendon Press.

Huang, Y. (2009). Taiwanese Confucianism. *Contemporary Chinese Thought, 41*(1), 3–9.

Im, T., et al. (2013). Revisiting Confucian bureaucracy: Roots of the Korean Government's culture and competitiveness. *Public Administration and Development, 33*, 286–296.

Jacques, M. (2011, February). How China will change the way we think: The case of the state. *TransAtlantic Academy Paper Series.*

Jan, C.-Y. (2010). History and context of public administration in Taiwan. In E. M. Berman et al. (Eds.), *Public administration in East Asia: Mainland China, Japan, South Korea, Taiwan* (pp. 497–516). Boca Raton, FL: CRC Press.

Jingjit, R., & Fotaki, M. (2011). Confucian ethics and the limited impact of the new public management reform in Thailand. *Journal of Business Ethics, 97*(suppl. 1), 1–73.

Johnson, I. (2016, June 8). China's memory manipulators. *The Guardian.* Retrieved from https://www.theguardian.com/world/2016/jun/08/chinas-memory-manipulators.

Jordan, S. R., & Ip, E. C. Y. (2013). Demystifying the Hermit Kingdom: The constitution and public administration in North Korea. *International Review of Administrative Sciences, 79*(3), 544–562.

Kim, P. S. (2012). A historical overview of Korean public administration: Discipline, education, association, international cooperation and beyond indigenization. *International Review of Administrative Sciences, 78*(2), 217–238.

Lee, E. W. Y. (2011). History and context of public administration in Hong Kong. In E. M. Berman (Ed.), *Public administration in SouthEast Asia, Thailand, Philippines, Malaysia, Hong Kong, and Macao* (pp. 239–253). Boca Raton, FL: CRC Press.

Lim, S. G., & Lim, J. H. (2015). *The leader, the teacher and you. Leadership through the third generation* (6th pr.). Singapore: World Scientific.

Liu, H. (2007). Influence of China's imperial examinations on Japan, Korea and Vietnam. *Frontiers of History in China, 2*(4), 493–512.

Lo, S. H. (2014). The study of public administration in Hong Kong and Macao: Evolutionary paths and implications. *Asian Journal of Political Science, 22*(1), 20–44.

Lord, C. (2003). *The modern prince: What leaders need to know now.* New Haven: Yale University Press.

Louie, K. (1980). *Critiques of Confucius in contemporary China.* New York: St. Martin's Press.

Ma, C., Xu, Y., & Chan, J. L. (2015). Wang Anshi and Confucian public management—A rejoinder. *Public Money and Management, 35*(4), 253–254.

MacGregor, N. (2011). *A history of the world in 100 objects.* London: Allen Lane.

McHale, S. F. (2008). *Print and power. Confucianism, Communism, and Buddhism in the making of modern Vietnam.* Honolulu: University of Hawaii Press.

Mittler, B. (2013). "Enjoying the four olds!" Oral histories from a "Cultural Desert". *Transcultural Studies* (University of Heidelberg), *2013*(1), 177–215. Retrieved from http://heiup.uni-heidelberg.de/journals/index.php/transcultural/article/view/10798.

Murray, J. K. (2009). "Idols" in the temple: Icons and the cult of Confucius. *The Journal of Asian Studies, 68*(2), 371–411.

Nguyen V. T. (2008). *Van Mieu—Quoc Tu Giam and famous Confucius' sayings.* Hanoi: n.p.

Nurkse, R. (1952). Trade fluctuations and buffer policies of low-income countries. *Kyklos, 12*(3), 141–154; Epilogue: pp. 244–265.

Nurkse, R. (1964 [1953]). *Problems of capital formation in underdeveloped countries* (9th impr.). Oxford: Basil Blackwell.

Ono, S. (1962). *Shinto—The Kami way.* Tokyo: Tuttle.

Painter, M. (2003). Public administration reform in Vietnam: Problems and prospects. *Public Administration & Development, 23*(3), 259–271.

Painter, M., & Peters, B. G. (Eds.). (2010). *Tradition and public administration.* London: Palgrave Macmillan.

Pierre, J. (2013). *Globalization and governance.* Cheltenham: Elgar.

Podger, A., & Yan, B. (2013). Public administration in China and Australia: Different worlds but similar challenges. *Australian Journal of Public Administration, 72*(3), 201–219.

Pollitt, C. (2015). Towards a new world: Some inconvenient truths for Anglosphere public administration. *International Review of Administrative Sciences, 81*(1), 3–17.

Pollitt, C., & Bouckaert, G. (2011). *Public management reform: A comparative analysis: New public management, governance, and the Neo-Weberian State* (3rd ed.). Oxford: Oxford University Press.

Public Administration Review (2010). R. O'Leary, & D. M. Van Slyke (Eds.). Special issue on The Future of Public Administration in 2020, *70*(Suppl. s1).

Quah, J. S. T. (2010). *Public administration Singapore-style.* Emerald: Bingley.

Raadschelders, J. C. N. (2013). *Public administration: The interdisciplinary study of Government.* Oxford: Oxford University Press.

Rose-Ackerman, R. (2017). What does "Governance" mean? *Governance, 30*(1), 23–27.

Rosemont, Jr., H. (2013). *A reader's companion to the Confucian* analects. New York: Palgrave Macmillan.

The Scholar as Gentleman (2017) = Exhibition room in the Asian Civilizations Museum Singapore description. Retrieved from http://acm.org.sg/collections/galleries/scholar-in-chinese-culture.

So, B. W. Y. (2015). Exam-centred meritocracy in Taiwan: Hiring by merit or examination? *Australian Journal of Public Administration, 74*(3), 312–322.

Suleski, R. (2008). Confucius: The organization of Chinese society. In D. Jones (Ed.), *Confucius now: Contemporary encounters with the Analects* (pp. 253–290). Chicago: Open Court.

Tan, S.-H. (2008). Modernizing Confucianism and "New Confucianism". In K. Louie (Ed.), *The Cambridge companion to modern Chinese culture* (pp. 135–154). Cambridge: Cambridge University Press.

Tan, S.-H. (2011). The *Dao* of politics: Li (Rituals/Rites) and laws as pragmatic tools of government. *Philosophy East and West, 61*(3), 468–491.

UNPAN (2017) = United Nations Public Administration Network. Retrieved from http://www.unpan.org/.

Wang, A. (1935). The Wan Yen Shu, or memorial of a, myriad words [1058]. In H. R. Williamson, *Wang An Shih: A Chinese statesman and educationalist of the Sung Dynasty* 1 (pp. 48–84). London: Probsthain.

Weber, M. (2008 [1922]). *Wirtschaft und Gesellschaft: Die Wirtschaft und die gesellschaftlichen Ordnungen und Mächte, Nachlass* 2: *Religiöse Gemeinschaften*, MWS I/22. Tübingen: Mohr Siebeck.

Welch, E., & Wong, W. (1998). Public administration in a global context: Bridging the gaps of theory and practice between Western and non-Western nations. *Public Administration Review, 58*(1), 40–49.

Xiao, H., & Li, C. (2013). China's meritocratic examinations and the ideal of virtuous talents. In D. A. Bell & C. Li (Eds.), *The East Asian challenge for democracy: Political meritocracy in comparative perspective* (pp. 340–362). Princeton, NJ: Princeton University Press.

Xu, Y., Ma, C., & Chan, J. L. (2014). Wang Anshi's *Wanyanshu* as the origins of modern public management? *Public Money and Management, 34*(3), 221–226.

Yao, X. (2001). Who is a Confucian today? A critical reflection on the issues of Confucian identity in modern times. *Journal of Contemporary Religion, 16*(3), 313–328.

Yesilkagit, K. (2010). The future of administrative tradition: Tradition as ideas and structure. In M. Painter, & B. G. Peters (Eds.), *Tradition and public administration* (pp. 145–157). London: Palgrave Macmillan.

Zarrow, P. (2008). Social and political developments: The making of the twentieth-century Chinese State. In K. Louie (Ed.), *The Cambridge companion to modern Chinese culture* (pp. 20–45). Cambridge: Cambridge University Press.

Zhang, W. (2017, March 1). For China's one-party rulers, legitimacy flows from prosperity and competence: The West still underestimates Beijing's ancient social contract with "Heaven". Berggruen Institute, Philosophy + Culture Center. Retrieved from http://philosophyandculture.berggruen.org/ideas/for-china-s-one-party-rulers-legitimacy-flows-from-prosperity-and-competence.

CHAPTER 3

Rethinking Public Governance in the Asian Century: Grand Discourse Vs. Actual Reality

M. Shamsul Haque

Introduction

In recent years, there has emerged an unprecedented global discourse on the idea of an 'Asian Century', following the earlier propositions of the Chinese Century (Rees-Mogg 2005) and the Indian Century (Halliwell and Morley 2008), as well as the debates on Asian Miracles and Asian Values (Hoon 2004; Thompson 2004). In general, the idea of Asian Century symbolises the re-emergence of Asia as one of the world's most significant regions in terms of its impressive economic progress, its increased share of global GDP, and its huge productive workforce. In line with the forecasts that very soon Asia will be the world's largest producer and consumer of goods and services and account for nearly half of the world's output, the current twenty-first century is being advocated as the 'Asian Century' (ADB 2011a; Cheung 2012; Government of Australia 2012). It is claimed that "Asia's rise is changing the world" (Government of Australia 2012, p. 1). Some recent reports reinforced

M. Shamsul Haque (✉)
Department of Political Science, National University of Singapore,
Singapore, Singapore
e-mail: polhaque@nus.edu.sg

S. Bice et al. (eds.), *Public Policy in the 'Asian Century'*, International Series on Public Policy, https://doi.org/10.1057/978-1-137-60252-7_3

this concept of the Asian Century, which include *Asia 2050: Realizing the Asian Century* by the Asian Development Bank (2011); *Imagining Asia 2020: Make Way for the Asia Giant* by the Research Team of DBS Bank (2011); and *Australia in the Asian Century* by the Australian Government (2012).

With the rise of Asia's global significance, there has also been a proliferation of research on Asian economy, society, politics, and culture in major disciplines, including Economics, Sociology, Political Science, History, and so on (Haque 2013). While, the post-War expansion of social science studies on Asia was largely due to the emergence of postcolonial states, Cold War tensions and regional conflicts, and the region's integration into the world capitalist markets (Sterckx and Luca 2009), the current academic interest is largely because of Asia's rising economic and political power. In particular, there has been a significant increase in academic publications exploring the intellectual and policy implications of the Asian Century for international law (Fidler 2005), international relations (Cox 2012), development studies (Schmitz 2007), and so on. There is also increasing attention paid to the idea of the changing world order caused by the rise or emergence (re-emergence) of the Asian powers (Brooks and Wohlforth 2009; Dadush and Stancil 2010; Drezner 2007). In addition, the significance of the Asian Century debate has also intensified due to growing speculations on the declining economic and political powers of the West (Western Europe and North America) in relation to the rise of Asia (see Cox 2012; Kappel 2011; Kimmage 2013; Kupchan 2012).

The role played by the state-centric public governance that spearheaded development plans and institutions sits behind the rise of economic development and expansion of political power in Asia, compared to other regions (Kurlantzick 2011; Cheung 2012). There have been considerable studies, debates, and publications on the role of public sector management in accelerating economic development in many countries in East Asia and Southeast Asia, such as China, Japan, South Korea, Taiwan, Indonesia, Malaysia, Singapore, and Thailand (Doner et al. 2005; Cheung 2005). Many Asian leaders are "increasingly confident, no longer hesitate to advertise their interventionist [developmental] model—or to criticise the models of others" (Kurlantzick 2011, p. 27). More specifically, the existing literature, in general, tends to attribute spectacular Asian economic progress to the role of the so-called developmental state (explained below) characterised by a unique mode of governance (politics, administration, and business) (Beeson 2001; Regnier 2011).

These claims of Asian progress vis-à-vis Asian governance have serious implications for rethinking the academic domains of public policy and administration, as well as for the practical policy reforms adopted by governments worldwide, in line with the Asian success stories. With regard to the need for questioning the taken-for-granted Western concepts and theories in policy studies, Bice and Sullivan (2014, p. 539) emphasise that "the construct, content, and conduct of policy studies must respond to the challenges and opportunities of the 'Asian Century.'" However, there are serious controversies over the authenticity of the grand rhetoric of the Asian Century itself, on the one hand, and the reality of actual Asian achievements (beyond economics), on the other. Questions can also be raised about the uniqueness of the Asian brand or model of public governance attributed to such achievements. This chapter uses a critical approach in attempting to address these controversies or puzzles.

Emergence of the Asian Century: Advocacy and the Reality

Historically, Asia has always received global intellectual attention as the region represents the birthplaces of major religions, scientific discoveries, economic wealth, and great civilisations (for details, see Sommer 2006). However, for nearly five centuries, the hegemonic Western powers dominated the world economy, politics, and culture (especially Britain in the nineteenth century and America in the twentieth century). This led to a certain regional drive in Asia to reclaim its past civilisational glory in the current century, under the construct of the Asian Century, based on the region's unprecedented economic progress (Sommer 2006; Kurlantzick 2011). Related to this Asian reassertion, especially in the global ideational or normative order, is the recent discourse on so-called "Asian Values". Here, Asian Values tend to be distinguished from hegemonic Western political and moral values (e.g. individualism, liberalism, rights, and rationality) by prioritising the values of collectivism, communitarianism, filial piety, and political loyalty embedded in and compatible with the Asian context (Campbell 2007; Hoon 2004).

However, compared to such civilisational, ideational, and normative claims of Asian power and uniqueness, the contemporary debates have been largely guided by evidence-based economic and political considerations. For instance, recent claim to the Chinese Century highlights the rising economic and geo-political dominance of China in the twenty-first century (Rees-Mogg 2005; Elliot 2007). Similarly, the rhetoric of the Indian Century refers to India's potential for global economic dominance in the current century (Halliwell and Morley 2008). On the other hand, the idea of America's Pacific Century, touted by Hillary Clinton (2011), emphasised the global rise of Asia as led by the US through economic and strategic investment. Such economic and strategic benchmarks of global dominance or leadership are also embedded in the Asian Century perspective. This section examines the validity of Asian Century claims based on relevant empirical indicators.

Economic Performance: Growth, Income and Markets

Asia accounted for about 58 percent of the global economy in the 1850s, which declined to only 15 percent in the 1950s after a century of colonial intervention. Since then, rapid economic development has boosted the Asian share of global output to 27 percent in 2010 (ADB 2011a, p. 15). With continuing economic resurgence, it is estimated that Asia's share of global GDP will nearly double from 27 percent (2010) to 51 percent by 2050, a surge that is expected to strengthen the region's leading global economic position (ADB 2011a, p. 1). In comparison with the US economy, it was estimated that the total GDP of ten Asian economies (China, Korea, Singapore, Hong Kong, Taiwan, Malaysia, Indonesia, Thailand, Philippines, India) would be equal to the US GDP of $17 trillion by 2016, and it is predicted to be 17 percent more than US GDP by 2020 (Research Team 2011, p. 11).

The significant increase in Asia's share of global GDP is integral to the region's unsurpassed rate of economic growth compared to other regions. During the period 1990–2010, the average annual growth rate of GDP in Asia was 7.0 percent (including 9.9 percent in China and 6.4 percent in India), which was more than double the 3.4 percent growth rate in Latin America and the Caribbean (ADB 2012, p. 38). This was also reflected in significant increases in the levels of average income, which almost doubled in every decade (Research Team 2011, p. 12). It is estimated that with the upsurge of Asia's total GDP to $148 trillion (half of the global GDP) by 2050, the per capita income will also increase to $38,000 (PPP), a figure equivalent to the current average income level in Europe (ADB 2011a: 2).

Such an unprecedented expansion of wealth and income in Asia will have profound impacts on regional and global markets. These impacts may include a massive expansion of foreign direct investments in Asian countries, emergence of Asian transnational firms investing in other regions, increased Asian needs for importing industrial raw materials and building urban infrastructures, and greater Asian markets for high-value consumption goods demanded by its rising middle class (Government of Australia 2012, p. 40). It is highlighted that "Asia will not only be the world's largest producer of goods and services, it will also be the world's largest consumer of them" (Government of Australia 2012, p. 1). For instance, the food market has overwhelmingly expanded: it is estimated that Asian food consumption will increase by 45 percent by 2020, amounting to a total value of nearly $3 trillion, of which China alone will account for $1.48 trillion (Research Team 2011, p. 4). By 2020, the housing market in China will expand by 2.2 times to $3.7 trillion. In the world's largest automobile market in China, the number of vehicles will increase from 18 million (2011) to 30 million units (Research Team 2011).

This expansion of markets is largely due to the rising income level in Asia. Between 1990 and 2010, Asia's average per capita GDP increased significantly from $1,633 to $5,133. The proportion of the population living on or below the $1.25-a-day poverty line fell from 53.9% in 1990 to 21.5% around 2008, as 716 million people were lifted out of poverty. Seventeen countries reduced poverty by more than 15 percentage points in the period (ADB 2012, p. 38). In particular, the expansion of consumption markets in Asia is due to a drastic increase in the income of the middle class, which is likely to expand from 525 million (2011) to about 1.74 billion people in the foreseeable future (Research Team 2011). It is highlighted that "Asia's expanding middle class, like its Western counterpart, will seek to enjoy a better quality of life. This will drive the sale of durable goods such as refrigerators, cars, televisions, and mobile phones" (Research Team 2011, p. 24).

Institutions, Demographics and Other Considerations

Reflecting the unparalleled expansion of Asia's wealth, income, and consumption is its assertiveness in building regional financial institutions often spearheaded and led by China. One such institution is the the

Asian Infrastructure Investment Bank (AIIB) proposed by China in 2013 as a multilateral development bank to help build infrastructure in the Asia-Pacific region (Economist 2014). The AIIB has a capital of $100 billion and started operation after its ratification by 10 member states in 2015. Today, it has the memberships of 52 states. Another major multilateral financial institution is the New Development Bank (NDB) which represents the recently established cross-regional group known as the BRICS (Brazil, Russia, India, China, and South Africa). The NDB has an initial authorised capital of $100 billion, and it aims to support both infrastructure and development projects through loans and guarantees, and to build global networks of partnerships with multilateral development institutions and banks (Desai and Raymond 2014). It is observed that the AIIB and the NDB championed by leading Asian countries (especially China) are parallel competing international institutions such as the World Bank and the IMF led by the US (Cohn 2012; Desai and Raymond 2014). In addition, China's President Xi Jinping launched an ambitious initiative in 2013, known as 'One Belt, One Road' (OBOR), which represents the new twenty-first century version of the ancient Silk Road trade links connecting Asia, Africa and Europe and promoting trade among them. The recent Belt and Road Forum for International Cooperation held in Beijing was attended by 28 heads of state and government leaders (Zhao 2017).

Another dimension of Asia's global economic influence is its demographic figure, as it accounts for nearly 60 percent of the world population, and has seven of the world's most populous countries (ESCAP 2016). This situation significantly determines the share of global labor supply, as well as the size of consumption markets. It is found that between the 1980s and early 2000s, the world's labour supply almost doubled; in 2012, this labor pool included 3 billion workers; and about 50 percent of the new labor supply came from Asia. At the same time, the growth rate of new workforce declined in the Western World (Torres 2013; Freeman 2010). This demographic power of Asia is globally significant because, as the region's rising economic expansion absorbs its workforce, there is increasing global competition for human resources pools among non-Asian countries, especially due to the aging population in developed nations.

All of the above economic indicators of Asia—including its increasing share of global GDP, enhancement of average per capita income, rising number of middle-class population, huge expansion of consumption markets, establishment of major financial institutions, and global share of workforce or labor supply—demonstrate the rising economic power and influence of Asia with significant implications for the existing world economic order based on Western (especially American) dominance. Beyond the rising significance of Asia's economic power, the region also has increasingly become highly influential in military power as it accounts for 3–4 nuclear powers (China, India, Pakistan, and North Korea), potential for more permanent memberships (beyond China) in the UN Security Council (India and Japan), large size of military establishments, and huge arsenal of modern weapons challenging Western powers (Kurlantzick 2011).

While the discussion above offers credible evidence—including rising economic supremacy, demographic significance, and military/security power—of legitimacy for claiming the Asian Century, there are many questions, controversies, and limitations that need to be seriously taken into consideration. In fact, there are scholars who question whether there is or will be an Asian Century after all (Sommer 2006; Groff 2012; Kurlantzick 2011).

Questioning the Asian Century: Origins, Challenges and Hazards

First, how 'Asian' (indigenous) is the Asian Century? In addition to the role played by internal stakeholders (especially the state), there are major exogenous factors accounting for Asian high economic performance, including the global capitalist integration of national economies, infiltration of transnational capital (e.g. foreign investment), and rapid expansion of information technologies. The origins of most of these factors are Western (i.e., non-Asian). For instance, it was found in 2006 that among the largest 500 MNCs investing in Asia and contributing to its economic growth and employment, about 179 were American and 148 European, and they operated in all major sectors, including energy, car manufacturing, pharmaceuticals, banking, information technology, and so on (El-Ojeili and Hayden 2006, p. 65).

In China, foreign-invested enterprises account for more than 50 percent of its exports and imports, 30 percent of industrial output, 22 percent of industrial profits, and 10 percent of employment (World Bank 2010). Some empirical studies demonstrate that in 2004, the exports of foreign-invested enterprises in China was $339 billion, which represented 57 percent of the country's total exports (Zhang 2005, p. 1). From their study on FDI, Han and Guo (2004, p. 58) conclude that rapid economic growth in China "is a result of both internal forces (continuing improvements of human capital and upward momentum of growth) and external forces (large foreign capital inflows)" (Han and Guo 2004, p. 57). This is also the case in other Asian countries with high growth rates. Thus, the current unprecedented rate of economic growth in Asia (one of the main benchmarks for claiming the Asian Century) could have been impossible without the massive influx of foreign investment and technology transfer.

In addition, the Asian model of development guiding contemporary economic policies, institutions and activities is largely based on a Western outlook of progress that prioritises utilitarian economic growth, competition, and consumerism. The benchmarks and achievements of current Asian development initiatives are in line with a Western-style industrialisation of economy, modernisation of society, and urbanisation of living. Even consumption patterns are rapidly changing in major Asian cities based on a Western-centric globalised lifestyle. It is observed that with the rapid economic and income growth and rise of consumerism, there is a dramatic shift in Asian diets from traditional local foods to more Western-style foods (Pingali 2004; EIU 2011). By 2002, the share of supermarkets in processed or packaged food market reached 33 percent in Southeast Asia and 63 percent in East Asia, and there has been a drastic increase in fast-food chains in these regions (Pingali 2004). Similarly, between 2000 and 2014, Asian demand (as percentage of global demand) drastically increased from 14 percent to 36.8 percent for imported telecoms and IT equipment, from 10 percent to 22 percent for domestic electrical appliances, from 12.5 percent to 29 percent for audio and video equipment, and from 8 percent to 41 percent for car sales (EIU 2011, pp. 8–9).

Second, how homogeneous and convergent or conflict-free are Asian countries to generalise them under the Asian Century banner? In reality, Asian countries are extremely heterogeneous in terms of their territorial and population size, level of economic development, political systems, and so on. For instance, Asia has countries with some of the world's largest (e.g., China and India) and smallest (e.g., Singapore and Maldives) territorial size; and largest (e.g., China and India) and smallest population size (e.g., Brunei and Maldives). With regard to the level of development, there is significant diversity. While Japan, Singapore, and South Korea can be categorised as high-income developed nations, China, Malaysia, Thailand, Sri Lanka, Indonesia and the Philippines are considered middle-income countries, India, Vietnam, and Indonesia are categorized as developing countries, and Cambodia, Bangladesh, Myanmar, and Nepal are considered low-income countries (Regnier 2011; Coclanis and Doshi 2000).

There are significant political differences within Asia as well. While there are presidential systems of democracy in South Korea, Indonesia and the Philippines; there are parliamentary systems in Japan, India, Bangladesh, Pakistan, and Malaysia. Meanwhile, communist governments rule in China, Vietnam, and North Korea and there are absolute monarchies in Brunei, Qatar, and Saudi Arabia (Coclanis and Doshi 2000; Regnier 2011).

These forms of territorial, demographic, economic, political, and ideological diversities have implications for conceptualising a common Asian identity inherent in the idea of Asian Century. For instance, while it may give a greater sense of pride to economically affluent and/or territorially and demographically influential nations (e.g., Japan, Korea, China, and India), the Asian Century may not bear much meaning to economically poor and/or small-size powerless countries (e.g., Laos, Cambodia, and Maldives). There are, in fact, tendencies of exercising power and influence by regional powers, such as India and China, which are often perceived by neighbors (e.g. Taiwan, Hong Kong, Bhutan, Nepal) as unjust or unfair, sparking intra-regional tensions. The sense of Asian solidarity or unity needed to claim the validity of the Asian Century is also questionable, as there are various forms of cross-national conflicts in Asia. Although the Cold-War hostility has subsided, there are still uneasy relationships between China, Vietnam and North Korea and non-communist countries in Asia. More importantly, there are severe deep-rooted and historically inherited tensions between Pakistan and India, between South and North Koreas, between Taiwan and China, between Japan and China, and among Iran, Iraq, Syria, Lebanon, and Israel. All of these intra-regional tensions, conflicts, and even wars pose serious challenges to the realisation of the Asia Century.

Third, the model of Asian development associated with the Asian Century has potential adverse consequences that should be explored and seriously taken into consideration. For instance, in the process of achieving high economic performance, the situation worsened for many Asian countries with regard to external economic dependency, financial crises, economic inequality, social exclusion, and environmental degradation. All of these adverse consequences may render the possibility of the Asian Century unrealisable.

During the recent decades of Asia's spectacular economic growth accelerated by huge foreign direct investment, the degree of foreign ownership increased and the patterns of production, consumption, and workforce development were adjusted to facilitate such export-led growth. In the process of integrating national economies into the transnational capitalist system, external dependence and vulnerability accentuated for most Asian countries. As some of these countries experienced severe challenges of financial crises in the late 1990s, the rescue operation through foreign loans expanded their external debt, which worsened their external dependency further. It is reported that the total external foreign debt of Indonesia is \$133.8 billion, India \$107.9 billion, China \$84.2 billion, and the Philippines \$54.2 billion (Worldatlas 2017).

Another concern related to economic-growth-driven Asian development is the worsening situation of income inequality. Although most countries in major regions of Asia experienced a significant reduction in the level of poverty during 1990–2010 (United Nations 2013), by 2006, the number of people living in urban slums reached 550 million in Asia (El-Ojeili and Hayden 2006), which could be largely due to the rapid urbanisation and growing urban-rural disparity and economic inequality. Some recent studies on the rising inequality of per capita income measured by the Gini Coefficient, found that between the 1990s and 2000s, the Asia-wide Gini coefficient increased from 39 to 46, much worse than the OECD countries with figures ranging between 25 and 35 (ADB 2012, pp. 50–52). In China, in particular, the Gini coefficient increased from 32.4 in 1990 to 43.4 in 2008 (ADB 2012, p. 45). Thus, while growth-led development in Asia has drawn global attention for three decades, its adverse consequences for worsening inequality creates doubts in the actual virtue of such development.

In addition, the rapid pace of urbanisation, industrialisation, and hazardous production and consumption, which has been an integral part of high economic growth rates in Asia, has serious implications for the regional and global environment. As discussed above, in East and Southeast Asia, there has been an unprecedented expansion of consumption markets for environmentally hazardous processed foods, electronic appliances, and automobiles. It is no surprise that between 1990 and

2010, the amount of CO2 emission increased from 1 billion to 3 billion metric tons in South Asia and 3 billion to 9 billion metric tons in East Asia (United Nations 2013, p. 44). It is reported by the WWF (2012, p. 32) that during the recent two decades (period of high economic growth) in the Asia-Pacific region, extensive coastal development (where intensive foreign investment was made) led to "the destruction of many major coastal habitats, including corals, mangroves, seagrasses, wetlands, and salt marshes". It was also estimated that by 2015, China and India were likely to have the highest Ecological Footprints (indicator of ecological degradation) amounting to 37 percent of the global increase, and that countries like Japan, Indonesia, Pakistan, and South Korea were to be among the world's top 20 countries with high Ecological Footprints (WWF 2012, p. 25). The point here is that the environmental costs of Asia's intensive economic growth based on hazardous industrialisation and urban development deserve serious attention, and may lead us to ponder whether the economistic model of Asian development associated with the Asian Century is unquestionably praiseworthy from an ecological point of view.

Centrality of the State and Public Governance in Asian Development

This chapter has already highlighted that state-centric public governance has played a most crucial role in the rise in Asian development. In particular, in East Asian cases (e.g., Korea, Japan, China and Taiwan), the statist tradition is widely accepted due to a Confucian administrative culture that prescribes a paternalist mode of governance in which the bureaucratic elites are encouraged to play a key role in policy-making role (Cheung 2012). In contrast, "free market explanations" have been rejected by many scholars (Petras and Hui 1991). However, it is necessary to explore more diverse interpretations to deal with other Asian regions (especially South and Southeast Asia) and to locate (at least briefly) the patterns of public governance in its historical evolution and formation.

Historical Formations of the State and Public Governance

First, during the colonial phase of the state and governance in different parts of Asia, the formation of the "colonial state" led to the replacement or drastic restructuring of pre-colonial governing systems characterised by the dominance of Europeans exercising an indirect rule, often co-opting the native elite from local affluent families (Cooke 2003). Under the colonial state, the administrative system reflected certain Weberian bureaucratic principles (hierarchy, technical qualification, and rule of law) but adjusted to the local social and cultural contexts (Harris 1990). Such a framework of governance could be observed under the British colonial rule in South and Southeast Asia (Common 2001). In line with the priority of law and order and administrative discipline under the colonial rule, the centralised hierarchical structures also characterised the Dutch rule in Indonesia, the Spanish rule in the Philippines and the French rule in Indochina (Harris 1990; Sharp 1954).

Second, the post-colonial phase witnessed certain variations in the formations of the state and governance among the Asian regions. In South Asia, the state was defined as a "post-colonial state" dominated by the bureaucratic-military oligarchy which came to exercise significant autonomy from dominant social forces and to mediate between diverse power blocs (Alavi 1972). Very similar frameworks of state governance emerged in countries like Thailand (and perhaps Indonesia) which was characterised as a "bureaucratic polity" (Riggs 1966). However, the most widely discussed postcolonial state formation is the so-called "developmental state" in East and Southeast Asia (especially Japan, South Korea, Taiwan, and Singapore, and Malaysia), which possesses features such as a centralised structure, interventionist roles, alliances with the private sector, and a competent bureaucracy (see, Pierre Chap. 13 of this volume; Vu 2007; Loh 2005). Among these major postcolonial frameworks of state governance in South, East and Southeast Asia, the most common feature of the administrative system is its interventionist developmental role which received priority in the postcolonial context and required rapid socio-economic development in decolonised societies lacking private entrepreneurs and functional market systems.

Third, in line with the contemporary globalisation of transnational capital, disenchantment with the state-centric model, proliferation of pro-market (neoliberal) ideology, and triumph of market forces, the current phase of state formation is largely interpreted as the "neoliberal state". This neoliberal state prescribes the reduction or restructuring of governance in favor of a greater primary role played by business enterprises and other non-state actors (Robinson 2001; Liow 2011). Under such a neoliberal state, the domain of public governance tends to pursue pro-market policies (e.g., privatisation, deregulation, liberalisation), facilitation of the business sector's role, and businesslike reforms in public management such as managerial autonomy, financial discretion, and performance-based management, which are encapsulated as the so-called New Public Management (NPM). Most countries in Asia, including the communist governments of China and Vietnam, have been affected by the global trends of such a market-centric neoliberal state formation and businesslike public management, and at least partially, they embraced some of the basic tenets of this market-led state and governance (Khoo 2005; Common 2001).

In adopting this neoliberal mode of governance, governments in Asia were not only persuaded often by domestic experiences of public sector crises and public demands for alternatives, they were considerably pressured or influenced by international agencies such as the IMF, the World Bank, the UNDP, the WTO, and bilateral donors (Regnier 2011; Loh 2005; UNDP 2005). For instance, some of these agencies provided financial assistance to carry out reforms in public policies, organisations, finance, and management in countries such as Bangladesh, India, Pakistan, Sri Lanka, Cambodia, China, Indonesia, Philippines, Thailand, and Vietnam (UNDP 2005; World Bank 2004).

In the above context, most countries in Asia embraced the market driven model of public governance despite their cross-national variations in the degree of adopting different dimensions of the model. For instance, Bangladesh, South Korea, Singapore, Malaysia, Thailand, and the Philippines introduced reforms such as privatisation, outsourcing, managerial autonomy result-based budgets, performance measures, and so on (UNDP 2005; ADB 2011b). Although Indonesia and Japan have been relatively slow in reforming the public sector, they adopted some divestment initiatives, autonomous administrative units, target-based budgeting, result-oriented management, and performance measurement (ADB 2011b). Under the communist system, China and Vietnam also introduced drastic market-driven reforms to downsize ministries and departments, privatise state enterprises, outsource services, devolve financial management, and create businesslike administrative units (Xue and Zhong 2012; Vasavakul 2002).

The Developmental State and the Asian Century

The above discussion on the historical stages of evolving modes of governance demonstrates considerable shifts in its nature and role in Asia. However, it is the developmental state model that has been allegedly central to the realisation of rapid economic development, especially in East and Southeast Asia. Despite the recent trend towards the neoliberal pro-market restructuring of the state in Asia discussed above, there is still a common tendency among scholars to highlight the continuing role of developmental states in pursuing the so-called "governed market" model in the region (Cheung 2012, p. 211). This section of the chapter delineates the basic features of such a developmental state and its current status within the prevalent context dominated by transnational corporations and global and regional markets.

In general, the features of a developmental state in Asia include: (a) a close intermingling between the state and the market (in a governed market system); (b) collaboration and interlocking between the public and private sectors without losing each sector's autonomy; (c) the state's role to network and negotiate with diverse business groups while maintaining its distance from their sectional interests; (d) existence of a centralised but meritocratic and capable bureaucracy endowed with considerable autonomy; and (e) policy priority in favor of economic growth and industrialisation (Painter 2005; Ahn 2004; Mabasa and Mqolomba 2016). Under the developmental state, while the state bureaucracy is characterised by meritocracy, competence-based recruitment, competitive remuneration, and permanent tenure, it goes "beyond the Weberian ideal by promoting linkages with private actors, particularly business and, ideally, labor as well" (Doner et al. 2005, p. 335).

Some scholars conducting studies on state bureaucracy in the 1960s and 1970s, highlighted the developmental role of public bureaucracy in developing countries like India, Malaysia, Indonesia, Thailand, and Singapore, which they interpreted as "development administration" involved in long-term development plans related to nation-building and economic development through decentralisation and participation (Polidano 1999; Wong 2004; Hsueh 1970). The developmental state and development administration emerged in certain historical contexts in Asia, such as the ideological acceptance of state intervention, the need for rapid socioeconomic modernisation in the postcolonial atmosphere, and the established tradition of a centralised paternalistic government as found in Confucian political culture (Onis 1991; Mabasa and Mqolomba 2016; Painter 2005).

Among Asian countries, there is a greater consensus about the existence of a developmental state in Japan, South Korea, Taiwan, and Singapore, whereas Malaysia, Indonesia, the Philippines, and Thailand are categorised as intermediate developmental states (Ahn 2004; Doner et al. 2005; Beeson 2001). More recently, communist countries, such as China and Vietnam, are being interpreted as developmental states (Regnier 2011). In communist China, in particular, there are relevant signs of a developmental state, including the Confucian political culture legitimising state control, massive pro-market reforms carried out under the auspices of the state, utmost priority given to rapid economic growth or development, state-led but pro-market industrial strategies and trade policies, and export-led industrialisation (Mabasa and Mqolomba 2016). Thus, "most scholars contend that China only became a developmental state after commencing its economic reforms" (Mabasa and Mqolomba 2016, p. 78).

The limitation of the abovementioned views of the proponents of the developmental state and its continuing role in Asia's economic development is relatively insensitive to the real-life scenario of state and public governance that has undergone significant, market-driven reforms reinforcing the primacy of market forces in the region. In this regard, Beeson (2001, p. 490) emphasizes that even if the distinctive characteristics of the developmental state are less prevalent in cases like Korea and Japan, "it is entirely possible that they will continue because they are so deeply institutionalised". Kim (2011, p. 168) also suggests that "Asian developmental states have quite resiliently adapted to neoliberal globalization. . . Asian developmental states would never give up control of their economies for neoliberal restructuring. Works on Korea also point out that the developmental state in that nation has neither disappeared nor become weakened."

However, such strong statements in favor of the usual continuation of developmental state and governance seem to overlook the reality of drastic market-led policy reforms (privatisation, deregulation, and liberalisation) and pro-business restructuring of public sector management (outsourcing, agencification, and managerial autonomisation) adopted by Asian states. Thus, there is certainly a need for more critical rigorous, studies on the changing nature and role of the state and governance in Asia and its implications for the realisation of the Asian Century. In particular, if Asia's remarkable economic development has resulted from the role played by the developmental state, any significant change in such a state formation would be likely to affect the sustainability of economic development.

Indigenising Public Governance for an Authentic Asian Century

It has been discussed in this chapter that the rise of the Asian Century debate has been largely based on Asia's spectacular economic performance in terms of the growing regional share of global GDP, increasing per capita income, expansive consumption markets, comparative advantage in large demographic size (human capital), and creation of multilateral institutions. While all these positive economic evidences appear to be in favour of claiming the Asian Century, there are other major factors that raise questions about this claim. For instance, export-led economic growth tends to perpetuate Asia's external dependency, worsened further by external foreign debt. In the process of economic growth, most Asian countries have experienced increased levels of income inequality. In addition, growth-led development based on hazardous industrialisation and urbanisation has serious implications for regional and global environmental degradation. In this regard, some scholars highlight some of the undesirable consequences of rapid economic development under the developmental state in China, such as "income inequalities, environmental degradation . . . rural poverty, massive urban migration, the repression of worker rights, and the reduction of social security nets for the poor" (Mabasa and Mqolomba 2016, p. 78). All of these negative consequences of the Asian model of economic development deserve due attention in appraising the Asian Century.

Behind the Asian economic miracles is the leading role played by the state and public governance. Thus, the chapter has analysed the nature and role of the state and governance in Asia at three historical phases of state formation, including the colonial state, the postcolonial developmental state, and the incipient neoliberal state. However, as there is a common tendency among Asian scholars to highlight the continuing role of the developmental state in achieving rapid economic development, the chapter illustrates the main tenets of such a state, and suggests the need for exploring how the developmental state may have been restructured by recent drastic market-oriented reforms in governance.

In order to overcome the limits of the Asian development model underlying the Asian Century, it is essential to transcend the narrow economistic view of development and redefine it as a more multidimensional concept covering political, cultural and environmental concerns as well. It should be a development model that does not accentuate external dependency, income inequality, and environmental degradation. The realisation of such development would also require an appropriate framework of governance that is indigenously constructed in line with local needs and realities of Asian countries—it should not be externally imposed by international actors as found in the case of colonial-bureaucratic, postcolonial-developmental, and current neoliberal public management models of governance discussed in this chapter.

Such externally inherited or imposed administrative models created wide-ranging gaps between administration and society. As the borrowed administrative models lacked indigenous roots, their application to governance often produced dysfunctional outcomes such as excessive bureaucratic power and administrative elitism in many Asian countries (Cheung 2005; Abueva 1970). Similarly, the values of imposed or imitated Western administrative models (e.g., efficiency, specialisation, impartiality, and meritocracy) are compatible with Western cultural norms (e.g., individualism, division of labor, competition and achievement), but they mismatch with Asian cultural values, including collective values, paternalism, loyalty, seniority, and reciprocity (Cheung 2005; Sharp 1954; Harris 1990). Thus, there is a need for contextualising (indigenising) public administration systems in Asia, but there are serious challenges or constraints in building indigenous administrative knowledge.

Challenges to indigenising public administration include, first, the continuing colonial legacy in academic research on Asian public administration that assumes the superiority of Western knowledge and backwardness of local knowledge (see, Moloney Chap. 11 of this volume; Candler et al. 2010). There is also the dominance (epistemic colonialism) of the US over the public administration field which discourages the recognition of national and local experiences (Candler et al. 2010). Another barrier to indigenisation is the fact that there is inadequate representation of Asia in knowledge production in the public administration field—comparative studies on the field's leading journals show that there are serious degrees of underrepresentation of Asia-focused articles, Asian scholars as authors, and Asian academics as editors and editorial board members (Ko and Prameswaren 2010). In addition, most of the premier journals and book publishers are located in Western countries, especially the US and the UK. Thus, in building indigenous knowledge and profession of public governance and administration in Asia, it is imperative to deconstruct Western-centric intellectual hegemony, utilise Asian local knowledge, and expand Asian representation in research and publications.

In short, while we must recognise Asia's remarkable economic achievements and perhaps support the idea of the Asian Century as a fair ideational alternative to the past British Century and American Century, we should still unbundle this grand claim of the Asian Century. It is crucial to objectively assess the validity and consequence of its inherent economic development model and to explore the nature and limits of its supporting modes of public governance. Proceeding a step further, we may need to rethink the Asian development model, make it more context-driven and people-centered, explore a more indigenous mode of governance to enforce the new development model, and thus, make the Asian Century truly Asian.

References

Abueva, J. V. (1970). Administrative reform and culture. In H. B. Lee & A. G. Samonte (Eds.), *Administrative reforms in Asia* (pp. 21–47). Manila: Eastern Regional Organization for Public Administration.

(Asian Development Bank) ADB (2011a). *Asia 2050: realizing the Asian century.* Manila: Asian Development Bank.

(Asian Development Bank) ADB. (2011b). *Framework for results-based public sector management and country cases.* (Report of ADM Project Asia-Pacific Community of Practice on Managing Development Results). Manila: ADB.

(Asian Development Bank) ADB. (2012). *Asian development outlook 2012. Confronting rising inequality in Asia.* Manila: Asian Development Bank.

Ahn, S,-G. (2004). The transformation of Northeast Asian states in the era of globalization: Regulatory state or flexible developmental state? *Korean Journal of International Relations, 44*(5), 135–148.

Alavi, H. (1972). The state in post-colonial societies: Pakistan and Bangladesh. *New Left Review, 74*, 59–81.

Australian Government. (2012). *Australia in the Asian Century*. White Paper, October. Canberra: Australia in the Asian Century Implementation Task Force, Department of the Prime Minister and Cabinet.

Beeson, M. (2001). Globalization, governance, and the political-economy of public policy reform in East Asia. *Governance: An International Journal of Policy and Administration, 14*(4), 481–502.

Bice, S., & Sullivan, H. (2014). Public policy studies and the "Asian century": New orientations, challenges, and opportunities. *Governance, 27*(4), 539–544.

Brooks, S. G., & Wohlforth, W. C. (2009). Reshaping the world order: How Washington should reform international institutions. *Foreign Affairs, 88*(2), 49–63.

Campbell, C. (2007). *The easternization of the West: A thematic account of cultural change in the modern era*. Boulder, CO: Paradigm Publishers.

Candler, G. G., Azevedo, A., & Albernaz, R. O. (2010). Towards global scholarship in public affairs. *Public Administration, 88*(3), 836–850.

Cheung, A. B. L. (2005). The politics of administrative reforms in Asia: Paradigms and legacies, paths and diversities. *Governance, 18*(2), 257–282.

Cheung, A. B. L. (2012). Public administration in East Asia: Legacies, trajectories and lessons. *International Review of Administrative Sciences, 78*(2), 209–216.

Clinton, H. (2011). America's Pacific century. *Foreign Polic,*. 11 October.

Coclanis, P. A., & Doshi, T. (2000). Globalization in Southeast Asia. *Annals of the American Academy of Political Science, 570*, 49–64.

Cohn, T. H. (2012). *Global political economy: Theory and practice*. New York: Routledge.

Common, R. (2001). *Public management and policy transfer in Southeast Asia*. Aldershot: Ashgate Publishing Limited.

Cooke, B. (2003). A new continuity with colonial administration: Participation in development management. *Third World Quarterly, 24*(1), 47–61.

Cox, M. (2012). Power shifts, economic change and the decline of the west? *International Relations, 26*(4), 369–388.

Dadush, U., & Stancil, B. (2010). *The world order in 2050*. Washington, DC: Carnegie Endowment of International Peace.

Desai, R. M. & Raymond V. J. (2014, July 17). What the new bank of BRICS is all about. *The Washington Post*.

Doner, R. F., Ritchie, B. K., & Slater, D. (2005). Systemic vulnerability and the origins of developmental states: Northeast and Southeast Asia in comparative perspective. *International Organization, 59*(2), 327–361.

Drezner, D. W. (2007). The new new world order. *Foreign Affairs*, March/April.

(*Economist* Intelligence Unit) EIU. (2011). *Rising consumption, rising influence: How Asian consumerism will reshape the global electronics industry*. London: *The Economist* Intelligence Unit Limited.

Elliott, M. (2007, January 22). China takes on the world. *Time Magazine*. Retrieved from http://content.time.com/time/magazine/article/0,9171,1576831,00.html.

El-Ojeili, C., & Hayden, P. (2006). *Critical theories of globalization*. Basingstoke: Palgrave Macmillan.

(Economic and Social Commission for Asia and the Pacific) ESCAP. (2016). *ESCAP population data sheet*. Bangkok: United Nations Economic and Social Commission for Asia and the Pacific.

Fidler, D. P. (2005). The Asian century: Implications for international law. *Singapore Year Book of International Law, 9*, 1–17.

Freeman, R. (2010, March 5). *What really ails Europe (and America): The doubling of the global workforce. The Globalist*. Retrieved from https://www.theglobalist.com/what-really-ails-europe-and-america-the-doubling-of-the-global-workforce/.

Government of Australia. (2012). *Australia in the Asian century: White paper 2012*. Canberra: The Government of Australia.

Groff, S. P. (2012, April 18). Will this be the 'Asian century'? *The Guardian*. Retrieved from https://www.theguardian.com/global-development/poverty-matters/2012/apr/18/asia-century-globalisation-success-governance.

Halliwell, M., & Morley, C. (2008). *American thought and culture in the 21st century*. Edinburgh: Edinburgh University Press.

Han, G. L., & Guo, S. (2004). Political economy of FDI and economic growth in China: A longitudinal test at provincial level. *Journal of Chinese Political Science, 9*(1), 43–62.

Haque, M. S. (2013). Public administration in a globalized Asia: Intellectual identities, challenges, and prospects. *Public Administration and Development, 33*(3), 262–274.

Harris, P. (1990). *Foundations of public administration: A comparative approach*. Hong Kong: Hong Kong University Press.

Hoon, C. Y. (2004). Revisiting the Asian values argument used by Asian political leaders and its validity. *Indonesian Quarterly, 32*(2), 154–174.

Hsueh, S. S. (1970). Technical cooperation in development administration in South and Southeast Asia. In E. W. Weidner (Ed.), *Development administration in Asia* (pp. 339–365). Durham: Duke University Press.

Kappel, R. (2011). *The decline of Europe and the US: Shifts in the world economy and in global politics*. GIGA *Focus* International Edition 1/2011.

Khoo, B. T. (2005). Capital control and reformasi: Crises and contestations over governance. In F. L. K. Wah & J. Ojendal (Eds.), *Southeast Asian responses to globalization* (pp. 83–109). Institute of Southeast Asian Studies: Singapore.

Kim, S. (2011). Globalization and national responses: The case of Korea. *International Review of Public Administration, 16*(2), 165–179.

Kimmage, M. (2013). *The decline of the west: An American story.* 2012–2013 paper series No. 4. Washington, DC: Transatlantic Academy.

Ko, K., & Prameswaren, K. (2010, October 7–8). *Knowledge accumulation of Asian public administration: In progress or static?* Paper presented at the KAPA 2010 International Conference, Seoul, Korea.

Kupchan, C. A. (2012, March 20). The decline of the West: Why America must prepare for the end of dominance. *The Atlantic.* Retrieved from https://www.theatlantic.com/international/archive/2012/03/the-decline-of-the-west-why-america-must-prepare-for-the-end-of-dominance/254779/.

Kurlantzick, J. (2011). The Asian century? Not quite yet. *Current History, 110,* 26–31.

Liow, E. D. (2011). The neoliberal developmental state: Singapore as case study. *Critical Sociology, 38,* 241–264.

Loh, K. W. F. (2005). Globalization, development and democratization in Southeast Asia. In F. L. K. Wah & J. Ojendal (Eds.), *Southeast Asian responses to globalization* (pp. 17–54). Institute of Southeast Asian Studies: Singapore.

Mabasa, K., & Mqolomba, Z. (2016). Revisting China's developmental state: Lessons for Africa. *Strategic Review for Southern Africa, 38*(1), 69–84.

Onis, Z. (1991). The logic of the developmental state. *Journal of Comparative Studies, 24*(1), 109–126.

Painter, M. (2005). Bureaucratic autonomy and administrative reform capacity in East and Southeast Asia. In A. B. L. Cheung (Ed.), *Public service reform in East Asia* (pp. 231–254). Hong Kong: The Chinese University Press.

Petras, J., & Hui, P.-K. (1991). State and development in Korea and Taiwan. *Studies in Political Economy, 34,* Spring 1991.

Pingali, P. (2004). *Westernization of Asian diets and the transformation of food systems: Implications for research and policy.* ESA Working Paper No. 04–17. Rome, Italy: The Food and Agriculture Organization.

Polidano, C. (1999). *The new public management in developing countries.* IDPM Working Paper no. 13. Institute for Development Policy and Management, University of Manchester, UK.

Rees-Mogg, W. (2005). This is the Chinese century. *The Times,* 3 January.

Régnier, P. (2011). Developmental states and hybrid regimes in South-East Asia: The socio-economic and political challenges of global crises (1998–2008). *Asien, 120,* 10–27.

Research Team (DBS Bank). (2011). *Imagining Asia 2020: Make way for the Asia giant.* Singapore: DBS Bank Ltd.

Riggs, W. F. (1966). *Thailand: The modernization of a bureaucratic polity.* Honolulu: East-West Center Press.

Robinson, W. I. (2001). Social theory and globalization: The rise of a transnational state. *Theory and Society, 30,* 157–200.
Schmitz, H. (2007). The rise of the east: What does it mean for development studies? *IDS Bulletin, 38*(2).
Sharp, W. R. (1954). Some observations on public administration in Indochina. *Public Administration Review, 14*(1), 40–51.
Sommer, T. (2006). Is the 21st century going to be the Asian century? *ASIEN, 100,* 70–78.
Sterckx, R., & Luca, D. (2009). *Asian studies in the humanities: Visions for the future.* France: European Science Foundation.
The Economist. (2014, November 11). Why is China creating a new 'World Bank' for Asia. Retrieved from http://www.economist.com/blogs/economist-explains/2014/11/economist-explains-6.
Thompson, M. R. (2004). Pacific Asia after 'Asian Values': Authoritarianism, democracy, and 'good governance'. *Third World Quarterly, 25*(6), 1079–1095.
Torres, R. (Ed.). (2013). *World of work report 2013: Repairing the economic and social fabric.* Geneva: International Labour Organization.
(United Nations Development Programme) UNDP. (2005). *Trends and challenges in public administration reform in Asia and the Pacific.* Bangkok: UNDP Regional Centre in Bangkok.
United Nations. (2013). *The millennium development goals report 2013.* New York: United Nations.
Vasavakul, T. (2002). *Rebuilding authority relations: Public administration reform in the era of Doi Moi.* Hanoi: Report commissioned by the Asian Development Bank.
Vu, T. (2007). State formation and the origins of developmental states in South Korea and Indonesia. *Studies in Comparative International Development, 41*(4), 27–56.
Wong, J. (2004). The adaptive developmental state in East Asia. *Journal of East Asian Studies, 4,* 345–362.
World Bank. (2004). *Nepal: Country assistance strategy, 2004–2007.* Kathmandu: The World Bank, Nepal Office.
World Bank. (2010, July 16). Foreign Direct Investment—The China story. Retrieved from http://www.worldbank.org/en/news/feature/2010/07/16/foreign-direct-investment-china-story.
Worldatlas. (2017). Countries with the most external debt. Retrieved from http://www.worldatlas.com/articles/countries-with-the-most-external-debt.html.
WWF International. (2012). *WWF report 2012: Ecological footprint and investment in natural capital in Asia and the Pacific.* Manila: Asian Development Bank.

Xue, L., & Zhong, K. (2012). Domestic reform and global integration: Public administration reform in China over the last 30 years. *International Review of Administrative Sciences, 78*(2), 284–304.

Zhang, K. H. (2005, June 25–26). *How does FDI affect a host country's export performance? The case of China.* Paper presented at the International Conference on WTO and the Asian Economies III, Xi'an Jiaotong University, China.

Zhao, B. (2017, May 10). *China's 'one belt, one road' initiative: "A new silk road linking Asia, Africa and Europe".* Montreal: Centre for Research on Globalization.

CHAPTER 4

Weber and Confucius in East Asia: The Great Experiment

Jill L. Tao

Introduction

Nations in East Asia have a long tradition of what has been referred to as "Confucian bureaucratic culture" (Frederickson 2002, p. 614). This has been both a point of pride and contention for these nations as they have moved from traditional societies, in a Weberian sense, to more modern, post-industrial economies and more democratic political regimes. China, however, despite its historical role as the source of Confucian thought, teachings and influence, has rejected the tenets of Confucian teaching more severely than its neighbors, South Korea and Japan. Especially under former Communist Party Chairman Mao Zedong, Confucian philosophy and the so-called 'feudal thinking' that it epitomised were rejected, and later during the Cultural Revolution of the 1960s, more radical rejection was associated with violence (Bianco 1971).

In Korea, in the aftermath of the Korean conflict of the early 1950s, the government was reeling from the effects of the war, and

J.L. Tao (✉)
Department of Public Administration, Incheon National University,
Incheon, South Korea
e-mail: j.tao.808@gmail.com

S. Bice et al. (eds.), *Public Policy in the 'Asian Century'*, International Series on Public Policy, https://doi.org/10.1057/978-1-137-60252-7_4

was compelled to essentially start from scratch. Building a new Korean national identity was both a response to the attack from the north (e.g. how is the South different from the North? It was previously one people, and is now two) and a rejection of the years of occupation by the Japanese and subsequent military rule by the US after the end of World War II (Kim 2012). The country's most recent indigenous governing system had been during the late Choseon Dynasty (ending in 1897), which, towards its end, had seen increasing criticism of the formalism that had become synonymous with the behavior of the ruling elite. This critique was captured by *Sil-hak*, a Confucian reform movement that emphasised 'practical learning' and a more egalitarian approach to rule (see Kim 2012, pp. 219–220, on the writings of Chong Yak-yong). It is important to note that this critique was not a rejection of Confucianism, simply a shift in focus to attempt to create a more flexible system of governing that could adapt to the rapid changes that were occurring in Korea at that time. So when a new government formed in the 1950s, it incorporated several influences from outside of Korea, but it had an essential Confucian core that remained intact.

Both China and Korea have been influenced at different points in the twentieth and twenty-first centuries by the writings of Max Weber, especially in the field of public administration. But Weber, who is often seen as the spokesperson for modernisation, is perceived as both a student and a critic of Confucianism and its 'bureaucratising effects' on society. As both China and Korea search for ways in which their provision of public service might be improved, each nation has expressed some ambivalence toward Weberian perspectives. This ambivalence can be traced to two sources: one, an attempt to protect what is seen as an indigenous system of governing, and therefore, one that is more culturally appropriate; and two, a misreading, perhaps, of what Weber's ideal types mean for 'Confucian bureaucratic culture'. However, there may be far less distance between Confucius and Weber than one might think. This chapter will attempt to examine Confucian approaches to governing within two different contexts: within Korea, where these approaches have never quite been fully rejected; and within China, where the rejection was absolute and highly political. These contexts will be examined through Weber's depictions of modernisation, or the 'rationalisation of value spheres', which includes a depiction of bureaucracy as an ideal type. The ways in which Weber's depiction of this ideal type differ from traditional authority approaches may offer some insight into where the mismatch between Confucian systems of thought and Weberian ideals can cause confusion. I will then use the perception of corruption to illustrate how this conflict in ideals manifests this confusion, and then will highlight some practical implications for policy.

China and the West and Confucianism

Chinese intellectuals were no strangers to the writings of German philosophers at the turn of the twentieth century (Bianco 1971). But the West, in contrast, knew remarkably little about China, partly because of the isolationist stance of the country over long periods of time, including a ban on international trade during the Ming dynasty. Max Weber, with his publication of several essays on the world's religions, was actually responsible for a resurgence in interest in China and Confucianism, especially within Europe. But much of his writing, and indeed, the basis for his conclusions about modernisation and the rise of capitalism in the West, but not in the East, were based on very limited sources: poorly translated, and often unsubstantiated accounts of life inside China (Radkau 2011). That said, Weber's inductive approach to his development of theories of human behavior and social structures have incorporated a perspective on bureaucracy that uses China as a heuristic for understanding traditional legitimacy. This reasoning is based on his understanding of Confucianism and the role it played in Chinese society and government. One of the key characteristics that Weber examines is the prevalence of bureaucratic forms and the relative importance of bureaucrats within Chinese society.

Weber's conception of bureaucracy is an oft cited and as often misunderstood notion of the social structure that exercises authority within a given society. The roots for this conception were developed over a period of many years, and mostly as commentary on the logical progression of 'modernisation' and the rise of capitalism. These ideas were most famously articulated in his seminal work *The Protestant Ethic and the Spirit of Capitalism*, originally published in 1905 shortly after his first (and only) visit to the United States (Coser 1977, pp. 237–239). The theme of this work was by no means unique to Weber (see Felix Rachfahl's critique for a notable list, nicely summarised by Chalcraft and Harrington 2001, pp. 89–90). But his reasoning was focused, as noted by Radkau (2011), on a moralistic core in the public sphere:

> "What was at issue was …*how* the connection between Protestantism and capitalism should be conceived. The idea suggested itself that the link between the two was not so direct but passed through a shared third element. And for an educated liberal this was likely to be the Enlightenment and modern science, both of which had developed mainly on the ground of Protestantism that was also especially favourable to the advance of secularism. However, it is precisely vis-à-vis Rachfahl's alternative picture of the genesis of capitalism that the distinctiveness of Weber's thesis appears most sharply. For Weber sought the origins of capitalism not in the Enlightenment and the process of secularization, nor in the dissolution of religious attachments, but on the contrary in religious passion…he was convinced that the modern vocational ethic must have sprung from a powerful instinctual force, and he located this neither in the Enlightenment nor in philosophical idealism but in the realm of religion. (p. 185)

For Weber, the connection between religious fervor and vocation remained a powerful link, one belied by later interpretations of the 'ideal' bureaucrat as 'relentlessly objective'. The times were those of Frederick Taylor and the machine, the ultimate manifestation of a perfect work ethic for some, but not for Weber. He was, at best, ambivalent about the future of modern society and its embrace of capitalism, and the specter of the iron cage was his harbinger for the modern industrial worker. This is why his later work turned east, to more 'traditional societies' with distinct roots for bureaucratic systems.

Weber's Ideal Manifestations of Authority

Weber's notion of the 'ideal type' of legal-rational authority was bureaucracy, and as an ideal type, it had certain characteristics that helped manifest the theoretical underpinnings of this kind of legitimacy. The main characteristics are six, as put forward in the Gerth and Mills translation (1946) and focus on the primacy of rules, the importance of expertise, and the application of reason to the execution of one's duties (pp. 196–198). As the name implies, the basis for authority in the modern state was a body of law, or rules, that carried power quite separately from the body or individuals who were responsible for the drafting of the law or rules. It is this dispossession of the law that gives it an objective nature, which Weber refers to as follows: "The theory of modern public administration, for instance, assumes that the authority to order certain matters by decree—which has been legally granted to public authorities—does not entitle the bureau to regulate the matter by commands given for each case, but only to regulate the matter abstractly" (Gerth and Mills 1946, p. 198). In other words, there should be an overarching principle that can be applied in a general fashion to cases that are deemed similar.

Weber's conception of the nature of this 'modern officialdom' differed from 'traditional' systems in this separation of law from its makers. As he explains,

> Bureaucracy, thus understood, is fully developed in political and ecclesiastical communities only in the modern state, and, in the private economy, only in the most advanced institutions of capitalism. Permanent and public office authority, with fixed jurisdiction, is not the historical rule, but the exception. This is so even in large political structures such as those of the ancient Orient, the Germanic and Mongolian empires of conquest, or of many feudal structures of state. In all these cases, the ruler executes the most important measures through personal trustees, table-companions, or court-servants. (Gerth and Mills 1946, p. 196)

Weber saw repudiation of certain components of 'traditional bureaucracy' as necessary for true modernisation to take place. In particular, he saw he personal nature of law and power in traditional societies as being antithetical to the modern state. The modern state was, in his eyes, a manifestation of rationalisation, where cause and effect were linked in a systematic way, and this meant that the individual must be capable of engaging in this process in order to function properly in society.

In his study of the world's religions, which included Taoism and Confucianism, he saw societies that had developed such religions as capable of becoming modern and achieving rationalisation. Eisenstadt (1986) called such societies 'axial' in reference to what Jaspers (1948) called 'the Axial Age'. But, as Bellah (1999) states:

> Rationalizing potentialities exist in all the axial civilizations, but, according to Weber, it was several tendencies within Western Civilization that led to the decisive breakthrough into modernity, the third of his major evolutionary stages, one characterized by a high degree of rationalization in every sphere and the increasing disjunction between the spheres. Although Weber used the term "capitalism" as his most frequent way of referring to modern society, he by no means considered economics the key to the entire complex. He attributed to the Protestant Reformation, particularly in its Calvinist and sectarian forms, a key role in the emergence

> of modernity; especially through its relentless criticism of magic and its methodical organization of ethical life in an effort to transform the world. (Bellah 1999, p. 279)

The 'spheres' Bellah references here and their 'disjunction' are key to grasping how Weber sees a 'modern' bureaucracy as opposed to a 'traditional' one. There are six spheres: the kinship sphere: the economic sphere; the religious sphere; the erotic sphere; the political sphere; and the intellectual sphere (Oakes 2003, p. 29). As society evolves, these spheres separate and become ever more distinct, and tensions between them can drive an evolution to a new social form. In more traditional societies, such as China, Weber interpreted much of what he read as overlap between spheres, and the importance of the kinship sphere in all others was not conducive to modernisation in his eyes. This is why he concluded that China, while it embraced Confucian norms, would never become a 'capitalist' society, since the bonds of kinship would prohibit business relations with those outside one's own circle. Kinship enables a given group to exercise its own authority over members, meting out punishment, for example, for transgressions against other members. This is why one only engages with others from the same group—authority ends at the group's edge, and the norms and expectations of behavior are different beyond that boundary. Thus there is no recourse for enforcing an obligation beyond the limits of kinship. For Weber, modern capitalism required the ability to move beyond kinship boundaries by recognising and honoring the rules of external trade.

There are two important observations to make of Weber's conclusions. The first is his underestimation of China's size, complexity and diversity. To say there is 'one China' or a unified 'Chinese' approach to conducting affairs of business or state is a caricature that does little justice to the China of Weber's time or the modern version. Weber saw the importance of kinship ties within Chinese society as emblematic of a feudal society (a view with which Mao concurred), and therefore a barrier to modernisation. This was only partly true, since there were places within China where such ties were looser than in others, the coastal regions and urban areas, for example, where international trade was vigorous and lively. But for Weber, rooted in the European transition to a more technologically and industrially driven society, the bonds of kinship were shackles rather than supports.

The second observation is with regard to Weber's conception of evolution. He is not saying more evolved forms are more desirable than traditional forms. He is simply describing what he sees as a progression from a less fragmented and perhaps more holistic societal arrangement to one that is more structurally diverse, where new social forms may create tension with older ones. These areas of tension appear to have held some fascination for Weber, since he saw them both as an impetus for progress (modern science, technological advances) and as a source of human misery (destruction of familial ties, social alienation, industrial loneliness). It is, as Radkau (2011) outlines, this perception of the capitalist motivation to accumulate wealth as an internalised drive, not something external, that leads Weber to his conception of the 'iron cage' in which modern man finds himself. And as the name implies, this is not necessarily a natural or comfortable place for mankind to be.

Confucius and Chinese Bureaucrats

Confucian thinking, as outlined in the *Analects* and in the works of later Song dynasty scholars, such as Zhuxi (朱熹) is articulated as an understanding of how people interact with the world around them (Rarick 2007). It is the nature of this relationship between mankind and the natural world that serves to guide the relationships between people. What is natural is that which does not require learning, that which is innate. But how this manifests itself is through thought and emotion, which can have both positive and negative influences on the outside world. George Frederickson (2002) has articulated many of the principles of Confucian thought that hold interest for Western students of public administration, but he does not address Weber's conceptions of ideal types in this discussion. It is worthwhile, however, to revisit his perceptions of the important tenets of Confucian systems of thinking and juxtapose these with both the Weberian ideal and the thinking of current Chinese intellectuals on Confucianism and its potential role in shaping public service.

Frederickson's account of the Confucian approach to public service is introductory and broad, but it serves to highlight the distinctions between this approach and what Frederickson characterises as a 'Western' approach in some detail. He engages in this comparison through the lens of ethics and the idea of bureaucratic morality. He provides a breakdown of these differences by directly comparing 'Western' and 'Eastern' approaches to the characteristics of what he calls 'bureaucratic morality'

(Frederickson 2002, p. 623). He does so to illustrate the central focus of his article: understanding the role of the Confucian bureaucrat and his internalisation of a moral code of conduct. Frederickson highlights the important distinctions between behavior and intent, and how these manifest the characteristics of virtue. The most important distinction, in his opinion, is between intelligence (the recognition of right and wrong) and righteousness, which is doing right, as distinct from doing what is proper. Propriety is what has been accepted by society at large as appropriate behavior if one is doing right. But this distinction recognises that society can sometimes be wrong. As Frederickson puts it, "One is intelligent if one knows that murder is wrong. One is righteous if one does not murder. It is especially important, however, that one does righteous things for the right reasons. Righteousness always trumps propriety, and the righteous act done with a pure and unselfish heart is greater than mere serviceable goodness" (pp. 621–622).

Although Frederickson refers to his list of characteristics as representing an 'ideal type' of Confucian thought, he does not reference Weber or his conceptions in his comparison. If one compares the characteristics of the ideal bureaucracy to the characteristics of Confucian thought articulated here by Frederickson, however, there is one characteristic that seems consistently distinct (see Table 4.1). Confucian systems focus on virtue and its different types, and this forms the core that helps explain not just *how* people behave but how they *should* behave. It is inherently normative and intended to be so. This is why Frederickson refers to his rendition as an ideal type. Weber's ideal bureaucracy is also normative, but the norms articulated through bureaucracy's characteristics are the logical outcomes of a society based on legal-rational authority. Thus, Weber is describing a system that should exist if such authority truly holds sway. It is a predicted future, based on a distinct set of values important to modernisation, and the supreme value is rationalisation.

As Table 4.1 illustrates, the Weberian ideal and the general understanding of 'western' conceptions have some overlap but there are important distinctions, especially with regard to Confucian concepts. Two concepts, in particular, are worth highlighting because they play an important role in understanding the following discussion of how Confucian values can lie underneath the surface of what appears to be 'Western' or 'Weberian' approaches to public authority. The first is with respect to the instruments of governance, and is discussed by Frederickson in some detail: that Western and Weberian conceptions are

Table 4.1 A modified comparison of approaches to bureaucratic morality in Weberian, Western and Confucian thought

Subject	*Weberian thought*	*Modern western thought*	*Confucian or East Asian thought*
Instruments of governance	Laws, rules and documents (files)	Constitutions, laws, regulations	Man, judgment
Power	From the law and reason	From authority, from position	From morality; from position, by example
Purpose	To apply expertise to the proper implementation of rules	Efficiency, effectiveness, equity	Understanding, to do good
Rules and roles	Clear and hierarchical	Ambiguous	Clear
Processes	All management based on written documents (files). Strict separation between public and private resources	Good management, total quality, scientific, decision making	Moral conventions, intuitive, judgmental, moral action
Values	Expertise and rationality	Neutrality, policy advocacy	Virtue
Education	Expertise	Knowledge, skills	Understanding, virtue
Structure	Hierarchy and jurisdiction	Fluid, loosely coupled, ambiguous	Hierarchy, clear
Qualities	Vocation, judgment	Competence, judgment	Virtue, judgment
Aspirations	To master and rise (promotion)	To serve, to lead	To do good
Standards	Laws, rules, clear delineation and execution of tasks	Constitutions, laws, regulations, codes of ethics	Moral conventions, self-cultivation, virtue

Adapted from Frederickson (2002), p. 623. Weber's tenets added by author

similar, and constitute the basis of the 'rule of law', or as John Adams outlined in the Constitution of the Commonwealth of Massachusetts, "A government of laws, not of men" (1780). The Confucian approach, however, places the instruments squarely in the hands of men, and this is rooted in the Confucian notion that man is part of nature and therefore inherently good (Rarick 2007). This distinction highlights the importance of the character of those who rule in a Confucian context, where a good man[1] may be the source of laws. In the Weberian context, the law has legitimacy because it comes through a vetting process that has been accepted by a majority of the people under its rule with appropriate representation across society. Therefore, no individual is above the law nor can he or she unilaterally change it. In the broader Western context, however, constitutions outline the distribution of power and its institutions in society, and governance is thereby guided by whomever drafts such constitutions.

The second important distinction can be found in the processes used by bureaucrats. Within the Weberian context, bureaucrats are bound by two limits: rules and the separation of public and private spheres. A bureaucrat is a public official, and therefore his or her private affairs have no place inside the office that he or she occupies. In the Western context, there is instead a collection of practices that emphasise the particular area of expertise a particular bureaucrat may hold and exercise within the confines of his or her position. But in the Confucian context, the discretion of the individual official reigns supreme. This is not necessarily a contradiction with the Weberian ideal, but the explicit distinction between rules and person is not articulated. Moral convention may be the external imposition of societal rules and values, but the source and relative worth of those values are decided by the individual. Thus, for two different individuals to come to the same conclusion, they would have to be educated in the same way and to have followed similar paths to the understandings that they bring to bear on a particular subject.

The conclusions that we may draw from such observations are as follows: first, these three types of officials (Weberian, western and Confucian) may look and behave in similar ways at first blush—all recognise hierarchy as a means for organising complex actions; all value education and experience and the knowledge such things impart; and all are concerned with carrying out their duties in ways that are seen by society to have merit. However, the second conclusion renders the first as superficial; the source of one's legitimacy and therefore the reach of one's power in Western and Weberian systems differs substantially from Confucian systems, especially in the Weberian context. An official has no jurisdiction outside of his or her position. For example, just because someone is a ranking bureaucrat does not necessarily make him or her a good parent. Parenting falls within the private sphere, and is irrelevant to whether one can fulfill his or her public duties. But within a Confucian system, such an expectation does exist. The duties that one performs at home and in public are similar, and thereby behavior should reflect that similarity. This means that if one scolds a child for improper behavior, one may also scold a junior colleague in the same way. Thus, similarities in structure and appearance between Weberian and Confucian systems are not necessarily indicative of the differences that lie beneath the surface. This is why examining the distinct environments where Confucianism has been attacked and embraced can provide a better understanding of how it is manifested in the behavior of public officials.

Modern China, Rejection and Return to Confucian Values

Mao's rejection of Confucian ideals began much earlier than the overt campaign during the Cultural Revolution and the rule of the Gang of Four. As a student in Changsha and later as an organiser of peasant guerilla units in the skirmishes between the early Communist recruits and the Kuomintang, Mao had been highly critical of 'feudalism', especially the components that perpetuated conditions of abject poverty for the poorest peasants and relative comfort for those who owned the land. The landed class was extremely diverse in China, with some landowners in the Western provinces living barely better than their tenants, where others in the east and north fared much better (Bianco 1971). But the burden of relatively rigid class structures was often cited as too difficult to reform in a better way, especially during a time of warfare. Mao saw this as an excuse, which he later referred to in his rejection of the Soviet and Marxist models of communism, where revolution lay in the hands of the urban labor class. China's urban laborers were much better off than their peasant counterparts and knew it. Thus, they had little incentive to pursue new structures, and were far too disparate to organise in a meaningful way. Mao saw revolution as only possible with the peasantry, whose living conditions had deteriorated over the last part of the ninteenth and early parts of the twentieth century (Bianco 1971). Caught between starvation and crushing debt, they had little to lose. So, for Mao, the rejection of old class structures was in part a rejection of the Confucian value system: to seek virtue was a lofty ambition, but it was often used to hide less virtuous intentions. In the public sector, this often led to corruption and the entrenchment of an aristocracy that helped its own rather than seeking broader well-being (Adler 2011).

After the revolution and the military victories of the Communists were cemented with the establishment of the People's Republic of China in 1949, the rule of the Chinese Communist Party (CCP) depended greatly on its ability to show that a newly reconstructed society would reap benefits unknown to previous generations. This meant a strong and thorough rejection of 'feudal' ways, which included redistributing land, often by force, and dealing harshly with those who objected. Confucian ideals and values were quickly determined to be too risky for those who wished to live longer lives, and so the revolution attempted to undo over 2500 years of social conditioning within a relatively short time. The fact that the CCP was at all successful in this endeavor speaks volumes to both the tenacity and the use of both force and reward of early party leaders. It also clearly highlights the desperation of the peasants who supported them.

Aside from class structure there were specific components of the political aspects of Confucianism to which the CCP objected. The deference to elders and gender-bias were key components, since both had been written into law over centuries, thus making change more difficult. By the time the Cultural Revolution had run its course, and at the height of the rule of the Gang of Four, Confucius and his teachings were held in such low regard that they were described as follows:

> Confucius was a reactionary who doggedly defended slavery and whose doctrines have been used by all reactionaries, whether ancient or contemporary, Chinese or foreign, throughout the more than 2000 years since his time. The bourgeois careerist, renegade and traitor, Lin Piao was a thorough devotee of Confucius and, like all the reactionaries in Chinese history on the road to their doom, he revered Confucius, opposed the Legalist School and attacked Chin Shih Wang, the first emperor of the Chin dynasty (221–207 B.C.). He used the doctrines of Confucius and Mencius as a reactionary ideological weapon in his plot to usurp Party leadership, seize state power and restore capitalism in China. (Adler 2011, p. 7)

The understanding of capitalism here is what might be called 'crony capitalism' today. This is very much in keeping with Weber's perspective of the inability of a Confucian China to engage in modern markets, where trade occurs between strangers and transactions are driven by profit-maximisation for individuals and little else. The fusion between the political and economic spheres was where Weber also found China lacking in its ability to modernise.

But the China of today is a far cry from either the China of Weber's studies or Mao's China. How have the 'marketisation' policies of the last twenty-five years affected Weber's predicted future? Has China's rejection of Confucian thinking helped make the opening of markets with international trading easier? This is a difficult question to answer with a simple examination of China's recent history, which is never really simple. To offer what Weber called 'understanding through opposition' (Radkau 2011), it is perhaps constructive to compare what is currently articulated by Chinese scholars on approaches to management in the public sector—which oversees the opening of trade to other countries–with scholars' views on management from a context that is still very much steeped in Confucian thinking, South Korea. By examining the context of public bureaucracies in South Korea, where neo-Confucianism ensconced many of the traditions against which Mao and the CCP railed, it will become clearer as to what Weber meant by 'rationalisation' and modernising the state, and why he saw Confucian states as unlikely to modernise.

Korea and Confucianism

Anyone who has visited South Korea within the last decade would have difficulty concluding that it was not a 'modern' state. With a high degree of urbanisation (91.6% of the population lives in urban areas, according to a United Nations 2011 report), a highly efficient infrastructure, including global shipping and transportation capacity, South Korea functions at most levels as part of the developed world. Its government is highly centralised and unitary, so the degree of control exercised by the national government over affairs of state and economy is considerable. Yet it has done so in apparent contradiction of Weber's predictions, since the public sector (and indeed much of private sector corporations as well) has firm roots in Confucian ideals and values. So, was Weber wrong?

A closer examination of the Korean system may help answer this question. There is remarkably little literature on Confucian influences on Korean management, either public or private, and this in itself may be telling. But recent attempts to chronicle the history of public service in Korea have generated some interesting observations.

Kim (2012) notes that in the 1990s, a growing interest in 'Koreanisation' of public administration developed, in addition to the idea of indigenisation. As he explains, "The terms Koreanization and indigenization sound similar, but have slightly different connotations...In general, Koreanization implies that the pattern of development needs to reflect the Korean values and behavioral factors of Korean public administration" (Kim 2012, p. 229). This does not mean a return, as he puts it, "to old Confucian values. Instead, it could be seen as a way to find Koreans' own identity and realization of remaining relevant with a reasonable synthesis between domestic and foreign ideas" (p. 228). But unfortunately, he does not elaborate further on what the more modern values might be.

The pervasive influence of Confucian values in East Asia was addressed by Frederickson, but in an overarching manner, with little attention paid to particular approaches within nations. More recently, however, Im et al. (2013) have examined how the neo-Confucian teachings of the late Chosun dynasty still resonate in the current Korean civil service. Here, the focus is on indigenisation, but from a historical perspective that attempts to document where Confucian tenets may conflict with prescriptions from public administration theory borrowed from the West. The authors discover "a good deal of continuity between these unique features of the Chosun administration and the contemporary state, including the relationship between the state and society and the individual behavior of government officials" (p. 294). Some of the most important are those articulated in the moral obligations of the state. But the manifestations of these obligations play out in three ways:

> Much like the structure of state–society relations, the organizational culture of the South Korean bureaucracy today contains many features that derive from the country's Confucian heritage. In particular, the low substitutability of employees, a cultural acceptance of bureaucratic discretion, and a promotion-driven incentive system can be understood as key features of the Korean bureaucracy that distinguish it from Western models. (Im et al. 2013, p. 292)

Unlike Frederickson, Im and his co-authors clearly have the Weberian legal-rational model in mind as the epitome of 'Western' thinking. And the distinctions they articulate go a long way toward highlighting the different conceptions of the behavior of a public official within a Confucian system and one adhering to Weber's legal-rational tenets. The insights offered into why a Korean public official may behave in ways that would not make sense within a Weberian logic are compelling. Since a Confucian system internalises rules within individuals through learning and study, each individual in the system may have a unique set of skills that s/he brings to her/his organisation. This is what Im et al. mean when they describe 'low substitutability of employees'. Rather than having the position dictate the skills of the occupant, as the Weberian system is often interpreted as requiring, the occupant defines the position.

This articulation of the Confucian basis for public officials and their behavior is probably the most important because it highlights both the ideal of the ancient regimes and how far the current practice has both been adhered to and deviated from. Key to the training of public officials and their subsequent execution of duties was the idea that a proper education would provide them with the appropriate tools to do what was necessary. As Frederickson states, "In the Confucian states, it is assumed that both governmental and family investments in education will reap cultural, social, and especially economic benefits... Through education, one could become a good official, part of the ruling elite. In this way, Confucius built an enduring link between education and political power" (2002, p. 618).

However, this approach is prone to the same problem that Weber identifies in modern societies, where the means for producing something of value (say, capital) become ends in and of themselves. This is where Weber's idea of the means becoming the ends in modern society is both prescient and predicted by Confucius himself. As Im et al. explain:

> Just as a whole-of-the-person approach reduces substitutability in government organization, greater individuation of employees also makes any failures on the job inseparable from personal failures on the part of the offending employee. The emphasis in Korean culture on "saving face" motivates employees to avoid exposing themselves to criticism or fault wherever possible. As such, Korean culture tends to produce a highly "bureaucratic type" that relies upon the rules and regulations of the organization in the process of carrying out their duties. This reliance on rules reduces the chances that one would have to act in a discretionary manner, thereby opening his or herself up to censure should the discretionary action produce negative or unintended consequences. Thus, reliance on the rules allows bureaucrats to preserve their honor and reputation within a system where personal relations go deeper than formal organizational ties, a behavior grounded in the deeper cultural context of the bureaucracy

> rather than a respect for the legal–rational authority base of the organization in the Weberian sense of term. (Im et al. 2013, p. 293)

Herein lies the heart of the distinction—the source of the laws, rules and regulations that Weber saw as the basis of modern society was not a monarch or a benevolent aristocracy, learned or otherwise. In Europe, the social contracts between rulers and the ruled had long since soured. As in China, the obligation of the ruling class to care for those less fortunate has been abandoned. Once that social contract was broken, and the bonds of *noblesse oblige* rent asunder, any law based on traditional authority would be challenged. The source of Weber's legal-rational authority was not a monarchy offering decrees for the population but rather laws arrived at through the consultation and competition of democratic political systems. Without this key component undergirding legal-rational authority, it would be easy to mistake one set of laws and rules for another.

So, the Korean system has managed the task of producing a modern economy with some deference to Confucian norms (the dominance of *chaebol*, the large corporations led by powerful families, for example). But it has done so with a burgeoning development of its political systems at the same time (Kim 2012), which may mean that Weber was not too far off the mark. How does this help us to understand what may happen in the future in Korea, and what the implications are for China? Again, a comparison may be useful.

China and Korea: Quasi-Confucian?

China has been attempting 'marketisation' within a communist context, which may seem odd for a country that used to denounce 'running dog capitalists' and saw the accumulation of wealth as 'spiritual pollution' (Snow 1937). However, the CCP leadership after Mao's death saw the need to try alternatives from state-centric models, especially to stimulate growth and then provide better distributions of societal resources. Both of these goals are very much in keeping with the CCP's central concerns: address abject poverty and maintain the social contract between the Party and the people. The real question is whether this constitutes capitalism as a manifestation of Weber's rationalisation.

In South Korea, as discussed above, there are lingering shadows of Confucian structures within public service, but as the nation has moved towards more democratic manifestations of governing, the rules of the state have reflected this movement. In China, there have been calls to re-introduce Confucian values in public service sectors as wealth has increased and the privileges (and excesses) associated with political power have become more obvious. If Weber's conception of legal-rational authority is correct, then we might expect to see a number of things develop in both countries as markets and political systems evolve. Before addressing where these systems may go in the future, summarising where they are now with respect to manifestations of Confucianism and Weberian rationalisation is a logical precursor.

Where Are We Now?

Thus far, Weber's legal-rational authority and Confucianism have been presented as separate and somewhat contradictory ideals for administrative systems. They have, however, both been manifested to different extents in the two countries examined, and now we have a better idea as to what brings us to the twenty-first century and how these ideals might play out in the two systems. But until now, one key component of societal change has been left unexamined, and it seems appropriate to address it here, since it is pertinent to where both countries may go in the future. This is the question of industrialisation, and its impacts on social ties, especially those considered central to Confucianism, such as the relations between members of the family. As industrialisation has moved societies into the era of mass production and consumption, the impact on familial and social networks has been well-documented by sociologists (e.g. Durkheim's *anomie*), as well as its impact on public institutions and whether or not they suffer dysfunction (Merton 1940). This is where the parallelism of Confucian norms in both public and private settings runs into difficulty.

As societies industrialise, the role of government in this process can take many forms. In China, the communist state played the role of family organiser, restructuring social ties in ways that included pulling women into the industrial labor force in a public and official way (Cooke 2001). The concerted effort to make women equal partners in the new state was an open rebuke of the fundamental division between male and female roles in Confucian society. Although this rebuke has not been as successful as first envisioned (Kanthor 2016), compared to the status of women in South Korea, Chinese women have, to date, fared much better (Cooke 2010). This can be linked directly to Confucian norms, and their repudiation in Mao's China.

The Confucian model of societal relations is premised on the family and the roles played within this sphere, which Weber acknowledges as distinct from the public sphere. However, as Arendt (1958) argues, the family can never be viewed as a democratic unit, and the inherent conflict between an autocratic head, no matter how benevolent, and pluralistic models, creates dysfunctions in the fabric of society. As Merton notes (1972), the opportunity for a state to rewrite social relationships presented by industrialisation can render very different sets of conditions within public organisations. And in East Asia, depending on how firmly the state adheres to Confucian norms, one of the clearest manifestations of such adherence presently can be found in the role women play in public organisations. One might argue that 'modernisation' in East Asia must face this question head on, as the state plays a mediating role between the increasingly separate public and private spheres Weber predicts. If Confucianism is brought back in its original form as a governing template, there will be a heavy cost for precisely this reason. The social structures that underlay relationships in Confucian times have changed substantially, in both overt (e.g., visible roles for women in public institutions) and covert (e.g., restructuring of generational family ties) ways. The fit will be a difficult match, given these changes, and may require substantial rethinking by states looking for a path forward.

That said, does the Weberian ideal offer a viable alternative? One might argue that Weber's cautionary tale of modernisation does, at least, give form and name to the pitfalls that lie along the path toward greater reliance on law and empiricism, and an articulation of what may be lost when we label individual discretion as inherently undesirable. In his discussions of different systems of jurisprudence and the exercise of justice, Weber notes that the discretion exercised by judges in traditional systems can favour the poor in a way that brings equity to an inequitable system (Weber 1954). Empirical justice systems, in contrast, offer no such path. Thus, if society becomes less equitable, a legal-rational system will simply make things worse. From his nineteenth century vantage point, Weber was peering around the arc of history, buoyed by his analysis of the past to try and see what brave new world the rapid change of his age might bring. The modernism he saw was technological in form, advancing through the discoveries of science, and offering exciting possibilities for what was to come. But it lacked a solid grounding in human social structures, which is precisely what confounded his observations and necessitated the creation of ideal types. Weber saw mankind as driven, but not necessarily by the same natural benevolence presupposed in Confucianism. The darkness of rationality, especially in its nineteenth century German context, lies in its separation from compassion. So, while Weber's approach may recognise the rising influence of legal norms that push beyond national and cultural boundaries, the key to creating an administrative apparatus that is responsive to indigenous needs in non-western contexts lies in being able to produce rules that have a feel for their local conditions. This is where Confucian norms provide common ground, and where the two approaches might combine to form a quasi-Confucian, hybrid approach.

Conclusion: Where Might Quasi-Confucianism Lead?

If the twenty-first century truly is an Asian century, then there will have to be a reconciling of these approaches. Fortunately, as discussed thus far, they are not so far apart as might be expected. However, the problems lie in their similarity of form, and the conclusions drawn by those who think that structure dictates function, and can lead to misinterpretations of behavior. Thinking about how such differences may play out within the context of Chinese and South Korean administrative systems can be instructive in showing how the dissimilarities under the surface may be revealed and thus better understood, both inside and beyond the borders of East Asia. What might we expect as these systems move forward into a more interconnected and interwoven system?

First, higher levels of transparency will become crucial to maintaining public trust in both systems. Contrary to popular conceptions of the authoritarian state in China suppressing all dissent through force, or the Korean government being democratically responsive to its citizenry, both countries rely on the consent of the governed to maintain their rule. Bureaucrats play a key role in the perception citizens have of their governing classes and the relationship between those classes and the public at large. Expanding power, whether economic or political, may be the driving incentive behind the modern state, but when private interests violate and corrupt public trust, the law must reflect and enforce balance. This is in keeping with both a Confucian pursuit of virtue and a Weberian sense of vocation for public officials.

How the state accomplishes this may be seen by examining attempts to combat corruption in the public sector, which for both countries is a perennial concern. This is perhaps the stickiest issue to address, since the source of authority in a Weberian system and a Confucian system are quite different. A hypothetical example helps to illustrate this difference. In both systems, let us agree that corruption occurs when a public official uses the power of his or her office for personal gain. But how is this determined? From the outside, if a public official decides favorably in a case where a plaintiff is within the public official's network of relations, has corruption taken place? Within a Weberian system, the answer to this question might be answered by looking at the underlying laws or rules that guided the decision. If it appears that the rules have been executed objectively, then we may draw the conclusion that corruption is not an issue. But within a Confucian system, such scrutiny does not yield a ready answer. If we trust that the official is behaving with propriety, then we may conclude that no corruption has taken place. But if we do not know whether or not the official has propriety, then no such trust can be assumed. This gray area, where the manifestations of both proper and improper behavior might be one and the same, is an unresolved problem for Confucian systems. Thus, higher levels of transparency, and practice with explaining how and why decisions were reached may become more common.

Second, the role of the public sector as a supporter of markets will shift from direct financial backing (through state banks) to research oriented support. This has already begun in China, where significant portions of the national budget are being poured into research and design in all areas of the economy. Public officials have become more specialised in particular areas of expertise. This is not yet the case in Korea, but there have been recent movements in a similar direction. This is again a fusion of the Confucian value of filial piety, where the state is responsible for leading the way to a better life for the people, and the Weberian ideal of specialised expertise that requires training and mastery to execute.

Third, and perhaps most important, may be a loosening of the kinship ties that often drive bureaucratic behaviour. In China, the expression "*you guanxi keyi cai hou men*" (有关系可以开后门, or "if you have connections, you can open the back door") illustrates the importance of personal relations to getting government bureaucrats to respond to requests for assistance. In Korea, these ties are illustrated by the way in which information is shared within an organisation. If no formal relationship exists between people, then rarely does an informal relationship develop to help overcome some of the structural barriers to communication. This can often slow down the exchange of information necessary for individual bureaucrats to complete tasks or expedite their fulfillment of duties. As these ties loosen and more informal ties are made that smooth communication, formalism may decline (some would argue it has already declined too far in China). This will be the most disruptive change in South Korea, since many social norms are premised on the formal relations between individuals.

At the end of this examination, as indicated at the outset, there is far less distance between Confucius and Weber than one might think. However, the world that Weber foresaw is one that had been rejected by Confucius as unsustainable and out of sync with the natural world, and therefore, out of balance with heaven (*tian* 天). Weber would have agreed, since he drew small pleasure from watching the efficient exercise of industry in his own nation, and saw the ways in which empire could become little more than an instrument of war. But if Confucian values can inject sustainability into Weberian rationalisation, this may be a path worth pursuing. Weber himself might concur.

Note

1. The use of the male term only here is intentional—Confucianism is very clear on distinct roles for men and women in society, and this should not be overlooked.

References

Adler, J. A. (2011, April 14). *Confucianism in China today*. Unpublished paper presented at Pearson Living Religions Forum, New York City.

Arendt, H. (1958). *The human condition*. Chicago: University of Chicago.

Bellah, R. N. (1999). Max Weber and world-denying love: A look at the historical sociology of religion. *Journal of the American Academy of Religion, 67*(2), 277–304.

Bianco, L. (1971). *Origins of the Chinese revolution 1915–1949*. Translated by Muriel Bell. Palo Alto, CA: Stanford University.

Chalcraft, D., & Harrington, A. (2001). *The protestant ethic debate: Max Weber replies to his critics, 1907–1910* (pp. 89–90). Liverpool: Liverpool University Press.

Cooke, F. L. (2001). Equal opportunity? The role of legislation and public policies in women's employment in China. *Women in Management Review, 16*(7), 334–348.

Cooke, F. L. (2010). Women's participation in employment in Asia: A comparative analysis of China, India, Japan and South Korea. *The International Journal of Human Resource Management, 21*(12), 2249–2270.

Coser, L. A. (1977). *Masters of sociological thought: Ideas in historical and social context.* New York: Harcourt, Brace and Jovanovich Publishers.

Eisenstadt, S. E. (Ed.). (1986). *The origins and diversity of axial age civilizations.* Albany: SUNY Press.

Frederickson, H. G. (2002). Confucius and the moral basis of bureaucracy. *Administration and Society, 33,* 610–628.

Gerth, H. H., & Mills, C. W. (1946). *From Max Weber: Essays in sociology.* Oxford: Oxford University.

Im, T. B., Campbell, J. W., & Cha, S. Y. (2013). Revisiting Confucian bureaucracy: Roots of the Korean governments' culture and competitiveness. *Public Administration and Development, 33,* 286–296.

Jaspers, K. (1948). *The origin and goal of history.* London: Routledge and Kegan Paul.

Kanthor, R. (2016). Holding up half the sky: Women speak out on the status of feminism in China. *TakePart.* Participant Media. Retrieved from: http://www.takepart.com/feature/2016/07/29/women-china.

Kim, P. S. (2012). A historical overview of Korean public administration: Discipline, education, association, international cooperation, and beyond indigenization. *International Review of Administrative Sciences, 78*(2), 217–238.

Merton, R. K. (1940). Bureaucratic structure and personality. *Social Forces, 18*(4), 560–568.

Merton, R. K. (1972). Insiders and outsiders: A chapter in the sociology of knowledge. *American Journal of Sociology, 78*(1), 9–47.

Oakes, G. (2003). Max Weber on value rationality and value spheres. *Journal of Classical Sociology, 3*(1), 27–45.

Radkau, J. (2011). *Max Weber: A biography.* Translated from German by Patrick Camiller. Malden, MA: Polity Press.

Rarick, C. A. (2007). Confucius on management: Understanding Chinese cultural values and managerial practices. *Journal of International Management Studies, 2*(2), 22–28.

Snow, E. (1937). *Red star over China.* New York, NY: Random House.

Weber, M. (1954). *On law in economy and society.* Cambridge, MA: Harvard University.

CHAPTER 5

Disciplining Democracy: Explaining the Rhythms of Myanmar's First *Hluttaw*, 2011–2016

Nicholas Farrelly and Chit Win

Dr. Nicholas Farrelly is a Deputy Director in the Bell School of Asia Pacific Affairs, The Australian National University. Chit Win was a PhD candidate in the same institution. His PhD research looked at the role of ethnic representatives inside Myanmar's legislature. This chapter is based on their joint field research and deep immersion in the culture and daily life of Myanmar's *Hluttaw*. The authors were granted special access to the *Hluttaw* complex, to its MPs, to the dynamics of life in what is still one of the world's newest legislatures. We are very thankful to all of those who facilitated this access, especially the Speaker of the *Amyotha Hluttaw* U Khin Aung Myint, Deputy Director General of the *Amyotha Hluttaw*, Daw Thida Tun, and all of the other staff and MPs who offered their insights and support. We hope this explanation of the *Hluttaw* helps to explain their work and will be of benefit to future generations intrigued by the daily practice of legislative power in Myanmar from 2011 to 2016.

N. Farrelly (✉) · C. Win
Coral Bell School of Asia Pacific Affairs, Australian National University, Canberra, Australia
e-mail: nicholas.farrelly@anu.edu.au

C. Win
e-mail: chit.win@anu.edu.au

S. Bice et al. (eds.), *Public Policy in the 'Asian Century'*, International Series on Public Policy, https://doi.org/10.1057/978-1-137-60252-7_5

Introduction

It is early 2014 in Nay Pyi Taw and the Director General of the *Pyidaungsu Hluttaw* (Myanmar's Union Assembly), U Kyaw Soe, calls the assembly to attention. The cavernous chamber hushes. In the observers' gallery a large contingent of opposition National League for Democracy (NLD) supporters, resplendent in matching outfits, are overshadowed by a slightly more numerous group from the then-governing Union Solidarity and Development Party (USDP). In Myanmar's legislature, their colours and uniforms designate belonging: black is reserved for the power in the parliament; white is for officials and the USDP; any other colour means non-USDP; and colourful costumes are worn by ethnic minorities. In the observers' gallery, the NLD wear *pinni* jackets over their white shirts with dull coloured *longyi* (sarong). This brown-coloured, rough cotton clothing was worn as a sign of patriotism or rebellion against authorities during the colonial period. Myanmar's democratic forces maintain this tradition as a sign of their consistent opposition to the former military regime. The USDP members, in their own uniforms, strike a more imposing posture. Each wears a white shirt, many with a party lapel pin, and a green *longyi*. It is a uniform that takes inspiration from the official culture that nurtures many USDP members: they tend to be teachers, local government workers and part of family networks with strong military ties. In this uniformed spectacle, two of Myanmar's most important political lineages—one of the democratic movement and one of the *athwinpyaung* (transitional) establishment—are fodder for the evening's television broadcasts. They are not mobilised by accident: it all takes planning, purpose and financial wherewithal. As preparations for the 2015 general election are beginning to build momentum, these different visions of Myanmar's history will soon meet in direct competition. In the meantime, Myanmar's *Hluttaw* in 2014 is contested, transitional ground.

In the *Hluttaw* as the hush descends, the shuffling of paper stops. Then, a senior clerk, standing near the over-sized main door, bows to the Director General, giving the signal that the Speaker's arrival is imminent. Moments later more than 1000 chairs push back as the assembled members of the Union Assembly (hereinafter referred to as MPs), and all those sitting in the observers' gallery, stand to attention. The sound of the heavy wooden chairs scraping the floor is one that reverberates loudly: it is the sound of the legislature in motion. The Speaker follows a man carrying a golden mace, as another attendant helps him to his seat. Wearing a black gown with gold trim, a silk *longyi*, and velvet slippers, the Speaker strides confidently to his throne on the high stage in the middle of the chamber. The configuration of the chamber offers an echo of the grandest classroom imaginable. The Speaker has unquestioned authority and the members address all of their remarks directly to him. The adversarial seating of the Westminster system is ignored in favour of a system where there is one *saya* (teacher), and many *tapyit* (students). With the greeting of "*Ahlone Mingalabar*" ("good morning everyone") from the Speaker, the MPs respond with a rousing "*Mingalabar*".

And with that procession and ritual, another ordinary day commenced in Myanmar's extraordinary legislature, one of the world's most surprising and exhilarating places to study the evolution of representative politics and public policy formation. The first *Hluttaw*, elected on 7 November 2010 and then revitalised through by-elections on 1 April 2012, brought together voices from across Myanmar's geographic, cultural and political spectrum until their terms ended on 29 January 2016. This first group of MPs was tasked with gently unraveling five decades of direct military control. As such, the business of the first *Hluttaw* was weighty, comprehensive and formed by what we argue became a new style of Myanmar policy discipline, shaped by an emerging set of legislative practices. It is notable that the very first order of business each day in the *Hluttaw* was a roll call of absentees. Those who failed to register for the day's legislative debates were always mentioned by name. This could be more than one quarter of the legislators. The only exception to the trend of absenteeism was among the military, who were allocated 25 percent of the seats under the 2008 constitution. They attended the *Hluttaw* habitually.

Under these conditions, we seek to understand how a Myanmar style of discipline informed the functioning of the country's first *Hluttaw*. The core research for this chapter was undertaken from January to April 2014, in the ninth session of the *Pyidaungsu Hluttaw*. Yet to speak of one *Hluttaw* is to miss some of the subtleties of this new institution. Under the 2008 constitution, it is divided, somewhat conventionally, into a bicameral *Pyithu Hluttaw* (Peoples' Assembly or lower house) and *Amyotha Hluttaw* (Nationalities Assembly or upper house). These two houses sit jointly, on a regular basis, as the *Pyiduangsu Hluttaw* (Union Assembly or combined house). During the first *Hluttaw*, the Speakers of the two houses shared responsibilities as speaker/chairman of the combined house. For the first 30 months this task was shouldered by U Khin Aung Myint, a former Minister of Culture in the State Peace and Development Council (SPDC) and a retired Major General in the Army, who enjoyed a reputation as a thoughtful, moderating influence. He was followed by Thura U Shwe Mann, the erstwhile Speaker of the lower house, who previously held more senior positions in the former military regime including as Chief of General Staff of the Army, Navy and Air Force. Thura U Shwe Mann was, for a time, considered a contender for the Presidency after the 2015 election. Obviously, the electoral triumph of the NLD at the 8 November 2015 election dampened those ambitions. In the aftermath of that vote, U Khin Aung Myint and Thura U Shwe Mann hold much less significant positions now that the USDP is no longer in charge.

With the NLD government taking tentative steps towards consolidating a democratic culture in Myanmar, it is easy to forget what came before. Helpfully, it was under the leadership of U Khin Aung Myint and Thura U Shwe Mann that the scholarly treatment of Myanmar's new legislative institution commenced. Most of early analytical attention focused on the composition of the legislature and on its formal outcomes. One important research paper was the International Crisis Group's "Not a Rubber Stamp: Myanmar's Legislature in a Time of Transition", which acknowledged that the *Hluttaw* quickly became more robust and autonomous than expected, though there remained many problems with individual and institutional competency (ICG 2013). The Open Myanmar Initiative offered a quantitative appraisal of the performance of MPs based on their questions and motions, and the executive government's response to their requests. Furthermore, there has been inevitable interest in the ways that the legislative apparatus has managed to incorporate different political strands (Kean 2014), from the stridently democratic, to former ethnic rebels, to the most rigid ideologues of the old military dictatorship (Egreteau 2014, 2015). Since members of the Union Assembly first took their seats in January 2011, and with NLD leader Daw Aung San Suu Kyi's participation after the by-election in 2012, there has been more international awareness of the legislature and its "proactive" role in Myanmar's future (Fink 2015; Than Than Nu 2014).

It is clear, however, that the day-to-day rhythms of the first *Hluttaw* have yet to be fully explored, and there is a need to more effectively understand how this institution was constructed from the ground up. It evolved quickly. In this chapter we seek to analyse its development, starting with the 2010 election campaign and ending with the preparations for the fresh cohort of MPs who joined the institution after the 2015 election. In the cycle of the first *Hluttaw* many lessons were learned. We hope to provide some inside analysis of the role of the new legislature in an evolving set of policy practices. Given the difficult trajectories of societies emerging from long periods of authoritarian rule, there is much to be gained from a close examination of Myanmar's recent history. As we consider the big picture of public policy in the Asian Century, it is worth looking at the vernacular details of a political and legislative system that has grappled, in such a courageous way, with the onerous requirements of more open and democratic government.

In our research for this chapter, we were in the fortunate position of working and living alongside MPs in the first *Hluttaw*, engaging with *Hluttaw* staff on a daily basis, and enjoying the company of many other figures associated with the *Hluttaw*'s development. These interactions provided special opportunities to analyse the political, cultural and economic character of the new legislature. This chapter begins by introducing a conceptual discussion of the rhythmic quality of the first *Hluttaw* as it set about disciplining Myanmar's transition from a policy perspective. This is followed by an analysis of where members of the *Hluttaw* came from. This basic demographic, economic and geographical overview helps to explain the variety of trajectories that brought individuals to serve in Nay Pyi Taw. We then turn to a discussion of the elections, in 2010 and 2012. Some MPs were elected in relatively open contests, while others faced no competition for their seats. Explaining these different situations helps to clarify the limited democratic quality of the legislative institution that existed from 2011 to 2016. The major analytical sections of the chapter follow with an explanation of the key groups in the *Hluttaw*, their parliamentary practices and their daily life in Nay Pyi Taw.[1]

Explaining the Rhythms

Myanmar's first *Hluttaw* was the linchpin of an experiment in political change that is still underway. The *Hluttaw* complex, with its distinctive roofs and gargantuan buildings, was designed as the centerpiece of the new administrative capital, Nay Pyi Taw. It is impossible to ignore the way that this system is changing the way that people think about politics. To help clarify the rhythmic aspects of these changes, we suggest there are three key analytical categories worthy of further consideration in any discussion of the changing dynamics of policy and power. We dwell on patience, representation and order. More generally, the development of this new legislature gives the people of Myanmar a chance to see how "Myanmar style" public politics can operate. We expect that these different aspects of the rhythms of legislative life will change over time, especially now that the NLD commands such a strong majority in the second *Hluttaw*.

First of all, life in the first *Hluttaw* required patience. Nothing tended to happen quickly and there was a need to wait for the opportune moment to present itself, with MPs required to pass the time in anticipation of events and future activity. Life in Nay Pyi Taw gave MPs a chance to examine the country's political, economic and cultural life from a variety of perspectives. They could sit together, talking, and taking the pulse of the nation. They absorbed large quantities of news media, especially newspapers and journals. These helped to reflect their own experiences of national politics, but also often challenged their views on what was occurring. There was sometimes great consternation when they read reports which suggested journalists appeared to have misunderstood a specific set of issues. Some MPs worked hard to get their message across while others were inclined to take the path of least resistance. They were prepared to wait for an opportune moment, or simply for the expiry of their term in 2016. For some, their attendance in Nay Pyi Taw was sufficient: they were representing their people and providing a chance for the entire system to become more inclusive and democratic.

Second, the system of politics established in Nay Pyi Taw has been predicated on representation and participation. From 2011 to 2016, MPs were expected to be part of the overall process of political change and to work collaboratively. There was a clear structure to their participation and in many cases mere attendance was sufficient. This approach encouraged some to decide that their time was better spent elsewhere. Absenteeism among MPs became a major issue, and one that frustrated senior legislative leaders. Yet it was a product of the way that the theatrical aspects of the *Hluttaw* itself undermined the confidence of individual MPs in having their voices heard. For many, there was a sense that nobody would miss them in Nay Pyi Taw and that they could more profitably pursue political or commercial activities in Yangon, or elsewhere. Many MPs were also being invited to travel abroad and so they were given a chance to see how other legislatures work. In light of these experiences, some decided that the heavily regimented *Hluttaw* system was not in keeping with more "democratic" practices. With their relatively high social status, they may have often felt that sitting in the *Hluttaw* without being encouraged to actively take part in legislative debate was an inefficient use of their time.

Third, the *Hluttaw* served to order people through categories, uniforms and transportation. On every sitting day MPs wore, and still wear, their relevant attire. For an ethnic Naga MP that might, for example, be a tall helmet, replete with bird feathers, and a crisp black jacket. For MPs from the USDP it would be a silk *longyi*, a crisp white shirt, a coloured *taikpone*, which is a straight-cut jacket, and a silk head-piece, called a *Gaung Paung*. Almost everyone was immediately recognisable by the clothes they wore. Some ethnic parties wore the same interpretation of their traditional ethnic dress, while others gave a degree of flexibility in the clothing worn. In all cases their clothes helped to clarify categories of belonging and ownership. Even transportation, especially that which was reserved specifically for MPs, gave them a sense of a specific status and of being part of a transformative moment in the country's political and policy history. With these analytical categories in mind, the rhythms of the first Hluttaw need to be looked at in detail.

Where Did MPs Come from?

The logic of the *Hluttaw*'s national representation meant that members of the first *Hluttaw* were drawn from across the country. The greatest concentrations of MPs came from the densely populated Bamar-majority Regions of Yangon, Mandalay, Ayeyarwaddy, Sagaing, Bago and Magwe. The ethnic-majority States, places like Kayah, Chin, Kayin and Mon States, are much less densely populated. High mountains and remote village tracts characterise their terrain. In any case, all areas of the country were designated within constituencies. In the *Pyithu Hluttaw* these constituencies were based on administrative township boundaries. There were 330 elected constituencies in the lower house, with 110 other seats, 25% of the total seats, reserved for military nominees. In the *Amyotha Hluttaw* there were 168 constituencies, 12 seats each for 14 States and Regions, and they are not based strictly on township-level boundaries. The military representation took 56 seats, a quarter of the total. These were formed by the amalgamation of different lower house units. It led to some overlaps between representational duties and functions. Upper house seats were identified by a number: Yangon Region Constituency

No. 7, for instance. That constituency took in the lower house constituencies of Thanlyin, Kyauktan, Dala and Seikkyi Kanutto Townships, which were represented by 4 lower house MPs.

The MPs of the first Hluttaw came from all parts of the country meaning that travel was an important part of their duties. Seventy-five percent of the elected representatives had their permanent address in their constituency and around 15% of them had settled either in Nay Pyi Taw, Yangon or Mandalay. Some 10% of the MPs lived in larger towns close to their constituencies. Those who hailed from distant corners spent most of their time in Nay Pyi Taw or Yangon. It was time consuming, troublesome, and expensive to return home regularly. Indeed many MPs, based on the economic and cultural sway developed over the decades, maintained second residences in Yangon. They may have only returned to their constituencies, whether those are in Rakhine State or Tanintharyi Region, when they had a long break from other responsibilities.

As a political institution established under the military regime, the age structure of the first *Hluttaw* presented some interesting dynamics. The average age of MPs was 57 and with only 6% female representation, the *Hluttaw* could generally be regarded as an "old men's club". The oldest member was 80 and the youngest was 26.[2] About 40% of the MPs were aged in their 60s considering the relatively low average life expectancy of Myanmar, many of them were not able to participate in the 2015 election. Moreover, apart from age and health reasons, many MPs were not interested in running for a second term because they felt that they had done their duty as requested by their parties, their constituencies or their ethnic groups. This is partly due to the candidate selection strategies by the parties as detailed later in the chapter. The fact this first term would be the last term for most of the MPs, created an attitude of "*tar won kyae*" ("doing what is right for the country"), rather than taking populist approaches in order to get re-elected. On the other hand, there were a sizeable number of MPs who lost interest and got frustrated confined in Nay Pyi Taw for five years away from their families and businesses (Fig. 5.1 and Table 5.1). One ethnic MP told us:

> I feel lonely and uncomfortable living at the dormitory in Nay Pyi Taw. I am a diabetic person and the food at the guest house is oily and not suitable for me. At the same time, I don't know and don't want to cook. I have my business in Yangon and being in Nay Pyi Taw during the parliamentary sessions that are held three times a year each lasting about two months

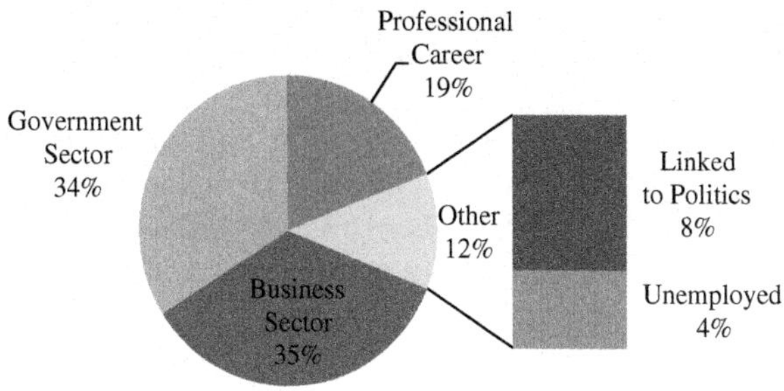

Fig. 5.1 Occupational background of *Hluttaw* representatives

Table 5.1 Socio-economic breakdown of the MPs at the *Pyidaungsu Hluttaw*[d]

Occupation[a]			*Political experience*[b]	
Business			Party cadres	14%
1. Local level	35%	24%	National convention participants	12%
2. State and regional level		7%	BSPP	7%
3. National level		4%	Local administration	7%
Government			Culture/ethnic/militia leader	5%
1. Civil servants	34%	17%	SPDC leadership	4%
2. Education (teachers/university lecturers)		12%	Civil society	4%
3. Military and police		5%	Political activists	4%
Others Professions			Tycoons/businessmen	2%
1. Agriculture (e.g. farmers)	19%	8%	Senior government officials	2%
2. Medical/engineers		6%	Senior military officials	2%
3. Lawyers		4%	1990 elected representative	2%
4. Academic		1%	Academics	2%
Professions Linked to Politics[c]			Negligible experience	40%
1. Political appointee	8%	4%		
2. Party/activist/journalist		4%		
Unemployed	4%			

[a]Importantly the notion of "occupation" refers to the profession that has profound influence on a MP's life, not necessarily their most recent employment

[b]Some MPs may overlap in their political experience

[c]The term "professions linked to politics" refers to professions where practitioners may gain political experience due to the nature of their working environment

[d]Based on the *Hluttaw*'s data on 477 elected MPs at the *Pyidaungsu Hluttaw* as of November 2013

made me lose a lot of business opportunities. I don't know how I'll survive for another two years.

The socio-economic breakdown of the MPs and their education qualifications also shaped the *Hluttaw* and the way it ran. A sizable number of MPs came from local areas where their occupation was predictable enough: they were predominately merchants and traders, while civil servants and education personnel were the second and third largest groups, while as little as 4% were involved in politics or were those who gained political experience due to the nature of their working environment such as journalists and political commentators. According to the biographical information provided by the *Hluttaw*, MPs were engaged more in local administration than party politics. It is interesting to note that about 12% of the MPs, mostly from the USDP, attended the National Convention that drafted the 2008 constitution which paved the way for elections in 2010. However, the opposition NLD had 16% of their MPs who won in the 1990 General Election and 30% of them classified themselves, by profession, as *"Nain-ghan-yay Hloat-shar-thu"* (political activists). Another notable fact is that a significant number of MPs were active in the Burma Socialist Programme Party during the socialist regime, and these experienced figures tended to chair important standing committees in the *Hluttaw*.[3] One of the greatest contributions of these BSPP members was that they could easily conceptualise various issues as most of them had undertaken advanced political training courses during the socialist period, which ended in 1988. That background had significant influence in shaping the *Hluttaw* as we saw it from 2011 to 2016 (Fig. 5.2 and Table 5.2).

The education qualification reveals the "learning by doing" nature of the *Hluttaw*. More than half of the MPs had undergraduate degrees with only eight doctoral degree holders and not one held a degree in political science, as the subject was not taught in Myanmar for many decades from the 1980s onwards. The ruling USDP possessed the most and the least educated MPs. All eight PhD holding MPs were from the USDP, specialising in medicine, engineering and computer science. And more than 10% of its MPs, or more than half of the Master's degree holders, were also from the USDP. But its share of high school dropout MPs was quite high too. For instance, 44 USDP MPs did not have a chance to pursue advanced education after high school and 13 others did not finish high school. At the same time, ethnic parties concentrated their

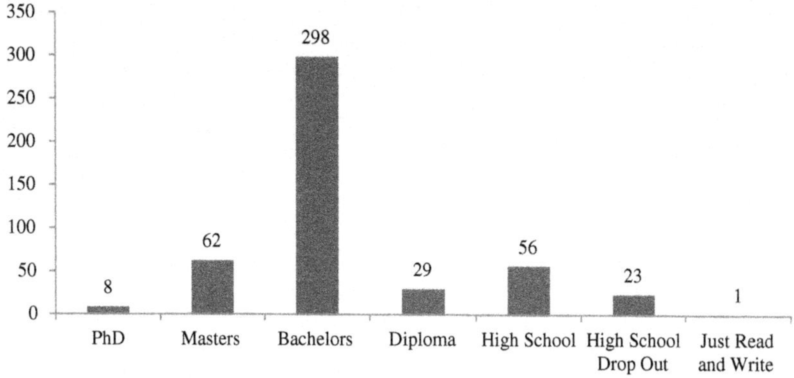

Fig. 5.2 Educational qualifications of *Hluttaw* representatives

Table 5.2 Education qualification of the MPs in the *Pyidaungsu Hluttaw*[b]

Education qualification	*Total*	*USDP*		*NLD*		*Ethnic parties*	
	477 seats	*347 seats*	*71*	*45 seats*	*9*	*76 seats*	*16*
	Total (%)	*Total (%)*	*Within USDP (%)*	*Total (%)*	*Within NLD (%)*	*Total (%)*	*Within ethnic parties (%)*
PhD	2	100	2	0	0	0	0
Graduate	13	67	12	3	30	6	5
Undergraduate	62	75	66	5	58	14	58
Graduate Diploma	6	30	3	0	5	43	17
High School	11	80	13	1	7	13	9
High School Dropout	5	54	4	<1	<1	29	9
Read and Write	<1	<1	<1[a]	0	0	0	0

[a]He is an ethnic USDP MP from Shan State and used to be the militia leader in his area

[b]Based on the *Hluttaw*'s data on 477 MPs at the *Pyidaungsu Hluttaw* as of November 2013

candidate selection on undergraduate or graduate diploma holders. This is partly because educated ethnic elites were requested by their ethnic parties to present themselves at the 2010 election along ethnic lines. For their part, 30% of the opposition NLD MPs were Master's degree holders and a about a quarter of them were medical doctors, meaning that it had the most educated representation. The best educated MPs were usually government employees at one point or were from the education sector whereas, in general, local militia leaders, ethnic leaders and local businessmen were less well educated, at least in a formal sense.

Election Time

When the General Election was held in late 2010 for the first *Hluttaw* most of the opposition led by the NLD, including ethnic political elites, boycotted the election. But some NLD members willing to take their chances regardless of the credibility of the election split themselves from NLD and formed the National Democratic Force (NDF). Ethnic civil society groups from Mon, Rakhine and Shan States also felt that unless they seized the opportunity, the USDP would legitimise themselves by setting up ethnic proxies as "legitimacy gap fillers" and therefore decided to contest by setting up new ethnic parties. Their main strategy was securing votes from people who did not want to vote for USDP, or securing votes along ethnic lines.

The way that candidates were selected to stand for the *Pyithu Hluttaw* or the *Amyotha Hluttaw* showed the variety of regional and party approaches. In 2010, there were not many candidates willing to take a chance on the new legislative system. Instead they were often nominated by other local powerbrokers to take on the responsibility. Ethnic parties had a hard time finding suitable candidates, as many hopefuls were still afraid of being imprisoned for engaging in party politics. Some of the ethnic elites who were engaged in non-political areas such as promotion of traditional literature and culture were asked to contest the election.[4] For its part, the USDP took experienced party cadres and senior members of the SPDC regime, and also recruited retired headmasters, teachers and public servants who were engaged in the social and religious affairs of their village or town. The fact that teachers are revered in Myanmar, and that they are commonly perceived as obedient to the administration, made them the best choice for the USDP. Next, some prominent business tycoons also became the favourites of the USDP as they could contribute to party fund-raising. To name a few: *Pyithu Hluttaw* MP U Htay Myint aka Yuzana U Htay Myint was chairman of Yuzana Co. Ltd and was one of the wealthiest property developers in Myanmar; *Pyithu Hluttaw* MP U Aung Zaw Win was chairman of Shine

Construction Company, a leading property developer in Yangon; and *Amyotha Hluttaw* MP U Khin Shwe aka Zaygabar U Khin Shwe was chairman of Zaygabar Group of Companies and owned the Mingalardon industrial zone. All of them were close to the former military regime.

In contrast, the NLD candidates for the 2012 By-Election tended to be loyal members of the party who had provided years of service to Daw Aung San Suu Skyi and the democratic activist effort. The selection of candidates by the NLD in preparation for the 2012 vote happened very quickly. While the party leadership prevaricated about whether to endorse the political system by offering candidates for election they needed to find compelling individuals, steeped in the history and hardship of the NLD, to take on these positions. Some emerged from the ranks of former political prisoners, while others were life-long activists, blooded in the underground politics of the past quarter century. Looking at their backgrounds, in all cases they must have received Daw Aung San Suu Kyi's personal imprimatur.

More generally, in conversations with MPs, what emerged was profound arbitrariness about their nomination to take on particular roles. In 2010, the USDP was seeking to consolidate its control but it was starting from a modest base of experience in terms of its formal party history. In many respects the filling of elected positions took a similar character to how the SPDC government, and its civilian wing, the Union Solidarity and Development Association (USDA), had mobilised personnel during earlier phases of political development. Local community leaders, public servants and teachers who were directed to take part in public rallies of the USDA in supporting government policies such as the Seven Stage Road Map and the constitution were carefully observed and potential hopefuls were selected. Those USDP candidates who failed to win seats in 2010 disappeared from the scene.[5]

In the 2010 election, campaign strategies were different from one party to another and from one candidate to another depending on the constituency. For example, a USDP candidate who was of a senior military or civilian administrative background may have used his incumbent power to influence the constituency. The USDP was heavily involved in setting up low cost health clinics, low interest cash loans and upgrading neglected streets into concrete paved streets in many cities and towns. Such tactics were quite apparent in downtown Yangon where the USDP paved one side of the road with a promise that the other half would be realised after the election. In the villages, its funding went to construct artesian wells.[6] On the other hand, ethnic candidates promoted the importance of ethnic identity and other Bamar dominant parties such as the NDF and National Unity Party relied on a vote of dissent against the USDP. And during the by-election in 2012, Daw Aung San Suu Kyi's portrait was sufficient to secure the votes for NLD members.

It is worth emphasising that the 2010 General Election, from which most MPs for the first *Hluttaw* were elected, was neither free nor fair. It was conducted at a time of great uncertainty and consternation in Myanmar politics. At the time it disappointed those who had hoped that democratic reform would entail more radical and immediate changes. Regional and election watchdogs wrote a number of papers on the credibility Myanmar's 2010 General Election. All of them identified irregularities in the campaign of the USDP. One of the most serious accusations was the surprise number of advance votes. In some constituencies, the USDP met strong contenders from the NDF and ethnic parties, and the results were not in favor of the USDP until advance voting ballots were brought in. However what followed the 2010 election has continued to surprise observers. In its immediate aftermath, Aung San Suu Kyi was released from house arrest. She then re-launched the NLD and throughout 2011 there were moments of confidence building and reconciliation between Aung San Suu Kyi and the government. The *Political Parties' Registration Law* (2010), one of the main reasons why the NLD boycotted the 2010 election, was amended paving the way for Daw Aung San Suu Kyi to enter into politics. In 2012 the National League for Democracy was the overwhelming winner, taking 37 *Pyithu Hluttaw* seats, and all but one of the other seats that were contested. This gave it a respectable presence in the *Hluttaw* and provided the foundation for the strong majority they received after the 2015 General Election.

Key Groups in the *Hluttaw*

Within the Hluttaw, there were a number of key groups that had specific roles or obligations. These groups were distinguished usually in clothing, speech and manner, ensuring that everyone was well aware of their position in the hierarchy and their appropriate contribution to the overall effort of political and legislative action. After the 2015 General Election the shape of these groups changed in ways that will require attention in future studies.

The Speakers

Unlike other parliaments, the Speakers in the first *Hluttaw* were the power centre in their own chambers. In addition to the fact that they used to be the senior figures in the SPDC regime, their sincere motivation and commitment to the *Hluttaw* made them not only *conductors* but also *commanders* of the *Hluttaw*. They controlled the agenda and the proceedings of the sessions, they could also significantly influence parliamentary debates, bill drafting and even voting outcomes. They did so through physical gestures and direct/indirect remarks to show their positions. As *Amyotha Hluttaw* Speaker, U Khin Aung Myint said in an interview with us:

> MPs told me that I never smile but they still love me. Every day, I have to closely observe the mood of the MPs inside the chamber. Should there be any tension arisen from the debate I have to intervene by breaking the ice with some jokes.

On the other side, MPs suggested to us that they knew how to decode the Speakers and quite rarely dared to confront them. On the other hand, both Speakers earned the respect of most MPs as they were able to increase the status of the *Hluttaw*. One non-USDP MP from the *Pyithu Hluttaw* said:

> Even though I don't like the system, I trust the sincere commitment of the two Speakers. One is a commander and another is a thinker. Together it made the perfect leadership.

The enthusiasm of the Speakers can be given some credit for the pace and scope of reform and the robustness of the evolving legislature culture.

USDP

As the USDP held 347 seats or 71% of the total seats in the *Pyidaungsu Hluttaw*, interactions between its factions were important. Though the Central Executive Committee, comprised of senior figures from the SPDC government guided its political mission, it had its own interest groups. According to our analysis, USDP MPs could generally be grouped as (i) remnants of the SPDC regime who were former ministers, deputy ministers, military generals and senior public servants; (ii) party cadres; (iii) business entrepreneurs associated with the USDP; (iv) retired public servants; and (v) ethnic members. And these groupings, in some cases, were further divided into informal factions: hardline, reactionary and progressive factions depending on their career experience and political and economic ambitions. In a different direction, businessmen MPs could be regarded as the guardians of "cronyism". They were in the *Hluttaw* for one simple reason: to entertain senior members of the USDP and in return gain some economic favours like in the old days of direct military rule. In fact, things often did not turn out according to their expectations as the influence of senior USDP MPs on the government faded as time went by and they had no other choice but to continue entertaining them. Nevertheless, they resisted some of the reform process as in the case of foreign direct investment law and telecommunication law in 2012 that allowed significant foreign ownership and management. USDP ethnic MPs struggled to reconcile their ethnic interests and party policies. However, according to what we observed during the plenary sessions, they were important brokers between the USDP and ethnic parties.

NLD

Looking at the numbers alone, the 45 members of the NLD led by Daw Aung San Suu Kyi in the first *Hluttaw*, representing 9% of the total seats, could be regarded as a minor party. But due to Daw Aung San Suu Kyi's history and status it was more like an opposition party than a minor party. Each day in the *Hluttaw* Daw Aung San Suu Kyi would sit quietly. In the plenary, she would be surrounded by the other Chairs of the Affairs Committees, mostly former senior military personnel from the USDP, as they would sit together in the front row. Daw Aung San Suu Kyi herself opted to maintain a relatively low profile in the *Hluttaw*. She spoke on a number of occasions related to education and about the activities of the rule of law committee of which she was the chair. She was, however, notable in other respects for her non-participation. Though she encouraged her NLD MPs to actively participate in debates, her quiet gestures were also hard to read, even, we were repeatedly told, for her colleagues. When President U Thein Sein spoke on 26 March 2014, she did not applaud. She may have been the only person in the room. Was she distancing herself from legitimising the first *Hluttaw* in which she could only play a minor role? One of the plausible explanations is that since all of her movements, as well as her words, are closely watched, she may have feared that she could be misinterpreted.

Ethnic Parties

One of the significant aspects of the first *Hluttaw* was the role of ethnic parties. There were 16 ethnic parties. The SNDP was the largest, having 4% of the total seats: 22 of the 76 seats held by the ethnic parties. In general, Myanmar's eight national races except Kayah had one or more ethnic parties. In addition, the Wa and Pa-O from the Shan State also had a presence in the *Hluttaw*. Ethnic parties could generally be classified as either pure ethnic parties or as alliance parties of the USDP. Regardless of party affiliation, ethnic minorities knew each other and sometimes they were related by blood. Many of them had combat experience, either as insurgents or through having lived in conflicted areas. In fact, this made them understand the nature of the military and they were often well received and respected by military representatives. Most of the ethnic MPs were not politically associated with the former military regime or the opposition. Rather, they were more closely linked with Myanmar's various ethnic armed groups. Most of them were not keenly interested in regular plenary sessions. According to our observations, they frequently skipped the plenary sessions and rarely read documents distributed to them. To them, their presence had already made the *Hluttaw* legitimate and they were interested in local level issues, for instance the welfare of their ethnicity and constituency. They usually asked for investments in infrastructure such as roads, bridges, schools and hospitals. Occasionally, they would ask for the promotion of their literature and culture. After years in Nay Pyi Taw, some of the ethnic MPs became prominent, involved not only in debates of national standing but they also held important positions such as chair or secretary of the affairs committee in the *Hluttaw* and they were regularly consulted by the Speakers.

Other Groups

Apart from the USDP, NLD and ethnic parties, there were two minor parties in the *Hluttaw* and their backgrounds are totally different: the NDF and the NUP. Had NLD participated in the 2010 General Election without Daw Aung San Suu Kyi, it could easily have secured votes of dissent against the USDP. That was the case for the NDF, a splinter party from the NLD after the latter decided to boycott the election. In the earlier days of the first *Hluttaw*, NDF MPs were the symbol of opposition; a defiant demonstration to the rest of Myanmar that all your discontent can be discussed inside the *Hluttaw*. They were critical of the government and observing from their participation in the committees and in the plenary sessions, most of them became influential MPs. For its part, the NUP was an anomaly in the *Hluttaw*. They were neither seen to be for nor against the USDP government. Most of them were in their 60s and 70s, and represented remnants of the BSPP leadership, the ruling party during the socialist era. Their presence in the first *Hluttaw* was hardly noticeable since they did not interact much with other MPs.

There were no observable Buddhist or Christian blocs in the *Hluttaw*. But there was a small Muslim group with three Muslim MPs who were members of the USDP. All of them were successful businessmen. The trio always consulted each other about representing their identity, as one Rohingya representative told us. During the Rakhine conflict, one of these Muslim MPs, U Shwe Maung, representing Buthidaung township in northern Rakhine State, became the centre of attention as he lobbied on behalf of his constituents.[7]

Military

As we learned in interviews with military officers, the military cohort, allocated 25 percent of seats, regarded themselves as "guardians" of the constitution. Contrary to some impressions, military MPs did occasionally speak in the *Hluttaw*. They were well-organised and only deigned to intervene when they anticipated key military or government interests were at stake. The military MPs were drawn from commands across the country and sought to shadow the representative functions of elected MPs. The highest military rank in the *Hluttaw* was a Brigadier-General, a Deputy Commander in their command headquarters. Attendance among military MPs was, as mentioned earlier, very high. During the start of every session, scores of military MPs were replaced because of promotions and transfers. But there were also some military MPs, mostly junior ranking officers, according to their language, *pait-mi* or "stuck", since the beginning. According to the MPs that we interviewed, the role of the military in the *Hluttaw* changed significantly over the years.

In the beginning, the military representatives appeared to be spying on the movements of the elected MPs. The ice started to melt soon after the MPs treated them with respect, especially non-USDP MPs. Over time, they interacted amicably with other MPs and openly discussed substantive matters. The military used to vote in one bloc on sensitive matters and was open to individual choice on less sensitive matters. But it is interesting to note that with the NLD inside the *Hluttaw*, the military started to vote as a bloc regardless of the sensitivity of the issue. The military presence reminded everyone in the first *Hluttaw* that the military was watching and for the sake of everybody's interest, it was best not to awaken the *sleeping giant*. It was believed that this strong perception in the *Hluttaw* encouraged non-USDP MPs to take moderate or cooperative approaches with the USDP.

Features of the *Hluttaw*

The Hluttaw Compound

For visitors the first notable feature of the *Hluttaw* is its size and layout. Walking along unnecessarily high, long and wide corridors, one can feel the institutional power of the *Hluttaw* and start to question how a relatively poor country like Myanmar decided to pour its scarce resources to build a legislature of such scale. Viewing the *Hluttaw* from the Google Earth, the 150-hectare compound resembles a "*Palin*", the royal throne of the ancient Burmese kingdoms. It has 31 buildings of various sizes representing the 31 planes of existence in Buddhism with committee buildings at the base to the *Pyidaungsu Hluttaw*, the highest authority, at the top. The VIPs and the MPs enter from the 22-lane *Yazar Htarni* (Royal Abode) road crossing the bridge, a symbol of separation from ordinary lives. The President's Office, the *Hluttaw* compound, and the residences of the President, the Vice-Presidents and the Speakers are all in one big compound and all separated by bridges.

The building layout of the *Hluttaw* may also reveal the original design of the legislative apparatus. The *Pyidaungsu Hluttaw*, the *Pyithu Hluttaw*, the Reception Hall, the Dining Hall and the Culture Theatre are connected with corridors while the *Amyotha Hluttaw* stands alone implying that the initial idea of the constitution on the number of houses was different from the current one. Moreover, apart from the Speakers and the Deputy Speakers, MPs did not have their own offices in the beginning. Furthermore, staff members did their paper work from an office located outside the *Hluttaw* compound. All point towards the idea that the *Hluttaw* may have been physically designed to act as a rubber stamp. But that did not last. The *Hluttaw* became more robust and then struggled against the constraints of the buildings. For instance, committee meetings were held in a complex of buildings a few hundred metres from the chambers. And since the *Hluttaw* still prefered paper-based bureaucracy, even internal correspondence needed vehicle transport from one building to another. Some initial renovation and redesign was already happening in 2014 and 2015, with more planned for the years ahead.

Seating Plan

Everything in the first *Hluttaw*, even the seating plan, tried to ensure that party affiliation did not unduly influence MPs. Scars of internal divisions during the parliamentary era still haunted the *Hluttaw*. The seating in the chambers resembled neither the Westminster nor the Congressional systems. At the *Pyidaungsu Hluttaw*, it was divided into three wings: the *Pyithu Hluttaw*, the *Amyotha Hluttaw* and the military representation, all facing towards the Speaker. First, the chairs of the committees of both *Hluttaw* sat in the front rows respectively. After them, MPs from the *Pyithu Hluttaw* sat according to their committees. MPs from the *Amyotha Hluttaw* sat in accordance with their States and Regions. The military would sit in hierarchy. The system tried to mingle everyone in the chamber apart from the military representation. It encouraged MPs to develop a kind of camaraderie between the members of the various *Hluttaw* Committees and the States and Regions they represent regardless of their party affiliation. Frequently, committee members voted in blocs though they are from different parties. A classic example was the voting on the electricity rate hike that was debated on 25 March 2014. All the 15 members of the Investment and Industrial Development Committee voted together against the rate hike while most of their party MPs voted in favor of the hike.

Corridor Interactions

Corridor meetings were as important as the plenary sessions in the first *Hluttaw*. During plenary sessions, most of the MPs did not talk unless they had tabled a motion or a question to speak on behalf of the committee. But MPs used attendance registration and recess sessions to express their views and informally debate other issues. Every morning, before the start of the plenary sessions, MPs exchanged their ID card with electronic voting cards and meeting documents. Some civil service organisations tabled their papers during the attendance registration. It was also a ripe moment for journalists to arrange or conduct interviews after looking at the agenda. Observers also wandered curiously around the corridors. Everybody is looking at every other person. This was the best time for MPs to show the public, the observers, that they were truly doing something important. One of the most interesting times during our *Hluttaw* observations was the coffee breaks. Everyone gossiped about the plenary session along the corridors, in the toilet, at the smokers' corner, as well as in the coffee shop. There you could really see the reaction of the MPs on the issues discussed though they may have sat silently inside the chamber.

Questioning

In the earlier days of the first *Hluttaw*, a typical job of a MP meant raising questions on behalf of the constituency. Even though the quality and relevance of the question exhibited the capacity and the interest of that MP, it was imperative for an MP to keep asking questions if he wanted to be seen as an active member. After decades under the authoritarian regime questioning the government was seen as a privilege in the *Hluttaw*. In general, most of the questions were on constituency development or reducing bureaucratic red tape.[8] Occasionally, the government responded in a vague manner with confusing numbers. For instance, according to one ethnic MP, the government ministries responded using units that were not familiar to the MPs such as the use of billions and millions rather than *lakh* (hundreds of thousands), or kilograms rather than in tonnage making them confused. Over time, MPs and the government got smarter. MPs articulated their questions while the government threw the ball back citing the need for legislation or budget approval from the *Hluttaw*. Some questions, for instance raised by Rakhine Muslim and Rakhine Buddhist MPs were deemed sensitive with respect to ongoing communal violence, and so they were barred from publicly questioning the government in the *Hluttaw* plenary. Rather, they received written responses from the relevant government agencies. According to the *Hluttaw* procedures, questions from MPs were screened by the Speakers. Some were rejected outright citing irrelevance or inappropriateness. Some sensitive matters were categorised as "non-asterisk" meaning that it could be asked through a written request to the government and it may then receive a response in writing. If the Speakers put an asterisk on the question, it meant that it could be tabled in a plenary session.

Voting Practices

In the *Hluttaw*, voting results were significantly influenced by the Speaker's decision on the choice of voting method between oral voting, show of hands, and secret ballot. Though secret voting was used for sensitive issues, for formalities or less contentious issues oral voting was preferred. MPs were expected to say "*Tha Bawtu Bartae*" meaning "Yeah" when asked "*Tha Bawtu Bathala*" or "Do you agree?" It would be followed by "Is there anyone who disagrees?" and one could raise his or her voice if they disagree. During our observation in the *Hluttaw*, we only saw a handful of instances where a motion was opposed through voice voting. Following Myanmar customs, MPs were usually timid and afraid of becoming *a-pae-khan* or an "outcast" in the *Hluttaw.* MPs complained that though they did not like a motion, in order not to upset the Speaker and end up being framed as not cooperative, they would rather sit silently. If the Speaker uses voice voting, it can be decoded as the motion needs to be adopted. If a show of hands is applied it means "stand up if you dare" and usually only a few would stand up to oppose the motion.

Committee and Commission Meetings

Various standing and ad hoc committees of both *Hluttaw* also consolidated their own styles. All MPs in the first *Hluttaw* were involved in at least one of the committees. During *Hluttaw* sessions, the afternoon was reserved for committee meetings. In the beginning, the committees played small roles, literally just writing reports. However, depending on the type of committee and the competency of the chair, some gained significant roles in the *Hluttaw.* They started to hold direct consultations with government agencies and gave recommendations to plenary sessions. Likewise, the government also began to engage with various committees and avoided misunderstanding at the plenary sessions. Whenever there was an argument within the chamber, the recommendation of the committee was taken into account before calling for a vote. MPs from minor and ethnic parties were also appointed as chairs and secretaries of the various committees depending on their career experience and participation in the *Hluttaw*. However, since the NLD came into the *Hluttaw* in mid-2012, the ruling party seemed reluctant to share those positions with other parties. The *Hluttaw* still lacked institutional support for research skills and therefore tried to solve the gap in its own way by creating expert commissions. There were two expert commissions: *Commission on Special Affairs and Legal Assessment* for the *Pyithu Hluttaw* and *Political, Economic and Social Affairs Commission* for the *Amyotha Hluttaw*. Both commissions consisted of experts from the legal, public finance, economics and education sectors. They were mostly retired senior public figures. A few prominent businessmen and political analysts were also in the commissions. They give advice to the Speakers and the committees especially on current issues and bills.

Media

The media were an almost constant presence at public events. During *Hluttaw* sessions they were crammed into two observers' galleries on either side of the *Hluttaw* chamber. From there they could watch proceedings on television, or through a narrow window. For the first 10 minutes of each session they would usually hustle to get fresh footage of legislative proceedings. At other times they would be ready to interview MPs who made themselves available. Over time, there was increasing enthusiasm for dealing with the media and helping to shape the news of the day. When major speeches were given, MPs would expect to be interviewed. These were then broadcast on the state-run news media, especially MRTV and the National Races Channel, but also on a number of private networks. Media groups that were long exiled from Myanmar have returned in recent years, and even had an active presence around the first *Hluttaw*.

Life in Nay Pyi Taw

For a politically motivated person, it was financially quite lucrative to be become an MP in the first *Hluttaw*. The monthly salary of an MP was initially 300,000 kyat (roughly $310) per month. For some this is the most they had ever earned. For others it was a token amount, one they would easily spend on one evening's entertainment. They also benefited from a daily allowance when parliament was sitting: that is 10,000 kyat (or $11). This helped to pay for their food and accommodation. They could usually eat meals for less than 1500 kyat, and accommodation only cost 2000 kyat per night, a heavily subsidised rate. This left them with some extra pocket money. At the beginning of the first *Hluttaw*, MPs were offered, at a subsidised price, like in the old days of the socialist regime, to buy a "Myanmar mini", an 800 cc Chinese automobile re-assembled in Myanmar. As expected, many of them sold their cars at market price taking the profit.

Having meals and coffee together at the *Hluttaw* was often considered as important as the plenary sessions. At the *Hluttaw*, there were a number of restaurants and cafes. These served simple meals, including fried rice, curries, noodles and pastries. For morning tea, many MPs would enjoy a steamed bun and a tea or coffee. In the Myanmar style, either beverage is milky and sweet. Attendants ensured that the MPs had a comfortable period between sessions. Some MPs, especially male MPs, would congregate in a vast underground precinct adjacent to the toilet facilities. There was a "smoking room" with comfortable "*Hluttaw*" embossed seats. It was a place where MPs could meet away from the roaming television cameras, and in an environment that gave them a chance to cross party lines. In this subterranean space it was common to see military MPs canvassing for ideas among those from other parties, and for powerbrokers to be discussing issues with leaders from other parties. It was a convivial atmosphere, and one that helped to explain why so many matters in the *Hluttaw* itself were well understood before debate began.

Apart from the official functions at the *Hluttaw*, life of an ordinary MP from 2011 to 2016 in Nay Pyi Taw was totally different from legislative counterparts outside Myanmar. First of all, every action in Nay Pyi Taw was influenced by the vast distances in the city. Unless one owned a car, mobility in Nay Pyi Taw was limited and it was only recently that vehicles have become a utility rather than a luxury. Some MPs had a car for travelling around Nay Pyi Taw while many others still relied on the transportation provided by the *Hluttaw* to attend plenary sessions. The chair of a committee was provided with a car. On a regular day, you could see a bus line up at the Nay Pyi Taw Development Committee Guest House or simply "*Sipin Yeiktha*", located 8 km away from the

Hluttaw. Non-USDP MPs from different chambers and different ethnicities gathered in the meeting point at around 8:30 a.m. USDP MPs were also ferried from their dormitories at the USDP party headquarters, 13.5 km away from the *Hluttaw*. Upon their return, they could be confined in their compounds and they would be at the mercy of the car owners to get out of the compound.

There were three compounds where MPs were accommodated.[9] As mentioned, *Sipin Yeiktha* is a huge compound which can accommodate any visitors from across the country. It is said to have capacity for 1000 visitors a night. There, non-USDP MPs lived in air-conditioned dormitories, about 20 square metres, with a bathroom attached. In the early days, it was triple occupancy but that was later reduced to single occupancy. Originally, they also had to return to the dormitories during the parliamentary recess. That was amended and the MPs could settle in their own room and even bring their families to live with them. Initially, the compound resembled more of a detention centre except that it had restaurants and convenience stores. No visitors were allowed. No cars could come in. MPs were searched by security personnel before boarding the buses and they were not allowed to bring cameras, phones, computers and other electronic equipment. All had to be bagged in a clear plastic bag. But those restrictions became a thing of the past.

Eventually, many MPs felt comfortable bringing family members to Nay Pyi Taw. The presence of family members had its own reasons. First of all, after years of confinement, family members, especially wives of older MPs, came to live with them in order to take care of their housekeeping. In the compound, they were grouped based on party and geographical location. Female MPs lived together in a separate row of dormitories. The NLD got the most remote place in the compound. The USDP MPs were also housed in the same compound for a few months and they were later transferred to the USDP party headquarters. The best time to visit *Sipin Yeiktha* was in the evening around dusk just before dinner where you could see MPs casually walking, chatting and some cooking dinner while young local journalists tried to get MPs' opinions on recent events. Non-USDP MPs nicknamed their compound as "*Minmanaing Yeiktha*" ("*Rebellion Guest House*") symbolising their connections with armed insurgents in their political careers.

On the other hand, the USDP party headquarters offered more comfort but lacked the flavour offered by the *Sipin Yeiktha*. It was largely off limits to outsiders and located at the southern edge of Nay

Pyi Taw. There was more security awareness compared with *Sipin Yeiktha* and everything was a lot more organised. Three were large two-storey buildings accommodating over 300 USDP MPs. One building each was reserved for the male MPs from the *Pyithu Hluttaw* and the *Amyotha Hluttaw* respectively while the other one was for the female MPs and reserved rooms for visiting USDP MPs from other States and Regions. They lived in single air-conditioned rooms that they furnished to make more comfortable. Facilities such as grocery stores, restaurants, hair salons and laundry service were provided at a subsidised rate. Unlike the non-USDP accommodation, there was wi-fi available in the rooms and in the common area there were reading and meeting rooms and a gym, but it was mostly deserted. USDP MPs could watch over 300 international and local TV channels. However, the atmosphere was different from the *Rebellion Guest House*. It was a lot quieter as the room doors were always shut. There were strict dormitory rules such as no guest can stay overnight unless approved by the dormitory managers. Strangely, during breakfast and dinner, none of the MPs talked about politics and the conversations were mostly about their families.

There was also accommodation for the military MPs. It was in an area nestled inside the main military zone on the eastern edge of Nay Pyi Taw. Apart from the military representatives, nobody has really seen what is inside and how they are accommodated. According to them, they follow their usual military barrack regulations and they have to do their assigned homework.

On particular occasions, large-scale meals were organised in Nay Pyi Taw to which MPs were invited. In early 2014 there were, for example, dinners held for Shan State Day and Chin State Day. These events at the Myanmar International Convention Centre brought together hundreds of people. Heavily monitored by the news media, much of the attention was focused on the top tier political players, especially Thura U Shwe Mann, U Khin Aung Myint and Daw Aung San Suu Kyi. At these dinners, and many other events, these three notable personalities sat together at the central table. For the first minutes of any event they were surrounded by a scrum of cameramen and by some others keen to get a picture of the historic trio. At a time when politics was defined by patience, representation and order, these occasions offered the public a glimpse of the Nay Pyi Taw legislative culture was growing according to its own peculiar rhythms.

Conclusions

Myanmar's first *Hluttaw* proved that transitions from military dictatorship to new forms of government can occur rapidly, and unexpectedly. The formation of a new institutional culture introduced very significant changes to Myanmar society. These changes will not end with the first *Hluttaw*. There is a chance that the institutional, economic, political and cultural conditions described in this chapter will be obliterated by what is yet to happen, especially now that Daw Aung San Suu Kyi's NLD now has the weight of numbers after the 2015 General Election. But the very deliberate efforts to evoke earlier systems of power in Myanmar society, especially those with monarchical or socialist designations, gives the *Hluttaw* an historical foundation, whatever happens. Future legislative cultures will likely draw on a similar array of cultural concepts, especially where they are rooted in Myanmar's dominant Theravada Buddhist heritage.

The situation analysed here therefore remains in flux and it is far too early to judge what will come of the legislative culture once it gains some greater equilibrium. The early phase may prove indicative of trends that will follow. On the other hand it may be impossible for the practices established during the first legislative period to be followed by subsequent governments. The NLD, as an example, has previously stated its policy of returning the functions of the administrative capital to Yangon. While this will likely prove unfeasible, it is clear that many Myanmar civil servants are quietly in favour of the idea. It is also conceivable that legislative power is diminished over time. The speakers of the first *Hluttaw*, Thura U Shwe Mann and U Khin Aung Myint, both retired military figures, sought to create a legislative context that could weather dissenting voices.

This chapter is ultimately a study of one aspect of life in Nay Pyi Taw under the previous government. The new city has many critics and the system of government disciplined by the *Hluttaw* is part of a much wider story of political change and spatial re-designation. In Nay Pyi Taw, the *Hluttaw* has come to signify the role of the Myanmar people in the transformations underway in Myanmar society. Many justifiably bemoaned the fundamentally unrepresentative character of its members after the 2010 General Election. There were also good reasons for criticising its practices and its hesitation to deal with some of the most challenging issues in Myanmar society, such as federalism and communal conflict. Nonetheless the first *Hluttaw* offered a glimpse of the potential for Myanmar to create its own form of representative democracy, with a robust legislative culture and an awareness that unelected elites will need to take a lesser role in the country's government. Thura U Shwe Mann is now one of many USDP figures relegated to much lesser standing now the NLD controls the legislature. In 2015, he failed even to win back his own seat. Such developments show that the first *Hluttaw* generation presented the Myanmar people with one version of more participatory politics, but it will be up to the next generation to come up with something better.

The broader lessons from Myanmar's experience are relevant to any country that faces an historic process of political and economic change. In the Asian Century, more countries will experiment with different political formations, including carefully managed legislatures, constrained, in this case, by a long history of military dominance in politics. Seeking to find an appropriate speed and intensity of reform was one of the jobs taken on by the first *Hluttaw*. While critics can find many areas for improvement, the fact is that the experiment in legislative politics undertaken from 2011 to 2016 has provided a reasonable foundation for the expansion of democratic politics under the NLD government. The peaceful transfer of power, including the top positions within the *Hluttaw*, sets a precedent for Myanmar's rising generations of political leaders. There is no doubt the system remains fragile in key respects and there is still the possibility the military will re-assert its control.

As a final point, Myanmar's bold changes would not have been possible without the active support and encouragement of foreign governments. The consensus among the near neighbours—countries like China, India, Thailand and Singapore—has been that Myanmar's reforms will have benefits beyond its borders. More distant foreign powers, such as the United States, European Union and Australia, have been similarly pragmatic as they have sought to offer financial and diplomatic backing to the various groups looking to shift local horizons. From a policy perspective, there has been no single driver of the change process, and it is worth emphasising the overwhelmingly vernacular character of the reforms. In response to what they see in Myanmar, dictators from elsewhere in Asia will consider whether their own societies could profit from such maneuvers. At the same time, the region's few strong democracies can still hope that Myanmar will, at some stage, become a full member of their modest club. As the rhythms of Myanmar's first *Hluttaw* show, it is only with patience, representation and a sense of local priorities that such a system of government can thrive.

Notes

1. Originally, the *Pyidaungsu Hluttaw* consisted of 498 elected representatives and 166 military nominees for a total of 664 representatives. After the establishment of the *Hluttaw* in 2011, some joined the cabinet relinquishing their representative status and some passed away. A by-election was held in 2012 to fill these seats. At the end of the eighth session of the *Hluttaw* in November 2013, there were 477 elected representatives and 166 military nominees with a total of 643 representatives.
2. Data provided by the *Hluttaw*. This information can also be obtained from *Parliaments of Myanmar* published by the *Myanmar Times*.
3. There were 31 MPs who identified themselves as a product of BSPP. About half of them were members of standing committees and other important ad hoc committees such as international relations, peace, rule of law and the like. Two of them chaired the most important committees: the bill committees of the *Pyithu Hluttaw* and the *Amyotha Hluttaw* respectively.
4. Some ethnic groups have their own cultural associations that operate at the local as well as national level. For example, the Kachin, Chin, Mon, Rakhine and Shan have their own *Traditional Literature and Culture Association/Committees* that are well known in Myanmar. Some sub-ethnic groups such as Rawang, Lisu and others also have their own associations.
5. For example, in the 2010 election, there were three famous election contests in Yangon where the USDP lost to the NDF: *Pyithu Hluttaw* Pazundaung constituency USDP candidate Dr. Tin Tun Oo lost to U Aung Zin from NDF; *Pyithu Hluttaw* Sanchaung constituency USDP candidate Dr. Paing Soe lost to U Soe Win from NDF; *Amyotha Hluttaw* Yangon constituency no. 4 USDP candidate U Myat Thu aka Takatho Myat Thu (a political commentator) lost to Dr. Mya Nyana Soe from NDF. Dr. Paing Soe who was then a deputy minister for health was appointed as a member of Nay Pyi Taw Council as a consolation prize while others no longer appeared wearing the USDP hat. Most of the losing USDP candidates were either party cadres or local popular figures.
6. In rural areas of upper Myanmar, water is a scarce commodity and therefore digging artesian wells is a popular campaign tactic. It can cost around 2,200,000 Kyats, around US$2300, to dig and install. Most of the funding for such projects came not from the USDP but from the candidate's own arrangements. Such projects can be financed through the help of wealthy local donors.
7. In the midst of sectarian violence in Rakhine State, he submitted a motion for an amendment of the 1982 Citizenship Law on 25 July 2012 that was harshly rejected by the *Hluttaw* (Source: New Light of Myanmar on 26 July 2012)

8. According to OMI statistics, *Pyithu Hluttaw* MPs tend to ask questions related to infrastructure, governance with a focus on being a check and balance to the government, whereas *Amyotha Hluttaw* MPs ask about infrastructure, health and governance with an intention to satisfy the constituency need. Source: OMI (2014).
9. This description is based on direct personal experience. Chit Win was provided with accommodation both at Nay Pyi Taw Development Committee Guest House and the USDP Headquarters Guest House where he spent two months at each guest house in 2014.

Bibliography

English Language Publications

Egreteau, R. (2014). The continuing political salience of the military in post-SPDC Myanmar. In N. Cheesman, N. Farrelly, & T. Wilson (Eds.), *Debating democratization in Myanmar* (pp. 259–284). Singapore: Institute of Southeast Asian Studies.

Egreteau, R. (2015). Who are the military delegates in Myanmar's 2010–2015 Union Legislature? *SOJOURN: Journal of Social Issues in Southeast Asia, 30*(2), 338–370.

Fink, C. (2015). Myanmar's proactive National Legislature. *Social Research: An International Quarterly, 82*(2), 327–354.

International Crisis Group. (2013). Not a rubber stamp: Myanmar's legislature in a time of transition. *Asia Briefing* (Vol. 142). Yangon: International Crisis Group.

Kean, T. (2014). Myanmar's parliament: From scorn to significance. In N. Cheesman, N. Farrelly, & T. Wilson (Eds.), *Debating democratization in Myanmar* (pp. 43–74). Institute of Southeast Asian Studies: Singapore.

Than Than Nu. (2014). From exile to elections. In N. Cheesman, N. Farrelly, & T. Wilson (Eds.), *Debating democratization in Myanmar* (pp. 93–108). Institute of Southeast Asian Studies: Singapore.

Myanmar Language Publications

1. ကပ္ပတိန်သာစိန်၊ ခေတ်တစ်ခေတ်၏လွှတ်တော်သို့။ ၂၀၁၂၊ အောင်သီဟစာပေ။
2. ကျော်ဝင်း၊ ဖက်ဒရယ်မူ၊ သဘောတရားနှင့်လက်တွေ့ (Federalism: Theory and Practice)၊ ၂၀၁၃၊ ရန်ကုန်၊ တကောင်းစာပေ။
3. ကျော်ဝင်း၊ မြန်မာ့နိုင်ငံရေးလေ့လာဆန်းစစ်ချက် (၁၉၄၈-၁၉၈၈)။ ရန်ကုန်၊ ဂန့်ဂေါ်မြိုင်စာပေ။
4. ပြည်ထောင်စုသမ္မတမြန်မာနိုင်ငံတော်လွှတ်တော်များ (၂၀၁၃ ခုနှစ်) ပြည်သူ့လွှတ်တော်ကိုယ်စားလှယ်များ၊ အမျိုးသားလွှတ်တော်ကိုယ်စားလှယ်များ။ ရန်ကုန်၊ MCM Books Publishing။ ၂၀၁၃
5. ပွင့်လင်းမြန်မာရှေ့ဆောင်၊ လွှတ်တော်စောင့်ကြည့်လေ့လာရေးအစီရင်ခံစာအမှတ် (၁)၊ မြန်မာ့လွှတ်တော်ကိုကိန်းဂဏန်းအခြေပြုချဉ်းကပ်လေ့လာချက် (ပထမအကြိမ်မှ ဆဋ္ဌမအကြိမ်ထိ ပုံမှန်အစည်းအဝေးများအတွင်း မေးခွန်းများလေ့လာချက်)၊ ၂၀၁၄၊ ရန်ကုန်၊ ပွင့်လင်းမြန်မာရှေ့ဆောင်။
6. မြန်မာသံတော်ဆင့်အပတ်စဉ်သတင်းစာတွေ့ဆုံမေးမြန်းခန်းများစုစည်းမှု (၁)၊ အစိုးရ၊ လွှတ်တော်၊ ပါတီများ နှင့် မီဒီယာ။ ရန်ကုန်၊ မွေ့သံတော်ဆင့်စာပေ။ ၂၀၁၃။
7. မောင်သိန်းညွှန့် (ကော့ကရိတ်)၊ ဒီမိုကရေစီလွှတ်တော် နိုင်ငံရေး နှင့် ကျွန်တော်။ ၂၀၁၂၊ သင်းစာပေ။
8. မောင်ရေစက်၊ မြန်မာ့လွှတ်တော်ပုံရိပ်၊ ၂၀၁၃၊ ရန်ကုန်၊ မေသံတော်ဆင့်စာပေ
9. ဖေအာင်ဒင်၊ မြန်မာနိုင်ငံ၏ ပြည်ထောင်စုလွှတ်တော်ကိုအနီးကြည့် အဝေးကြည့်၊ ၂၀၁၃၊ ရန်ကုန်၊ ခေတ်ပြတိုက်စာပေ။
10. ဦးကြည်မြင့် (လသာ)၊ ဒုတိယအကောင်းဆုံးနဲ့လှပတဲ့စိတ်ကလေး။ ၂၀၁၂၊ ရန်ကုန်၊ မိုးမြင့်ကြယ်စာပေ
11. ဦးကြည်မြင့် (လသာ)၊ ပြည်သူ-လွှတ်တော်-အစိုးရ၊ တြိဂံ နှင့် ဆဌဂံ၊ ၂၀၁၃၊ ရန်ကုန်၊ မိုးမြင့်ကြယ်စာပေ

CHAPTER 6

Science and Technology Policy in the Asian Century

Paul H. Jensen and Lauren A. Palmer

Introduction

There is growing understanding that a vibrant innovation ecosystem is an important element of a healthy and prosperous nation, and that scientific research in turn underpins a healthy innovation ecosystem. What is less known is what the role of government is in nurturing this ecosystem. While many argue that government policy should play a strong role in guiding and promoting innovation (see Arrow 1962 for the seminal contribution here), there are others who counter that innovation is best left to the market (Davidson and Potts 2016). This debate really hinges on the existence of market failures, although it has become increasingly topical to think about the role of national innovation systems and the notion of 'systems failure' (Dodgson et al. 2011). In this Chapter, we

P.H. Jensen (✉)
Faculty of Business & Economics, The University of Melbourne, Melbourne, Australia
e-mail: pjensen@unimelb.edu.au

L.A. Palmer
Australian Council of Learned Academies, Melbourne, Australia
e-mail: Lauren@acola.org.au

S. Bice et al. (eds.), *Public Policy in the 'Asian Century'*, International Series on Public Policy, https://doi.org/10.1057/978-1-137-60252-7_6

explore recent experiences (and experiments) in Australia and Asia with science and technology (S&T) policy, with a specific emphasis on the different ways in which the boundaries of government intervention in the market have been defined. For example, we will consider how university-industry collaboration occurs across different nations and the effect that it has on the diffusion of new technology into practice. This will include consideration of the ways to bridge the university-industry divide, the degree of collaboration between academic and industrial researchers, and the role of government programs designed to stimulate university-industry collaboration.

Given these insights, we reflect on what S&T policy can tell us about public policy in the Asian century and how we might manage the ongoing tension between national interests and global prosperity. We also delve into recent Asian experiences with S&T policies, examining a range of national programs in China, Singapore, India, Japan and South Korea, that have been introduced and the characteristics of their success. One particularly interesting initiative, the Innovation Growth Lab (IGL), which is designed to provide funds to researchers using randomised controlled trials to evaluate the effects of specific government innovation programs, is also outlined.

Innovation has many definitions but it is here defined as '*the implementation of a new or significantly improved product (good or service), process, new marketing method or a new organisational method in business practices, workplace organisations or external relations*'.[1] At its most fundamental level, innovation is people-centred: it is the result of creative individual(s) with complementary skills and knowledge collaborating to develop new ways of doing things and to take them to the market. An increasingly important part of this process revolves around collaboration—across firms, states and countries—working together to speed up the innovative process and to diffuse the knowledge created as quickly as possible to gain the competitive advantage. It is well-known that the team size is increasing in scientific activity, and it is becoming equally apparent that taking scientific ideas to market is being conducted by teams of people.

Scientific, engineering, and technical innovation can address issues of global importance and lead to products and services that allow countries to be productive and maintain international competitiveness. Businesses, small-medium enterprises (SMEs), multinationals, start-ups, publicly funded research institutes and universities all compete and cooperate with one another to be more innovative and to gain and maintain a competitive advantage in market opportunities. The availability of resources, such as financial and human resources, play an important role in determining an organisation's research and innovation activities and outputs (OECD 2014b). Universities, governments and industry are key enablers of change in the innovation system and recognise the importance of innovation to their competitiveness. As a result, they look at ways to be more innovative and grow the innovation system through investing and developing programs that facilitate collaboration, translation of research and innovation.

In the Section of this Chapter, 'Returns to Collaboration', we provide an examination of the rationale underpinning the notion that there are returns to different types of collaboration (e.g. interdisciplinary collaboration, university-industry collaboration). While collaboration is often talked about in positive terms, it is important to understand the mechanisms that drive the potential gains. In the Section 'Barriers to Collaboration', we discuss some of the barriers to collaboration. In the Section 'International S&T Policy Programs', we provide an overview of the different types of programs observed in Asia and Australia, and the degree to which these programs have successfully promoted collaboration and innovation outcomes. Finally, we provide some conclusions and policy implications in the 'Conclusions' Section.

Returns to Collaboration

Typically, substantial education is required for individuals to expand the knowledge frontier (Jones 2008). As innovation continually pushes the boundaries of knowledge, and vice versa, there is the potential for increased educational burden on future innovators. This effect, known as the 'burden of knowledge' (Jones 2008), can lead to individuals needing to increase and access new knowledge to be innovative. As a consequence, it is taking longer for an individual to reach the knowledge frontier—where once upon a time it was conceivable to reach the frontier straight out of your Ph.D., it is now commonplace for scientists to work for several years after their Ph.D. in someone else's lab before they are ready to start their own lab. Thus, the age at which great invention occurs is steadily advancing.

Increasing knowledge can be done in two ways: through individuals broadening their range of knowledge, or by individuals narrowing their knowledge to a specific area (Jones 2008). Broadening knowledge can be time intensive as it requires further education and/or training and this time dependency can lead to delays in the innovation process. Alternatively, by becoming more specialised in a certain area, individuals can develop a deep understanding in a particular field and are able to collaborate with other individuals who have the required knowledge base to value add and overcome knowledge gaps in the innovation process. But this process also indicates that there are returns to collaboration: as it becomes harder to reach the frontier, there are returns from working with others in order to undertake innovative research.

Jones (2008) analysed a rich data set (of previous work and new data) to demonstrate innovator behaviour—including age of first invention, specialisations, and teamwork patterns—to show that the distance to the frontier of knowledge can vary over time and be dependent on the field of innovation (Jones 2008). He has also demonstrated via examination of 19.9 million papers in the Institute for Scientific Information (ISI) Web of Science database over five decades and 2.1 million patents, that publications in the sciences and engineering are to a greater extent being published by teams of researchers rather than individuals (Wuchty et al. 2007). Further research has highlighted that teamwork and collaboration has been increasing since the 1950s (Wuchty et al. 2007) or even as early as the early 1900s (Zuckerman and Merton 1973). This demonstrates the opportunities for researchers to collaborate with peers to generate knowledge and translate research. However, not all collaborations are equal; some can enhance productivity, whilst others can result in high transaction costs, unfinished projects or unsatisfactory results that inhibit productivity (Lee and Bozeman 2005).

Research and development has typically been viewed as geographically constrained with many universities and incubators becoming known as the go-to location for their research excellence in certain fields and locations (e.g. Silicon Valley as a high-tech innovation and development hub). However, the links between scientific and technological research and location is weakening and as a result the tyranny of distance is declining (Jones et al. 2008). Cheaper air travel means that researchers and innovators are more mobile than ever before, providing significant opportunities for individuals to access the knowledge, resources and technologies needed to drive their research and innovation agendas forward. Additionally, technological advances such as email and videoconferencing have allowed greater access to geographically distant researchers and potential collaborators. Policies that support programs and funding to encourage researchers to collaborate with international and national peers will be important in continuing to assist researchers to be more mobile and to facilitate knowledge exchange through collaboration and international networks.

Collaboration networks can be built through a variety of different mechanisms including through the dissemination of information (e.g. conference presentations and posters, scientific publications, sharing of data), access to resources, technology and facilities (e.g. specialised equipment, laboratories, patents, grant funding), and talent and knowledge exchange (e.g. advancing and sharing knowledge for innovation, diaspora of educated and knowledgeable students and researchers, solving issues of global importance, interactions with industry and research institutions). Such collaboration is important in changing the speed of knowledge diffusing into practice.

Although it seems obvious that collaboration is an increasingly important feature of the innovation landscape, it is worth stopping to ask: why are there positive returns to collaboration? At the scientist-scientist level, we have seen that teams are getting larger, and larger teams are doing the most important research (Wuchty et al. 2007). Furthermore, Adams et al. (2005) find that the size of scientific teams has increased by 50 percent over the period 1981–1999. But why would university-industry collaboration matter? One reason is that when university researchers and industry researchers get together, they might ask different (e.g. more applied) types of questions. This could be good for the economy, but it is worth noting that we actually do not know what the optimal mix of pure versus applied research is, and it is likely that doing more applied research limits the time available to conduct basic research, i.e. there are trade-offs. It may also be the case that collaborations between university researchers and industry scientists might speed up the translation of knowledge into practice. And this could be of substantial benefit to society because the speed of diffusion has important productivity implications. However, there is no strong evidence suggesting that this is, in fact, empirically true. So, it is important to be aware that the case for increasing collaboration—particularly between universities and industry—does not have much of an empirical basis.

Interdisciplinary Collaboration

Whilst science and technology are integral in addressing issues of global importance, they cannot do so in isolation. The humanities and social sciences are an important element in addressing global challenges and multidisciplinary approaches can provide the comprehensive knowledge needed to solve global challenges. There are many examples where a diverse range of people with varying expertise have come together to collaborate and innovate on projects of global importance, where the required knowledge was greater than one individual. The large hadron collider (LHC), the world's largest and most powerful particle accelerator capable of advancing understanding of physical laws by testing different theories of particle physics and high energy physics, is an example of such an innovation. The LHC took ten years to plan and build, and involved over 10,000 scientists, engineers and technicians from over 100 countries. The LHC now conducts interdisciplinary research, with several collaborative projects utilising the particle accelerator.

Likewise, the Human Genome project is another example of a multidisciplinary project in which the collaborative efforts across disciplines have achieved results that one individual and one discipline could not have achieved alone. The research program involved 20 institutes across six countries with the goal to map and better understand human genomes. A small portion of the project was dedicated to studying the ethical, legal and social issues related to the increased knowledge and availability of genetic information that result from the project's outcomes.

These examples demonstrate the role of international and interdisciplinary collaboration to bridge knowledge gaps and overcome the burden of knowledge in order to advance scientific and technological research, development and innovation.

The Role of Universities and Publicly Funded Research Organisations

Universities and publicly funded research organisations are also an integral part of the innovation ecosystem, as bodies assisting in the creation of skilled graduates, new knowledge, and knowledge exchange. Universities and publicly funded research organisations aim to undertake research in areas of global importance, generate new knowledge, enable and encourage innovation, and form partnerships with industry, government and other research organisations to commercialise ideas.

Increasing mobility of researchers and the desire to gain talented knowledge is leading to universities, organisations, industry, and even other countries competing to attract and retain talented individuals. Since 1975 there has been a nearly universal increase in the frequency of collaborations between authors based at different universities throughout the United States of America (Jones et al. 2008). These bodies understand the risks of losing their best and brightest, but also the benefits of attracting strong individuals from overseas and national research organisations. The internationalisation and globalisation of universities and higher education, through for example student mobility and fostering attractive and competitive research environments to draw highly qualified researchers, has played a role in the global competition for talent (Heitor 2015; OECD 2014b; Turpin et al. 2008). Attracting and retaining talented individuals can typically be done in two ways: via integrating small to medium enterprises (SMEs) and new firms into global value chains or through national research ecosystems that encourage direct foreign investment (OECD 2014b). Regarding the latter of these pathways, there is a focus on increasing the attractiveness and competitiveness of national research systems through increasing research infrastructure, strengthening universities' capacity, branding activities, developing improved learning environments and education products, mobility schemes, and opening the research system to provide job opportunities for talented foreign researchers (OECD 2014b).

The mobility of researchers and students plays a significant contribution to building international networks (Turpin et al. 2008). The internationalisation of higher education is increasing and in 2011 the number of international students worldwide had doubled since the year 2000 (OECD 2014b). This increasing internationalisation has opened doors for researchers to increase their knowledge networks and access knowledge that previously may not have been easily accessible.

However, tenure, academic promotion policies and key performance indicators (KPIs) for university researchers do not necessarily encourage or support collaboration with other researchers or industry. Therefore in order to capture the benefits of collaboration, incentives to facilitate collaboration need to be reviewed at the research institution level and changed to encourage better collaboration with industry. Supplementing internal research and development efforts by collaborating with industry, publicly funded research institutes, universities and external suppliers and competitors, would promote important knowledge exchange that could lead to greater innovative processes. There are a number of pathways that can be taken by universities in terms of their research outputs: (i) the research idea can remain within the university confines or be published in a journal but the research is of no practical benefit to others, (ii) the research idea is publicly available and can be used by others, or (iii) the research idea is a partnership with industry and has potential to create a pathway to commercialise a research idea. The first pathway is not ideal as it doesn't lead to research translation or positive knowledge exchange, however, the other two pathways lead to better results and can change the speed at which knowledge is diffused into practice. A lack of industry engagement at the university level can result in the research ideas staying within academia, with less chance of commercialisation.

The Role of Industry

Universities collaborate to translate research into commercial outcomes, build valuable contacts and networks, improve graduate outcomes, and enhance knowledge transfer. On the other hand, industry tends to seek collaborations to access specialised technology, facilities and knowledge, share costs of research and development (thereby reducing innovation risks), gain access to skilled individuals, and access public funding.

Collaboration between research institutes and industry has the potential to increase productivity performance through the creation of new ideas, products and services for the market. However, there are several barriers to university-industry collaboration, including, but not limited to: issues around IP (use, access, management and ownership); mismatch in expectations from either party (fast commercial returns versus basic research); financial barriers; and lack of incentives for researchers to collaborate with industry (Bell et al. 2015; Bruneel et al. 2010). In Australia, the government provides a number of services to connect industry with researchers including: Connecting Australian-European Science and Innovation Excellence (CAESIE), R&D Tax Incentive, the CSIRO Small and Medium Enterprise Engagement Centre and Flagship Collaboration Fund, the ARC Linkage Schemes and Industrial Transformation Research Program.

The Role of Government

Governments potentially play an important role in influencing incentives and setting appropriate long term innovation policies that support research and innovation to nurture a nation's productivity. However, this is a highly contested point of view, with many debating that the arguments in favour of direct government intervention typically fail to see the costs and overstate the benefits of such intervention (Davidson and Potts 2016). In most countries, however, governments do provide both indirect and direct financial support to encourage collaboration, research translation and innovation. Indirect support can be provided through tax incentives (both corporate and personal) whereas direct support can be provided through funding received through debt financing systems (e.g. loans, credit guarantees, debt sharing mechanisms, etc.), competitive grants, repayable loans, early stage financing and innovation vouchers. Recent Organisation for Economic Co-operation and Development (OECD) data demonstrates that Australia is overly-reliant on indirect support (Bell et al. 2015; OECD 2015). Yet, without getting into the detail of whether or not there is a strong rationale for government intervention in the innovation market, one thing is clear: the level of evaluation of government S&T programs is weaker than in other areas of public policy such as education, labour and health. We basically do not know the effectiveness of most S&T policy programs, despite allocating hundreds of millions (even billions) of dollars into such programs. Recent initiatives such as the *Science of Science and Innovation Policy* (National Science and Technology Council 2008) in the United States have slowly started to change this, but most countries are lagging behind the United States. Julian Lane and colleagues have been leading the way on this front, producing new datasets that greatly improve our ability of do rigorous evaluations on a range of S&T policy programs (Lane 2009, 2010).

Many nations also support innovation via fiscal incentives. In 2015, there were 28 OECD countries that provided tax relief for business research and development expenditures (OECD 2014b). Within some of these OECD countries R&D tax incentives are used to encourage collaboration. There is evidence that suggests government tax incentives can attract foreign research and development Centres and can lead to greater competition between countries (OECD 2014b). Indeed, many of the countries that have adopted R&D tax incentives have higher rates of business collaboration with public sector research organisations (Bell et al. 2015).

Looking to Australia, in 2015 the Australian Government undertook a consultation process as part of the Tax White Paper to examine support for research and development including the Australian R&D Tax Incentive (Ferris et al. 2016). The Australian R&D Tax Incentive is a broad-based entitlement program aimed to help businesses offset the cost of undertaking research and development. The incentive is open to businesses who are conducting eligible research and development in all sectors and of any size with the aim of incentivising and encouraging businesses who previously may not have actively participated in innovation and research activities to collaborate with researchers and research institutions.

In addition to direct and indirect financial support, it is argued that governments can support innovation through investing in services that support science, engineering, research, education and infrastructure services (such as research laboratories, and digital infrastructure). Additionally, governments can nurture the innovation ecosystem through encouraging and/or providing incentives for industry and businesses to invest in research translation and innovation and by reducing or removing regulatory barriers (Australian Government 2015e). An important and well known element to developing better networks and innovation processes is to improve the interaction between publicly funded research organisations and universities with industry. What is less well known is what the role of government is in nurturing the innovation ecosystem long-term. Additionally, there is a financial limit to what governments can provide, so where do the current boundaries to government intervention lie and where in the future should they sit?

Barriers to Collaboration

There are systematic barriers in many nations with respect to collaboration and innovation including a lack of incentives for researchers to collaborate with business, financial barriers for SMEs to collaborate (including limited stable/long-term strategic funding), low levels of technically skilled personnel, and regulatory burdens. Geographical isolation, particularly in the case of Australia, may also pose challenges due to the time and financial costs associated with international travel. However, as previously mentioned the tyranny of distance is weakening and cheaper travel and advances in information and communication technologies can more readily facilitate knowledge exchange (and other exchanges) between researchers.

Tsukada and Nagaoka (2015) have investigated patterns of international research collaboration for European and East Asian countries, and found that communication with international researchers using the English language, a popular language in scientific and technical fields, can be a barrier for some countries in the Asian region (McKenzie et al. 2015; Tsukada and Nagaoka 2015). Therefore, improving English language skills, as well as second languages for English speaking researchers, could assist in developing more meaningful and effective scientific collaborations with the Asian region (McKenzie et al. 2015).

As previously noted, the research and innovation process is taking longer due to an increasing knowledge base and this changing pattern in the innovation process is currently not supported by appropriate policies and funding. To date, numerous international innovation systems and the professional services that support them have been hindered by short term and unstable policy and funding settings. Many programs to support research and innovation are typically three year contracts, making it more difficult for researchers to develop their research ideas into innovative products and services. Additionally, to be competitive and secure funding to undertake research, development and innovation in their chosen fields, researchers typically need to have already produced results and findings from their research.

The lack of stable long-term research, innovation and productivity polices and funding has presented a barrier for a prosperous longstanding innovation system in Australia. For instance, the Australian Government funded an International Science Linkages (ISL) program over ten years, which supported Australian scientific researchers from both the public and private sector to collaborate with international counterparts on innovative science and technology research, with the purpose of contributing to Australia's economic, social and environmental wellbeing. In 2010, the ISL program underwent an independent review by an Australian based consulting firm, Allen Consulting (now ACIL Allen). The independent review noted that the ISL program was the *'Australian Government's leading mechanism for increasing Australia's participation in international research, for strengthening strategic partnerships between the Australian and overseas research communities, and for facilitating access by Australian researchers to global technology and science facilities'* and was noted as a key element to the Government's innovation policy agenda at the time (Australian Government 2011). Additionally, the first recommendation of the review stated that the ISL program should be renewed and funding should be increased to $20 million AUD per annum (Australian Government 2011). However, despite the recommendation, the 2011 Australian Federal Budget did not contain funding for the ISL Program, and the existing funding ran out in June 2011. In its place, much shorter term initiatives were introduced targeting specific countries including a research collaboration program with China (the Australia-China Science and Research Fund) and a joint fund initiative with India (the Australia-India Strategic Research Fund) (Smith 2011; Australian Government 2015c). The Australia-India Strategic Research Fund is now one of India's greatest sources of support for international science and is also Australia's largest fund for bilateral research (Australian Government 2015b). In moving forward, a whole-of-government approach will be important to secure stable long-term funding to assist in maximising Australia's innovation dividend from scientific research and to ensure the longevity of such programs.

International S&T Policy Programs

The UK Innovation Growth Lab (IGL), established in 2014, aims to '*enable, support, undertake and disseminate high impact research that uses randomised trials to improve the design of the programmes and institutions that help make our economies more innovative and entrepreneurial*' (Innovation Growth Lab 2015). IGL notes that there is significant investment in initiatives to help foster innovation. With 12 partners from across the globe, IGL currently support 16 trials through the IGL grants programme. Examples of trials include: trialling different instruments to increase business-university links and technology transfer; exploring how to best design research labs to encourage collaboration; testing several interventions to support high-growth entrepreneurs, including training, co-working spaces, mentoring and coaching; and studying how to incentivise employees to contribute new ideas. Through trialling programs at a small scale and evaluating their effectiveness, or by making small changes to existing programs, a better understanding of improving the design of innovation programs and initiatives can be gained resulting in the potential minimisation of wasting resources in the process (Bravo-Biosca 2015).

Looking to the United States of America (USA), the successful Small Business Innovation Research (SBIR) Program encourages small business to engage in federal research and development that has commercialisation potential (SBIR 2015). Established in 1972, the SBIR Program has had long-term stability. Its mission is to *'support scientific excellence and technological innovation through the investment of Federal research funds in critical American priorities to build a strong national economy'*. Through fostering and encouraging small businesses to engage in research and development, the program stimulates high-tech innovation and promotes entrepreneurship in businesses. The SBIR programs are supported through money sought from federal agencies which possess a research and development budget exceeding $100 million USD. These federal agencies, 11 of which are part of the SBIR program, are required to allocate 2.8 percent of their research and development budget annually towards the SBIR program.

The USA and countries within Europe have long held advantages in collaboration in scientific fields. There are a number of international knowledge networks that provide examples of direct government action including Switzerland's knowledge network Swissnex; the German Academic International Network (GAIN); the Geneva International Academic Network (GIAN); and Canada's International Science and Technology Partnerships (ISTP). Such initiatives have been key tools for national science and technology action (Heitor 2015). However, new countries of increasing significance are emerging in the Asian region which will present greater opportunities for Australia to collaborate with the region.

The Asian region's close proximity to Australia and recent growth presents additional opportunities for deeper engagement. Between 2008 and 2014, China was Australia's third largest collaborator with 21,058 joint papers. Australia's other major partners included the USA (first), UK (second), Germany (fourth) and Canada (fifth). Over the same period, Australia was Singapore's third largest partner with 4,166 papers (UNESCO 2015).

Australia

In Australia, innovation varies across sectors and despite the continuing dialogue that innovation is important to business, Australian exporters do not perform highly across a number of innovation indicators compared to the country's OECD counterparts (Australian Government 2014). There are a number of factors that might cause poor business research and innovation outcomes and these issues vary across countries. For example: Australia has a small manufacturing industry predisposing the country to lower levels of R&D expenditure compared to larger overseas manufacturing sectors; Australia has a significant number of small to medium enterprises which are susceptible to innovation risk; and, larger companies enjoy a high proportion of foreign direct investment, increasing reliance on overseas innovation (Withers et al. 2009). As noted, other countries will face a different set of challenges in achieving their S&T objectives: in developing Asian economies, for example, improving the capabilities of the workforce, and human capital formation more generally, will likely be of fundamental importance.

Poor levels of new-to-market innovation in Australia limits the country's capacity to build international competitiveness and participate in global value chains (Australian Government 2014). Strengthening global relationships, particularly with Asia, through encouraging and facilitating smarter collaboration between business and between businesses and universities and publicly funded research organisations will be important for improving Australia's innovation ecosystem and the country's productivity.

The Australian Research Council (ARC), an Australian government entity, is one of the main bodies for funding competitive research in Australia and provides research advice to the government. The ARC Linkage scheme plays an important role in encouraging partnerships, both nationally and internationally, between researchers and business, community organisations, industry, and other publicly funded research agencies (Australian Government 2015a). The ARC Linkage schemes '*aim to encourage and extend cooperative approaches to research and improve the use of research outcomes by strengthening links within Australia's innovation system and with innovation systems internationally*' (Australian Government 2015a). However, the success rates of applicants across all ARC schemes has been declining and has decreased by almost half since 2002 to 17.8 percent. The success rate of Linkage schemes specifically have been steadily decreasing—for example: the Linkage Infrastructure Equipment and Facilities scheme has dropped from 55.1 percent in 2002 to a 41.5 percent success rate in 2015, and the Linkage Project scheme has dropped from 51.8 percent in 2002 to 35.9 percent success rate in 2014. The percentage of Australian companies listed on

ARC Linkage funded projects, however, remains relatively stable with the largest partners listed as government (local and state) followed by Australian private companies. The total amount of cash provided by Australian private companies is greater than that of the local and state government partners, indicating good engagement with private companies at this level.

Additional incentives and programs supported by the Australian Government include the Entrepreneurs' Programme (an Australian Government flagship initiative announced in 2015, funded at $484.2 million AUD over the next five years, with the aim to provide practical support and advice to entrepreneurs and business) and Industry Growth Centres (established in five growth sectors in Australia where a competitive advantage already exists).

In 2015–2016, the Australian Government committed approximately $9.7 AUD billion to support science, research and innovation. Of this commitment approximately $1.8 billion AUD was intramural expenditure[2] going towards Australian Government research and development and federal research agencies such as CSIRO and Defence Science and Technology Group. The remainder was for extramural expenditure[3] in the business enterprise sector (e.g. industry research and development tax measures and business innovation); the higher education sector (e.g. ARC, higher education research and development, performance based block funding); and in the multisector category (e.g. National Health and Medical Research Council, Cooperative Research Centres, etc.) (Australian Government 2015d). The majority of this funding was dedicated to supporting public research and business innovation through tax incentives.

To compliment these programs, in late 2015 the Australian Government released its National Innovation and Science Agenda (NISA) which has four pillars aimed at supporting Australian entrepreneurs; increasing collaboration between industry and researchers; developing and attracting world-class talent; and embracing innovation and agility in the way Australia conducts business. The NISA aims to build on key initiatives and to continue to support certain programs already in place. It also includes new initiatives aimed at encouraging a more innovative and entrepreneurial economy. For example, NISA will continue to support the establishment of Industry Growth Centres in five key areas of competitive advantage: Advanced Manufacturing; Food and Agribusiness; Medical Technologies and Pharmaceuticals;

Mining Equipment, Technology and Services; and Oil, Gas and Energy Resources. The Agenda outlines a number of measures to support innovation, however as the program is still in its infancy, is too early to review the effectiveness of these.

China

The Chinese economy has grown substantially over recent years and is currently the world's second largest economy in terms of GDP. During the period 2008–2012, China doubled its spending on research and development following a slower growth over the period 2001–2008 (OECD 2014b). In 2014, China spent 2.05 percent of GDP on research and development, investing slightly more than the European Union (1.94 percent of GDP). According to China's Science and Technology Minister Wan Gang, the country's research and development fund reached 1.34 trillion Chinese yuan in 2014, of which the private sector provided 76 percent, offering support and easier access to funding for scientific and technological researchers to innovate (Yingqi 2015). Additionally, China's research collaborations with other countries has been growing rapidly within the Asian region since 2000; in particular, China's research collaboration with Australia has grown more than tenfold since 2000, eightfold with Taiwan, tenfold with South Korea, and since 1999 has grown fourfold with Japan (Adams 2012).

China has a number of programs to support research and development which are mainly provided through four entities: The Ministry of Science and Technology (MoST); the National Natural Science Foundation of China (NSFC); The Chinese Academy of Science (CAS); and the China Scholarship Council (CSC) (Zhang 2014). Within each of these entities there are a number of programs that support research and development for the scientific and technological fields. In addition, China has a number of laws and regulations that provide legal guidance and guarantees to promote the transformation of scientific and technological achievements (National People's Congress of the People's Republic of China 1996; National People's Congress of the People's Republic of China 2008; Gao 2015). The country also has a number of new initiatives to support innovation such as the 'Made in China 2025' program which aims to use subsidies and mandates to encourage manufacturing companies to upgrade faculties to be environmentally sustainable and innovative (The Economist 2015), however these initiatives have not been operating for long enough to be able to comment on their effectiveness. In addition to the aforementioned initiatives, China has ongoing five-year plans that outline strategies for growth. In early 2016, China released its 13th five-year plan (2016–2020) for economic and social development of which innovation is a key principle. The 13th five-year plan suggests creating an innovation-driven system with markets playing a key role in allocating resources (The State Council 2015). With respect to Australia's relationship with China, the Australian government encourages collaboration through the Australia-China Science and Research Fund providing opportunities for Australian researchers to collaborate with China.

India

India is also at the forefront of a number of scientific and technological fields. The country is large and diverse and innovation is seen as critical to socio-economic development (OECD 2014b). Whilst India is a rapidly growing emerging economy, its growth rate has slowed in recent years (OECD 2014b). In 2011, the country spent 0.82 percent of GDP on research and development. India has developed a sizeable publicly funded research and development structure in the areas of science, technology and innovation (Abhyankar 2014). The country however has a complex and large national innovation ecosystem with many individuals and institutions partaking in research and innovation (Abhyankar 2014). In the past, these institutions have operated independently of one another; however more recently there has been a greater push to connect the institutions and programs together to harness the country's innovation potential (Abhyankar 2014).

In 2010, the Indian government declared 2010–2020 the 'Decade of Innovation' and in parallel the country established the National Innovation Council to develop a road map for promoting innovation (European Commission 2013). In 2013, India's Ministry of Science and Technology unveiled its new Science, Technology and Innovation (STI) policy to drive investment in science and in science-led technology and innovation in areas of socio-economic importance (Government of India 2013). The policy outlined key initiatives for strengthening India's innovation ecosystem and for enhancing entrepreneurship. Among other initiatives, the policy stated that research and development spending will increase to 2 percent over the five years since the establishment of the policy by creating a conducive environment that encourages the private sector to invest in research and development (Embassy of India 2013). India also had five-year plans which were overseen by the Planning Commission (Government of India). However, in 2014 in a speech by then Prime Minister Modi, it was announced that the Planning Commission would be disbanded, though the 12th five-year plan continued for 2012–2017 (UNESCO 2015).

The Ministry of Science and Technology has a number of initiatives to encourage and support innovation including: The India Innovation Growth Program; National Innovation Foundation; PRISM—Promoting Innovation in Individuals, Start-ups and Micro, Small and Medium Enterprises (MSMEs); Council of Scientific and Industrial Research Innovation Complexes; Patent Assistance Programs; Technology Business Incubators; Small Business Innovation Research Initiative; and Technology Development and Demonstration Program (Abhyankar 2014).

With respect to Australia's relationship with India, collaboration is encouraged and supported by the Australian Government through support from the Australian-India Strategic Research Fund, providing opportunities for Australian researchers to collaborate with India. Yet despite good programs, along with joint publications between Australia and India, India is not yet in the top three collaboration partners for Australia.

Japan

In 2014, Japan spent 3.58 percent of its GDP on research and development. Like India and China, Japan has five-year plans known as the Science and Technology Basic Plan. The Council for Science, Technology and Innovation is responsible for the formulation and implementation of the plan and the country is entering into the fifth Science and Technology Basic Plan (FY2016-22) (Council for Science Technology and Innovation 2015). In 1995, the Science and Technology Basic Law was enacted and it is in accordance with this that the Science and Technology Basic Plans (STBP) are formulated and implemented. The fifth basic plan recognises the burden of knowledge, noting that '*as the intellectual frontier expands, it is becoming increasingly difficult for individual organizations to produce all the knowledge and technology necessary for success*' and notes that it will be increasingly important to collaborate and bring people with diverse specialisations together (Government of Japan 2015a).

Japan experimented with innovative S&T policies via the creation of 'science cities' such as Tsukuba Science City back in the 1970s. This tentative first step crystallised into a sophisticated and expansive program of developing science cities in the 1980s known as Technopolis. This program was backed by the Ministry of International Trade and Industry (MITI) and resulted in the creation of 25 science cities across the country. The scale of this industrial and regional development program was unparalleled and it was heralded at the time as a major launching pad for Japan's technological development. Despite substantial support through the 1980s and 1990s, the program was disbanded in 1998. Suzuki (2004) argues that a range of both macroeconomic factors (e.g. unfavourable exchange rates) and organizational failures (e.g. bureaucratic conflict) contributed to the program's demise.

Since then, the STBP have progressed Japan's science, technology and innovation sector as demonstrated through, for example, rising numbers of researchers and publications; increasing investment in research; the growing number of patents being held; and steadily increasing joint research projects among universities, companies and research and development institutions since 1996 (Government of Japan 2015b). However, there are still several areas needing improvement including increasing industry-university collaboration; increasing research output; encouraging students to pursue research careers; and increasing public confidence in science and technology. In recent years Japan's research papers have decreased both qualitatively and quantitatively (in terms of their international rankings), and the science, technology and innovation sector is starting to fall behind other leading countries (Government of Japan 2015a). The fifth STBP has four pillars designed to address the gaps in science, technology and innovation: creating new value for the development of future industry and social transformation; addressing economic and social challenges; reinforcing the fundamentals for science, technology and innovation; and building a systemic virtuous cycle of human resource, knowledge, and funding for innovation.

In 2012, Japanese Prime Minister Shinzo Abe positioned innovation as one of the four key pillars for the country's growth strategy with the goal to make Japan the most innovation-friendly country in the world (Council for Science Technology and Innovation 2015). Shortly after in 2013, the Cabinet Office of Japan's Government announced the

Comprehensive Strategy on Science, Technology and Innovation. The strategy had a long-term vision and short-term programs to support science, technology and innovation policies. A number of actions have been taken since then including the establishment of an annual PDCA cycle directly linked to the budget establishment, the Cross-ministerial Strategic Innovation Promotion Program (SIP), establishment of the Impulsing Paradigm Change through Disruptive Technologies Program (ImPACT) and concerted efforts with respect to solving issues of importance (Council for Science Technology and Innovation 2015). The ImPACT program was developed with the aim of supporting and encouraging high-risk disruptive innovation that has the potential to be high-impact. An evaluation of the programs and system will be undertaken in 2019. The Cross-ministerial Strategic Innovation Promotion Program involves 10 themes addressing key societal and economic challenges for Japan and facilitates basic research through to commercialisation. The Comprehensive Strategy will be updated yearly, and considered in conjunction with the five-year plans, to enable flexible policy management (Government of Japan 2015a).

South Korea

South Korea was the leading OECD country in 2014 in terms of gross domestic spending on research and development at 4.29 percent of GDP. The country also has five-year plans, which were initially established in 1962 as economic development plans. The five-year economic and development plans ran from 1962–1996, each with principal objectives and a specific focus (e.g. infrastructure, heavy and chemical industries, high-tech industries etc.) introducing policies and resources to reach their principal objectives (OECD 2014a). South Korea underwent a significant economic change over the period 1962–1996; the introduction of the Technology Promotion Plan and the enactment of the Science and Technology Promotion Act, alongside the five-year plans, were major policy instruments and strategies that drove the South Korean economy from an agricultural economy to a leading industrial power (OECD 2014a). During this period (1962–1996) the *chaebols*—business conglomerates such as Samsung, LG and Hyundai—also played a key role in the country's economic development (OECD 2014a). Over this time, several scientific and technical institutes and policies were also implemented. In 1966, the Korean Institute of Science and Technology

(KIST) was founded and in 1981 KIST integrated with the Korea Advanced Institute of Science (KAIS) to form the Korean Advanced Institute of Science and Technology (KAIST).

However, shortly thereafter in 1989 the two separated with KIST re-establishing itself as an independent entity and KAIS remaining as KAIST (KAIST 2014b; KIST 2016). KAIST is a research focused university that aims to foster leading researchers in science and technology, undertake basic and applied research and support collaborations with other research institutions and industries (KAIST 2014a). In 1967, the Ministry of Science and Technology (now the Ministry of Science, ICT and Future Planning) was established as well as the Science and Technology Promotion Act. The Ministry of Science and Technology, known as MOST, was the central government agency accountable for scientific and technological policy (Chung 2011). In 1982, MOST initiated the first national research and development program which supported high-risk research in key priority areas that would actively drive economic growth including information technology, industrial technologies and new material technologies (Hanna 1999; OECD 2014a).

In 1999, South Korea announced a long-term strategic plan, 'Vision 2025: Korea's Long-term Vision for Science and Technology Development', which outlined 39 tasks, 19 recommendations and key national and science and technology indicators to advance Korea's Science and Technology development by 2025. Following announcement of Vision 2025, the Science and Technology Framework Law was created which formed the basis of the five year Basic Plans of Science and Technology (2003–07, 2008–12)(OECD 2014a). In 2013, then President Park Geun-hye announced in her inaugural speech her vision for the Creative Economy, defining it as '*the convergence of science and technology with industry, the fusion of culture with industry and the blossoming of creativity made possible by the breaking down of barriers between industries …*' (Park 2013). President Park identified specific areas that would be key priorities for the creative economy, namely science, technology and the Information Technology industry (Park 2013). The Creative Economy Action Plan has three goals, six strategies (each accompanied by three to five tasks totalling 24 tasks across the plan). The three goals are to (1) create new jobs and markets through creativity and innovation; (2) strengthen Korea's global leadership through a creative economy; and (3) creating a society where creativity is respected and manifested (MOSF 2013). Across these goals are the six strategies which include: creating an ecosystem that promotes the creation of start-ups; strengthening the role of SMEs and ventures in the economy and their ability to enter global markets; creating growth engines for new markets and industries; and strengthening innovation capacity of science technology and ICT (MOSF 2013).

Since September 2014, South Korea has established 17 Centres for Creative Economic Innovation (CCEI) to support the Creative Economy and improve the regional ecosystem. CCEIs are cooperative partnerships between private and public sectors (StartupKorea 2015). Entrepreneurs and start-ups are matched with leading Korean companies who offer expertise, mentoring and resources with the aim of fostering a conducive environment to nurture entrepreneurs and start-up companies as well as boost innovation of SMEs (StartupKorea 2015). Currently, each CCEI has a specific focus which draws on region specific resources. The CCEIs have provided support for prototype production as well as sales and distribution. Within the first 12 months since its establishment, CCEI supported 437 start-ups with this number projected to grow to over 2,500 by 2017 (StartupKorea 2015). A demonstration day held in late 2015 provided CCEI start-ups and entrepreneurs with the opportunity to showcase their products, allowing investors to identify new investment opportunities but also demonstrating the success stories of the CCEIs (MSIP 2015).

The South Korean Government has a National Science and Technology Council which has several main functions including the coordination and establishment of major S&T promotion policies and plans and financial support for technology innovation. It is the key body for making decisions on cross-agency science, technology and innovation policies (OECD 2014b). In addition the country has a Presidential Advisory Council on Science and Technology that identifies key national scientific and technological policy issues and makes recommendations and suggestions of ways to address the issues on a long-term basis (PACST 2014).

Singapore

In 1967, Singapore established a Science Council to encourage and drive science and technology and to build appropriate human resources to support scientific research and development (A*STAR 2011). The government replaced the Science Council with the National Science and Technology Board in 1991, following enactment of the Technology

Board Act in 1990 (Singapore Government 2013). Through the National Science and Technology Board, Singapore established five-year plans. The country's first plan, known as the National Technology Plan, had a budget of S$2 billion to set up Singapore's science and technology direction. This five-year plan was followed in 1996 with the National Science and Technology Plan, 2001 and 2006 as the Science and Technology plan, before the five-year plan changed to the Research, Innovation and Enterprise (RIE) Plan for 2011–2015. Singapore is now in its sixth five-year plan, the Research, Innovation and Enterprise 2020 Plan, and is committing S$19 billion over the life of the plan to support the translation of research and to build innovation capacity (National Research Foundation 2016c). The RIE 2020 plan will focus on four key priorities reflecting Singapore's key areas of competitive advantage: Advanced Manufacturing and Engineering; Health and Biomedical Sciences; Services and Digital Economy; and Urban Solutions and Sustainability. The National Research Foundation, under the Prime Minister's Office, determines the national direction of research and development initiatives. Within the four key areas, activities will be supported by three cross-cutting programs to ensure a strong pipeline of talent, excellent science and value creation (National Research Foundation 2016c). These programs are Manpower (10 percent of the total funding), Academic Research (15 percent), and Innovation and Enterprise (17 percent).

In 2002, The National Science Technology Board was renamed the Agency for Science, Technology and Research (A*STAR). The public sector agency, bridges the gap between industry and academia to form meaningful and productive collaborations that drive research to advance and translate scientific discovery and innovation. A*STAR has three key areas of strategic importance: Human Capital; Intellectual Capital; and Industrial Capital. Through concentrating on these key areas, A*STAR aims to build Singapore into a world-class scientific research hub. In 2011, A*STAR celebrated its 20th anniversary since its establishment as the National Science Technology Board under the Ministry of Trade and Industry. A*STAR develops and nurtures research talent in 18 biomedical science, physical science and engineering research entities and agencies (A*STAR 2011).

In 2013, Singapore's Prime Minister noted the importance of attracting national and international talent to boost the innovation system, stating that in order: '*To make further progress, we will need good people, we will need good research programmes, and then we will be able to get good outcomes. The good people [part] is most critical because first you must have the talent. And to sustain a vibrant research community, it means we have to attract international talent, as well as to nurture local talent. We need to do both*' (National Research Foundation 2016b). In this regard, Singapore has several research and development talent programs to attract talented scientists to undertake research in the country.

The National Research Foundation (NRF), established as a department in the Prime Minister's Office in 2006, is responsible for the direction of Singapore's research and development. The NRF funds initiatives and develops policies, strategies and plans for research, development and innovation. The NRF offers a large number of programs to support research and innovation including: Strategic Research Programmes, NRF Fellowship and NRF Investigatorship, Competitive Research Programme, Campus for Research Excellence and Technological Enterprise (CREATE), Research Centres of Excellence, National Innovation Challenges, Corporate Laboratory@University Scheme and National Cybersecurity R&D Programme. The NRF Fellowship and NRF Investigatorship both aim to attract and retain top scientists to undertake independent research and to support ground breaking high-risk research. For the NRF Fellowship, successful early career researchers are offered a five-year tenure-track position within a faculty at specific universities or research institutes including the Agency for Science, Technology and Research (A*STAR), the National University of Singapore, and Research Centres of Excellence (RCE) amongst others. The NRF Investigatorship supports mid-career researchers to undertake high-risk research (National Research Foundation 2016a). The NRF Strategic Research Programs supports research in specific areas to create new industries and encourage growth. The Competitive Research Programme encourages multidisciplinary research in areas of societal importance. The RCE allow researchers to conduct world-class research in key areas of long term strategic importance to the country and aims to attract and retain top scientific researchers, create new knowledge and train researchers and enhance graduate education. The National Innovation Challenge encourages and supports multidisciplinary research to address key challenges. Research supported by the National Innovation Challenge may result in commercial spinoffs both nationally and internationally.

The NRF specifically encourages university collaboration through CREATE. CREATE houses a number of research centres from various international universities to support interdisciplinary research in human systems, energy systems, environmental systems and urban systems. CREATE provides international universities a second home to facilitate collaborations with other universities within CREATE as well as local Singapore universities (CREATE 2014). The NRF Corporate Laboratory@University Scheme is a scheme specifically aimed at industry collaboration with Universities. The Scheme, launched in 2013, supports the establishment of foreign and local industry laboratories in Singaporean universities to facilitate and encourage university-industry research and development collaborations. The scheme is aimed at supporting the translation of research and development in the laboratory to the marketplace. In addition to promoting industry experience for university students, the scheme allows industry to access new knowledge to develop innovative services and products. The first corporate laboratory supported under the scheme was the establishment of a Rolls Royce Laboratory at Nanyang Technological University, a joint S$75 million investment which resulted in the tripling of existing projects between the collaborators over five years.

Singapore strongly recognises the importance of innovation and in addition to programs that support and encourage research and development, the country has an innovation and enterprise framework through the NRF to support growth in innovation and entrepreneurship. The National Framework for Innovation and Enterprise (NFIE) has two goals: to commercialise innovative technologies developed in research and development laboratories through the establishment of start-up companies, and to encourage universities to transform their research and development into commercial products for the market (i.e. to pursue academic entrepreneurship) (National Research Foundation 2014). The NFIE has a number of schemes to support these goals, including an Early Stage Venture Fund (in which S$10 million is provided to match funding provided by venture capital funds for early stage high-tech companies); Proof-of-Concept Grants (up to S$250,000 for technology proof-of-concept projects for researchers); Technology Incubation Scheme (co-investment from NRF of up to 85 percent capped at S$500,000 for Singapore-based start-up companies with the scheme co-investing the remaining 15 percent and providing mentorship and guidance); Global Entrepreneur Executives (aimed at attracting Global Entrepreneurial Executives in specific fields to relocate to Singapore); and the Innovation Cluster Programme (aimed at strengthening partnerships between universities, companies, government and research institutes to raise productivity, bring ideas to market quickly, create jobs and drive growth) (National Research Foundation 2014). The country also has a program through the Ministry of Trade and Investment that supports businesses to seize growth opportunities, build business capabilities as well as supporting start-up companies at different stages of growth (SPRING Singapore 2014).

Conclusions

In this Chapter, we explored recent experiences (and experiments) in Australia and Asia with science and technology policy. We examined the rationale for the existence of returns to collaboration in the first place—and whether there exists any barriers to collaboration. We considered how university-industry collaboration occurs across different nations and the effect that it has on the diffusion of new technology into practice, the degree of collaboration between academic and industrial researchers, and the role of government programs across a range of Asian countries designed to stimulate university-industry collaboration. What is clear is that a vibrant innovation ecosystem is an important element of a healthy and prosperous nation.

It is worth reflecting on what these Asian and Australian experiences with S&T policy can tell us about public policy in the Asian century. Most importantly, it demonstrates how all nations at different stages of development can learn from each other as they undertake national experiments in S&T policy. As there is very little empirical evidence to help guide innovation policymakers—relative to other areas of public policy such as health, labour and education—there is an exciting opportunity to collaborate across national borders to understand how to develop innovation policy. After all, innovation is one policy domain where there are potentially huge 'spillovers' so countries have a strong incentive to work together to share in the combined benefits of new knowledge. For example, the UK's Innovation Growth Lab (IGL)—which provides funds to researchers using randomised controlled trials to evaluate the effects of specific government innovation and entrepreneurship programs—is a centrally-coordinated international program of innovation experiments which can generate important new evidence on the effectiveness of S&T policies, which can then be shared amongst interested parties and countries. This type of initiative will provide a richer, evidence-based, rationale for future science and technology policies around the world.

Notes

1. Adopting the OECD definition of Innovation allows Australia to be systematically compared to OECD countries. OECD (2005) Oslo manual: guidelines for collecting and interpreting innovation data, 3rd edition, OECD and European Commission.
2. 'Intramural expenditure' is spending on R&D performed within Australian Government departments and agencies (Australian Government 2015d) "Science, Research and Innovation Budget Tables." Retrieved November, 2015, from http://www.industry.gov.au/innovation/reportsandstudies/Pages/SRIBudget.aspx.
3. 'Extramural expenditure' is spending on R&D performed outside the Australian Government (e.g. in universities, businesses or medical research institutes) (Ibid).

References

Abhyankar, R. (2014). The government of India's role in promoting innovation through policy initiatives for entrepreneurship development. *Technology Innovation Management Review, 4*(8), 11–17.

Adams, J. (2012). Collaborations: The rise of research networks. *Nature, 490*(7420), 335–336.

Adams, J., Black, G., Clemmons, J., & Stephan, P. (2005). Scientific teams and institutional collaborations: Evidence from U.S. universities, 1981–1999. *Research Policy, 34*(3), 259–285.

Arrow, K. (1962). Economic welfare and the allocation of resources for invention. In *The rate and direction of inventive activity: Economic and social factors*. Princeton, NJ: Princeton University.

A*STAR. (2011). *A*STAR: 20 years of science and technology in Singapore*. Singapore: A*STAR.

Australian Government. (2011). *Evaluation of the international linkages program: Executive summary and recommendations*. Canberra: Department of Innovation, Industry, Science and Research. Retrieved from https://industry.gov.au/science/internationalcollaboration/Documents/ISL_Evaluation_Executive_Summary_and_Recommendations.pdf.

Australian Government. (2014). *Australian innovation systems report.* Canberra: Department of Industry; Office of the Chief Economist. Retrieved from https://industry.gov.au/Office-of-the-Chief-Economist/Publications/Documents/Australian-Innovation-System/Australian-Innovation-System-Report-2014.pdf.

Australian Government. (2015a). *ARC funding opportunities.* Retrieved from http://www.arc.gov.au/linkage-programme.

Australian Government. (2015b). *Australia-India Strategic Research Fund (AISRF).* Retrieved from http://science.gov.au/international/CollaborativeOpportunities/AISRF/Pages/default.aspx.

Australian Government. (2015c). *Collaborative opportunities.* Retrieved from http://science.gov.au/international/CollaborativeOpportunities/Pages/default.aspx.

Australian Government. (2015d). *Science, research and innovation budget tables.* Retrieved from http://www.industry.gov.au/innovation/reportsandstudies/Pages/SRIBudget.aspx.

Australian Government. (2015e). *National innovation & science agenda.* Retrieved from https://www.innovation.gov.au/system/files/case-study/National%20Innovation%20and%20Science%20Agenda%20-%20Report.pdf.

Bell, J., Dodgson, M., Field, L., Gough, P., & Spurling, T. (2015). *Translating research for economic and social benefit: Country comparisons.* Report for the Australian Council of Learned Academies.

Bravo-Biosca, A. (2015). *Making innovation and growth policy more experimental: The first year of IGL.* Retrieved from http://www.innovationgrowthlab.org/blog/making-innovation-and-growth-policy-more-experimental-first-year-igl.

Bruneel, J., D'Este, P., & Salter, A. (2010). Investigating the factors that diminish the barriers to university-industry collaboration. *Research Policy, 39*(7), 858–868.

Chung, S. (2011). Innovation, competitiveness, and growth: Korean experiences. In B. P. Justin & Y. Lin (Eds.), *Annual World Bank Conference on Development Economics 2010, Global: Lessons from East Asia and the Global Financial Crisis.* Washington, DC: World Bank.

CREATE. (2014). *About CREATE.* Retrieved from http://www.create.edu.sg/about-create.

Davidson, S., & Potts, J. (2016). A new institutional approach to innovation policy. *Australian Economic Review, 49*(2), 200–207.

Dodgson, M., Hughes, A., Foster, J., & Metcalfe, S. (2011). Systems thinking, market failure, and the development of innovation policy: The case of Australia. *Research Policy, 40*(9), 1145–1146.

The Economist. (2015). *Still made in China: Chinese manufacturing remains second to none.* Retrieved from http://www.economist.com/news/

special-report/21663332-chinese-manufacturing-remains-second-none-still-made-china.

Embassy of India. (2013). *STI policy 2013 of India*. Retrieved from http://www.indianembassy.ru/index.php/science-technology/s-t-policy-of-india.

European Commission. (2013). *India*. Retrieved from https://ec.europa.eu/research/iscp/pdf/policy/india_comm.pdf.

Ferris, B., Finkel, A., & Fraser, J. (2016). *Review of the R&D tax incentive*. Canberra: Australian Government.

Gao, Y. (2015). *Measures that facilitate transfer of knowledge from publicly funded research organisations to industry in China*. Report for securing Australia's future project "Translating research for economic and social benefit: Country comparisons" on behalf of the Australian Council of Learned Academies.

Government of India. (2013). *Science, technology and innovation policy*. New Dehli: Ministry of Science and Technology.

Government of Japan. (2015a). Report on the 5th Science and Technology Basic Plan. Japan, Council for Science, Technology and Innovation. Cabinet Office, Government of Japan.

Government of Japan. (2015b). Brochure about the Council for Science, Technology and Innovation 2015. Cabinet Office, Government of Japan.

Hanna, N. (1999). *The East Asian miracle and information technology: Strategic management of technological learning*. Washington, DC: World Bank Publications.

Heitor, M. (2015). How university global partnerships may facilitate a new era of international affairs and foster political and economic relations. *Technological Forecasting and Social Change, 95*, 276–293.

Innovation Growth Lab. (2015). *Innovation growth lab*. Retrieved from http://www.innovationgrowthlab.org/innovation-growth-lab.

Jones, B. F. (2008). The burden of knowledge and the death of the renaissance man: Is innovation getting harder? *The Review of Economic Studies 76*(1), 283–317.

Jones, B. F., Wuchty, S., & Uzzi, B. (2008). Multi-university research teams: Shifting impact, geography, and stratification in science. *Science, 322*(5905), 1259–1262.

KAIST. (2014a). *About KAIST*. Retrieved from http://www.kaist.edu/html/en/kaist/kaist_010201.html.

KAIST. (2014b). *History*. Retrieved from http://www.kaist.edu/_prog/history/?site_dvs_cd=en&menu_dvs_cd=010202&site_dvs_cd=en&menu_dvs_cd=010202.

KIST. (2016). *History timeline*. Retrieved from http://eng.kist.re.kr/kist_eng/?sub_num=628.

Lane, J. I. (2009). Assessing the impact of science funding. *Science, 324*(5932), 1273–1275.

Lane, J. I. (2010). Let's make science metrics more scientific. *Nature, 464*(7288), 488–489.

Lee, S., & Bozeman, B. (2005). The impact of research collaboration on scientific productivity. *Social Studies of Science, 35*(5), 673–702.

McKenzie, C., Ito, T., Iwata, K., & Urata, S. (2015). Innovation in East Asia: Editors' overview. *Asian Economic Policy Review, 10*(1), 1–18.

MOST. (2013). *Creative economy action plan and measures to establish a creative economy.* Retrieved 2016.

Ministry of Science, ICT and Future Planning. (2015). *CCEI demo day.* Retrived from http://english.msip.go.kr/english/msipContents/contentsView.do?cateId=msse44&artId=1277769.

National People's Congress of the People's Republic of China. (1996). *Law of the people's Republic of China on promoting the transformation of scientific and technological achievements.* Geneva: World Intellectual Property Organization.

National People's Congress of the People's Republic of China. (2008). *Law of the people's Republic of China on progress of science and technology.* Geneva: World Intellectual Property Organization.

National Research Foundation. (2014). *National framework for research, innovation and enterprise.* Retrieved from http://www.nrf.gov.sg/innovation-enterprise/national-framework-for-research-innovation-and-enterprise.

National Research Foundation. (2016a). *NRF fellowship and NRF investigatorship.* Retrieved from http://www.nrf.gov.sg/about-nrf/programmes/nrf-fellowship-and-nrf-investigatorship.

National Research Foundation. (2016b). *R&D talent development programmes.* Retrieved from http://www.nrf.gov.sg/research/r-d-talent.

National Research Foundation. (2016c). Research innovation enterpise 2020 plan: Winning the future through science and technology. Research Innovation and Enterprise Secretariat. Singapore, National Research Foundation, Prime Minister's Office, Singapore Government.

National Science and Technology Council (U.S.). (2008). The science of science policy: A federal research roadmap. Report on the science of science policy to the Subcommittee on Social, Behavioral, and Economic Sciences, Committee on Science, National Science and Technology Council, Office of Science and Technology Policy. Washington, DC: Executive Office of the President, National Science and Technology Council.

OECD. (2014a). *Industry and technology policies in Korea.* Paris: OECD Publishing.

OECD. (2014b). *OECD science, technology and industry outlook 2014.* Paris: OECD Publishing.

OECD. (2015). *OECD science, technology and industry scoreboard 2015: Innovation for growth and society.* Paris: OECD Publishing.

PACST. (2014). *Presidential advisory council on science and Technology: Role and function*. Retrieved from http://english.pacst.go.kr/intro/en_estaBgRoles.do.

Park, G. H. (2013). *Opening a new era of hope. 18th Presidential Inauguraton Speech*. The Republic of Korea: Office of the President.

SBIR. (2015). *About SBIR*. Retrieved from https://www.sbir.gov/about/about-sbir.

Singapore Government. (2013). *National Science and Technology Board is formed*. Retrieved March, 2016, from http://eresources.nlb.gov.sg/history/events/9addb3d8-62eb-420a-a10a-3727f790259c.

Smith, B. (2011). Funding cuts to leave scientists out of the loop. *The Sydney Morning Herald*.

SPRING Singapore. (2014). *SPRING Singapore: Enabling enterprise*. Retrieved March, 2016, from http://www.nrf.gov.sg/innovation-enterprise/national-framework-for-research-innovation-and-enterprise.

StartupKorea. (2015). *What is Center for Creative Economic Innovation? (CCEI)*. Retrieved April, 2016, from https://www.startupkorea.com/page/en/about/about.jsp.

The State Council. (2015). *State councilor stresses importance of innovation for growth*. Retrieved January, 2016, from http://english.gov.cn/state_council/state_councilors/2015/11/20/content_281475238517660.htm.

Suzuki, S. (2004). Technopolis: Science parks in Japan. *International Journal of Technology Management, 28*(3–6), 582–601.

Tsukada, N., & Nagaoka, S. (2015). Determinants of international research collaboration: Evidence from international co-inventions in Asia and major OECD countries. *Asian Economic Policy Review, 10*(1), 96–119.

Turpin, T., Woolley, R., Marceau, J., & Hill, S. (2008). Conduits of knowledge in the Asia Pacific. *Asian Population Studies, 4*(3), 247–265.

UNESCO (2015). *UNESCO science report: Towards 2030*. Paris: UNESCO.

Withers, G., Denniss, A., & Yuan, M. (2009). Innovation financing and use of income contingent loans. *Australian Journal of Labour Economics, 12*(2), 145–165.

Wuchty, S., Jones, B. F., & Uzzi, B. (2007). The increasing dominance of teams in production of knowledge. *Science, 316*(5827), 1036–1039.

Yingqi, C. (2015). *R&D fund bolstered by private sector's input*. Retrieved from http://english.gov.cn/news/top_news/2015/10/28/content_281475221832122.htm.

Zhang, K. (2014). Overview of Chinese research & innovation programmes. *5th INCO Conference*. Athens.

Zuckerman, H., & Merton, R. (1973). Age, aging, and age structure in science. In R. Merton (Ed.), *The sociology of science: Theoretical and empirical investigations*. Chicago: University of Chicago.

CHAPTER 7

Humanising Bureaucracy: Clan-Oriented Culture in the Thai Civil Service

Marianna Fotaki and Rutaichanok Jingjit

Introduction

In 2002, Thailand's government implemented a drastic change program known as the Strategic Plan for Thai Public Sector Development. While its proclaimed objectives comprised several aspects, the central aim of the change program was to create a new form of management through

We would like to thank two anonymous referees and the participants of the Public Policy in the Asian Century Research Workshop (held on 5–6 May 2016 at the Melbourne School of Government, The University of Melbourne) for their very useful comments. Our gratitude goes to Dr. Sara Bice for her patience and guidance throughout the process and to Dr. Avery Poole for her diligent editing. The authors bear all responsibility for any remaining errors.

M. Fotaki (✉)
Warwick Business School, The University of Warwick, Coventry, England, UK
e-mail: Marianna.Fotaki@wbs.ac.uk

R. Jingjit
Department of Trade Negotiations, Ministry of Commerce, Bangkok, Thailand
e-mail: rutai31@gmail.com

S. Bice et al. (eds.), *Public Policy in the 'Asian Century'*, International Series on Public Policy, https://doi.org/10.1057/978-1-137-60252-7_7

the adoption of a result-based approach and a focus on performance (Painter 2004, 2006; Jingjit 2008).

The cumbersome structures and inefficient functioning of the Thai civil service became an increasingly critical issue. The international institutions, which became highly influential after providing financial aid to the country during the economic crisis, began to emphasise the importance of good governance in the late 1990s. As a result, various administrative reforms focusing on issues of compensation, the size of the public workforce, performance, management practices, reengineering of government agencies and personnel policies were already been implemented during this period. But the schemes were introduced in a piecemeal manner via pilot projects and did not appear to produce major changes to the civil service system. The Thaksin Shinawatra government's comprehensive reforms plan, phased in during his tenure as Prime Minister (2002–2005), drew its inspiration from the attempts aimed at transforming the public sector in the UK and other Anglo-Saxon countries (e.g. New Zealand). Although the reform of the civil service in Thailand appeared to be driven by multiple objectives, its core strategies "bore the unmistakeable stamp of New Public Management" (NPM) and were governed by the principle of 'managerialism' (Painter 2004). Comprising a set of doctrines with 'specific ideas about what should be done in administration' (Hood and Jackson 1991, p. 12), NPM (a term coined by a British scholar, Christopher Hood 1991) has been a worldwide phenomenon and a model for public sector reform since the mid-1980s (Hood 1996). With a strong focus on efficiency, client orientation, performance indicators and human resource management techniques, such reform stood in contrast with the values of bureaucracy. As an owner of a remarkably successful business empire, Thaksin condemned the country's bureaucratic systems as being outdated and instead favoured an entrepreneurial management style. The change program was expected to generate a new form of management through the adoption of a 'results-based' approach intended to decrease delays in the execution of various tasks, thus introducing greater flexibility in the system. Further, the focus on performance management (Painter 2006), was relied upon as a means of transforming the traditional bureaucratic culture.

Max Weber famously depicted the concept of ideal bureaucracy as integral moral institutions based on impartiality and fairness, embracing the ideas of impersonal, procedural, hierarchical and technical organisation. While Weber thought of such models, known also as 'classic bureaucracy', as the most efficient way of organising at the time, in the modern context, classic bureaucracy has been increasingly associated with inflexibility and inefficiency (Dingwall and Strangleman 2005; Duncombe et al. 1997; Hoggett 2006). Alternatives to bureaucracy have been proposed by liberalists (Bartlett and Ghoshal 1997; Kanter 1990; Senge 1990) as well as from various critical management perspectives (Du Gay 2000, 2005; Clegg et al. 2005; Maravelias 2007), and by feminist scholars (Ashcraft 2001). Researchers have opposed the idea that organisations should be governed via strict, impersonal rules and led by a centralised authority as they advocated less hierarchical and more flexible forms of organising (Peters 1989; Morgan 1991; Quinn 1992; Kanter et al. 1992). Such shifts would be better facilitated by embracing various forms of flexible post-bureaucratic management, evidenced in all modes of organising, including public administration (PA) (Boyne 2003; Greener and Powell 2008; Hood et al. 2001; Pollitt and Bouckaert 2000), with significant changes in organisational culture, such as empowerment of employees (Osborne and Plastrik 1997; Child and McGrath 2001) and the decentralisation of authority (Child and McGrath 2001; Josserand 2004). Overall, the expectation for the post-bureaucratic organisation was to promote a shift to more innovative and flexible organisations: with cohesion obtained through cross-cutting networks of various kinds with the management acting as catalyst for such change (Hedlund 1994; Josserand 2004; Josserand et al. 2006).

However, the rationale and ideology underlying many of the NPM reforms has been questioned by defenders of the bureaucratic ethos (Du Gay 1996, 2000; Ten Bos 1997) and by PA scholars (Hood 1991; Pollitt and Bouckaert 2000). Hood (1991), for example, opposes the logic of "public management for all seasons" addressing the issues of organisational inefficiency regardless of the context, while Pollitt and Bouckaert (2000) question such a 'one size fits all' approach as problematic because of the varying impacts of such reforms across national cultures. Moreover, Newman (2005) suggests that a "pure" form of bureaucracy strictly corresponding to the Weberian "ideal type" is rarely found, given that organisations tend to conflate bureaucratic attributes with other virtues and principles, rendering the whole idea of post-bureaucracy relatively unimportant. Josserand et al. (2006) suggest, that post-bureaucracy presents a new ideal-type as well as portraying an abstract representation of the desired changes.

Yet, there appears to be a consensus among scholars about the need to propose alternatives to classic bureaucracy with an aim of ensuring organisational survival. They tend to agree on the advantages of post-bureaucratic models of organising for achieving and sustaining corporate competitiveness (Ashcraft 2001; Dunleavy et al. 2006; Budd 2007) and about the importance of giving employees high degrees of 'responsible autonomy' to enable them to cope with a more volatile workplace (e.g. Adler 2001; Applebaum et al. 2000). Some critics of bureaucracy argue that it must be replaced with novel organisational forms (e.g. Cheney 1995; Deetz 1992) while others point to the potential of hybrids (e.g. Ashcraft 2006; Harris 2006; Salaman 2005). However, despite the focus on developing a more effective, novel form of organisation, there is a dearth of empirical studies on the hybrids that already exist in different contexts. The exploration of this issue in an international context might yield fruitful results because bureaucracy tends to accommodate itself to the exigencies and underlying values of the wider society in which it is situated (Clegg 1994). As Clegg (1994, p. 150) elucidates: 'Even when one is dealing with economic rationality and organisations constructed in support of rationality, there is no escape from values' (Clegg 1994, p. 150).

This chapter seeks to contribute to these discussions about hybrid organisational forms, as part of a wider debate about the merits and demerits of bureaucratic and post-bureaucratic organisations. We do so by examining a distinct manifestation of bureaucratic forms outside a Western setting, and addressing the effects of introducing NPM-type reforms in several public organisations in an East Asian context. We focus here on Thailand's reforms that had as their explicit aim an intention to modernise public services introduced after 2002, and focus specifically on the reasons for their limited outcomes in the settings studied. Given the heated debate regarding the values and problems associated with bureaucracy, and its recent widespread dismissal in favour of the market-based forms of organising that NPM propagates, this chapter addresses the following questions: What are the attributes of the organisational culture in public organisations in non-Western environments? And how far do they diverge from the ideas associated with classic bureaucracy? To what extent (if at all) have these attributes been altered by the NPM-type of reform carried out in the Thai civil service specifically? Which (if any) aspects of national culture exerted a significant influence upon the intended new mode of organising, thereby facilitating and/or impeding the intended changes?

The value of this chapter lies first, in its contribution to a greater understanding of the hybrid forms of bureaucratic organisations and their significance in explaining the limited outcomes of market-driven reform, especially via NPM. Second, the chapter highlights the cause of such failure, which as we argue, is entrenched in the deep-seated roots of clan-oriented culture that dominates the Thai civil service. Clan is an anthropological term denoting an attachment to the real or perceived ties of kinship and/or descent present within a group of people. For such group formation 'it does not matter whether an objective blood relationship exists' (Weber 1978, p. 389). While reducing the differences between individual and organisational goals and creating a strong feeling of community, clans, according to Ouchi (1980), tolerate high levels of ambiguity in performance evaluation that cannot withstand the scrutiny of contractual relations. As we have argued elsewhere (Jingjit and Fotaki 2010), clan-based culture can also lead to favouritism, nepotism and patronage. Despite the negative attributes of the clan present in the Thai civil service, this characteristic also tends to humanise bureaucratic structures through its emphasis on collegiality and informal structures, coexisting with the officialdom and the perseverance of seniority. The conclusions that emerge from our study reveal the realities of bureaucratic organisations in the Thai public sector. The study shows, specifically, how far the notion of an impersonal, inflexible and rule-bound institution characterised the settings studied. It provides clarity about the extent to which cultural values in various public organisations have (or have not) been altered through the implementation of the market-driven type of reform of NPM developed in Anglo-Saxon countries.

We commence with a review of the relevant literature on bureaucracy and NPM, followed by a summary of the research methodology. The next section reports on the findings obtained from research conducted in six public organisations in the Thai civil service at the central government level. This is followed by a discussion of the reasons for distinct manifestations of hybrid bureaucratic models in an East Asian setting that result from the translation of universal bureaucratic values into different contexts. Finally, the chapter stresses the influence of local cultural and religious values to suggest potential explanations for the persistence of idiosyncratic bureaucratic hybrids and limited cultural change under NPM reforms.

Origins and Rationales of Public Bureaucracy

The model of ideal bureaucracy advocated by Max Weber was a fundamental structure that greatly valued impartiality and fairness, allowing an organisation to be considered as a form of moral institution. His approach to organising comprised various key characteristics including rules, specialisation, meritocracy, hierarchy, separate ownership and accountability (see Weber 1947). Building on Weber's proposition, Du Gay (1996, p. 125) also stresses the importance of the bureaucratic ethos as a crucial moral and political resource in liberal democratic regimes. In a similar vein, Ten Bos (1997, p. 1012) argues that bureaucratic structures protect people both inside and outside organisations but that the moral predicament of organisational members does not reside in the rules per se, but how individuals relate to these.

Critiques of Bureaucracy

As organisations began to face new challenges, the viability and rationale for retaining the traditional bureaucratic model of organising, in both the public and private sectors, was increasingly questioned. Such challenges emerged from an increasingly unstable external environment owing to significant political and economic changes, as well as technological advancement (Hood 1991; Lovell 1995; Osborne and Gaebler 1992). Various scholars discuss potential strategic approaches to shifting away from bureaucracy towards more favourable alternatives. Such critiques of bureaucracy can be divided into two major camps: the counter-bureaucratic (Heckscher 1994; Le Grand 2007a, b) and the hybrid schools (see also Ashcraft 2001, 2006; Salaman 2005; Harris 2006; Josserand et al. 2006).

Counter-Bureaucratic Arguments

Counter-bureaucratic arguments are largely underpinned by the contention that power is intrinsically vested in a limited group of influential members within a bureaucratic organisational setting. Many scholars who promote the concept of empowerment, present in participatory (Mansbridge 1973; Rothschild and Russell 1986) and other more democratic (Cheney 1995; Deetz 1992) modes of organising, reject this view. Their work can be traced back to the work of Burns and Stalker

(1994) who argued in favour of replacing the bureaucracy model with an "organic" type of alternative emphasising cooperation and teamwork. They proposed various novel configurations (Davidow and Malone 1992; Heydebrand 1989), involving partnership and network-based organisational forms (e.g. Snow et al. 1993; Lowndes and Skelcher 2002). Heckscher (1994), who coined the term "post-bureaucracy" to differentiate it from conventional bureaucracy, advocated an "interactive" model in which the stringent exercise of power was replaced by a focus on two-way dialogues. Trust and independence are the basis of the interactive model: it is also underpinned by the principle of corporate success to be achieved through collaboration. Within the public sector specifically, it has been argued that government organisations could replace the command-and-control system with a market-based management model focusing on competition and greater use of contracts (e.g. Harrison 1993; Le Grand 2007a, b; Light 1997; Saltman and Von Otter 1992).

Hybrid Forms of Organisation

The hybrid school, on the other hand, is essentially centred on the critique of the inflexibility that characterises traditional rigid bureaucracies (Courpasson and Clegg 2006; Jingjit and Fotaki 2010; Christensen and Laegrid 2011; Denis et al. 2015). Inflexibility is ill-suited to the modern context as it undermines an organisation's performance and jeopardises its ultimate survival. Unlike those in the previous group, the proponents of bureaucratic hybrids do not entirely rebuff bureaucratic values but argue for forms of management that strategically combine "traditions" with "adaptations" (see Christensen and Laegrid 2011 for a review). The concept of a hybrid originates in the recognition that although bureaucracy has been significantly challenged, leading to widespread attempts to substitute the traditional form with alternative configurations, it has not been entirely discarded (see e.g. Heckscher and Donnellon 1994; Du Gay 2005). Therefore, while certain bureaucratic elements are abandoned or inhibited, others are still largely maintained in modern corporations—a phenomenon epitomised by numerous post-bureaucratic organisations (e.g. Ashcraft 2006; Harris 2006; Salaman 2005). This is partly because of various intrinsic difficulties involved in the transformation of large, complex bureaucratic organisations, such as inventing a different corporate identity and altering entrenched organisational philosophy (Josserand et al. 2006). Moreover, the evidence suggests that extensive post-bureaucratic pressures meet with severe resistance and skepticism from organisational members (Harris and Wegg-Prosser 2007). Thus, according to various scholars, hybrids are likely to be the consequence of shifting the emphasis in favour of post-bureaucratic forms as well as the potential answer to overcoming the limitations of classic bureaucracy (Maravelias 2007; Robinson 2015). However, viewed from a critical distance, the post-bureaucratic model is a curious mix of characteristics that seem to be incompatible (Grey and Garsten 2001). This is because a post-bureaucratic model requires a strong corporate culture that commits and unites employees all-the-while assuming that the post-bureaucratic organisations will be simultaneously open, flexible and constantly in flux. As Maravelias argues, the risk of post-bureaucracy is its tendency to make freedom a privilege of those with potential and of pushing others into vicious circles of opportunism.

Moreover, empirical research provides evidence concerning a range of novel activities that tend to involve "the invocation of alternative sources of authority and legitimacy" (Casey 2004, p. 61), emerging in the context of organisations that remain somewhat bureaucratic in a changing environment. A similar proposition was articulated by Ouchi, whose "ideal" type Z organisation is a hybrid that includes a rigid, individualistic type A and a participatory, consensual type B (Ouchi 1981; Ouchi and Jaeger 1978). Another perspective of the hybrid considers it as a dynamic process rather than a static organisational form characterised by new attributes that deviate from bureaucratic rigidity. This might include traits such as decentralisation and a flatter structure (Putnam 1983). Hybrid processes can thus be viewed as able to unite competing ideologies (Bahrami 1992; Gottfried and Weiss 1994) and to arbitrate the organisational paradoxes and tensions that exist, for instance, between the usual need to secure control and stability and the attempt to enhance flexibility and encourage innovation (Bushe and Shani 1991). Latent positive effects of hybrid organisational forms are usually depicted in relation to the corporate motive of securing and maintaining competitiveness. Berg (2006), for instance, highlights how such organisational forms combine both the values of the traditional procedural bureaucracy and other newly introduced concepts, such as customer focus, participation and professional pride. Koppel (1999) portrays various hybrid government institutions as bearing a significant resemblance to private corporations that are less rule-bound and more flexible, enabling them to effectively pursue organisational goals at lower costs than traditional agencies.

In contrast to this common viewpoint, Ashcraft (2001) argues for feminist bureaucracy as a distinct style of management—introducing the idea of the so-called "organised dissonance"—that fundamentally differs from the general assumption of a hybrid in that it does not necessarily require the resolution of competing organisational forms. On the contrary, we suggest, contradiction is largely accepted and even actively employed in this type of dissonant organisation. For instance, we have demonstrated in a related article that a combination of hierarchical and clan-based cultures was largely unadulterated in the Thai public service despite the introduction of Western NPM reforms aiming to introduce business-like management into PA (Jingjit and Fotaki 2010). This, we argued, was a result of religious values (both, Confucian and Buddhist), imbuing an organisational culture in the Thai bureaucracy prior to the reforms. This is in line with the literature suggesting that any significant organisational change is risky unless accompanied by a genuine transformation in the underlying value system (Schwartz 1992). As Schwartz (1992) points out, there is a common agreement among theorists across disciplines that a study of culture needs to concentrate primarily on values. One reason for this is that it has been suggested that values represent the core of culture (Deal and Kennedy 1982, 1983).

The Research Context and Analytic Framework

This chapter focuses on the Thai civil service during the period following a stringent public management reform considered to be one of the most remarkable efforts to transform the public sector in Thai history. The reforms were implemented over five years (2002–2007). The crucial aspect of the reform was the adoption of private management practices in pursuit of efficiency that reflected elements of NPM philosophy (Jingjit 2008). Originating in the belief that cultural change is a highly complex process, the current research set out to examine the deep-seated organisational culture of public organisations in the specific context of the Thai civil service and how this was modified following the introduction of the public management reform. Specifically, we examine the extent and pattern of cultural change following the introduction of the public management reform in Thailand through the viewpoints of civil servants themselves.

The main research framework guiding the data collection was adapted from the Competing Values Framework (CVF) originally developed by Quinn and Rohrbaugh (1981). The model is composed of two core

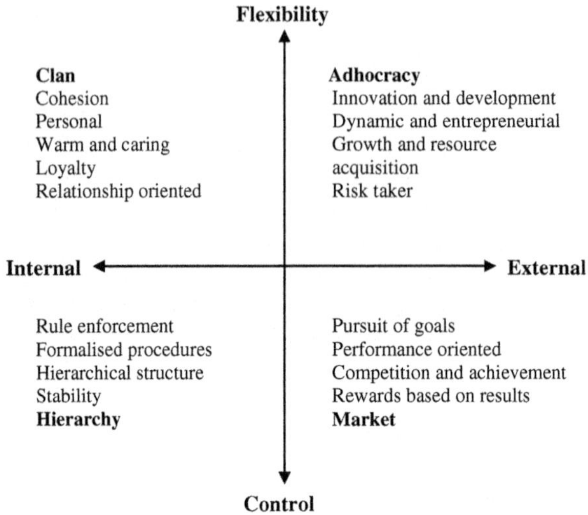

Fig. 7.1 The competing values framework (adopted from Zammuto and Krakower 1991)

dimensions—an internal versus external orientation and a control versus flexibility orientation. An internal focus refers to an emphasis on integration, information management and communication, whereas growth, resource acquisition and interaction with the external environment are critical in organisations with an external focus. Along the second dimension, a focus on control means that stability and cohesion are crucial, while adaptability and spontaneity are highly valued in an organisation that concentrates on flexibility. From these two dimensions, four models can be identified—internal process model, rational goal model, human relations model, and an open system model. Authors such as Zammuto and Krakower (1991) and Cameron and Quinn (1999), who later adopted their framework to examine organisational culture, referred to the four models as four cultural categories. These categories are illustrated in Fig. 7.1. This framework corresponds to the features of the pre-existing bureaucratic organisations as well as the intended pro-market changes that this chapter examines. At the same time, the framework combines features of traditional non-Western bureaucracy as represented in the Thai civil service. Thus, according to Zammuto and Krakower (1991), hierarchy is a combination of internal orientation with a focus on control. Market model culture, alternatively, is a mixture of control and external focus, and is dominated by the organisational aim of enhancing productivity and a competitive clan culture. A clan model with an internal focus and flexibility is characterised by high trust, teamwork, employee involvement, empowerment and corporate commitment to employees. Adhocracy, meanwhile, has flexibility but is externally focused, offering a form of organisation based primarily on the idea that innovation and adaptation are the keys to corporate success.

Research Design: Data Collection and Analysis

The study was conducted between 2006 and 2008 and supplemented with additional data following the aftermath of a major public sector reform launched in Thailand in 2002. We used a mixed method to collect the data and the results were triangulated. The triangulation of quantitative data was obtained from two sources: twenty-one face-to-face interviews and an open-ended section in the questionnaire. The main rationale for conducting a survey was that the data would provide more representative results than the use of in-depth interviews alone. The use of a self-completed questionnaire also helped to avoid the socially acceptable responses that are often given in face to face interactions. The material elicited through the survey was employed as a critical counterpoint to the interview data and as a means of acquiring qualitative data (in the open-ended section). Overall, the findings acquired through the combination of a mix of qualitative and quantitative methods appear to effectively validate, complement and extend one another. For reasons of space we are not reporting on the results of the survey in this article. We solely focus on the findings explored through qualitative interviews and open ended sections of the questionnaires.

Face-to-face, in-depth and semi-structured interviews were conducted with twenty-one informants representing diverse Thai public services, with roles ranging from the middle to top management levels. This method of interviewing was beneficial for exploring in depth the issues identified through the quantitative survey due to the 'open discovery' nature of this technique. The semi-structured format allowed us to alter slightly the issues raised and the matters explored from one interview to the next whenever new elements were revealed (Collis and Hussey 2003). This was advantageous for our study (Maykut and Morehouse 1994). The interview questions were based on seven key

Table 7.1 Core interview and questionnaire items

Seven key elements
1. Dominant organisational characteristics
2. Leadership style
3. Personnel management
4. Organisational cohesion
5. Strategic emphasis
6. Success criteria
7. Organisational rewards

aspects, designed to provide a thorough depiction of the culture in the Thai civil service (see Table 7.1).

Representatives from six government departments[1] from different ministries participated in the initial interviews. This evidence, along with the survey results from six comparative cases, helped us to examine how contextual and institutional factors influenced the implementation of the NPM-type reforms in Thailand. We included departments of different sizes and with varying functions of public services (see Table 7.2). The core structure comprising the open-ended questionnaire was drawn from key issues investigated in the survey, in which 1,362 civil servants took part. The questionnaire includes a section for detailed answers to seven open-ended questions, which correspond to the interview schedule (see Table 7.1).

The interviews in each organisation were conducted with public employees from different functional divisions. A stratified sampling was employed to select participants for the survey to ensure that the sample contained civil servants from all levels of the organisational hierarchy in the same proportions as in the full population. The informants participating in the face-to-face interviews were chosen from and/or suggested by their respective organisations on the basis of their knowledge and expertise, comprising 12 male and 9 female civil servants whose seniority levels varied from grade six to nine and age ranged from 35 to 56. All individuals' names have been omitted and the names of the organisations were replaced by the letters A-F to ensure anonymity (provided in brackets after the quotations). All interviews were tape recorded and transcribed in full. Both the interviews and the survey were carried out in the Thai language and were then translated into English.

Table 7.2 Research sites for the initial interviews and the survey (2006–2008)

Departments	*Functions*	*Ministries*
1. Office of the civil service commission (OCSC)	Policy	Prime Minister's office
2. Revenue department (RD)	Transfers (revenue and benefits)	Ministry of finance
3. Royal irrigation department (RID)	Physical construction and services	Ministry of agriculture and cooperatives
4. Department of industrial works (DIW)	Regulatory and services	Ministry of industry
5. Food and drug administration (FDA)	Licensing and regulatory	Ministry of public health
6. Department of highways (DOH)	Physical construction and services	Ministry of transport

We undertook thematic analysis of the data from the open-ended part of the questionnaires as well as the interview materials that were collected based on the aforementioned seven core aspects. These processes comprised the interpretation and categorisation of the raw data into themes (Kellehear 1993) structured according to the Competing Values Framework (CVF). All the statements and responses were judged on whether they were indicative of any of the features of the CVF and their alterations after the reform implementation. Additionally, attention was paid to identifying the dynamic relationships that could be found among the different categories and detecting emerging themes influencing the core component of the CVF model.

Hybrid Bureaucratic Forms: The Concurrence of Hierarchy and Clan Models

The research found that prior to the reform implementation in 2002, the culture of the organisations studied was concurrently dominated by hierarchy and clan models, corresponding with the lower and upper left hand sections of the graph (see Fig. 7.1). The bureaucratic hierarchical attributes were manifested in various aspects of organisational life. Civil servants strove to follow all formalised rules and procedures which governed organisational functions systematically and without fail. Although this approach usually resulted in substantial delays, the interviewees often justified and defended it as an appropriate mechanism for dealing with mistakes and preventing failures, because of an outstanding value placed on the constructed concept of security. This feature is illustrated by the following statement extracted from the open-ended section of the questionnaire:

> It was important to strictly follow formal rules in order to play safe, although it significantly slowed work down. (Q68 RD)

Thus, the presence of an extensive system of rules was due to a long-established tradition that usually resulted in the creation of additional regulation whenever a new fault was discovered to prevent it from recurring in the future. One of the interviewees elucidated this point as follows:

> In the past, formal detailed rules strictly governed what people did because when mistakes were found, new rules were established to prevent them from happening again in the future. This led to a build-up of rules without any removal of those that were outdated which explained why there was such a high number of regulations. As a result, work was slow and ineffective. (Interviewee 3 FDA)

This practice led to an accumulation of various rules over time, because there were few attempts to abolish policies that had become obsolete. As a result, one respondent (Interviewee 3, E) described that 'work was slow and ineffective'. Particularly in large organisations, such as the DOH (Department of Health), work was significantly slowed down due to multiple layers of red tape. However, civil servants tended to tolerate the situation and appeared to consider it an organisational norm, as revealed by one of the civil servants:

> Because this organisation is very large in comparison to other government departments and hierarchical and there were usually long procedures, work was slow but civil servants did accept this. (I1 DOH)

Furthermore, all the government departments studied were characterised by strong hierarchical features. This was due to their heavy reliance upon formalised internal organisational structures in which managerial and operational staff were relatively distant in terms of rank. The organisations' "obsession with control" (Mintzberg 1980) was also reflected in the emphasis placed upon the principle of clear allocation of work according to functional lines in order to ensure that individuals undertook their duties as officially assigned. At the same time, the success criteria were primarily defined by cost-effectiveness and budget control criteria.

However, the public organisations studied in the aftermath of introducing the NPM reforms in 2002 were not only traditionally bureaucratic and hierarchical, but were simultaneously dominated by clan-based values (see Table 7.2 summarising the principal attributes of the hybrid model of organising). Mutual generosity appeared to be a common feature in the workplace and relationships among organisational members were primarily based on cooperation, participation, shared understanding and respect for each other. The prevalence of such attributes was found to have significantly affected the pattern of bureaucratic culture. For instance, although prime importance was given to specific task allocation to individuals, civil servants often carried out additional work outside their job descriptions, motivated by the norm that it was crucial to assist one another:

> People in all levels in the organisation worked together to complete a common mission like the *long khak* tradition when members of the entire community work in cooperation to harvest rice. People tended to do more than just what was specifically required by their job descriptions because they often asked each other for help and they usually helped each other out. (Interviewee, 13 DOH)

Despite the dominance of formalised rules, a great deal of flexibility was often allowed within informal networks of civil servants. Interviewees revealed that relationships among organisational members were rather informal and underpinned by widespread kinship values. The communities found in the organisations studied could therefore be portrayed as large extended families whose members were linked by close personal ties and were highly familiar with one another. This idea was partly reflected by the way in which most civil servants addressed each other as brother or sister, even if this meant occasionally overriding the rules:

> Rules can be bent to help one another. We have sympathy towards each other. For example, people are allowed to go to see doctors during working hours without being formally reported as absent... We were like family members and our relationships were like those found in families. (Interviewee, I1 RD)

Furthermore, the distinct culture typified by an elevated concern for people's well-being could be seen both in the extensive forms of institutionalised welfare provision, which did not merely cover individual employees but also their parents, children, and spouses, and in the conventional norm of having a job for life. The security of employment in the civil service was perceived to be remarkably higher than in the private sector, especially for older employees who were more likely to lose their jobs in private firms, whereas within the civil service they could expect to benefit from the well-established pension scheme. Overall, the organisational culture was characterised by a significant degree of compromise associated with the notions of informality, familiarity, flexibility and various forms of intensive interpersonal communication, underpinned by a kinship mentality rather than a rigid exercise of power. This was because the ultimate aim was to acquire and maintain a pleasant working environment in which mutual generosity constituted an organisational norm:

> It was not only work but people's feelings were also considered. When we worked, we treated one another like family members rather than like bosses and subordinates, so there were a lot of compromises and flexibilities. In dealing with most situations, we discussed informally rather than just using formal authority. Our policy was that everyone should be happy and help each other. (Interviewee, I1 FDA)

In addition, the pervasiveness of the clan-type culture during the pre-reform era could be partially explained by the fact that a substantial number of civil servants shared similar educational backgrounds. For instance, a significant majority of public employees in the DOH and the RID (Royal Irrigation Department) in the past graduated from the same institutions. In the former, most personnel were trained in engineering and received their degrees from Chulalongkorn which is one of the country's most prestigious universities. As for the latter, the main group of officials were technicians who graduated with a degree in agriculture, and many had been educated in the colleges and schools that belonged to the department itself.[2] Therefore, most civil servants had already formed strong bonds when they were students and then continued in their professional life as civil servants. In other words, common attitudes and mindsets had already been formed among these public officials even before entering the civil service, which significantly facilitated the establishment of a clan culture in the organisations. As one interviewee indicated:

> In the past, 80-90% of civil servants shared a similar educational background; therefore, they usually had close personal relationships which were maintained when they started to work at the department. (I1 DOH)

The Perseverance of the Hybrid Bureaucratic Model Despite Modest Changes

At the time of conducting this study, the combination of hierarchy and clan cultural values remained largely prevalent in the organisations investigated, despite a five-year reform period since the program's initiation in 2002 and completion in 2005. Importantly, however, there was evidence of modest alterations. With regard to bureaucratic culture, a number of extensive (and probably quite a few obsolete) procedures still remained intact, given that highly complex and time-consuming legislative changes are required to bring about any major transformations in the civil service. Bureaucratic attributes, including rule conformity and clear separation of tasks, continue to be emphasised in the public organisations examined following the reforms. Further, virtually all departments studied remained considerably hierarchical with work being assigned along stringent command and control structures.

As with the hierarchical culture, clan-based values were still prevalent in the organisations examined in the aftermath of the reform. We were able to observe only a slight modification of clan-based values' inclusion in personnel development, knowledge and learning within the criteria for organisational success. The kinship feelings underscoring the norm of mutual generosity in the pre-reform period continued to be a major part of organisational life, in which the notions of teamwork, participation and a mutual exchange of ideas continued to be highly valued. Some respondents highlighted that these aspects of the organisational culture were closely related to the general Thai way of life. For instance, the caring aspect of leadership was viewed as being consistent with underlying societal norms characterised by informality and relaxed attitudes:

> Thai people are usually relaxed and informal. Bosses who are harsh to subordinates are seen as not having pity or sympathy; it's like bullying children. (Interviewee, I3 DIW)

The organisational culture was thus characterised by a significant degree of compromise associated with the notions of informality, familiarity, flexibility and intensive communication underpinned by a kinship mentality rather than a rigid exercise of power. This was because the ultimate organisational goal was to acquire and maintain a pleasant working environment in which mutual generosity constituted an organisational norm. This was further illustrated by a following response to the question 'What brought the civil servants in your organisation together?':

> It was not only work but people's feelings were also considered. We worked like a family rather than bosses and subordinates, so there was a lot of compromise and flexibility. We loved each other. We talked rather than exploiting authority. Our policy was that everyone should be happy and help each other. (I1 FDA)

The Persistent Influence of Local Culture

In addition to the dominating hierarchical and clan-based cultural values, there is another group of cultural attributes that interviewees referred to as commonplace in all six departments studied. These are seniority, patronage, a dependent relationship-based set of norms and nepotism.

Seniority System

Mutual relationships between individual civil servants are principally governed by the close observance of a seniority structure, which has a crucial impact upon the way in which the examined organisations operated. According to many respondents, this aspect of organisational culture has the effect of preventing civil servants from being results-focused. For instance, there exists a general view that public officials are often promoted on the basis of seniority rather than performance and 'there was not much consideration given to work results' (Questionnaire, 40 DIW). Furthermore, as one of the respondents explains:

> In the past, the basis for promotion was the seniority system and it was largely up to personal feelings or subjective judgements of the superiors. Other formal factors that were required to be taken into consideration for promoting employees were rather abstract, therefore the process was highly subjective. (Interviewee, I3 DOH)

Although some respondents observe that the value the organisations placed on seniority has slightly declined following the reform, the majority assert that the use of the seniority system is still the most and/or the only important criterion for assigning status and distributing rewards in the organisations. Several respondents highlight that the seniority system has positive effects as it is considered a glue binding people in organisations together. For instance, an answer to the question: 'What brought the civil servants in your organisation together?' was: 'The important factor was the seniority system which fostered unity among us' (Questionnaire, 34 RID).

This statement indicates the informant's belief in the seniority system as an integral part of the societal culture, and remains an important norm in the organisations studied. Accordingly, in respondents' views the concept of seniority appears to have contributed significantly to the prevalence of a clan culture as it represents the core mechanism providing the structure for interpersonal relationships. This also reflects the prevalent way people relate to each other in the Thai society more generally. For instance, the way public officials address one another as '*younger* brother/sister' or '*older* brother/sister' is common outside of the public services.

Patronage and the Dependent Relationship-Based Set of Norms

A large number of respondents indicated that their organisations are significantly influenced by elements of the patron-client system, and a strong presence of informal "cliques", partially encouraged by favouritism and nepotism. While the prevalence of these close, personal networks might be a facet underlying clan culture, several respondents see them as a source of widespread bias that occurred through the allocation of hierarchical rewards. For example, individuals believe that their opportunities to obtain promotions and salary increases are largely dependent upon the degree of closeness between the assessors and the assessed. Many informants emphasise that these relationships are often influenced by favouritism, which does not encourage the civil servants to be results-oriented, given the widespread view that a person will be promoted if he/she focuses on pleasing his/her superiors:

> Although in theory it was a merit system, it wasn't in practice. People who worked hard, the bosses didn't see it, whereas those who provided extra services to them got two-grade salary increases.[3] There were a lot of people like that who did certain favours for their bosses. Some bosses were very biased. (Interviewee, I3 RD)

The patron-client system and the presence of powerful cliques persisted in all the organisations studied, after the reforms. Moreover, the same norm continues to influence how the perceptions of employees are being managed, particularly regarding their career advancement. A large number of respondents reveal that promotion opportunities still do not depend on individuals' results or performance at work:

> The assessments for promotions are unclear, lack transparency and are unfair. Some people get a two-grade salary increase every year whereas others never get one even once in 10 years despite the fact that they both have the same responsibilities. A person's value depends on which group he or she belongs to. If the leader of that group is powerful, the person would get promoted. (Questionnaire, 76 DIW)

Nepotism is another strongly dependent relationship-based norm that remains prevalent during the post-reform era. Organisational leaders often display bias in prioritising their own relatives when delegating tasks. Many informants believe that nepotism has persisted in the Thai civil service because it has largely failed to attract new graduates due to relatively low salaries. Therefore, a number of people who were attracted to working in government departments were those whose parents or relatives were also civil servants. The major reason why many such people enter the civil service is their expectation of moving to highly favourable positions because of their family connections:

> Not many people really want to be civil servants. People who choose to be civil servants are either those whose family members are civil servants or those who cannot get a job in the private sector. (Interviewee, I2 RD)

Unsurprisingly perhaps, organisational rewards including salary increases and promotions do not represent an effective mechanism for motivating civil servants to put more than merely the minimum effort into their work. Some respondents explained that newcomers who had recently entered the civil service may be enthusiastic about producing results at first; however, this is unlikely to continue once they have absorbed the organisational norms:

> Powerful people exert a strong influence on the promotion procedures. So, rather than relying on performance and results as the main factors to

> judge whether a person should get promoted, favouritism and the spoils system are common, which discourages civil servants from working hard. Newcomers may be enthusiastic at the beginning but the more they take in the system, the more inactive they would be. (Interviewee, I1 RD)

It is important to note that, according to some respondents, this set of established norms underpinned by informal relationships of high dependency, appeared to form part of the fundamental characteristic of the Thai culture in general with regard to fairness or transparency:

> Thai people are not fair. Western people are more transparent, work is assessed more fairly and people get promotions according to results. Thai people are not like that; some people don't do any work. They just try to please their bosses. (Interviewee, I3 RD)

The Roots of Entrenched Clan-Oriented Cultural Values

The findings indicate that the culture of the public organisations investigated is governed by a hybrid bureaucratic model emerging during the post-NPM reform period. This model is characterised by the co-domination of hierarchical and clan-based cultural types that is based on a combination of the 'vertical control and command' along with 'orientation towards the person' dimensions, with the former corresponding to a hierarchy culture, while the latter could be viewed as being comparable to the clan culture of the CVF model (see, Fig. 7.1). In relation to the existing literature on culture in organisations, this distinct model shows a significant resemblance to the "family culture" that formed part of the typology proposed by Tropanes and Hampden-Turner (1997). The study clearly demonstrates that although tasks were allocated following the hierarchy and strict lines of command, clan-based virtues, such as cooperation, participation, mutual understanding and respect, were also highly valued among organisational members. Thus, despite the dominance of formalised rules, civil servants often carried out additional work outside of their job descriptions to assist one another. The phenomenon could be viewed as "rule by connections" in which individuals' obligations are not only determined by the rule of law but are also fundamentally underpinned by the desire to cultivate their relationships with others (Flynn 1999, p. 36). In particular, such interpersonal connections, which are found to be significantly influenced by a spirit of kinship, strongly correspond to Flynn's (1999, pp. 36–44) notion of "expressive" ties that usually generate mutual emotional commitments among members of Asian societies.

The findings presented in this study portray a conspicuous bureaucratic hybrid. This hybrid is situated at the intersection of typical bureaucratic characteristics, such as rationality and hierarchy, with modes of organising and specific cultural values, including respect for seniority, collectivism and benevolent paternalism. In other words, the bureaucracy examined is largely influenced by a clan- and relationship-based set of norms, while maintaining certain core characteristics of an ideal bureaucracy. These traits include, governance by formalised rules and procedures; allocation of tasks to individuals rather than reliance on personal initiative; and hierarchical distance among various ranks of civil servants. One of the potential explanations for the prevalence of these values in Thai public organisations might be the impact of national culture, as has been suggested by Schröter (2000, p. 200). According to this argument, organisations are naturally bound to their national cultures, i.e. "they are embedded in societal cultural patterns which in turn influence the ways they deal with salient managerial problems such as authority, uncertainty or participation". The cross-cultural research conducted by Hofstede (1980) and House et al. (2004, pp. 469, 474) confirms that, like many Asian states, Thailand is a *collectivist* rather than *individualist* society, which implies that the notion of the 'group' is highly valued.

In order to elucidate the prominence of a collectivist cultural profile of public organisations in Thailand it is essential to take the region's deeply-embedded ancient philosophies into consideration and to consider their relevance for neighbouring countries, notwithstanding the degree of caution required when making such generalisations. Buddhist and Confucian ways of life are among the most influential ideologies, which are fundamentally centred upon the notion of human relations and related attempts to generate and maintain harmonious societies. The values related to core Confucian concepts evidenced in public service organisations in the findings of this research correspond to Hofstede and Bond's (1988) argument that Confucianism constitutes the prominent philosophy shaping many Asian cultures. For instance, the prevalence of the seniority system and the ways in which kinship values governed interpersonal relationships between civil servants reflected key Confucian concepts regarding proper conduct, deference for old age and the significance of family, although these are perhaps less dominant in the Buddhist tradition.

The paternalistic approach to leadership is compatible with another core Confucian teaching which stipulates that while followers are required to obey leaders, leaders need to exercise their authority benevolently and take care of their followers' wellbeing (Hill 2007). It is also linked to a crucial Buddhist doctrine involving the proper conduct between master and servant, forming a part of its teaching on six key relationships (Sivaraksa 1991, p. 203), with a primary focus on compassion in human relationships. The influence of such traditions extends to the relationships between individual employees and the organisation, and thus to the custom of 'job for life'. This established practice, which is comparable to the Chinese concept of the 'iron rice bowl', could also be viewed as the product of Buddhism's emphasis on compassion in interpersonal relationships, in addition to compassion serving as an effective mechanism for maintaining a harmonious society. The integral link between these philosophies and the strength of clan-based cultural values is evidenced in the civil servants studied, especially regarding their benevolent paternalistic leaders as the centre of the organisation, securing its cohesion.

We suggest, that these features might be responsible for generating specific behaviours in civil servants, which in turn created distinctive bureaucratic attributes in the public service organisations studied. For instance, it was found that the corporate emphasis on vertical hierarchies tended to be principally governed by status- and respect-based relationships rather than the rigid exercising of formal authority. Despite Confucian and Buddhist ideas having a widespread influence throughout the region, we must simultaneously consider the moderating impact of cultural, political and linguistic diversity on the role of religious traditions and beliefs that shape the governance of public institutions.

Why Has There Been Only a Limited Cultural Change?

Although there are multiple potential explanations as to why the reform had only a limited impact on changing organisational culture in the Thai civil service, this article points to a modifying impact of the deeply entrenched values embedded in the national and/or regional culture. The essence of the argument goes back to Weber's original assertion about organisational analysis being always a cultural analysis, and an analysis of values (Weber 1978, quoted in Clegg 1994, p. 150). This study identifies a set of specific values, including deference to seniority and respect for kinship values, that are particularly durable aspects of culture. We argue that the combined effects of the seniority system and the dependent relationship-based set of norms on the core models of the CVF can be viewed as part of the explanation for the limited cultural change and the limited impact of NPM reforms in Thailand.

The limited impact of the NPM is also confirmed by other researchers. For instance, Mongkol (2012) argues that while some NPM-style initiatives, such as the restructuring of roles and functions, were implemented, others, such as downsizing or greater competition, were not tried at all. This conclusion corresponds with the findings of the research presented here, which identifies the notion of seniority and job security as having a crucial effect on fostering and maintaining a group-based culture in the organisations examined, and which could be jeopardised by the reforms. Although the reforms were viewed as a vital mechanism to bring organisational members together, they also appeared to produce a negative impact on the development of results-oriented values. For instance, organisational rewards in the form of promotions were largely distributed following the seniority structure rather than work outcomes. This finding confirms Burns and Bowornwathana's (2001) view that performance-related pay is less prominent than the seniority-based system in the Thai civil service. It also reiterates Flynn's (2000, p. 42) claim that the prevalence of the seniority concept in an organisational setting constitutes a cultural factor that might impede the adoption of a merit-based promotion scheme.

The set of dependent relationship-based norms was found to have a detrimental effect upon the development of a market-driven culture during both the pre- and post-reform eras. This negative relationship is particularly evident in the management of employees, including the process of task allocation and the prospects for individuals' promotions, which were somewhat related. The phenomenon is also identified by Bowornwathana (2007, p. 278), who highlights the effect of the patronage system on the lack of success in introducing performance measurement initiatives due to the superior patrons who usually manipulate the procedure in order to provide special favours to their clients. He argues that this phenomenon represents a noteworthy example of the adverse "reform hybrid" (ibid).

As such, collectivist societies may be developing a different type of bureaucracy that departs from the Western bureaucratic mode of organising conceptualised by Weber and developed by his followers. Different, advanced forms of bureaucracy existed in Asian countries before Weber's conceptualisation, although Western scholars, including Weber himself, had rather incomplete knowledge of how they functioned (see, Tao, Chap. 4 of this volume). Moreover, it has been suggested that while many Asian countries have often drawn on international experience as a source of ideas for public sector reform, especially that of states in the West, these were not uncritically replicated in Asian contexts (see, Turner, Chap. 9 this volume). However, we should not consider these as cases of indiscriminate policy transfer or products of international financial institutions' coercion. Rather, as Turner notes, 'it has been a process in which Asian leaders exercise a great deal of choice in what they transfer and then engage in a good deal of modification for application in an alien environment' (Turner, p. X).

Clearly, some of the features of classic Weberian bureaucracy—such as the hierarchical order of authority, fixed monetary salaries and administration as a full-time occupation—are present in the Thai civil service. However, this study shows that other significant attributes do not seem to take effect in practice, such as written rights and responsibilities; merit-based appointments and promotion systems; expert and technical training; and most importantly, the separation of office and person, which is characteristic of the clan organisations. This is also compatible with Ouchi's (1980) definition of the clan structure's ability to tolerate high ambiguity in performance evaluation. However, the literature does not always support our findings of the clan-based organisation being experienced as a warm, cozy environment (see, for example, Barker 1993). Paternalistic bureaucracy seems to be the dominant and enduring form of organisation in the Thai civil service because it reflects the values embedded in the national and, perhaps also, in the wider regional culture. Whether, and how far, the benevolent and humanising features of this paternalistic and familial type of bureaucracy override its negative features (e.g., favouritism, clientelism and nepotism, which may create a fertile breeding ground for corruption) is a question that needs to be empirically investigated. Another question is whether the findings of this study could potentially be generalised to other East Asian countries that have also been influenced by the same philosophical and religious systems over many centuries, particularly regarding the degree of collectivism? Examining from a comparative perspective the influences of national and/or regional culture on organisational culture in the context of reforms in public organisations could represent a promising avenue for future empirical research.

Conclusion

This chapter has presented forms of bureaucratic hybrids, comprising clan and hierarchy with some elements of post-bureaucracy, in public organisations in a non-Western context emerging from the implementation of an NPM-type reform in Thailand. Overall, the reform initiative did not manage to bring about a critical change. Instead, it appears to have merely resulted in a slight alteration in the overall cultural model in which hierarchy and clan cultural types continued to prevail. The study makes a theoretical contribution by filling significant gaps in the existing knowledge of bureaucratic hybrids and public management in an East Asian country, as it offers an explanatory framework for understanding the (im)possibility of its transformation in the context of organically embedded and deeply held values. The empirical findings highlight that public organisations are not merely driven by the characteristics associated with the classic hierarchical Weberian bureaucratic mode of organising, but may also be dominated by group-oriented values that are closer to clans. This brings into question the concept of bureaucracy as a monolithic superstructure that is bound to obliterate any informal relationships or networking. Given that the interpersonal relationships in such organisations are, to a great degree, governed by entrenched kinship values, the civil servants in this study do not present themselves as personally detached and strictly objective and dispassionate experts of the Weberian bureaucracy. We found for instance, that organisational leaders possessed the characteristics of benevolent patriarchs taking care of subordinates in return for securing their loyalty, which was underpinned by affective ties permeating different organisational structures (Fotaki et al. 2017).

Such a distinct bureaucratic configuration is governed by the values of collectivism and respect for status-based authority translating into seniority and patron-client systems, reflecting how the governance of public services has accommodated itself to the exigencies of the larger society. The dominant group-based norms underpinning this bureaucratic model were found to privilege the collective identity governing individuals' conduct in interpersonal relationships. This, as we have argued elsewhere, derives from the Confucian and Buddhist emphases on the harmony of the group, rather than the individual initiative and drive that the NPM reforms are meant to promulgate (Jingjit and Fotaki 2010). Unlike the vast majority of the existing literature that advocates hybrids as a means of achieving and securing competitiveness—an aim that is fundamentally underpinned by an assumption of utilitarian rationality—the chapter instead highlights a divergent organisational configuration that represents an 'organically grown' form of governance which may be serving quite different objectives. Finally, by clarifying the implications of underlying values, we underscore the role of cultural analysis in explaining the development of bureaucracy and its mutation into multiple organisational forms in accordance with a wider context. This hybrid organisational culture demonstrated a formidable resilience to NPM reform aimed at introducing post-bureaucratic logic to the Thai civil service—at least in the study detailed in this chapter—as it speaks to and coheres with deeply embedded values of the wider Thai society.

Notes

1. The detailed questionnaire refers to the quantitative aspect of the study and is not reported on here; the open- ended aspect of the questionnaire is structured along the seven dimensions outlined in the Table 7.1.
2. The RID possessed its own educational institutions.
3. 'Two-grade' is the highest salary increase in each year for Thai civil servants. There is usually a limited quota for the number of people who would be awarded this.

References

Adler, P. (2001). Market, hierarchy, and trust: The knowledge economy and the future of capitalism. *Organization Science, 12,* 215–234.

Appelbaum, E., Bailey, T., Berg, P., & Kalleberg, A. L. (2000). *Manufacturing advantage: Why high-performance work systems pay off.* Ithaca, NY: ILR Press.

Ashcraft, K. L. (2001). Organized dissonance: Feminist bureaucracy as hybrid form. *Academy of Management Journal,* 1301–1322.

Ashcraft, K. L. (2006). Feminist-bureaucratic control and other adversarial allies: Extending organized dissonance to the practice of "new" forms. *Communication Monographs, 73,* 55–86.

Bahrami, H. (1992). The emerging flexible organization: Perspectives from Silicon valley. *California Management Review, 34*, 33–52.

Barker, J. R. (1993). Tightening the iron cage: Concertive control in self-managing teams. *Administrative Science Quarterly*, 408–437.

Bartlett, C. A., & Ghoshal, S. (1997). *The individualized corporation*. London: Random House Business Books.

Berg, A. M. (2006). Transforming public services? Transforming the public servant? *International Journal of Public Sector Management, 19*, 556–568.

Bowornwathana, B. (2007). Governance reform outcomes through cultural lens: Thailand. In S. Kuno & I. Proeller (Eds.), *Research in public policy analysis and management*. JAI.

Boyne, G. A. (2003). What is Public Service Improvement? *Public Administration, 81*, 211–227.

Budd, L. (2007). From bureaucratic to post-bureaucratic: The difficulties of transition. *International Journal of Public Sector Management, 20*(6), 531–547.

Burns, J. P., & Bowornwathana, B. (2001). Asian civil service systems in comparative perspective. In J. P. Burns & B. Bidhya (Eds.), *Civil service systems in Asia*. Cheltenham: Edward Elgar.

Burns, T., & Stalker, G. M. (1994). *The management of innovation*. USA: Oxford University.

Bushe, G. R., & Shani, A. B. (1991). *Parallel learning structures: Increasing innovation in bureaucracies*. Reading, MA: Addison-Wesley.

Cameron, K. S., & Quinn, R. E. (1999). *Diagnosing and changing organizational culture*. Upper Saddle River, NJ: Prentice-Hall.

Casey, C. (2004). Bureaucracy re-enchanted? Spirit, experts and authority in organizations. *Organization, 11*, 59.

Cheney, G. (1995). Democracy in the workplace: Theory and practice from the perspective of communication. *Journal of Applied Communication Research, 23*, 167–200.

Child, J., & McGrath, R. (2001). Organizations unfettered: Organizational form in an information-intensive economy. *Academy of Management Journal, 44*(6), 1135–1149.

Christensen, T. & Laegrid, P. (2011). Complexity and hybrid public administration—Theoretical and empirical challenges. *Public Organization Review, 11*, 407–423.

Clegg, S. (1994). Weber and Foucault: Social theory for the study of organizations. *Organization, 1*, 149–178.

Clegg, S., Kronberger, M., & Pitsis, T. (2005). *An introduction to theory and practice*. London: Sage.

Collis, J., & Hussey, R. (2003). *Business research: A practical guide for undergraduate and postgraduate students*. New York: Palgrave Macmillan.

Courpasson, D., & Clegg, S. (2006). Dissolving the iron cages? Tocqueville, Michels, bureaucracy and the perpetuation of elite power. *Organization, 13,* 319–343.

Deal, T. E., & Kennedy, A. A. (1982). *Corporate cultures: The rights and rituals of corporate life.* London: Addison-Wesley.

Deal, T. E., & Kennedy, A. A. (1983). Culture a new look through old lenses. *The Journal of Applied Behavioural Sciences, 19,* 498–505.

Deetz, S. (1992). *Democracy in an age of corporate colonization: Developments in communication and the politics of everyday life.* Albany: State University of New York Press.

Denis, J. L., Ferlie, E., & Van Gestel, N. (2015). Understanding hybridity in public organizations. *Public Administration, 93,* 273–289.

Dingwall, R., & Strangleman, T. (2005). Organizational culture in the public services. In E. Ferlie, L. E. Lynn & C. Pollitt (Eds.), *The oxford handbook of public management oxford.* Oxford University Press.

Du Gay, P. (1996). Organizing identity: Entrepreneurial governance and public management. In S. Hall & P. Du Gay (Eds.), *Questions of cultural identity.* London: Sage.

Du Gay, P. (2000). *In praise of bureaucracy: Weber, organization, ethics.* London: Sage.

Du Gay, P. (Ed.). (2005). *The values of bureaucracy.* Oxford: Oxford University.

Duncombe, W., Miner, J., & Ruggiero, J. (1997). Empirical evaluation of bureaucratic models of inefficiency. *Public Choice, 93,* 1–18.

Dunleavy, P., Margetts, H., Bastow, S., & Tinkler, J. (2006). New public management is dead—Long live digital-era governance. *Journal of Public Administration Research and Theory, 16*(3), 467–494.

Flynn, N. (1999). *Miracle to meltdown in Asia: Business, government, and society.* USA: Oxford University.

Flynn, N. (2000). Managerialism and public services. In J. Clarke, S. Gewirtz, & E. McLaughlin (Eds.), *New managerialism, new welfare?* London: Open University in association with SAGE Publications.

Fotaki, M., Kenny, K., & Vachhani, S. (2017). Thinking critically about affect in organization studies: Why it matters (Editorial). *Organization, 24*(1), 3–17.

Grey, C., & Garsten, C. (2001). Trust, control and post-bureaucracy. *Organization Studies, 22,* 229–250.

Gottfried, H., & Weiss, P. (1994). A compound feminist organization. *Women & Politics, 14,* 23–44.

Greener, I., & Powell, M. (2008). The changing governance of the NHS: Reform in a post-Keynesian health service. *Human Relations, 61,* 617.

Harris, M. (2006). Technology, innovation and post-bureaucracy: The case of the British library. *Journal of Organizational Change Management, 19,* 80.

Harris, M., & Wegg-Prosser, V. (2007). Post bureaucracy and the politics of forgetting: The management of change at the BBC, 1991–2002. *Journal of Organizational Change Management, 20,* 290.

Harrison, A. (1993). *From hierarchy to contract.* Newbury: Policy Journals Ltd.

Heckscher, C. (1994). Defining the post-bureaucratic type. In C. Heckscher & A. Donnellon (Eds.), *The post-bureaucratic organization: New perspectives on organizational change.* London: Sage.

Heckscher, C., & Donnellon, A. (1994). *The post-bureaucratic organization: New perspectives on organizational change.* London: Sage.

Hedlund, G. (1994). A model of knowledge management and the N-form corporation. *Strategic Management Journal, 15,* 454–461.

Heydbrand, W. V. (1989). New organizational forms. *Work and occupations, 16,* 323.

Hill, J. S. (2007). Religion and the shaping of East Asian management styles: A conceptual examination. *Journal of Asia-Pacific Business, 8,* 59–88.

Hofstede, G. (1980). *Culture's consequences: International differences in work-related values.* Newbury Park, CA: Sage.

Hofstede, G., & Bond, M. H. (1988). The Confucius connection: From cultural roots to economic growth. *Organisational Dynamics, 16,* 5–21.

Hoggett, P. (2006). Conflict, ambivalence, and the contested purpose of public organizations. *Human Relations, 59,* 175–194.

Hood, C. (1991). A public management for all seasons? *Public Administration, 69,* 3–19.

Hood, C. (1996). Exploring variations in public management reform of the 1980s. In H. A. G. M. Bekke, J. L. Perry, & T. A. J. Toonen (Eds.), *Civil service systems.* Bloomington, IN: Indiana University.

Hood, C., & Jackson, M. (1991). *Administrative argument.* Aldershot: Dartmouth Publishing Co.

Hood, C., Rothstein, H., & Baldwin, R. (2001). *The government of risk: Understanding risk regulation regimes.* London: Oxford University.

House, R. J., Hanges, P. J., Javidan, M., Dorfman, P., & Gupta, V. (2004). *Culture, leadership, and organizations: The GLOBE study of 62 Societies.* Sage Publication.

Jingjit, R. (2008). *Analysis of organisational culture and outcomes of public management reform based on the competing values framework: The case of the Thai civil service.* Unpublished Ph.D. Thesis, University of Manchester, Manchester.

Jingjit, R., & Fotaki, M. (2010). Confucian ethics and the limited impact of the new public management reform in Thailand. *Journal of Business Ethics 97*(Supplement 1), 61–73.

Josserand, E. (2004). *The network organization, the experience of leading French multinationals.* Cheltenham: Edward Elgar.

Josserand, E., Teo, S., & Clegg, S. (2006). From bureaucratic to post-bureaucratic: The difficulties of transition. *Journal of Organizational Change Management, 19,* 54–64.

Kanter, R. M. (1990). *When giants learn to dance.* London: Unwin Hyman.

Kanter, R. M., Stein, B. A., & Jick, T. D. (1992). *The challenge of organisational change.* Reading, MA: Addison Wesley.

Kellehear, A. (1993). *The unobtrusive researcher.* St. Leonards: Allen and Unwin.

Koppel, J. G. S. (1999). The challenge of administration by regulation: Preliminary findings regarding the U.S. government's venture capital funds. *Journal of Public Administration Research and Theory, 9*(4), 641–666.

Le Grand, J. (2007a). *The other invisible hand: Delivering public services through choice and competition.* Princeton, NJ: Princeton University.

Le Grand, J. (2007b). The politics of choice and competition in public services. *Political Quarterly, 78,* 207–213.

Light, D. W. (1997). From managed competition to managed cooperation: Theory and lessons from the British experience. *The Milbank Quarterly,* 297–341.

Lovell, R. (1995). *Managing change in the new public sector.* London: Longmann.

Lowndes, V., & Skelcher, C. (2002). The dynamics of multi-organisational partnerships. *Public Managements-Critical Perspectives, 2,* 302–324.

Malone, M. S., & Davidow, W. H. (1992). *The virtual corporation structuring and revitalizing the corporation for the 21st Century.* New York.

Mansbridge, J. J. (1973). Time, emotion, and inequality: Three problems of participatory groups. *Journal of Applied Behavioral Science, 9,* 351–368.

Maravelias, C. (2007). Freedom at work in the age of postbureaucratic organization. *Ephemera, 7,* 555–574.

Maykut, P., & Morehouse, R. (1994). *Beginning qualitative research: A philosophic and practical guide.* London: The Falmer Press.

Mintzberg, H. (1980). Structure in 5'S: A synthesis of the research on organization design. *Management Science, 26,* 322–341.

Mongkol, K. (2012). Globalizing new public management: A pilot study from Thailand. *Research Journal of Business Management, 6,* 19–29.

Morgan, G. (1991). *Riding the waves of change.* San Francisco, CA: Jossey-Bass.

Newman, J. (2005). Bending bureaucracy: Leadership and multi-level governance. In P. Du Gay (Ed.), *The values of bureaucracy* (pp. 191–210). Oxford: Oxford University.

Osborne, D., & Gaebler, T. (1992). *Reinventing government.* Reading, MA: Addison-Wesley.

Osborne, D., & Plastrik, P. (1997). *Banishing bureaucracy.* Reading, MA: Addison-Wesley.

Ouchi, W. G. (1980). Markets, bureaucracies and clans. *Administrative Science Quarterly, 25,* 129–141.

Ouchi, W. G. (1981). *Theory Z: How American business can meet the Japanese challenge*. Reading, MA: Addison-Wesley.
Ouchi, W. G., & Jaeger, A. M. (1978). Type Z organization: Stability in the midst of mobility. *Academy of Management Review*, 305–314.
Painter, M. (2004). Governance. *International Journal of Policy, Administration, and Institutions, 17*, 361–386.
Painter, M. (2006). Thaksinisation or managerialism? Reforming the Thai bureaucracy. *Journal of Contemporary Asia, 36*, 26–47.
Pollitt, C., & Bouckaert, G. (2000). *Public management reform: A comparative analysis*. New York: Oxford University.
Peters, T. (1989). *Thriving on chaos. Handbook for a management revolution*. London: Harper Perennial.
Putnam, L. (1983). The interpretive approach: An alternative to functionalism. In L. Putnam & M. Pacanowsky (Eds.), *Communication and organizations: An interpretive approach*. Beverly Hills, CA: Sage Publications.
Quinn, J. B. (1992). *Intelligent enterprise*. New York: The Free Press.
Quinn, R. E., & Rohrbaugh, J. (1981). A competing values approach to organizational effectiveness. *Public Productivity Review, 5*, 122–140.
Robinson, M. (2015). *From old public administration to the new public service implications for public sector reform in developing countries*. Singapore: UNDP.
Rothschild, J., & Russell, R. (1986). Alternatives to bureaucracy: Democratic participation in the economy. *Annual Review of Sociology, 12*, 307–328.
Salaman, G. (2005). Bureaucracy and beyond: Managers and leaders in the 'post-bureaucratic' organization. In P. Du Gay (Ed.), *The values of bureaucracy*. Oxford: Oxford University.
Saltman, R. B., & Von Otter, C. (1992). *Planned markets and public competition: Strategic reform in Northern European health systems*. Buckingham: Open University.
Schroter, E. (2000). Culture's consequences? In search of cultural explanations of British and German public sector reform. In H. Wollmann & E. Schroter (Eds.), *Comparing public sector reform in Britain and Germany: Key traditions and trends of modernisation*. Ashgate.
Schwartz, T. (1992). Anthropology and psychology: An unrequited relationship. In T. Schwartz, G. M. White, & C. Lutz (Eds.), *New directions in psychological anthropology*. Cambridge: England Cambridge University.
Senge, P. M. (1990). *The fifth discipline: The art and practice of the learning organization*. New York: Double Day.
Sivaraksa, S. (1991). Being in the world: A Buddhist ethical and social concern. *Buddhist-Christian Studies, 11*, 200–210.

Snow, C. C., Miles, R. E., & Coleman Jr., H. (1993). Managing 21st century network organizations. In C. Mabey & B. Mayon-White (Eds.), *Managing change*. Sage.

Ten Bos, R. (1997). Essai: Business ethics and Bauman ethics. *Organization Studies, 18*, 997–1014.

Trompenaars, A., & Hampden-Turner, C. (1997). *Riding the waves of culture: Understanding cultural diversity in business*. London: Economist Books.

Weber, M. (1947). *The theory of social and economic organization*. NY: The Free Press.

Weber, M. (1978). *Economy & society*. Los Angeles: University of California.

Zammuto, R. F., & Krakower, J. Y. (1991). Quantitative and qualitative studies of organizational culture. *Research in Organizational Change and Development, 5*, 83–114.

CHAPTER 8

Urban Development in China: Moving from Urbanisation to Quality of Urban Life

Jong Youl Lee, Chad Anderson and Bo Wang

Introduction

China has followed a course of rapid economic growth during the twenty-first century noteworthy for being on a scale much larger than that of earlier waves of rapid industrialisation and economic development. Though the current worldwide slowdown has impacted its growth, the People's Republic of China has developed to a point in recent years that its huge exports, its latent market potential, and even its impact on the global environment make it a major regional and world

J.Y. Lee · C. Anderson (✉)
Department of Public Administration, Incheon National University, Incheon, Korea
e-mail: tishado@gmail.com

J.Y. Lee
e-mail: jylee@inu.ac.kr

B. Wang
Department of Public Administration, Guangxi University for Nationalities, Nanning, Guangxi, China
e-mail: wavesue@gmail.com

S. Bice et al. (eds.), *Public Policy in the 'Asian Century'*, International Series on Public Policy, https://doi.org/10.1057/978-1-137-60252-7_8

player on almost every issue. In recent years, however, China's rate of growth has slowed to the point that Chinese authorities have acknowledged a "new normal" of medium-high growth replacing the previous norm of perpetual explosive growth though it still easily outpaces the OECD average (OECD 2015, p. 18). Although some critics have pointed to underlying issues that could lead to crisis (Li 2011), it appears that China will continue to play a major and growing role in the world economy for the indefinite future.

One legacy of the rapid economic growth that followed market reform has been urban development on a massive scale, whether defined as expansion of cities or as their internal development. Urbanisation has returned to a pattern more typical of developing nations as cities of millions have sprung up very rapidly (Lee et al. 2013), while China is so large that it now represents the mainstream of urbanisation in the world (Wang 2015). Chinese cities have different local conditions and policies, and have pursued different development approaches as the market has been gradually liberalised. In contrast to an earlier emphasis on manufacturing, the City of Dalian, the "Silicon Valley of China," drives growth through technology and the cultural industry based on creative cultural contents, including content and programs for electronic media, but also performances, sports, and other creative industries (Lee and Wang 2013; Anderson et al. 2014; Wang and Anderson 2016).

The variety of policy approaches to urban development serves to counter criticisms of urban growth in general and Chinese growth in particular. Anti-growth critics highlight the emphasis on growth over quality of life like health, education, entertainment, (Clark 2004; Lee et al. 2012, pp. 47–49; Wu 2008, 2012), the destruction of nature, and the depletion of finite resources (Lee et al. 2012, pp. 290–293). These are important considerations when people are crowded into tall buildings that blot out traditional architecture in China while sprawl consumes farmland and pollution taints the life-giving land, air, and water. The challenge for China includes finding methods that answer critics of growth while delivering the benefits of urban development. The task is to respect the needs of people but not create new problems while developing the urban economy.

Even as late as the most recent 10th, 11th, and 12th Five-Year Plans, party discussions have centered on questions of urbanisation and expanding cities, such as moving populations, reforming the *hukou* system of registration, and the transfer of rural labour to urban areas (Wang 2015, pp. 56–65). Even though there is discussion of developing the economy inside of cities, much attention is still paid to urbanisation and moving people to cities at a time when China has already become an urban nation. This chapter argues that more attention needs to be paid to measuring and promoting development that pays attention to the quality of life inside the cities where the majority of Chinese now live.

This study uses data from 69 Chinese cities selected from every province for which data were available (the Xizang Autonomous Region was the only province or region unrepresented) covering the years from 2003 to 2013 in time series. The purpose is to examine the factors that drive urban development in China. In particular, the study asks whether traditional economic factors, education, environment, cultural industry, infrastructure, foreign direct investment (FDI), or government spending, each measured per capita, is most closely associated with urban development in the major cities of China during this time period. The study hopes to answer the question of what drives urban development in contemporary China.

Further, this study also considers results based on the most common Chinese measure of urban development, urbanisation level (the percentage of a district's population living in an urban area), and then compares them with the results for other common international measures of development. It argues that more attention to urban development by improving quality of life within cities (measured by GDP and income) is more desirable than emphasising moving more people into cities (measured by population density) or expanding cities (measured by urbanisation level).

This Chapter begins by looking at literature on urban development generally and then specific to China. Next, the Chapter compares the four measures of urban development (population density, GDP, income, and urbanisation level) with each other. It then looks at factors related to urban development through four linear regression models. Finally, the factors associated with development are compared under the different models and conclusions are drawn. In particular, the study detailed in this Chapter found that factors associated with urban development included alternative paths to development that could both urbanise and develop the local economy while promoting quality of urban life. It also found that attention to positive measures that developed Chinese urban economies also increased urbanisation. On the other hand, simply increasing an urbanisation level was associated with increasing air pollution, whereas attention to urban economic development measures did not.

Studies of Urban Development

Urban development is defined here broadly as growth to urban areas, including both the expansion of cities into new areas and the internal development of cities. The expansion of cities is also known as urbanisation (Wang 2015, pp. 18–20). Here the term urban development is used to mean both types of development. Urbanisation is used to specify urban expansion. Internal development or urban economic development is used to specify internal development. This chapter argues that as China is now an urban society more attention needs to be paid to the internal development of Chinese cities, particularly in ways that improve quality of life for residents.

The most traditional models of urban development stress "land, labour, and capital" as factors in urban development (Clark 2004). These models suggest that development is made possible through the development of unused land; the application of labour to build on the land; and the investment of capital to pay for the labour and the developments on the land.

Concerning land, location is a central consideration due to agglomeration economies where businesses concentrate for proximity to resources, transportation, production, or markets (Bruegmann 2005, pp. 22–23; Lee et al. 2012, pp. 311–315). The effect of location on urban development is a location triangle that constrains urban development according to land price and transport costs. At the same time, another way location may promote urban development is through the benefits of economies of scale created through the location of industry. Likewise, Meng (2006) stresses the need of a convenient transportation system for a city. While the growth and scale of development is restricted by the cost of transportation, location also further affects urban development through the convenience of transportation networks in promoting industry and industrial effects. This chapter uses public transportation and number of taxis and the area of the road network in a city to measure transportation as a factor in development.

Tiebout (1956) is famous for his hypothesis about the movement of people between urban areas. He asserted that people could "vote with their feet" by leaving an area they did not like and moving to an area they do like. Though he was addressing questions of choice among urban policies and urban services, this movement may be motivated by individual preferences in terms of work opportunity, or any of the different features or amenities offered by the city. This hypothesis supports a number of the theories discussed below by giving people agency in their relationship to the city, although the study detailed in this Chapter particularly uses variables measuring local expenditures on education, social welfare, science and technology, and the environment to consider the role of public services in urban development.

More recent versions of the application of labour in development have involved the concept of human capital in the form of investments in training and educating workers to become more productive. The increasing marketisation of China, including the successive and deepening effects of reform and the opening of the economy, have led to the typical problems of a market economy. These challenges include inequality and a need for specialised division of labour. There is still is a great difference and gap in urban development among China's different regions in terms of the availability of more productive skilled labour, with more skilled workers available on the East Coast than in the West. However, there has been more discussion of the role of human capital in this process outside of China. Schultz (1990) argued that attracting high-value labour is the key to urban development as it increases the value of the labour input. The rapid growth of human capital leads to an increasing share of the national income and a corresponding drop in the share of property. In addition, Lucas (1988) found that human capital development has strong positive externalities, as the communication between hi-tech employees and high-quality 'ordinary' workers leads to the spread of innovation that plays a role in increasing the efficiency of production. Unemployment is used in this study as a variable to consider the lack of employment opportunities, while education expenditures and university students consider the development of human capital.

Other theories have stressed the role of culture, and in particular, the creative class of innovative workers in contributing to the development of human capital through the mediating effect of social capital (Florida 2002, 2007) along the lines of Jane Jacobs' ideas of cities as engines of innovation (1969). Bin (2003) argued that the regional integration of urban networks plays an important role during urbanisation. Urbanisation is not only propelled by the manufacturing industry but by innovation in the service industry. Others have further argued for the role of consumption and non-market amenities and collections of amenities in developing social capital on the path to developing human capital (Clark 2004; Silver et al. 2006; Clark et al. 2014). The development of the culture industry in Dalian, for instance, actively promoted the fusion of cultural resources, capital, technology, talents and other factors—especially the fusion of the tourism and health industries (Wang 2003; Wang and Anderson 2016). This study uses university students as a proxy for the creative class, includes green space and pollution as positive and negative natural amenities, movie theatres as a constructed amenity, and also includes foreign and domestic tourists.

Another motive for urban development is to make the city self-financing through the development of industry. Changes in the population are due to industrial development and lack of opportunity elsewhere. There are both 'push' and 'pull' factors moving people to a city (Bluestone et al. 2008, pp. 86–90; Small 2002; Lee et al. 2012, pp. 59, 74). As technology is developed and shared on farms, for example, not as many farmers are needed, so they go to cities to search for jobs and places to live. At the same time, city life has many advantages that are attractive and draw rural citizens. They move to cities for work as well as for new amenities unavailable in rural areas. New products and services available in cities eventually give rise to new industries centered on them. For example, Hong et al. (2000) advocates that the thrust of urban development should shift from secondary industry (for export) to tertiary industry (for local consumption) on the basis of the increasing customer base for products and services located in Chinese cities. Therefore, what goods and services are produced plays an important role during the urbanisation process. This study includes the proportion of secondary industry (manufacturing) and tertiary industry (services).

Industrial development in industry need not be provided by domestic capital. Fengxuan Xue and Chun Yang (1995) assert that FDI has different effects on urbanisation in different cities, but that it is an important factor for promoting urban development, particularly in the absence of scarce domestic capital, which may not be accompanied by the expertise that may come with FDI. Luo Qian (2008) conducted an empirical study into the role of FDI on promoting urban development, which found that attracting FDI promoted urbanisation.

The literature also points to information and information technology as drivers of urban development. Deng and Li (2012) highlight the close relationship between urban development and an increase in information communications technology use and infrastructure. They found that for every 1% increase in ICT business volume alone when controlling for other factors, the rate of urbanisation increases 0.07%. Castells (1996) put forward information city theory, making up the so-called "information mode of development". This analyzes the influence of high technology industry on socioeconomic activities. Here, the world economy is seen as changing from being rooted in a 'dynamics of place' to taking root in a 'dynamic of flows.' This study included local expenditure on science and technology.

Drivers of Urbanisation in China: What the Literature Tells Us

Turning attention more specifically to China, Lee et al. (2013) looked at six measures of urban development in China in a database of 99 cities, particularly examining issues related to population measures and the housing market. The study used per capita GDP, regional gross production (RGP), and disposable income as dependent variables and ended up excluding housing price, population, and employment rate due to theoretical and practical reasons. In brief, this was because inflated housing prices and the existence of so-called 'ghost cities', used for investment, meant that housing price was not a reliable measure of development. Population and employment rate were also theoretically unreliable due to the discrepancy between measuring the registered and actual population. All three factors were further excluded for the practical reason that their results were not generally consistent with the other measures used.

Following this, Lee et al. (2013) argue that population density should be considered as a replacement for population; along with the more commonly used Chinese measure of urbanisation level, which is the proportion of a district's population living in an urban area. As for factors driving development, income from tourism was positively related to all three dependent variables. Fixed capital investment in creative cultural industries was related to GDP and RGP, and sprawl was related to disposable income. An increase in students was negatively related to GDP.

China is in the process of changing from an industrial society to a post-industrial society. Science and technology are crucial to industrial development but they cannot advance without the development of education, which is one of the main factors affecting competitiveness in this area (Lin et al. 2004). Zhao (2008), for instance, determined through statistical analysis that there was a long-term proportional relationship between science and technology investment and GDP in secondary industry.

Both per capita GDP (Dai 2001) and population density (Ladd 1992) are measures that have been used in studies to measure urban development in China. In addition, the two measures are different and may measure different aspects of development and match different policy aspects. For example, a per capita GDP model can show economic development while a population density model can show urbanised development. In theory, cities should maximise urban function and provide as many services and facilities as possible to ensure that residents can enjoy conveniences nearby. Such public facilities as hospitals, libraries, public green space, and road area should be closely aligned with population density.

The proportion of tertiary industry to GDP continually increases in the process of economic development. The development level of the tertiary industry depends on the level of national economic development and demographics (Roh and Lee 2013). Citing the World Bank Development Report and the United Nation Yearbook of National Accounts Statistics, Lin Ling (1995) listed the relationship between urbanisation level and industrial structure of 22 countries from high to low, and concluded that an increasing urbanisation level was accompanied by upgraded industrial structure. This resulted in a decisive economic development contribution of industrialisation to urbanisation level (Lin 1995). Meanwhile, increasing industrialisation and rapid tertiary industry development are predicted to play a more important part in the level of urbanisation (Lin 1995). For instance, per capita GDP shows a significant relationship to the development level of tertiary industry. Increasing GDP promotes the growth of the tertiary industry when the national economy level is at a lower level (Zuo and Li 2003).

There is widespread unauthorised migration in China known as the floating population in spite of government efforts to control population movements, including giving incentives for people to live at their official place of registration (Small 2002; Wang 2015). As a result, the registered population is not equal to the actual population. Local governments and scholars tend not to use the official registered population statistics for calculating population, but instead adjust the registered population by subtracting out emigrants and adding in the immigrant population, following the formula:

$$R - M + I$$

where

R = registered population
M = population that has migrated away
I = migrant population resident for at least six months

This is the usual formula used by urban governments and scholars, though population is not always recorded using this formula in statistical yearbooks (Wang 2015).

The urbanisation level of China was 51.29% in 2011. The urban population is now more than 50% of the total population as compared to only 10.6% in 1949 and 20% percent in 1979 (Lee and Wang 2013). China's urbanisation has entered a period of acceleration in particular since the beginning of economic reforms in 1978. Many scholars (Han et al. 2013; Lee and Wang 2013; Wang 2015) view the urbanisation level of China as actually overvalued in official statistics since existing urban population statistics in China include a great deal of the rural population from residents living in rural areas within an urban district, which made the urbanisation level of China nine points higher than the actual urban population (Wang 2015).

The usual explicit measure of urban development as urbansation is urbanisation level, which is the proportion of the population that is urban, which is calculated by Chinese local governments and scholars by dividing urban population by total population where cities generally have rural areas included under their jurisdiction.

There are two issues with using urbanisation level to stand in for urban development. First, statistical yearbooks do not always list data in a consistent manner regarding population and adjusted population and urbanisation level below the provincial level and some cities appear to calculate urbanisation level to a different standard in different years. This makes it more difficult to assemble a city-specific data set as the urbanisation level needs to be recalculated when a city appears to use only registered population for urbanisation level (Wang 2015). Second, it is possible for urbanisation level to reach 100% as was the case in more than one city in Lee et al. (2013). This remains a useful measure within provinces, but becomes less useful when dealing with cities as more approach and achieve 100% urbanisation. No cities in this study were greater than 90% urbanised.

Statistical Analysis and Comparison of Urban Development Models

This study employs data from 69 Chinese cities from the years 2003 to 2013 to determine the factors that were most closely associated with four models of urban development over this period. These cities were selected from every province for which data were available (the Xizang Autonomous Region was the only province or region unrepresented) on the principle of having the largest, the median, and the smallest city by population. This is done through GLS time series regression analysis. This study uses four dependent variables used to represent development: population density and urbanisation level to represent urbanisation, and per capita GDP and average annual pay to represent urban economic development. Variables representing traditional economic factors, human capital development, urban amenities, infrastructure, FDI, and government spending are compared to determine the factors most closely associated with urban development in the major cities of China during this time period.

Dependent Variables

The study presented in this Chapter employs a hedonic regression to estimate and separate the component factors predicted to drive urban development. Even though housing price is frequently employed as a market-based dependent variable in a hedonic regression to indicate development (Lee 1997; Clark 2004), it is excluded from consideration in the study due to the theoretical and practical issues raised in Lee et al. (2013). This study endorses instead the choice of alternative variables from that study, namely GDP and disposable income. Average annual pay was instead used as a proxy for disposable income. This study uses population density to test its usefulness in the Chinese context, partly in response to the work of Mehedi and Lee (2014), which argues for the use of the variable in a study of cities in Bangladesh. Finally, this study uses urbanisation level as the major measure of urbanisation in China.

There have been questions raised concerning the reliability involved in the calculation and reporting of population data noted above to take account of the floating population (Lee et al. 2013; Wang 2015), which would affect urbanisation level as well as population density. It is difficult to depend on the accuracy of household registration figures that do not

Table 8.1 Comparison of dependent variables using pearson correlations

	Urbanisation level %	*Population density*	*Per capita GDP*	*Average annual pay*
Urbanisation level %	1			
Significance				
N	759			
Population density	0.415***	1		
Significance	0.000			
N	759	759		
Per capita GDP	0.691***	0.295***	1	
Significance	0.000	0.000		
N	759	759	759	
Average annual pay	0.577***	0.305***	0.783***	1
Significance	0.000	0.000	0.000	
N	759	759	759	759

***Correlation is significant at the 0.001 level (2-tailed)

take consistent account of unauthorised population movements. It could be argued that the figures used for 'out-migrants' and 'in-migrants' may be little more than estimates in many cases. Furthermore, it is unclear that all cities consistently use the standard formula in reporting the data (Song and Zhang 2002). As a result, one of the aims of this study is to examine the consistency of the different urban development measures.

Table 8.1 shows the results of a Pearson correlation of the possible dependent variables selected for the study in order to indicate the compatibility between the selected dependent variables. All of the variables positively correlated with all of the others at a significant level and the relationships ranged from a low of 0.295 to a high of 0.783. Population density appeared to have the weakest link to the other measures of urban development, with correlations of 0.415 with urbanisation level, 0.295 with per capita GDP, and 0.305 with average annual pay. This is not surprising, given the issues given with population data in China. Urbanisation level was considerably more consistent with the other variables, with a 0.691 relationship with per capita GDP, and 0.577 with average annual pay. Per capita GDP and average annual pay, as variables verified in previous studies directly or in proxy, were the strongest and correlated with each other at the strongest level, 0.783. None of the variables were excluded from the study, but these last two were viewed as the strongest ones for measuring economic developments that improve the urban quality of life.

Models

With the selection of the dependent variables, the models were selected using the following formula:

$$
\begin{aligned}
Y = {} & \beta_0 + \beta_1 x_1 + \beta_2 x_2 + \beta_3 x_3 + \beta_4 x_4 + \beta_5 x_5 + \beta_6 x_6 \\
& + \beta_7 x_7 + \beta_8 x_8 + \beta_9 x_9 + \beta_{10} x_{10} + \beta_{11} x_{11} + \beta_{12} x_{12} + \beta_{13} x_{13} \\
& + \beta_{14} x_{14} + \beta_{15} x_{15} + \beta_{16} x_{16} + \beta_{17} x_{17} + \beta_{18} x_{18} + \beta_{19} x_{19} + \varepsilon
\end{aligned}
$$

where

Y = Population density (population in units of 10,000 per square kilometer).

= Per capita GDP (gross domestic product divided by total population).

= Average annual pay (mean annual remuneration in RMB).

= Urbanisation level (urban population divided by total population).

and

β_0 = Constant.

x_1 = Unemployment (% workers without work in the labour market).

x_2 = University students (number of students divided by total population).

x_3 = RSI (secondary industry as a proportion of GDP).

x_4 = RTI (tertiary industry as a proportion of GDP).

x_5 = Green space (per capita public green space in square meters).

x_6 = Movie theatres (per capita number of movie theatres).

x_7 = Road area (per capita area of roads in square meters).

x_8 = FDI (per capita foreign direct investment in $USD).

x_9 = Public transportation (per capita number of public transportation vehicles).

x_{10} = Taxis (number of taxis operating divided by total population).

x_{11} = Education (per capita local government education spending in RMB).

x_{12} = Social welfare (per capita local social welfare spending in RMB).
x_{13} = Science/Technology (per capita local public science/technology spending in RMB).
x_{14} = Pollution (per capita industrial sulfur dioxide emissions).
x_{15} = Environment (per capita local government spending on environment in RMB).
x_{16} = Domestic tourists (per capita number of visitors from mainland China).
x_{17} = Foreign tourists (per capita number of visitors from outside of mainland China).
x_{18} = East (located in the Eastern Coastal Economic Zone).
x_{19} = West (located in the Western Region).

Table 8.2 shows the summary statistics for all of the variables, dependent and independent. The number of observations was the same for all

Table 8.2 Summary of dependent and independent variables

Variables	*Obs*	*Mean*	*Std Dev*	*Min*	*Max*
Urbanisation level	759	54.089	15.916	21.1	90.0
Population density	759	503.43	450.73	16.0	3809
Per capita GDP	759	34262	27290	2559	256877
Average annual pay	759	30260	13962	8097	93997
Unemployment	759	4.6844	1.7616	1.30	9.90
University students	759	0.03134	0.03022	0.00017	0.12615
RSI	759	47.538	9.5022	19.8	73.3
RTI	759	42.152	9.9034	17.8	76.9
Green space	759	37.574	35.629	2.90	265
Movie theatre	759	0.03910	0.03315	0.00312	0.21326
Road area	759	11.196	7.9423	1.70	108
FDI	759	209.39	299.36	1.6233	2299.2
Public transport	759	0.00059	0.00145	0.00001	0.01695
Taxis	759	0.00119	0.00104	0.00007	0.00559
Education	759	771.56	732.74	68.897	5174.9
Social welfare	759	285.023	483.03	2.0533	3564.0
Science/Technology	759	137.33	413.36	0.57295	4382.2
Pollution	759	0.02072	0.02357	0.00006	0.21489
Environment	759	421.88	595.28	2.0746	4244.1
Domestic tourists	759	4.8806	4.0908	0.08052	24.233
Foreign tourists	759	0.15537	0.39003	0.00000	4.2773
East	759	33%	–	0.00	1.00
West	759	33%	–	0.00	1.00

variables, covering eleven years in 69 cities equaling 759. There was a good range of variance for all of the variables. The rationale for the dependent variables is discussed above. Unemployment was used in place of unavailable employment figures used in Lee et al. (2013) to represent economic opportunity. University student was used as a proxy for the creative class (Florida 2002; Florida 2007) as well as a proxy for education level (Anderson et al. 2015). Secondary (RSI) and tertiary industry (RTI) were used as measures of economic structure (Hong et al. 2000). Green space and movie theatre were included as measures of the impact of natural and entertainment amenities as well as of pollution as a negative amenity (Clark 2004; Clark et al. 2014). Road area was included as a measure of urban infrastructure (Anderson et al. 2015), and of sprawl (Lee 2012; Lee et al. 2013), along with public transport and taxis for transportation infrastructure (Renaud 1981). FDI is included here as generally asserted as having a strong relation to development in China (Xue and Yang 1995; Luo 2008; Anderson et al. 2015). Spending variables are included to measure different policy areas affecting urban development in the areas of education, environment, social welfare, and science/technology (Lin et al. 2004) to measure their respective impacts. Tourism, foreign and domestic, was found to have a big role in Zhang (2005), measuring some cultural industry effects, and are included here. Finally, dummy variables for the dynamic Eastern Coastal Economic Zone and the lagging underdeveloped Western Region are included to capture their unique dynamics that have frequently been theorised to differentiate them from the central part of the nation.

Regressions

Regressions were estimated for the four models with the results appearing in Table 8.3 and all of the significant results listed in Table 8.4. The model for population density showed significant positive results for science and technology at the 0.001 level, as well as environment and east at the 0.01 level, and university students and domestic tourists at the 0.05 level. Movie theatres and education had significant negative results, both at the 0.001 level (Table 8.4). The model with per capita GDP as the dependent variable produced significant positive results for university students, RSI, green space, road area, FDI, education, and domestic tourists at the 0.001 level, as well as movie theatres at the 0.01 level. Unemployment and foreign tourists had significant negative

Table 8.3 Regression results of random effects GLS regression with models for population density, per capita GDP, average annual pay, and urbanisation level as dependent variables

Independent variable	*Population density*		*Per capita GDP*		*Average annual pay*		*Urbanisation level*	
	Coef.	*p > z*	*Coef.*	*p > z*	*Coef.*	*p > z*	*Coef.*	*p > z*
Unemployment	1.04	0.592	−1352	0.000	−976	0.000	−0.742	0.000
University students	466	0.026	184980	0.000	66685	0.000	123	0.000
RSI	1.27	0.071	361	0.001	321	0.000	0.384	0.000
RTI	0.417	0.604	45.0	0.720	274	0.000	0.356	0.000
Green space	0.253	0.080	128	0.000	34.0	0.005	0.0351	0.001
Movie theatre	−790	0.000	56849	0.003	1977	0.862	−19.1	0.039
Road area	−0.996	0.062	811	0.000	107	0.041	0.132	0.001
FDI	0.020	0.136	22.6	0.000	−0.281	0.841	0.00641	0.000
Public transport	−54.9	0.975	319218	0.297	595387	0.002	−208	0.122
Taxis	−7400	0.365	−1348842	0.153	−2893558	0.000	2432	0.000
Education	−0.025	0.000	17.6	0.000	11.8	0.000	0.00125	0.007
Social welfare	−0.00149	0.868	−2.13	0.171	3.88	0.000	0.00150	0.030
Science/Technology	0.228	0.000	−2.69	0.253	−3.37	0.013	−0.00399	0.000
Pollution	−192	0.378	16739	0.579	1780	0.916	94.7	0.000
Environment	0.0229	0.002	−1.00	0.418	1.65	0.028	0.00138	0.014
Domestic tourists	1.92	0.033	503	0.001	983	0.000	0.373	0.000
Foreign tourists	−9.26	0.336	−11785	0.000	−9181	0.000	−3.23	0.000
East	203	0.006	4.10	0.999	−56.9	0.960	4.03	0.055
West	−118	0.105	−180	0.937	1485	0.170	1.11	0.588
Cons	389	0.000	−16780	0.066	−7771	0.138	7.87	0.096
Overall R-squared	0.430		0.867		0.773		0.740	

results at the 0.001 level (Table 8.4). The model for average annual pay was positive and significant for university students, RSI, RTI, education, social welfare, and domestic tourists at the 0.001 level, and for green space and public transport at the 0.01 level, and for road area and environment at the 0.05 level. Unemployment, taxis, and foreign tourists had significant negative relationships at the 0.001 level, and science and technology did as well at the 0.01 level (Table 8.4). Finally, the regression for urbanisation level showed positive and significant results for university students, RSI, RTI, public green space, FDI, taxis, pollution, and domestic tourists at the 0.001 level, while education and environment were significant at the 0.01 level, and social

Table 8.4 Statistically significant regression results

Independent variable	*Population density*	*Per capita GDP*	*Average annual pay*	*Urbanisation level*
	Coef.	*Coef.*	*Coef.*	*Coef.*
Unemployment		−1352***	−976***	−0.742***
University students	466*	184980***	66685***	123***
RSI		361**	321***	0.384***
RTI			274***	0.356***
Green space		128***	34.0**	0.0351**
Movie theatre	−790***	56849**		−19.1*
Road area		811***	107*	0.132**
FDI		22.6***		0.00641***
Public transport			595387**	
Taxis			−2893558***	2432***
Education	−0.025***	17.6***	11.8***	0.00125**
Social welfare			3.88***	0.00150*
Science/ Technology	0.228***			−0.00399***
Pollution				94.7***
Environment	0.0229**		1.65*	0.00138*
Domestic tourists		503**	983***	0.373***
Foreign tourists		−11785***	−9181***	−3.23***
East	203**			
Cons	389***			

***Significant at the 0.001 level
**Significant at the 0.01 level
*Significant at the 0.05 level

welfare at the 0.05 level. Unemployment, science and technology, and foreign tourists were significant and negatively correlated at the 0.001 level, and movie theatres was a negative correlation at the 0.05 level (Table 8.4).

The signs on most of the significant variables were positive, meaning that they increased in proportion to the dependent variable. The results were generally consistent across the dependent variables, though there were some notable differences. There was a contrast between negative results for unemployment for all dependent variables except population density. Population density and urbanisation level both had a negative result for movie theatres. Only population density failed to have a significant positive relationship with road area. Only urbanisation level had a positive result for taxis. Finally, urbanisation level was the only measure to have a positive correlation with pollution.

Measures and Drivers of Urban Development in China

The regression results were highly consistent for the four dependent variables and were reasonable in general, with some exceptions noted above and discussed below. All four models had high r squared values, suggesting good fit. The signs were generally going in the same direction from model to model, even for variables that were not significant, again with noteworthy exceptions. Urbanisation level had 16 significant variables, average annual pay had 14, per capita GDP had 10 and population density had only 7.

On almost every score, urbanisation level, average annual pay, and per capita GDP performed better than population density as measures of urban development. Not only did the former have more significant results, they had higher r squared values (although urbanisation level was between population density and average annual pay, and per capita GDP), and were more closely related to each other, though population density had a stronger relationship to urbanisation level (Table 8.1).

On a practical level, both population density and urbanisation level involve measures of population in China where the definition and measurement of population involves multiple steps. First, the household registration is consulted. Next, migrants not living at the local registered address must be subtracted from the registered population. Finally, unauthorised migrants living in the local jurisdiction must be added in.

Although this is fairly straightforward, it is not clear that the counting of out- and in-migrants is consistent and done to the same standard across jurisdictions. It may be no more than an estimate at this time in some cases (Lee et al. 2013; Wang 2015). This means that resident population statistics are very unreliable for the time being. In addition, there may even be incentives for inaccurate counts, as where services are based on registered population.

Both population density and urbanisation level are measures of population and not of the living condition of the population or of the city itself. There may be a good rationale for using population concentrations as a measure of urban development in an underdeveloped nation, such as Bangladesh where population equals urbanisation equals urban development (Mehedi and Lee 2014). In the case of Bangladesh, cities are by definition dense and the denser places are the more urban and more developed they become. This rationale does not make as much sense in China, which has surpassed 50% urbanisation. Here, more people are crowded into an already urban space, a situation which does not make it more urban or more developed.

The negative relationship between movie theatre and population density and urbanisation level for example, is opposite to the result for average annual income. This result suggests that more people in one place in China makes it *less* likely for there to be movie theaters, suggesting that population density or urbanisation does not really indicate the quality or developmental level of a concentrated population. This positive relationship between unemployment and population density also emphasises that tightly clustered groups of people in China are not necessarily better off. In the cases studied here, population density does not admit the possibility that there may be an ideal maximum density beyond which economic development declines. The historical experience of pseudo-urbanisation and crammed slums suggests that density levels that harm development need to be considered (Lee et al. 2012).

Urbanisation level does not have a density limit issue, though it does share a lack of concern for quality of social and economic development. It may make sense when a nation is underdeveloped to focus on urbanisation, as urbanised areas are likely to be more developed. However, China has passed the point where this is automatically the case. Chinese cities are increasing in variety as China becomes urbanised (Lee et al. 2013; Wang and Anderson 2016), meaning that there is likely to be more variation in urban development among urban areas, not some uniform state of development following complete urbanisation. Further, this study showed that urbanisation level was the only variable with a positive and significant correlation with pollution. This study argues that emphasis on improving the economic and social development level of cities will add more to the well-being of Chinese than will a focus on continuing to move more people into cities that are often already crowded. The People's Republic of China should be viewed and analysed as more of a mature but uneven economy that still requires a broad variety of analytical tools. The increasing emphasis on small and medium city development in the recent five-year plans is a good sign moving in this direction but, without an emphasis on economic opportunity and quality of life, small and medium cities will develop to share the same problems of pollution and congestion typical of big cities.

Moving to the independent variables, only three (university students, education, and domestic tourists) were significant among all of the dependent variables. The significance of university students may lend some support to the creative class explanation (Florida 2002, 2007), though it may just add support for the importance of education in human capital formation. At this time, the authors have been searching for a different variable to represent the construct of 'creative class' and have had to settle repeatedly for university students as a weak proxy. On the other hand, the results for local education expenditure were negative for population density but positive for the other variables studied, implying that simply measuring greater concentrations of people is not the best way to improve urban development outcomes in relation to education in China.

Previous effects of domestic, but not foreign, tourism were even more strongly reinforced, with the domestic tourist variable positive and significant for all dependent variables except for population density (Lee et al. 2013). This follows the stress that Clark (2004) placed on tourism as one of the top industries in the world. These results suggest that tourism promotion is playing an increasingly effective role in contributing to urban development. The effect of tourism is not limited to Beijing and a few other major sites but includes a robust domestic tourist trade that is related to development across a range of Chinese cities. In contrast, foreign tourism was negative for every dependent variable except for population density. Coupled with the strong domestic tourism results, this suggests a strong tourism industry in China that is not very oriented towards foreign tourists, who have different demands from the domestic market.

Unemployment was negatively associated with all dependent variables, except for population density, suggesting that more economic development comes with more employment opportunity (while dense concentrations of people are not necessarily centers of jobs). The economic variables measuring the level of secondary and tertiary economic activity relative to GDP (RSI, RTI) were positive across all dependent variables, though not significant for population density (or for per capita GDP in the case of RTI), reasonably suggesting that continued manufacturing and industrial development as well as services and the post-industrial economy continue to be paths to urban development in China, a major argument of Wang (2015).

Social welfare was positive with the two variables (annual income and urbanisation level) where it was significant. These suggest that cities are responding to demands of citizens for more well-being as incomes rise. On the other hand, science and technology expenditures were significant for three variables but negative for two of them (annual income and urbanisation level). This may function more as an investment fixed to population (increasing with density) more than associated with generating wealth or urbanisation, meaning it could decline in relative terms as incomes and urbanisation increase.

Infrastructure effects were supported with the road area in all of the models but population density. However, public transport only related to annual income, though taxis were negatively related to annual income, suggesting that less economically developed cities need more taxis to compensate for a weaker transportation infrastructure. Taxis were also positively related to urbanisation level.

Studies have frequently mentioned the importance of FDI to development in China (Anderson et al. 2015) but there were significant results only for per capita GDP and urbanisation level, offering only limited support for this common proposition. The dummy variables for the dynamic Eastern Coastal Economic Zone and the lagging underdeveloped Western Region did not have the expected effects. West had no significant relationships and East was only related to Population Density.

Conclusion

Population density is not as useful a measure of urban development in China in the way that it is in less developed nations where greater concentrations of people are more urban and more developed. Meanwhile, though urbanisation level is still a good measure and had the highest number of significant results in this study, China has become a majority urban nation so its usefulness is becoming limited as other studies have had cities that had a 100% urbanisation level, which will happen to more Chinese cities over time. Moreover, urbanisation level had a positive relationship with Pollution and a negative relationship with Movie Theatre. This suggests a need to start paying more attention to the positive development of cities for the quality of life of residents. GDP and average annual pay are generally available and do not seem to be linked to these negative factors although they have most of the same positive relationships as urbanisation level. A policy focus on improving urban economic development through increasing GDP and income will likely also promote urbanisation, developing cities but also paying more attention to resident welfare.

Both industrial and post-industrial paths to development continue to function and the development of transportation infrastructure can support this process. Cultural industry development in the form of continued tourism development oriented towards the domestic market that does not sacrifice other features of the city can develop and enhance features as suggested by amenity/scenes studies to develop the tourism market to benefit local residents, as well as visitors. Other policies that increase development include spending on education, especially higher education for human capital formation and to attract the creative class. Pollution continues to be an issue, with it even correlated to urbanisation level, while less pollution appears to be related to development, making environmental spending advisable. Policy makers can also shift from propagating heavily-polluting industries for development and shift to cleaner development and to cleaning up the pollution already in the environment.

The results regarding FDI appear to fly in the face of research into the factor's importance for Chinese development, though it was associated with GDP and urbanisation level. This may mean that more needs to be done to attract foreign investment to more parts of China and not just concentrate it on the eastern seaboard, or it may mean that FDI has a less important effect overall. Perhaps there just needs to be a lot more of it. More work should be done to clarify this important factor.

China has been undergoing a very rapid phase of development that has left it with striking accomplishments alongside the usual problems of urbanisation, including congestion, pollution, and loss of natural resources. These issues seem to be coming to a head at the same time as China is moving into its "new normal." Other nations, such as South Korea, have made the transition from a period of rapid development to a model of more balanced growth in a more livable environment. More attention to urban development by improving quality of life within cities (measured by GDP and income) is more desirable than emphasising moving more people into cities (measured by population density) or expanding cities (measured by urbanisation level). China scholars and Chinese policymakers have more knowledge than ever to contribute to and accelerate this process. Shifting to paying more attention to quality of urban life in promoting urbanisation and urban economic development will play a critical role.

References

Anderson, C., Lee, J. Y., & Wang, B. (2014, May 24). *What drives urban development in China?* Paper presented at Korean Association for Policy Studies, Seoul National University.

Anderson, C., Lee, J. Y., & Wang, B. (2015). Determinants of foreign direct investment in Chinese cities: Evidence from Liaoning province. *Korean Journal of Local Government & Administration Studies, 29*(4), 409–421.

Bin, H. U. (2003). Research on connotation of city network developing model in Changjiang Delta Region. *China Industrial Economy, 10*, 004.

Bluestone, B., Stevenson, M. H., & Williams, R. (2008). *The urban experience: Economics, society, and public policy.* New York: Oxford University Press.

Bruegmann, R. (2005). *Sprawl: A compact history.* Chicago: University of Chicago Press.

Castells, M. (1996). *The information age: Economy, society and culture, vol. i: The rise of the network society.* Oxford: Blackwell Publishers.

Clark, T. N. (2004). *The city as an entertainment machine.* Amsterdam: Elsevier.

Clark, T. N., Anderson, C., Byun M., Jang, W., Kim, S., Yoshiaki, K., Lee, J. Y., Navarro, C. J., Silver, D., & Wu, D. (2014). Karaoke together vs. bowling alone: Scenes illuminate how western rules can be transformed to drive development and democracy. In T. N. Clark (Ed.), *Can Tocqueville karaoke? global contrasts of civic participation, the arts and development* (pp. 15–30). Howard House, UK: Emerald.

Dai, H. Z. (2001). Study on the type of urban scale distribution and it's developing mechanism in China. *Human Geography, 16*(5), 40–43, 57.

Deng, C. H., & Li, G. P. (2012). Research on the impact of information upon urbanization: Positive analysis based on provincial panel data. *Journal of Xian University of Technology, 28*(1), 121–125.

Florida, R. (2002). *The rise of the creative class.* New York: Basic Books/Perseus.

Florida, R. (2007). *The flight of the creative class*. New York: Harper Collins.

Han, R. B., & Wang, L. N. (2013). Challenges and opportunities facing China's urban development in the new era. *China Perspectives, 2*, 15–27.

Hong, Y., Shen, K., & He, X. (2000). Study on the transformation of the economic growth mode. *Jiang Su Social Science, 2*, 71–79.

Jacobs, J. (1969). *The economy of cities*. New York: Random House.

Ladd, H. F. (1992). Population growth, density and the costs of providing public services. *Urban Studies, 29*(2), 273–295.

Lee, J. Y. (1997). Jutaeggagyeoge michineun yeonghyangyoinbunseog. *Hangughaengjeongnonjib, 9*(2), 337–351.

Lee, J. Y. (2012). Urban sprawl index and the factors affecting it: A comparison of Korea and China. *Hangug Geobeoneonseuhaghoibo, 19*(3), 67–86.

Lee, J. Y., & Wang, B. (2013, April, 19). *Impact of policy on urbanisation in China*. Paper presented at Korean Association for Policy Studies Conference at Myongji University, Seoul.

Lee, J. Y., Tao, J. L., & Anderson, C. D. (2012). *Urban administration: Issues and practices*. Seoul: Daeyong Moonhwasa.

Lee, J. Y., Anderson, C., & Wang, B. (2013, December 9). *Drivers of urban development in China: Measuring development and comparing models*. Paper presented at Public Policy in the Asian Century, Melbourne School of Government, The University of Melbourne.

Lee, J. Y., Anderson, C., & Wang, B. (2015, July 17). What determines cultural expenditures in local Chinese government in Liaoning? KAPA International Conference, Cheonan.

Li, M. (2011). The rise of the working class and the future of the Chinese revolution. *Monthly Review, 63*(2), 38–51.

Lin, L. (1995). *Urbanisation and economic development*. Wuhan: Hubei People's Publishing House.

Lin, Y., Hu, X., Wu, M. C., & Shen, Y. L. (2004). Comparative studies on science and technology competitiveness of 18 cities of China. *Science & Technology and Economy, 17*(3), 7–10.

Lucas, R. E. (1988). On the mechanics of economic development. *Journal of Monetary Economics, 22*, 3–42.

Luo, Q. (2008). Effect of FDI on urbanisation of China. *Research on Development, 4*, 19–23.

Mehedi, H., & Lee, J. Y. (2014). What affects urban development in Bangladesh? *Korean Journal of Local Government and Administration Studies, 28*(2), 1–19.

Meng, X. (2006, May). Urbanisation procession study-economic analysis on urban, urban group's development and the affecting factors based on space-time background. Ph.D. Dissertation, Beijing Normal University Institute of Economics and Business Administration.

OECD. (2015). National accounts at a glance. Retrieved from http://www.oecd-ilibrary.org/economics/ national-accounts-at-a-glance_22200444.

Renaud, B. (1981). *National urbanisation policy in developing countries*. Oxford: Oxford University Press.

Roh, J. Y., & Lee, J. Y. (2013). Urban industrial structure and its impact on development: The case of Incheon. *Journal of Korean Policy Studies., 13*(4), 21–35.

Schultz, T. W. (1990). *Human capital investment and urban competitiveness*. Beijing: Beijing Economic College Press.

Silver, D., Clark, T. N., & Rothfield, L. (2006). A theory of scenes. Available from http://sites.google.com/site/tncresearch/atheoryofscenes.

Small, K. A. (2002). Chinese urban development: Introduction. *Urban Studies, 39*(12), 2159–2162.

Song, S. F., & Zhang, K. H. (2002). Urbanisation and city size distribution in China. *Urban Studies, 39*(12), 2317–2327.

Tiebout, C. M. (1956). A pure theory of local expenditures. *Journal of Political Economy, 64*(5), 416–424.

Wang, B. (2015, December). *Three faces of urban development in China: State, market, and reform*. Ph.D. Dissertation, Incheon National University, Department of Public Administration.

Wang, B., & Anderson, C. (2016). The cultural contents industry in the development of Dalian. *Asian Journal of Cultural Policy, 3*(1), 18–31.

Wang, J. H. (2003, April). Research on social security system of urban-rural under population flow conditions–an empirical analysis of the floating population of Shanghai. Ph.D. Dissertation, Fudan University Institute of Population, Resources and Environmental Economics.

Wu, F. (2008). China's great transformation: Neoliberalization as establishing a market Society. *Geoforum*, 39, 1093–1096.

Wu, F. (2012, February 6). Urbanisation and its concerns. *China Daily*, 9.

Xue, F., & Yang, C. (1995). Urbanisation affected by foreign capital–case of Pearl River Delta of China. *City Planning Review, 6*, 21–27.

Zhang, H. C. (2005). Industrial factors promoting the competitiveness of city. *Commercial Economy Studies, 12*, 65–68.

Zhao, Z. J. (2008). The evidential analysis about the promoted effect to scientific and technical investment on GDP in China. *Mathematics in Economics, 25*(1), 58–63.

Zuo, X. G., & Li, Z. C. (2003). Analysis of the relationship between the development level of the third industry and per capita GDP and the proportion of agricultural population. *Statistics and Decision, 1*, 50–51.

CHAPTER 9

Public Sector Reform and National Development in East and Southeast Asia: Specificity and Commonality

Mark Turner

Introduction

From the first development decade of the 1960s, public sector reform has been a constant pursuit of Asian governments. Initially, it focused on the expansion of the scope of government and the number of public servants as the state filled functional gaps left by the departing colonial powers, or simply attended to the increasing demands of society on modern government. Much experimentation followed with a variety of efforts to improve performance through initiatives in areas such as restructuring, human resource management, and training and development. This was the era of big government when the state not only steered but also took on much of the rowing. Changes were incremental and non-threatening to public services. Some planned changes had the desired effect in states that were serious about reform but in many cases the initiatives failed to make the anticipated impact. This led to

M. Turner (✉)
School of Business, UNSW Canberra, Canberra, Australia
e-mail: mark.turner@canberra.edu.au

S. Bice et al. (eds.), *Public Policy in the 'Asian Century'*, International Series on Public Policy, https://doi.org/10.1057/978-1-137-60252-7_9

disappointment with big government and coincided with the rise of neoliberal ideologies that argued for the state to get out of business, to become lean and cut back on expenditure. Many new reform initiatives of a neoliberal nature were introduced by governments or imported by international financial institutions (IFIs) and other aid agencies. Changes were more significant although state institutions proved to be remarkably resilient to attempts to make radical transformations. But the general point is that since the beginning of the 1960s, constant attention has been paid to public sector reform in Asia and while the resources and enthusiasm devoted to it have varied over the decades, in every Asian country there has always been some reform activity.

Despite this common interest in public sector reform, Asia-Pacific states have often shown divergence in their approaches to public sector change, which is not surprising given the diversity of political economies, social conditions and cultures across the vast and highly populous region. Some of this diversity will be highlighted in this paper to show the need to understand the 'specificity' of public sector reform in countries that have different histories, institutional structures, levels of economic development, political regimes and cultures (Caiden and Sundaram 2004). These contexts need to be taken into account when trying to make sense of the multiple reform trajectories found in Asia. But one should not go too far down the road of exceptionalism as there are some important shared experiences and variations on common themes. Several of these themes are pursued in this chapter.

In the first section, the meaning of 'public sector' reform is explored. Then, commonalities and divergences evident in Southeast Asia are illustrated through a brief environmental scan of economy, polity and society in just one region of the 'Asian continent'. This is followed by observations on the persistency of bureaucracy in Asia and the long roots of multiple bureaucratic traditions. The next section deals with the relationship between policy transfer and public sector reform to illustrate how longstanding interest in such transfer is invariably complemented by selectivity in choice of what to transfer and local engineering to suit local circumstances. The widespread problems of accountability and corruption are dealt with next but empirical evidence demonstrates that there is wide variation from almost 'squeaky clean' to the worst in the world as far as corruption goes. Finally, we deal with government's numerous experiments with decentralisation. All are interested in re-engineering central-local relations but there are many ways in which this interest has been manifested—from radical decentralisation to lengthy conversations producing little action.

What is Public Sector Reform?

A first step in exploring public sector reform in East and Southeast Asia is to clarify what is meant by the term. Public sector reform, also often used interchangeably with public management reform, 'consists of deliberate changes to the structures and processes of public sector organizations with the objective of getting them (in some sense) to run better' (Pollitt and Bouckaert 2004, p. 8). The changes could be in structure such as splitting large organisations into smaller ones or devolving power and finance to local governments. Other changes might focus on the processes used to perform the tasks of public management such as speeding up the issue of licenses for setting up businesses, introducing IT solutions to budgeting or setting quality standards for health providers. There are also changes in human resource management (HRM), the systems used to recruit, promote, discipline, train, measure performance and reward employees of public organisations. Reforms can be to specific organisations or system-wide. They can be focused on one activity or cover multiple items across structure, process and HRM. Different combinations of measures will be used by governments according to their perceived needs and capacities, and the make up of these measures will vary over time. However, a narrative of improved government performance in terms of efficiency, effectiveness and quality is invariably used to justify and legitimate the reforms although this narrative may disguise political and ideological motives such as a preference for market solutions to policy problems, seeking legitimacy or a method of attracting votes (De Guzman and Reforma 1992).

Public sector reform is not new to East and Southeast Asia although some of the drivers of contemporary reform were much less evident in the early development decades of the 1960s–1980s. Now, there is frequently a message of 'urgency' from leaders about the need for reform due to the 'uncertainties and rapid changes taking place in the organizational environment' (Turner et al. 1997, p. 106). In East and Southeast Asia, leaders see public sector reform as making an important contribution to enhancing international competitiveness, a major policy goal in all the region's countries, and achieving the Millennium Development Goals and now the Sustainable Development Goals (SDGs).

Promoting good governance and satisfying citizens' demands for services provide additional motive force for public sector reform. Also, budgetary constraints place limits on government activities and encourage the search for efficiency with effectiveness.

Finally, when defining public sector reform care must be taken to avoid an exclusive focus on instrumental rationality that is only concerned with precisely calculated technical solutions for improving government operations. There is certainly a rational aspect to designing reforms but there is also a strong political component relating to interactions among stakeholders. The latter influence what changes are selected, how they are implemented, what resources are allocated and what priority is given. There will always be stakeholders who oppose reforms and will take steps to prevent or dilute them. As Caiden (1969, p. 8) astutely noted of public management reform almost half a century ago, it is 'an artificial inducement of administrative transformation against resistance'. This resistance may explain the poor performance of public service reform initiatives funded by donors (DFID 2013; IEG 2008).

Asian Diversity: Comparing the Countries of Southeast Asia

One of the arguments of this paper is that that there is a great deal that is specific to each country's public sector reform experience and that this is in large part explained by the diversity of the environments in which reform takes place. This diversity provides opportunities or challenges for particular reform prescriptions. It also indicates the inappropriateness or unacceptability of particular change initiatives.

In one short chapter it is impossible to deal with all the countries of East and Southeast Asia to demonstrate the enormous diversity that confronts the analyst and leads to many contrasting experiences in public sector reform. However, we can compromise and focus on Southeast Asia to illustrate the perils of generalisation among so many substantial differences. Such differences become even greater if East, South and Central Asia are added to the mix.

Geographical proximity is what binds Southeast Asia rather than similarity in politics, culture, demography and economy. This is clearly seen in the countries of the Association of South East Asian Nations (ASEAN), the longstanding regional grouping that has assiduously pursued a policy of non-intervention in the affairs of fellow members.

The economies of Southeast Asia span a wide range of the World Bank classification, from 'high income' to 'lower middle income' (see Table 9.1), with three countries Laos, Cambodia and Myanmar only recently graduating from the 'low income' to 'lower middle income' ranks. This variation is reflected in greatly contrasting Gross National Incomes (GNIs) per capita. On the high end is Singapore with US$52,100 in 2015 while at the low end is Cambodia, with a GNI of US$1,070.

The size of absolute GNI also varies considerably between countries especially because of great population differences. At one extreme is Indonesia, the fourth most populous country in the world, with 258 million people in 2015 while at the other is Brunei with a mere 423,000. There are great contrasts in between with the city state of Singapore housing only 5.5 million persons and Lao PDR with 6.8 million as compared to the Philippines with 101 million and Vietnam with 91.7 million. Overall there are about 630 million people in the relatively compact geographical area of Southeast Asia.

Despite considerable differences in GNI, in recent years all of the Southeast Asian economies (with the exception of Brunei) have enjoyed substantial and often sustained economic growth. In the period 2010–2014, their average annual rates of GDP growth ranged between 4.4% in Thailand and 8.5% for Lao PDR. Eight countries that accounted for the vast bulk of the region's economic activity had annual average GDP growth rates of above 5.7% between 2010 and 2014 making the region the most economically dynamic in the world.

While economic growth rates point to economic dynamism, global surveys which gauge the ease of doing business or the extent of economic freedoms paint a more mixed picture. Singapore is consistently rated at the top of these tables: first in the World Bank's 2016 *Doing Business* rankings and second in the Heritage Foundation-Wall Street Journal's 2016 *Economic Freedom*. Malaysia and Thailand are moderately well ranked in these global classifications but the other Southeast Asian countries are far behind. For example, Vietnam is ranked 90 out of 189 in *Doing Business*, the Philippines 103 and Indonesia 109 with each one allocated to the 'mostly unfree' category of the *Economic Freedom* ratings. The combination of excellent growth rates with mixed, often poor, rankings in the *Doing Business* and *Economic Freedom* tables suggest that most governments are still heavily engaged in the economy and that the market forces have not been unfettered. Even in top-ranking Singapore,

Table 9.1 Selected economic indicators for Southeast Asia

Country	*Population 2015*	*World Bank economy type 2015*	*GNI per capita (Atlas method current US$) 2015*	*GDP growth (annual average % 2010–2014)*	*Doing business ranking (189) 2016*	*Economic freedom 2016*	*Poverty head-count ratio at national poverty lines % of population*
Brunei	423,000	High income	37,300	1.27	84	Moderately free	
Cambodia	15.6 m	Lower middle income	1070	6.95	127	Mostly unfree	17.7
Indonesia	258.0 m	Lower middle income	3440	6.2	109	Mostly unfree	11.3
Lao PDR	8.0 m	Lower middle income	1730	8.5	134	Repressed	23.2
Malaysia	30.3 m	Upper middle income	10,600	5.72	18	Mostly free	0.6
Myanmar	59.0 m	Lower middle income	1280	7.5	167	No record	
Philippines	101.0 m	Lower middle income	3540	6.32	103	Moderately free	25.2
Singapore	5.5 m	High income	52,100	6.92	1	Free	
Thailand	68.0 m	Upper middle income	5,620	4.35	49	Moderately free	10.5
Vietnam	91.7 m	Lower middle income	1980	5.8	90	Mostly unfree	

Source World Bank 2016; Heritage Foundation 2016

there is considerable evidence that the government is an active and substantial player in the economy, especially through its government-linked corporations and statutory bodies (Shemirani 2011).

Southeast Asian countries have performed well in terms of improving the overall welfare of their populations. Political legitimacy is often tied to such achievement with governments frequently relying more on their economic performance than on guarantees of political freedoms. Indeed, organised labour is often weak or 'underdeveloped' with governments using a wide range of tactics: corporatist-style co-option, government sponsorship, high levels of regulation and outright repression (Ofreneo and Wad 2010).

But the welfare gains in Southeast Asia have been impressive. Poverty affected 45% of the population of the region in 1990 but had dropped to 14% by 2010. Country performance on poverty reduction has been varied as can be seen in Table 9.2. Myanmar, Lao PDR, Cambodia and the Philippines still have significant percentages of their populations living in poverty, perhaps surprising for the Philippines, a long-time lower middle income country. Life expectancy has increased everywhere providing clear indication of improved household conditions, nutrition and health services. Overall, unemployment is low with high labour force participation. Gender inequality varies and there has been limited progress in some of the region's countries such as Cambodia and Indonesia which are located in the bottom half of the UNDP gender inequality rankings.

Politically, historically and culturally there are similarities between some nations but more contrasts. This is significant as politics, history and culture provide the context and direction of institutional development which can have profound influence on public sector reform. All except Thailand were colonies but of different imperial powers including Spain, US, Britain, France and the Netherlands. The colonial inheritance can be seen in their institutions such as legal systems and politico-administrative arrangements. All colonies except Brunei received or seized political independence soon after the end of the Second World War starting with the Philippines in 1946 and culminating in Malaysia (then including Singapore) in 1957. The new states installed democratic governmental arrangements of varying types—for example, presidential and parliamentary—largely according to their colonial inheritance. However, many regimes slipped into authoritarianism through military coups, such as Burma and Indonesia in the 1960s, or revolutionary movements, such as Vietnam and Lao PDR in the 1970s.

Other states incorporated authoritarian elements into their democratic practice such as Malaysia and Singapore. The Third Wave of democratisation which commenced in Southeast Asia in 1986 with the overthrow

Table 9.2 Select indicators for politics and culture in Southeast Asia

Country	*Human development index (rank out of 180)*	*Life expectancy at birth 2014 and (1990)*	*Gender inequality index 2014 (rank out of 180)*	*Date of independence*	*Regime type*	*Political rights (Freedom House 2016) 1 most free 7 most unfree*	*Dominant religion*
Brunei	31 (very high)	78 (74)	n/a	1984	Politically closed authoritarian	6 Not free	Islam
Cambodia	143 (medium)	71(55)	104	1954	Hegemonic electoral authoritarian	6 Not free	Therevada Buddhist
Indonesia	110 (medium)	71 (63)	110	1949	Electoral democracy	2 Partly free	Islam
Lao PDR	141 (medium	68 (54)	n/a	1954	Politically closed authoritarian	7 Not free	Therevada Buddhist
Malaysia	62 (high)	75 (71)	42	1957	Competitive authoritarian	4 Partly free	Islam
Myanmar	148 (low)	65 (59)	85	1948	Ambiguous	6 Not free	Therevada Buddhist
Philippines	115 (medium)	69 (65)	89	1946	Electoral democracy	3 Partly free	Christian
Singapore	11 (high)	82 (76)	13	1965 (1957)	Hegemonic electoral authoritarian	4 Partly free	Mixed
Thailand	93 (high)	74 (70)	76	Not colonised	Politically closed authoritarian	6 Not free	Therevada Buddhist
Vietnam	116 (medium)	76 (71)	60	1954	Politically closed authoritarian	7 Not free	

Source UNDP 2016; Diamond 2002; Freedom House 2016

of President Marcos in the Philippines led to a resurgence of democratic practice. However, today no Southeast Asian country can be classified as 'liberal democratic'. Many are what Diamond (2002) describes as 'hybrid regimes' featuring varying mixtures of democratic and authoritarian features. At the democratic end of the regime continuum are the 'electoral democracies' of the Philippines and Indonesia, in the middle the 'competitive authoritarian' and 'hegemonic electoral authoritarian' regimes of Malaysia, Cambodia and Singapore, and at the authoritarian end the 'politically closed authoritarian' regimes of Brunei, Lao PDR, Thailand and Vietnam. The dominance of political regimes with at least some authoritarian characteristics suggests that incumbent parties and governments are keen to maintain their control over society and can intervene in the economy when they so desire.

One final and major aspect of variation among Southeast Asian countries is religion. There are four countries in which the majority of the population follows Therevada Buddhism, three in which Islam is dominant (including Indonesia, the most populous country), one (Philippines) in which Christianity is the major religion and one (Vietnam) where religious beliefs can be described as Confucianism-Taoism-Buddhism. Each religion provides values which strongly influence behaviour and which are used to legitimate power and authority structures. There are also minority groups in most Southeast Asian countries that follow alternate religious beliefs which may form the primary basis of identity. In some cases these identities have been used to mount armed challenges to the state as in Southern Thailand, the Southern Philippines, Aceh and West Papua in Indonesia, and among hill tribes in Myanmar. These internal conflicts have adverse effects on socioeconomic development in the regions concerned and public administration suffers.

The Persistence of Bureaucracy

Bureaucracy has long roots in many Asian societies and 'has been and continues to be a favoured organizational form' (Turner and Halligan 1999, 131). But, its origins are diverse, temporally differentiated and its manifestations vary in character. Thus, Farazmand and Balilaj (2015) have identified six indigenous models of public administration in their historical survey commencing with ancient Persia and early Iran where they see the first signs of bureaucratic organisation. Gladden (1972) traces Chinese bureaucracy to the Qin dynasty (221–206 B.C.) and dates merit entry and competitive examinations to the Han dynasty (206 B.C.–220 A.D.) while Heady (1984) describes China at around this time as a 'centralized bureaucratic empire' and attributes the 'staying power' of Chinese civilization to bureaucracy. Dreschler (2015) traces the widespread Confucian influence on effective public administration in China from ancient times to the present day and indicates its association with other contemporary national development success stories such as Singapore, Taiwan and South Korea. In Japan, the development of a civil bureaucracy with patrimonial characteristics was the work of the Tokugawa shogunate, that began in 1603 (Gladden 1972). And before European imperialists moved into Southeast Asia, other forms of state organization with bureaucratic features were being introduced into kingdoms and empires based on irrigated rice production (Wertheim 1993). Related structures bearing Chinese Confucian influence also entered into the northern parts of Vietnam. Meanwhile, bureaucratic origins as old as China can be found in the ancient Indian Mauryan Empire while other polities in South Asia subsequently adopted bureaucratic characteristics in their pre-colonial administrations (Eisenstadt 1972). Some features of these early bureaucracies were even continued by the British colonial and independence administrations, such as the overlord or collector which still forms the basis for contemporary field administration in India (Subramanian 1998).

The arrival of imperialist European powers in Asia brought the second wave of bureaucratisation. The areas previously unaffected by bureaucracy were gradually brought under the control of the imported bureaucratic mechanisms of the colonial state. Even those countries that had avoided imperial control, notably Thailand and Japan, also installed Western-style administrative arrangements to improve administrative efficiency and rebuff the attentions of the colonial powers. But the imported administrative structures and processes were not replicas of arrangements at home, but were geared to maintaining control over conquered populations and making the factors of production as easily available as possible to colonial business interests. Only towards the end of the colonial period were there 'belated efforts to extend the benefits of 'development' to native populations' (Turner and Halligan 1999, p. 132).

The postcolonial years in Asia were marked by the entrenchment and massive expansion of bureaucracy in both democracies and one-party states. It was widely viewed as the means to achieve the prime state objective of development. The state was not perceived as simply facilitating economic development by the private sector even in democracies. Rather, it assumed the leading role and was expected to both guide and participate in socioeconomic development. Such expectations of the state's prominent role in development had their antecedents in both pre-colonial and colonial bureaucratic forms. This gave rise to depictions of dynamic Asian states as 'developmental' (Johnson 1982), 'governed markets' (Wade 1990) and 'plan rationalism' (Henderson 2011) all of which indicated that 'state and market have always advanced in a fused fashion' (Cheung 2013, p. 251).

While the classic versions of these state-market arrangements have modified over time, plenty of examples of state intervention in the economy are still much in evidence today (Turner et al. 2013). The organisations of the state which have orchestrated the dynamic economic growth and welfare gains have often been bureaucratic in character. There has been a fondness among elite Asian public servants for the Weberian ideal type as a vehicle for government action as they could identify with its dimensions, even if reality was somewhat different. The administrative elite could engage in incremental change to fine tune their public sector organisations, often without challenging core elements. Even where public administration reform has been most evident, such as in South Korea, it is apparent that embedded indigenous models of bureaucracy have mediated reform especially involving policy transfer from the West (Im et al. 2013).

So what does public administration look like today after years of reform? As demonstrated in this volume and elsewhere, there is no one Asian public administration. There are multiple origins and trajectories and highly varied environments in which countries' public sector organisations operate. However, it is still possible to make some general points that may help to distinguish Asian public administration from Western theory and practice, with which it is so often unfortunately and ethnocentrically compared.

First, there is a preference for hierarchy. Delayering by reducing the number of levels in hierarchies has not been welcomed in Asian bureaucracies. Where there has been experimentation with such Western imports there has been resistance and disappointing results. Asian societies are generally 'high power distance' meaning that the less powerful defer to those in higher positions and see such behaviour as normal (Hofstede 1980; Blunt and Turner 2005). This aligns with the views of proponents of Asian values but clashes with those who see such Asian values as devices to shore up authoritarianism (Mahubani 2004; Milner 2004). However, this latter view ignores or perhaps downplays the historical legacy of Asian civilizations and seems to impose a Western frame of good governance and liberal democracy on Asian societies. The preference for hierarchy can also lead to risk avoidance especially at lower levels in the hierarchy with decision-making always being passed up the line to senior bureaucrats. This emphasises the concentration of power and authority in the higher ranks and also discourages innovation in public organisations where conformity is valued and commitment is oriented to maintaining one's employment in that organisation.

Second, and related to hierarchy, there is still a strong preference for a clear division of labour as manifested in position descriptions and charts of structures with neatly arranged boxes. But it is perhaps between organisational units that the division of labour is most clearly seen. Ministries, departments and other divisions demarcate their functional territories and defend them against intruders, thus making whole-of-government approaches far more challenging and less appealing than in the West. Horizontal communication is often for upper level public servants only.

Third, there is still a strong orientation to process as manifested in reliance on formal rules to guide behaviour. Streamlining has certainly been a policy choice for many years but has often encountered opposition, especially in implementation. The attachment to process is also linked to risk aversion, hierarchy and preference for the status quo. Fourth, all public services claim to practice merit-based employment in recruitment and promotion. There are exams, competency tests, specific training for particular levels and all the formal organisational paraphernalia that goes with merit-based employment. However, seniority still appears to be important for career advancement while patronage networks and loyalty may also influence job prospects. In many bureaucracies, opportunities for moving between ministries and departments may be severely limited and little practiced.

Fourth, the division between politics and administration is far more blurred in Asia than in Western countries and the Weberian ideal. The relative power of bureaucrats may vary between different countries and at different times but they are expected to be engaged in a joint venture with the political leaders. If they work together for national development and public sector reform they make a formidable team for change, while somewhat paradoxically defending the status quo and stability in their government organisations. However, the networks binding political and administrative leaders may also be mobilised against reform that they judge to be not in their best interests.

Fifth, there is a strong pragmatism among senior public servants. This is expressed in seeking accommodation with political leaders and choosing reforms originating in the West that might have chances of success on foreign soil. Pragmatism is also evident in building networks of support both within and outside of their organisations that will secure and sustain their positions of authority. The public service leaders will claim adherence to ideology when necessary but are also willing to make decisions in which national and organisational interests take precedence. The reformers are flexible as described in China where they allegedly have 'tried to embrace Lenin, Confucius, Weber and Thatcher all at the same time' (Cheung 2012, 276).

Sixth, certain values appear to be more deeply embedded in Asian bureaucracies than in the West. Prominent among these is loyalty. Although partially eroded through downsizing (generally on a modest level in Asia despite the rhetoric) loyalty is the cement of the Asian bureaucracy. It often operates through hierarchical networks that bind members of the organisation and involves reciprocity. The strong are expected to look after the weak and in return the weak give their unconditional support. Such loyalty can be expressed in a variety of behaviours ranging from predatory patron-client activities through to high levels of commitment to the organisation. Loyalty can also be demanded from political parties. This is especially the case in one-party states where deviation from the party line can be a risky business.

What has been erected so far is a model containing some of the common features of Asian public administration with some indication of where the features came from and how they fit together. However, two major elements are missing. These are the variations that are found in public administration across Asia and the nature and content of reforms that have taken place. In the space of a short paper like this, it is impossible to provide a comprehensive account of these phenomena across multiple countries. Thus, the focus is narrowed to three representative items which will provide insight into the processes at work in Asian public sector reform and the paradoxes and differences that occur. The first item deals with change by looking especially at New Public Management (NPM) while the second examines the issue of accountability and corruption. The third deals with territorial decentralisation.

Policy Transfer and Public Sector Reform in Asia

Asia has a long history of importing ideas and practices of public administration from Western countries (Weidner 1970; Esman 1972; EROPA various years). These innovations in management include a wide range of items such as performance management systems, IT-assisted budget processes, organisations with new functions (e.g., Ombudsman), human resource management (HRM) practices and many more. They have been viewed by leaders in Asia as new and potentially useful sources of thinking and practice in public administration. These managerial innovations have been acquired by Asian leaders as vehicles for giving momentum to modernisation and development through 'world class' public sector management. Western governments and academics in concert with IFIs have greatly assisted in this one-way flow of administrative solutions and have been complicit in depicting Asian public administration as a problem. As Cheung (2013, p. 252) has observed, the West has begrudgingly acknowledged '*economic* Asia' but '*political* Asia' is still characterised as a 'backwater', and while there is little appreciation of '*cultural* Asia'. Asia has been perceived as inferior and therefore a natural recipient of policy transfer. It is a situation in which Western academics, politicians and public sector managers have experienced difficulty or perhaps demonstrated myopia when trying 'to understand Asia within its own right and within its own history and civilization' (Cheung 2013, p. 250; Dreschler 2015).

Close scrutiny of Asian public administration's relationship with the West reveals a longstanding pattern. Governments in Asia seek knowledge of Western practices and innovations in public administration. They consider the appropriateness of these items for transfer to their own countries and select those which seem to suit their purposes. The choice will be influenced by evaluation of the contribution an innovation will make to bureaucratic performance, the degree of fit with domestic practice and the amount of opposition that would be generated. Pragmatism rules the process.

With developing countries in Asia, push factors have been very evident with IFIs and other donors vigorously promoting Western public administration solutions to Asian governments although passive resistance has often seen these imported practices failing to make much impression on well-established and self-confident organisations. For the more developed and larger countries of Asia, push factors have been less important but nevertheless still significant. These push factors have come with globalisation and the need to conform to international standards and also apply to the developing countries. However, the richer and larger countries have been able to exercise much more discernment in what they judge to be useful from the West.

To illustrate the points made above, we can consider one of the major policy transfers in recent years for public administration, that of NPM. It became a 'globalised' phenomenon which attracted much interest in Asian countries and which had enthusiastic exporters from its Western countries of origin and IFIs (OECD 1996).

In an earlier article on the transfer of NPM to Southeast Asia, I described it as 'the continuation of a well-established strategy. They [Southeast Asian leaders] select particular items and ignore others' (Turner 2002, p. 1494). During the transfer process items can be modified to varying degrees to suit a country's particular circumstances. These will be determined by a range of contingent environmental factors such as the political system, state strength, economic conditions, institutional history and culture. Similarly, Samaratunge et al. (2008) have stressed the importance of contextual factors in accounting for the relative success of NPM reforms in Singapore and Malaysia and their failure to achieve the desired results in Sri Lanka and Bangladesh. One major reason for differential performance appears to be that somewhat spongy concept of 'political commitment' (Samaratunge and Bennington 2002) but there are other factors which in combination have often led to 'mixed results at best' (Batley and Larbi 2004) or to the achievement of 'little' (Manning 2002; see also Turner et al. 2015).

In the case of Southeast Asia, NPM can be likened to 'a menu of practical initiatives' and the governments of Southeast Asia as the diners (Turner 2002). Among the diners there were various reactions to the menu. Some were 'enthusiastic' and consumed many items, but certainly not all. Singapore and Malaysia fell into this category. Then there were the 'cautious' diners who dabbled in a few of the NPM dishes. The Philippines, Thailand and Indonesia fell into this group. Finally, there were those who were 'unfamiliar' with the menu and were unwilling to sample much of what was on offer. These countries included Vietnam, Laos and Cambodia. Since that time, there has been more experimentation and a wider range of dishes has been tested by the 'cautious' and 'unfamiliar' diners. However, in no case has a Southeast Asian country attempted to replicate the experiences of the NPM originators. They have continued to investigate, observe and consider a range of public administration innovations of Western origin whether NPM or not and make choices based on the contingencies that they bring to the process.

Finally, it is useful to consider the experience of what happens when NPM items are imported into Asian nations and how domestic forces reshape those imports to suit local conditions and local interests. In a comparative study of NPM reforms in the Netherlands and South Korea, Bransden and Kim (2010, p. 368) demonstrate that while the reforms bear some similarities, their significance varies according to state-civil society relations. It is especially in the organisational reforms that this claim is borne out. For South Korea, Bransden and Kim (2010, p. 383) note that the reforms occurred at a specific juncture in the country's history—in the early years of democratisation and under the effects of the Asian Financial Crisis—so 'even minor changes of position represented a major step forward'. While each of these minor changes represented a large step forward in the South Korean context, this was not the case in the Netherlands.

The Korean comparison and the Southeast Asian experiences add weight to Cheung's (2013, p. 253) contention that Asian countries 'may defer to the instrumental superiority of Western institutions and practices', but once these have been mastered, they 'embed such instrumentality within their own indigenous cultures and values' so that what has been imported becomes itself indigenised. This is perhaps the experience of NPM in Asia.

Accountability, Corruption and Public Sector Reform in Asia

Despite receiving plaudits for dynamic economic performance and significant gains in human welfare, Asian countries also attract unwanted attention because of corruption. It is not a new problem but it seems to be one that does not go away. According to the latest 2015 Transparency International Corruption Perceptions Index only three Asian 'countries' appear in the top 20 least corrupt countries/territories of the 167 ranked in the world (see Table 9.3). These are the city state of Singapore (8), the Chinese Special Administrative Region of Hong Kong (18), and Japan (18). But most Asian countries languish in the lower reaches of the corruption league table. There is a very rough correlation with GNI per capita, the richer nations generally performing better than the poorer ones. For example, the three poorest performers in Southeast Asia are the three poorest countries—Myanmar, Cambodia and Laos. The best Southeast Asian performers are the highest in terms of GNI per capita—Singapore, Malaysia and Thailand. However, the correlation between level of perceived corruption and GNI per capita is far from being exact.

The issue of corruption in Asia came to attention during the first development decade (Myrdal 1968) and was noted rather than being seriously addressed. Only in the era of 'good governance' from the mid-1990s did IFIs, other donors and Asian governments themselves begin to take concerted actions on corruption. Strategies were developed to stamp out corrupt practices, agencies were established to specifically combat corruption, the World Bank and other donors began to threaten sanctions if corrupt practices did not cease while citizens, the media and NGOs added pressure on officials to do something about corruption.

One of the problems with corruption is that it often leads to public sector reform failure, however many initiatives are introduced. Corruption is associated with 'a particular constellation of reform inhibitors', prime among which is patronage (Turner 2013, p. 278). Patronage has a long history in rural East and Southeast Asia often binding landlords and tenants (Scott 1972). It builds on the 'personalization of power' (Khan 2005, p. 714) as an asymmetrical dyadic relationship between patron and client governing the flow of resources, exchanges and power relations (Eisenstadt and Roninger 1980). While the patron dominates the relationship, it is not in itself all bad, although it often may be. For example, Grindle (2012) has shown how patrons may enjoy the flexibility of selecting highly capable clients to enable the achievement of organisational goals. But, where government officials use state resources as their own property to draw on as needed then patronage loses its commitment to development goals. It can combine with five other phenomena to produce outcomes that adversely affect public administration reform. The first of these is weak accountability that leads to corruption or at least creates the conditions in which corruption can thrive. Second, if there is a hegemonic political regime (Diamond 2002), then it becomes difficult for domestic political actors to hold governments to account. Third, societal perceptions of the legitimacy of hierarchy and high power distance support the acceptance of patronage which in turn creates an environment for corruption. Fourth, low wages lead officials to seek membership of patronage networks where values of loyalty and trust far outweigh those relating to achievement. Also, low wages may encourage corruption in order to achieve incomes that are considered sufficient. Finally, bureaucratic dysfunctions play into the hands of patronage. Support for cumbersome procedures, lack of structural flexibility and other pathologies allow patronage to thrive as lower-level personnel seek security and upper level officials build their power. Within these patronage networks 'the state is treated as an extension of the property of the leader, and the leader rules with the help of clients who get a pay-off for this support' (Khan 2005, p. 174).

Table 9.3 Corruption perceptions index rankings and scores and GNI per capita for selected Asian countries

Country	*TI corruption perceptions index ranking (out of 167) 2015*	*TI corruption perceptions index score (0 = highly corrupt, 100 = very clean)*	*GNI per capita (Atlas method current US$) 2014*
Singapore	8	85	55,150
Hong Kong	18	75	40,320
Japan	18	75	42,000
Bhutan	27	65	2370
South Korea	37	56	27,090
Malaysia	54	50	11,120
Mongolia	72	39	4280
India	76	38	1570
Thailand	76	38	5780
China	83	37	7400
Sri Lanka	83	37	3440
Indonesia	88	36	3630
Philippines	95	35	3500
Vietnam	112	31	1890
Pakistan	117	30	1400
Timor Leste	123	28	2680
Nepal	130	27	730
Bangladesh	139	25	1080
Laos	139	25	1660
Myanmar	147	22	1270
Cambodia	150	21	1020
North Korea	167	8	n/a

Source Transparency International 2015

This is not to say that public sector reform success is impossible where patronage and corruption are well established. Far from it; in Indonesia there have been significant efficiency and effectiveness gains in important institutions specifically targeted for public sector reform such as the anti-corruption agency and the Ministry of Finance (DFID 2013). Also, in China there has been remarkable sustained economic success and improvements in citizen welfare despite a rising tide of corruption. The improvements are, however, in great part due to constant public administration reforms that have seen the orientation and practice of public administration change significantly since the People's Republic of China was established in 1949 (Xue and Zhang 2012). The bureaucracy has moved from being a Russian-style centralized model to one in which efficiency, flexibility and innovation are valued in the creation of an enabling environment for the economy and public services to citizens.

But citizens and governments are more concerned about corruption in the current era than they were in the past. They have expressed their voices often very loudly and accompanied it with actions. Seven out of ten people in East and Southeast Asian countries believe their government institutions to be corrupt according to the AsiaBarometer survey (Carlson and Turner 2008). Over half believe that politicians stop caring about citizens once elected while six out of ten persons see government officials as paying little attention to what people think. These views are now making themselves felt in democratic politics. Candidates all promise faithfully to stamp out corruption and to provide more responsive services. Entrenched political parties in countries such as Malaysia and Cambodia have seen massive political backlashes over corruption while China's political leaders have made the eradication of corruption a policy priority.

Decentralisation, Specificity and Endogenous Forces in Asian Public Sector Reform

Historically, centralisation has been a dominant theme in Asian state development. Rulers from early Chinese dynasties onwards have engaged in long-term nationalist projects to centralise the states that they have striven to create. Their aim has been to establish control over resources and people to achieve stability and consolidate the authority of the centre. It has often taken much effort to bring the peripheries under the centre's control (and still does today in some countries) but infrastructure development and the attractions of state services have often boosted centralisation projects. In East and Southeast Asia, it seems that it is only when that central control has been established can the matter of decentralisation enter the policy agenda. However, such consideration and subsequent actions have produced contrasting results across the region. We can see the full spectrum of possible central-local arrangements, ranging from marginal delegation of authority to radical experimentation. Such variation reflects the contrasting political economies and other environmental circumstances of the region's countries and illustrates the specificity that can be encountered in Asian public administration reform. A few examples will illustrate this.

Thailand

In all countries of Asia there is a discourse on decentralisation but its content and ensuing state actions have varied. In Thailand, for instance, there has been debate on decentralisation for many years and local government institutions have been in place over many decades. There have even been directives to decentralise in at least one constitution. While there has been some delegation of authority, the reality is of a centralised state where powerholders, including the bureaucratic elite, have prevented the devolution of significant power to local governments (Warr 2014; Chardchawarn 2010). The Thai military, national government politicians and the bureaucratic elite wish to maintain central command while big business is satisfied with this status quo. All 76 provincial governors are appointed by the Ministry of Interior while decentralisation legislation and rules keep local control in central hands.

Cambodia

In Cambodia, in the aftermath of the genocidal Khmer Rouge regime there was no state. All had been destroyed and the new government supported by Vietnam set about building the requisite government institutions. The object was to create a strong central government, a goal that was handed on to the democratically elected government that came to office after the 1991 Paris Peace Agreement. When the Cambodia People's Party (CPP) had established its hegemony in the late 1990s, its leaders decided it was time for decentralisation on a modest scale. The policy combined decentralisation (political) and deconcentration (administrative). Voluntary deconcentration moved at glacial speed largely because central ministries did not want their functions, budgets and powers reduced (Blunt and Turner 2005). On the political front, elected commune councils were a major innovation, the first locally elected governments in Cambodia's history. However, they were allocated very few powers and minimal budgets. What they did do, however, was to facilitate the building of CPP nodes in villages across the land, thus creating a vast network for the central party to monitor and dominate local affairs (Eng 2014). More recent attempts to deepen decentralisation—still on a modest scale—have led to foot-dragging by central ministries and limited power to the people. The new councils at district and provincial level are selected by representatives, not the public at large.

Indonesia

Indonesian decentralisation provides a radical contrast to Thailand and Cambodia. Perhaps the most centralised state in Southeast Asia under the authoritarian rule of President Suharto's New Order, Indonesia was badly affected by the 1997 Asian Financial Crisis. Economic troubles rapidly became political troubles and Suharto was ousted in favour of democracy. In the interim between the departure of Suharto and the election of a new president, legislation was enacted, in 1999, to dramatically change central-local relations. Most service delivery functions and the funds that accompanied them were decentralised to the districts which were placed under the control of elected councils in a multi-party system (Turner et al. 2003). Provinces still retained some functions but had much reduced significance and authority in local affairs. The radical decentralisation move reflected the political economy of archipelagic Indonesia where centrifugal tendencies had been evident from the birth of the republic. Decentralisation was a way of satisfying the local elites who represented these forces. And the choice of districts as the major winners was a deliberate move as they would not attempt to secede whereas provinces might if they were made powerful and wealthy (Turner et al. 2003). However, centrifugal tendencies did continue after implementation of decentralisation in 2001, as manifested in the large number of new districts and provinces that have been created (Fitrani et al. 2005). Further decentralisation is also being enacted with the decision to devolve significant funds and expenditure responsibilities to the village level (Lewis 2015).

China

A final example is China, a country that is more decentralised than most developing and transition states. It is also an authoritarian political system, an arrangement not normally associated with decentralisation. An interesting reform strategy has been the use of fiscal decentralisation as a tool of economic development—'a cornerstone of China's transition to market economy' (Shen et al. 2012) and a way to foster economic development while maintaining political control (Lin and Liu 2000; Landry 2008). Between 1949 and 1979, fiscal centralisation was prevalent with locally collected revenues going to the centre and no local discretionary spending allowed. With the decision to take the market route to development in 1979, there was an 'ad hoc decentralisation' whereby the state allowed increased fiscal autonomy to promote economic development, through 'market-preserving federalism' (Montinola et al. 1995). This had an adverse effect on central government revenue and a game of 'hide and seek' ensued. This involved subnational governments hiding funds and central government seeking them out, a situation that led to a fiscal condition of a 'weak trunk with strong branches' (Shen et al. 2012, p. 9). In 1994, there were major reforms which involved the central state restoring its fiscal authority. The ratio of central government's revenue to total revenue leapt from 22% in 1993 to 56% in 1994 (Shen et al. 2012, p. 16). The situation is one in which expenditure remains decentralised with most service delivery functions devolved to subnational governments and revenue centralisation with provinces reliant on the centre for 67% of their resources (Shen et al. 2012, pp. 17–18; Wu 2012).

These few examples illustrate that decentralisation has been a very specific reaction to domestic conditions. It has been an endogenous affair with governments responding to domestic political forces and interests rather than exogenous ones. IFIs and foreign governments have not been involved in the basic design of decentralisation in Asian countries. Asian governments perceive it to be too important to delegate such decisions as it involves fundamental decisions about the design of the state. IFIs and aid donors have provided technical assistance but have been kept out of determining the structure and basic content of decentralisation arrangements. There has also been precious little policy transfer indicating that central-local relations are determined with reference to domestic considerations. These considerations are specific to each country. Furthermore, in the cases of Indonesia, the Philippines and possibly more Asian countries, local governments can be the sources of innovation in public sector management and governance. This demonstrates that innovation in public sector management in Asia does not necessarily derive from exogenous stimuli.

Conclusion

Public sector reform has been a constant activity for governments in Asia. It has been viewed as important for a variety of reasons including enhancing national competitiveness, saving money, addressing public demands for services, and providing legitimacy for political leaders. The sources of innovation in public service provision have been both endogenous and exogenous. It is, however, the latter that has attracted the most attention. The West has been viewed as the source of new and potentially superior methods in public administration, most recently as seen in the Asian interest in NPM. Western observers have often interpreted this interest as proof of convergence in public administration and the superiority of Western methods of addressing managerial and governance problems (Dreschler and Cheung 2013). However, Asian reality diverges from this view. Asian leaders acknowledge the instrumental value of many Western innovations but this has not meant that they uncritically accept all that emanates from Western countries. Indeed, the history of policy transfer has typically involved Asian leaders seeking out and selecting particular innovations in public administration which they regard as having utility in Asian contexts. Once the innovation is adopted, it is then adapted to suit the novel Asian surroundings. It is a process of filtering, first of ideas and then of what is useful.

Other reforms are authentically domestic as we have seen with decentralisation. But there is remarkably little curiosity in the West about Asian public administration and a casual disregard of how it is structured and operates despite the astonishing economic and social success of many Asian societies. Indeed, the 1997 Asian Financial Crisis was interpreted by many Western observers as the Asian bubble bursting and evidence of the unsustainability of Asian solutions to public policy problems. The return to dynamic economic growth and social progress in Asia has received a muted response from the West where most countries are struggling to extricate themselves from the damage still being caused by the Global Financial Crisis. But the export of Western public administration innovations continues as a one-way process. Certainly, Asian countries have become more interested in how success stories like South Korea, Japan, Singapore and China have reformed their public sector management. Perhaps it is time to consider whether Asia has innovations to offer to Europe just like in the nineteenth century when Cambridge University used China's imperial examination system as a model for the university's reform (Cox 2016).

References

Batley, R., & Larbi, G. (2004). *The changing role of government: The reform of public services in developing countries*. Basingstoke: Palgrave Macmillan.

Blunt, P., & Turner, M. (2005). Decentralisation, democracy and development in a post-conflict state: Commune councils in Cambodia. *Public Administration and Development, 25*(1), 75–87.

Bransden, T., & Kim, S. (2010). Contextualising the meaning of public management reforms: A comparison of the Netherlands and Korea. *International Review of Administrative Sciences, 76*(2), 367–386.

Caiden, G. (1969). Development administration and administrative reform. *International Social Science Journal, 21*(1), 9–22.

Caiden, G., & Sundaram, P. (2004). The specificity of public sector reform. *Public Administration and Development, 24*(5), 373–383.

Carlson, M., & Turner, M. (2008). Public support for democratic governance in Southeast Asia. *Asian Journal of Political Science, 16*(3), 219–239.

Chardchawarn, S. (2010). *Local governance in Thailand: The politics of decentralization and the roles of bureaucrats, politicians and the people*. Japan External Trade Organization: Institute of Development Economics.

Cheung, A. (2013). Can there be an Asian public administration? *Public Administration and Development, 33*(4), 249–261.

Cheung, A. B. (2012). One country, two experiences: Administrative reforms in China and Hong Kong. *International Review of Administrative Sciences, 78*(2), 261–283.

Cox, D. (2016, April, 30). Chinese take a punt on Cambridge. *The Guardian Weekly*, 15–21.

De Guzman, R., & Reforma, M. (1992). Administrative reform in the Asian Pacific region: Issues and prospects. In Z. Zhijian, R. De Guzman, & M. Reforma (Eds.), *Administrative reform towards promoting productivity in bureaucratic performance*. Manila: EROPA.

Department for International Development (DFID). (2013). *Summary report of the public sector governance reform evaluation*. London: DFID.

Diamond, L. (2002). Thinking about hybrid regimes. *Journal of Democracy, 13*(2), 21–35.

Dreschler, W. (2015). Paradigms of non-Western public administration and governance. In A. Massey & K. Johnston (Eds.), *The international handbook of public administration and governance*. Cheltenham: Edward Elgar.

Eisenstadt, S. (1972). *The political systems of empires*. New York: Free Press of Glencoe.

Eisenstadt, S., & Roninger, L. (1980). Patron-client relations as a model of structuring social exchange. *Comparative Studies in Society and History, 22*(1), 42–77.

Eng, N. (2014). *The politics of decentralisation in Cambodia: The district level.* Unpublished Ph.D. thesis, Monash University, Australia.

Esman, M. (1972). *Administration and development in Malaysia: Institution building and reform in a plural society.* Ithaca: Cornell University Press.

Farazmand, A., & Balilaj, A. (2015). Does Asia have a unique theory of public administration for all seasons? An exploratory essay. *Asia Pacific Journal of Public Administration, 37*(3), 143–160.

Fitrani, F., Hofman, B., & Kaiser, K. (2005). Unity in diversity? The creation of new local governments in a decentralising Indonesia. *Bulletin of Indonesian Economic Studies, 41*(1), 57–79.

Freedom House. (2016). *Freedom in the World 2016.* Retrieved from http://www.freedomhouse.org.

Gladden, E. (1972). *A history of public administration* (Vol. 2). London: Frank Cass.

Grindle, M. (2012). *Jobs for the boys: Patronage and the state in comparative perspective.* Cambridge: Harvard University Press.

Heady, F. (1984). *Public administration: A comparative perspective.* New York: Marcel Dekker.

Heritage Foundation. (2016). *Index of Economic Freedom.* Retrieved from http://www.heritage.org/index/about.

Henderson, J. (2011). *East Asian transformation: On the political economy of dynamism, governance and crisis.* London: Routledge.

Hofstede, G. (1980). *Culture's consequences: International differences in work-related values.* Beverly Hills: Sage.

Im, T., Campbell, J., & Cha, S. (2013). Revisiting Confucian bureaucracy: Roots of the Korean government's culture and competitiveness. *Public Administration and Development, 33*(4), 286–296.

Independent Evaluation Group (IEG). (2008). *Public sector reform: What works and why?* Washington, DC: World Bank.

Johnson, C. (1982). *MITI and the Japanese miracle: The growth of industrial policy, 1925–1975.* Stanford: Stanford University Press.

Khan, M. (2005). Market, state and democracy: Patron-client networks and the case for democracy in developing countries. *Democratization, 12*(5), 704–724.

Landry, P. (2008). *Decentralized authoritarianism in China: The Communist Party's control of local elites.* Cambridge: Cambridge University Press.

Lewis, B. (2015). Decentralizing to villages in Indonesia: Money (and other) mistakes. *Public Administration and Development, 35*(5), 347–359.

Lin, J., & Liu, Z. (2000). Fiscal decentralization and economic growth in China. *Economic Development and Cultural Change, 49*(1), 1–21.

Mahbubani, K. (2004). *Can Asians think?* Singapore: Times Editions.

Manning, N. (2002). The legacy of new public management in developing countries. *International Review of Administrative Sciences, 67*(2), 297–312.

Milner, A. (2001). *What's happened to Asian values?* (Working Paper). Faculty of Asian Studies, Australian National University. Retrieved from https://digitalcollections.anu.edu.au/bitstream/1885/41912/2/values.html.

Montinola, G., Qian, Y., & Weingast, B. (1995). The political basis for economic success in China. *World Politics, 48*(1), 50–81.

Myrdal, G. (1968). *Asian drama: An inquiry into the poverty of nations.* New York: Pantheon.

Ofreneo, R., & Wad, P. (2010). Industrial relations and labour market conditions. In R. Rasiah & J. Schmidt (Eds.), *The new political economy of Southeast Asia*. Cheltenham: Edward Elgar.

Organization for Economic Cooperation and Development (OECD). (1996). *Integrating people into public service reform.* Paris: OECD.

Pollitt, C., & Bouckaert G., (Eds.). (2004). *Public management reform: A comparative analysis.* Oxford: Oxford University.

Samaratunge, R., & Bennington, L. (2002). New public management: Challenge for Sri Lanka. *Asian Journal of Public Administration, 24*(1), 87–109.

Samaratunge, R., Alam, Q., & Teicher, J. (2008). The new public management reforms in Asia: A comparison of South and Southeast Asia. *International Review of Administrative Sciences, 74*(1), 25–46.

Scott, J. (1972). Patron-client politics and political change in Southeast Asia. *American Political Science Review, 66*(1), 91–113.

Shemirani, M. (2011). *Sovereign wealth funds and international political economy.* Farnham: Ashgate.

Shen, C., Jin, J., & Zou, H. F. (2012). Fiscal decentralization in China: History, impact, challenges and next steps. *Annals of Economics and Finance, 13*(1), 1–51.

Subramaniam, V. (1998). The administrative legacy of ancient India. *International Journal of Public Administration, 21*(1), 87–108.

Transparency International. (2015). *Corruption Perceptions Index 2015.* Retrieved from https://www.transparency.org/cpi2015/.

Turner, M. (2002). Choosing items from the menu: New public management in Southeast Asia. *International Journal of Public Administration, 25*(12), 1493–1512.

Turner, M. (2013). Why is it so difficult to reform some Asian bureaucracies? Building theory from Cambodian practice. *Public Administration and Development, 33*(4), 275–285.

Turner, M., & Halligan, J. (1999). Bureaucracy and the alternatives in East and Southeast Asia. In K. Henderson & O. Dwivedi (Eds.), *Bureaucracy and the alternatives in world perspective.* Basingstoke: Macmillan.

Turner, M., & Hulme, D. (1997). *Governance, administration and development: Making the state work*. Basingstoke: Macmillan.

Turner, M., & Podger, O. (2003). *Decentralisation in Indonesia: Redesigning the state*. Canberra: Asia Pacific Pres.

Turner, M., Hulme, D., & McCourt, W. (2015). *Governance, management and development: Making the state work*. London: Palgrave.

Turner, M., O'Donnell, M., Suh, C. S., & Kwon, S. H. (2013). Public sector management and the changing nature of the developmental state. *Economic and Labour Relations Review, 24*(4), 481–494.

UNDP (United Nations Development Programme). (2016). *Human Development Report 2016*. New York: UNDP.

Wade, R. (1990). *Governing the market: Economic theory and the role of government in East Asian industrialization*. Princeton: Princeton University.

Warr, P. (2014, September, 22). Why Thailand must decentralise. *East Asia Forum'*. Retrieved from http://www.eastasiaforum.org/2014/09/22/why-thailand-must-decentralise/.

Weidner, E. (1970). Development and innovation roles. In E. Weidner (Ed.), *Development administration in Asia*. Durham: Duke University Press.

Wertheim, W. (1993). *Comparative essays on Asia and the West*. Amsterdam: VU University Press.

World Bank. (2016). World Bank Website. Retrieved from http://www.worldbank.org.

Wu, A. (2012). Economic miracle and upward accountability: A preliminary evaluation of the Chinese style of fiscal decentralisation. *Asian Review of Public Administration, 20*(1&2), 104–120.

Xue, L., & Zhong, K. (2012). Domestic reform and global integration: Public administration reform in China over the last 30 years. *International Review of Administrative Sciences, 78*(2), 284–304.

CHAPTER 10

A Capabilities Framework for a Globalised Public Service

Sara Bice

Introduction

This book has so far made clear that the very concept of 'public policy' is changing in light of complex global problems and the breakdown of barriers that historically delineated between the local and the global. This chapter explores that context by turning the focus to the public servants whose daily work makes public policy possible. Today's public administrators and policymakers face challenges of climate change, global health epidemics, terrorism, migration and economic failure while still retaining the charge of providing sound government and services at the national,

The capabilities model presented in this chapter is indebted to the work of Ms Angela Merriam. Please see, Bice and Merriam (2016). 'Defining Asia Capabilities for Australia's Public Service', *Australian Journal of Public Administration*. The chapter is also indebted to the research assistance of Ms Joanna Hanley, University of Melbourne, whose work contributed greatly to thinking on global leadership and cultural intelligence.

S. Bice (✉)
Melbourne School of Government, University of Melbourne,
Melbourne, Australia
e-mail: sara.bice@unimelb.edu.au

S. Bice et al. (eds.), *Public Policy in the 'Asian Century'*, International Series on Public Policy, https://doi.org/10.1057/978-1-137-60252-7_10

state and local levels. This progressively complex policy environment is encapsulated throughout this volume in terms of the 'Asian Century'. It might also be thought of as the felt implications of globalisation. Either way, it is clear that we need to rethink the ways that we do policy and, with that, what it takes to be a successful public servant in the Asian Century, the twenty-first century.

This chapter pursues the above challenges by addressing a central question: What are the skills, knowledge and capabilities critical to effective public administration in the Asian century? It draws upon a 12-month research study with Australian public servants to introduce a research-based framework of capabilities for a globalised public service. The chapter surveys relevant 'Asia literacy' and 'Asia capabilities' literature and analyses in-depth interviews with Australian public service leaders on this issue. In so doing, it contributes to a growing body of scholarly composition concerning the nature of public service work in the twenty-first century (Denhardt and Denhardt 2015, 2009; Dickinson and Sullivan 2014; Dickinson et al. 2015; Needham et al. 2014; Shergold 2013; Drechsler 2013; The University of Birmingham 2011) and to a similarly emergent literature concerning the intersections of 'Western' and 'Asian' public administration (Drechsler, Turner and Moloney in this volume; Drechsler 2013; Haque 2013, 2007; Bell 2010; Turner 2002).

The research findings presented in this chapter stem from an earlier paper (Bice and Merriam 2016) that considered the knowledge and skills necessary to equip Australia's public servants—those individuals 'directly employed by government who operate on the border between the political executive and the population' (Dickinson and Sullivan 2014, p. 3)—to be more 'Asia-capable'. The Asia capabilities project was itself catalysed by a series of Government initiatives, including a major White Paper on 'Australia in the Asian Century' (DFAT 2012). Much of this early research and commentary initially concentrated on 'Asia literacy'—defined primarily in terms of Asian language proficiency—but eventually expanded to incorporate broader values and skills, although these were poorly defined. To progress our thinking about what Asia capabilities might mean from an Australian perspective, the Melbourne School of Government undertook a 12-month project to better define these rather vague 'Asia Capabilities'. Meanwhile, colleagues in the UK and Australia were advancing notions of a 'twenty-first century' public servant (Needham et al. 2014). We also became attuned to a nascent but clearheaded scholarship about the work of business and organisation scholars on global leadership and cultural intelligence (CQ) (Earley and Mosakowski 2004; Rosen et al. 2000). This chapter presents the Australian research findings and integrates them with these two broader fields of research to suggest an emergent capabilities framework for a globalised public service.

The chapter presents a strong starting point for understanding the capabilities necessary to facilitate successful participation in a globalised policy environment. At the same time, the framework remains untested and is particularly limited in two, important ways. First, any notion of 'global' is necessarily problematic. Just as the collective term 'Asia' belies tremendous diversity, 'global' is at once suggestive of the universal while also encompassing a multiplicity that can never really be pragmatically accounted for or managed. Secondly, the research that underpins the initial framework presented here was undertaken within Australia, with Australian public servants. While these individuals hail from a variety of backgrounds and experiences, further development of the framework requires engagement with other, especially Asian, countries. Otherwise, the research may only further reify the 'west to the rest' approach that Drechsler warns about earlier in this volume.

Some of the suggestions made throughout this chapter may appear obvious, but they risk being ignored if not clearly articulated and set within the context of a framework that can add value across departments, agencies and a variety of relationships and activities. For example, is being a capable public servant in a globalised environment a task that simply requires awareness of one's own specificity while operating in diverse contexts? Or is it about working within inescapable values or 'hypernorms'? Are there individual attributes or skills critical to success? Are these inherent in particular personalities or can they be acquired through study, experience or training? And are such skills necessary across the whole of government, or are they best concentrated within particular, especially outward-facing departments or agencies? These are but a few of the myriad questions engaged as the chapter seeks to understand whether and how global capabilities represent a strategic endeavour to support successful public management in the Asian Century.

The Twenty-First Century Public Servant

The work of this chapter takes place within a limited but growing literature concerned with better understanding both the lived experience of twenty-first century public administrators and the ways in which our theorising about public administration must necessarily shift to remain relevant to dynamic, globalised environments. It is valuable briefly to review these contributions here, as they set the scene for the relevance, utility and (arguably) necessity of a capabilities framework for a globalised public service.

Concerns about diverse countries' abilities to engage with one another are coloured by a shifting policymaking environment where public administrators and policy scholars are seeking to (re)define what it means to be a public servant in the present day. Key influencing factors include: changes in the public administration workforce (Grimshaw et al. 2002; Corby 2000); evolving citizen expectations of government and new forms of citizen engagement (Denhardt and Denhardt 2015; Newman et al. 2004; Needham 2008); increased emphasis on ethics and values (Hebson et al. 2003; Brereton and Temple 1999) requirements for more non-hierarchical organisational structures; and legacies of New Public Management (NPM) that promote generic over technical skills (Needham et al. 2014). As Dickinson et al. (2015, p. 24) argue, public administrators of the twenty-first century face clear and agreed challenges related to "problem complexity, financial constraints, IT developments, employment flexibility, and industrial relations." To these challenges, Bice and Sullivan (2014) add operating effectively in a policy environment in which certain, traditionally local, issues have become global. Today's public servants must therefore be equipped for global engagement, with roles in a variety of policy areas holding the potential to influence economic development, global health, environment and security.

The role of the twenty-first century public servant demands difficult trade-offs, with a stronger focus on policy over service delivery and development of particular skills, including "international literacy" which reflects the increasing interactions between "public services and global influences and specific attention to the need for 'Asia capability'" (Dickinson et al. 2015, p. 25). It also appears likely that as the key tasks of public servants shift from service to policy, the cohort will shrink and these individuals will require a range of technical, human and conceptual skills that build upon but are substantially different to those demanded of past public administrators (Dickinson and Sullivan 2014). This situation leads Dickinson and Sullivan (2014) to suggest four new roles for public servants this century: curators, commissioners, foresighters and storytellers. Space to delve into these roles in any depth is limited here. What is important, however, is that these new role types represent shifts in the general expectations about what public servants can and will do within their occupations. The chapter asserts that novel or different skills and experiences, or at least novel combinations of existing ones, will be required to support these emergent roles. Indeed, Dickinson and Sullivan (2014) make a start towards outlining these, but the idea requires better articulation and stronger theoretical support.

Global Leadership and Cultural Intelligence

Business and management scholars have made substantial advances in understanding the skills and capabilities necessary for successful operation in globalised environments (Mendenhall 2012). Driven by their subjects' need to respond to rapidly changing financial markets, the identification of causal links between socio-cultural diversity and global economic performance and by increased multinationalisation, the theories and frameworks developed by these researchers show applicability and promise for public administrations undergoing aligned shifts. Importantly, and presumably because the nature of public administration has transformed in more recent years, business literature appears to be ahead of policy scholarship in its consideration of global skills, capabilities and leadership. It is important to keep in mind, however, that while these literatures offer pertinent and helpful insights as we begin to consider a 'globalised' public service, the work of business remains distinct to that of the public service. There will be great opportunity in future development of global leadership theory targeted specifically at public administration. Nevertheless, the business literature's notions of 'global leadership' and 'cultural intelligence' are particularly salient, and it is worthwhile briefly introducing them here.

Traditional leadership theories remain mostly bound to domestic markets, while *global* leadership offers a capability considerably distinctive to these traditional conceptualisations (Vesa 2002). Global leadership is distinguished by a primary focus on cross-cultural interaction with others from diverse countries (Juhnee and McLean 2015). Importantly, it "transcends [even] a multi-country comparison of domestic leadership approaches" or more homogenised notions of 'universal leadership' models (Junhee and McLean 2015, p. 240) to suggest a suite of global literacies, including personal, social, business and cultural skills (Rosen et al. 2000). As such, it aligns with the concerns of certain public administration scholars who emphasise the need for 'public administration with a global perspective' as distinctive to the learnings and leadership styles possible through adopting a comparative public policy perspective (Gulrajani and Moloney 2012).

In many ways global leadership focuses on the 'negative leadership space'; that is, it is concerned with the ways in which leaders respond effectively to the novel or unknown, including how they may react to culture shock or knowledge deficits inherent to operating in disparate environments (McCall and Hollenbeck 2002). Consequently, global leadership also emphasises the centrality of relationships and personal networks, which certain scholars argue are made possible through strong capabilities that are learnable, as opposed to inherent (Julsrud and Gjerdacker 2013).

The assertion that global leadership capabilities can be attained through training and practice, rather than simply lying dormant within individual personalities, is supported by related studies of CQ. CQ is visible when, "occasionally, an outsider has a seemingly natural ability to interpret someone's unfamiliar and ambiguous gestures in just the way that person's compatriots and colleagues would, even to mirror them" (Earley and Mosakowski 2004, p. 139). While such high CQ may appear 'natural', studies suggest that the ease with which those who display high CQ engage in diverse environments usually belies considerable experience and, sometimes, explicit training (Kivland and King 2015). In other words, the "capability to adapt effectively to new cultural contexts" can be taught (Earley and Ang 2003, p. 59). As a result, employers now pay more attention to CQ "as a way to synergize differences in international organizations and to build capacities adapted to the strategic outlook of markets", (UNESCO 2009, p. 178).

When applied to the public sector, global leadership and CQ literatures provide a helpful framework for considering the skills, attitudes and experiences that support successful operation in a globalised environment. These might include: behaviours that support multinational team members; flexible working styles; capacity to pick-up on behavioural cues; reproduction of cultural knowledge and behaviours; problem-solving and strategic approaches to new hurdles; and the capacity to put others at ease through empathy and a desire to reach shared understanding (Junhee and McLean 2015; Berke et al. 2008). Research suggests that these skills, attitudes and capabilities can be built through dedicated training (Earley and Peterson 2004), especially of the type that supports the development of habits (Kivland and King 2015). Given the longer-term nature of such endeavours, it is important to consider whether and how public administrations might better support such training throughout individuals' career paths. There is a depth of experience and stability of habit to be gained through dedication to this style of capacity-building. It may also contribute to administrations' capacities to build and retain strong talent.

The business literature also focuses on the importance of global experience to developing global capabilities, in addition to an emphasis on habit-forming and skills-based training. Perhaps unsurprisingly, studies confirm that in order to build a global capacity, it is helpful for people to undertake work in globalised environments. As McCall and Hollenbeck (2002) put it, people learn to 'be global' from doing global work. Rosen and colleagues (2000) further explain how doing such global work helps business executives to develop 'global literacies', an idea reflected directly in the public service arena, at least in the Australian case (Bice and Merriam 2016). Much like the changes in the contemporary public policy environment, a concern for global literacies in business was spurred by the development of 'borderless economies' and a slippage between markets that were historically more bounded by geography and culture (Rosen et al. 2000).

Clearly, both global leadership studies and CQ literatures offer insights that could be applicable to public administrators experiencing similar shifts in their roles and experiences, related to globalisation and the compression of policy issues across space and time.

Cases from Australia's Public Service

The study adopted a qualitative approach, involving in-depth, semi-structured interviews with 23 opinion leaders, working in or closely with Australian governments at Commonwealth, state and local levels, and one large group interview with 16 representatives of a major

Commonwealth government department. Interviewees represented all levels of government across three states, Victoria, New South Wales and Queensland, and the Australian Capital Territory. In-depth interviews provided a method appropriate to the study's aim of outlining a relatively new area of consideration, giving us the ability to open discussion on a topic that was relatively under-researched. Use of a semi-structured interview instrument allowed us to explore themes and ideas as they emerged in each discussion, and supported interrogation of new ideas (Flyvbjerg 2001).

Interviewees were selected based upon their knowledge of their own organisation's attention to Asia capabilities and their leadership within their organisations, related to these issues. While this resulted in rich information, it also seems to have contributed to strong congruence between interviewees' responses. For this reason, findings revealed largely homogenous views with little dissonance. Future research could involve public servants with more limited experience in global environments to expand the views, opinions and themes represented. The interviews lasted from 45 minutes to 1.5 hours and aimed to capture ideas about Asia capabilities from a wide scope of areas and perspectives. Departments represented through the interviews perform work in the areas of: national security; foreign affairs; trade; policing; justice; the arts; premier and cabinet; local government; state services; business and innovation; primary industry; education; sustainability and environment; regional development; public service commissions; and health and human services. The project was undertaken with university human research ethics approval, including provision of anonymity for interviewees.

Interviews were structured as in-depth conversations (Legard et al. 2003; Flyvbjerg 2001) about Asia capabilities, guided by an interview schedule centring on questions about organisational understanding of global capabilities; practice of Asia-specific capabilities; the components or qualities necessary for a public servant to be globally capable; perceptions of existing levels of capability within the organisation; the extent to which proposed skills or competencies can be taught or are innate; differences between Asia literacy and capability; the value of global or Asia capabilities to the organisation; and benefits and challenges. All interviews were fully transcribed and results analysed thematically using N*Vivo10 software (Bazeley and Jackson 2013).

Global Capabilities Framework

Other chapters in this volume point to the variety and depth of skills necessary to successful public administration in a globalised policy environment. From understanding the cultural values that underpin bureaucratic structures (Drechsler, Chap. 2 of this volume) to the role of intergovernmental decision-making in relation to non-communicable diseases (Kay, Chap. 12 of this volume), the contemporary policy environment is one that demands capabilities that are enriched and extended beyond those common to more traditional, domestic public service (Moloney, Chap. 11 of this volume).

Also in this volume, Mark Turner (Chap. 9 of this volume) describes the application of 'Western' policy models in a variety of Asian countries. His earlier work (Turner 2002) explained the ways in which Southeast Asian public administrators apply NPM as "choosing items from the menu". Adapting Turner's metaphor, a menu of 'global capabilities' is suggested here, as defined in the Australian study. This menu offers public administrators the opportunity to indulge fully or choose selectively for purpose, but ultimately illustrates the staples required for successful engagement in a globalised policy environment. The 'menu' builds on the global business leadership and cultural intelligence literatures reviewed earlier to consider two capabilities dimensions (global and specific) that incorporate four core elements (skills, attitudes, knowledge and experience), with each element comprising five components (see, Fig. 10.1).

Each of the four elements may be combined with others in a variety of ways, allowing individual administrators or agencies to determine their own best-fit selections. In this way the framework avoids being overly prescriptive. Rather it aims to clarify better the contours of an emerging discourse on public service capabilities, acknowledging the most commonly voiced narratives concerning the Asian Century, as arising from the literature and research interviews. These include political and sociological perspectives, encompassing such issues macro-economic shifts, the importance of scientific and technological cooperation with emerging innovation centres and the political leverage necessary to do so (Palmer and Jensen, Chap. 6 of this volume).

The menu incorporates two distinct dimensions of global capabilities. First, it captures a foundational level of 'generic' or globally-relevant capabilities characterised by skills and attitudes. Secondly, it denotes

Fig. 10.1 Global capabilities framework: Dimensions, elements and components

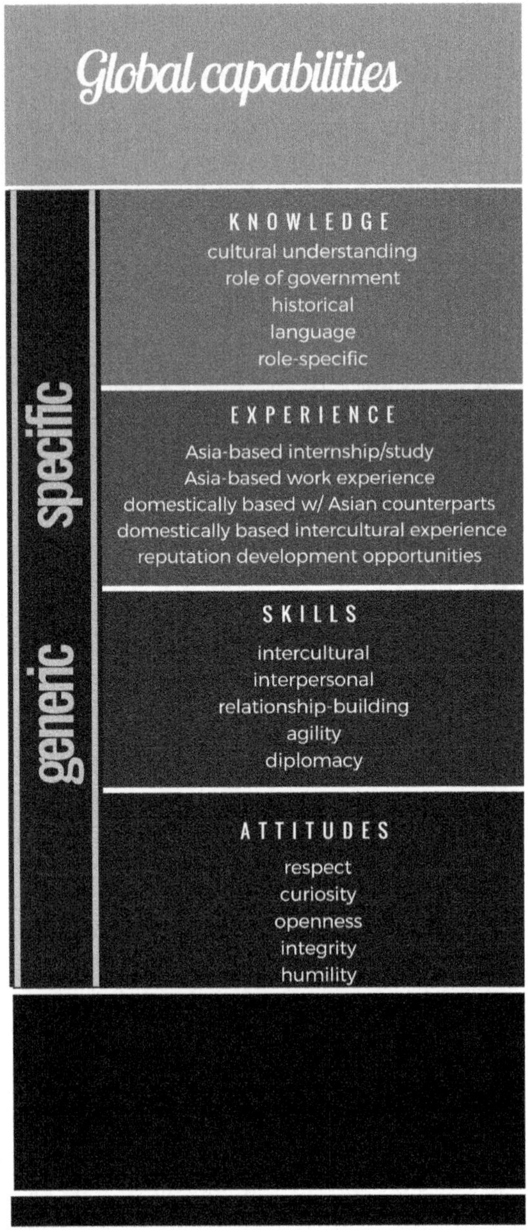

more specific knowledge and experience, usually applied at the country level. These two capability dimensions are necessarily interrelated, with strong feedback loops. Their relevance will vary according to a public administrator's role, department and level of government, among other things.

Elements and Components of Global Capabilities

The following section provides a concise overview of the four core elements of global capabilities and their five components, defining each and providing illustrative quotes from the analysis which support and explain their inclusion.

Specific Dimensions

Knowledge
Knowledge, in this dynamic context, is broadly applied and contextually idiosyncratic. Its core components, as derived from the research, are summarised below.

Cultural Understanding
When asked to list the "five core skills, competencies or capabilities central to Asia capabilities", almost all individual interviewees named awareness and understanding of specific Asian cultures. Going beyond travel guide titbits, this includes the "broad set of rules and expectations that people have that govern how you interact" (Interview 26); that frame what defines "context" (Interviews 2, 11, 13); "perspective, values and normative frameworks" (Interviews 20, 25); or knowing what will "matter to people at an emotional level, rather than a sort of formal, technical level" (Interview 20). Cultural understanding is, therefore, more about knowing, rather than doing.

Interviewees pinpointed foundational factors of cultural understanding about Asian countries, including cultural values, such as those regarding the individual versus collective, family versus state, or varying definitions of democracy. Yet painting Asia in such broad strokes also has its drawbacks. Not only does 'Asia' not possess any essential economic, political, legal or cultural characteristics in the same way that Europe does, values vary even within particular countries at "different times under different historical conditions and [at] particular, different institutional [levels]" (Interview 25). For Australian public servants, developing a layered cultural understanding of particular Asian cultures demands nuance.

Knowledge of Role of Government

Understanding the role of Asian governments and interactions among politics, economics, law, public policy and public management was mentioned by most of the interviewees. While politics and administration tend to be disassociated into disciplinary silos in theory (Svara 2001), interviewees expressed them as very much interrelated in the applied sense. This was articulated in a variety of ways, including discussion of understanding various systems or environments (Interviews 2, 22), especially economic (Interviews 2, 15, 20), political (Interviews 15, 22) or concerning public policy and management (Interviews 3, 4, 15). A lack of consensus and precision around language (e.g. interchanging 'politics' and 'policy' throughout discussions) may indicate a lack of consensus on analytical frameworks through which to understand these forces in Asia, or more generally. This is certainly an issue that has been raised in the literature (Cheung 2013, 2005; Haque and Turner 2013). As one interviewee who has spent a great deal of time working in various Asian nations emphasised, knowledge of the role of government in Asian countries is particularly pressing, as:

> ...the role of government is probably much greater in Asia than it is in Australia...[and] the role of government is very different to that of Australia and it's viewed differently and it's very important. (Interview 22)

Historical Knowledge

History was described as an important means of catalysing social interaction and developing trust (Interview 23); as a background for understanding contemporary institutions (Interview 26) and cultural values (Interview 9, 13), including important institutional values (Interview 25); and as part of the understanding necessary to develop key attitudes, such as respect (Interviews 1, 9). As one interviewee described, even a basic understanding of history can assist with sensitivity to and understanding of policies (or in this instance, lack thereof):

> I think giving the respect of understanding [a country's] history and the evolution is really important. Like, you'll have people [who] went to Vietnam, for example, 'Did you see all those people who didn't have helmets on their motorbikes?!'And I'm going, 'Those folks are probably bloody excited that they've got a way of getting to a job. (Interview 9)

Language

Further to the notion of Asia literacy, language skills were perceived as important, but not foundational to a global capability. Language is incorporated into the capabilities skill set here, however, as all interviewees discussed language. Even where interviewees felt that knowledge of an Asian language was not essential to successful engagement, they noted its usefulness. Where language skills were held, they were seen as but one component of the broader suite of necessary capabilities.

> You can have a degree of literacy around Asia if you know any language because it introduces you to a whole new culture and all that sort of thing. But capability, for us, is knowing how to do business in those markets and that's another layer on top. (Interview 18)

Many interviewees felt that Asian language capabilities remained relatively underutilised in their departments due to structural reasons. For example, several interviewees suggested that substantial Asian language skills existed within their departments but that the individuals holding these skills were rarely tapped for them because they were assigned to other roles. Better skills identification within the existing public administration workforce and greater role flexibility and opportunities may offer one means of allowing Australia's public service to make better use of existing language skills. This was certainly the case in the Australian context and it would be important to consider whether similar, structural barriers exist in other country's administrations.

Role-Specific Knowledge

The findings demonstrate that there is considerable value in public servants understanding the roles of their counterparts in Asian nations. For the Australian public servants interviewed, this role-specific knowledge encompassed often taken-for-granted but nevertheless critical understandings such as: the location of the role within the administrative system; functions of the role; reporting structures; authority and responsibility; managerial styles; and even day-to-day worklife. Interviewees discussed how understanding of others' roles assisted their ability to work more effectively with Asian counterparts, as they could align processes and expectations accordingly. One interviewee went further, describing how exposure to the daily work of public servants in a different environment (here, via an exchange program) created a deeper appreciation of the work being achieved:

> There's so many examples like that from within Asia, where, even from an objective measure, [if we] look at what they're achieving on a day to day basis, in terms of public service provision, it far exceeds what we would ever have to do because of our population size. (Interview 10)

Understanding others' roles is therefore often linked to experience, the next of the four core elements of global capabilities to which the chapter now turns.

Experience

Interviewees asserted that the practical learning garnered from experience engaging with Asian counterparts, businesses and clients is an important part of turning passive, academic learning into an active capability. As one interviewee summed up, "A lot of it, I think, is about being worldly and having life experience" (Interview 14). Importantly, in terms of recruitment into the public service, interviewees suggested that a willingness to have international experiences was most important, and that experience could be gained within a role. Lack of prior experience, therefore, need not preclude selection, but should be incorporated into opportunities offered to public administrators by their employers. Interviewees' discussions of the value derived from on-the-job experiences underline this point, below.

Moreover, several interviewees explained how the values and outcomes of experiences may be unpredictable and extend well beyond those which appear obvious or are expected. Interviewees asserted the need for organisations to invest in supporting public administrators' experiences within Asia or with Asian counterparts visiting Australia, as a critical and effective means of improving policy development and service delivery. The experience of one interviewee's colleague in China sums up this perspective well:

> [My colleague is] in a policy role [concerning] agribusiness policy, particularly some policies of trade with China. ...So he took [a scholarship] and stayed in China for six months. He took an extensive trip—not just in language—an intensive trip in China to all different places. [It was] in the winter [and he] experienced the cold, minus 30 degrees, and went to some remote villages and countryside, and then [he saw] the real sort of farmers and what the rural policies in China do and why that's important to Chinese farmers. And then he understands why an FTA [free trade agreement] with China is mixed up with a lot of agribusiness access issues. If he gets to see the rural farmers in China, he gets to see the poor areas, and he understands why this thing's stuck; the access, it's so difficult. So it's the first-hand information, understanding the culture and not just the language. (Interview 24)

Similarly to knowledge, however, the transferability of experience varies across space and time. For example, interviewees suggested that while experience in Vietnam may translate to improved capabilities in China, this may be less the case in India. Equally, experience in China thirty years ago may translate better to an understanding of contemporary North Korea than contemporary Shanghai, unless that knowledge is updated. Thus, experience may help to understand how cultural values, policies and practices shift over time. "There are different values used at different times under different historical conditions and particularly under different institutional instructions" (Interview 25).

Reputation Development

Interviewees also suggested that regular experience with Asian counterparts was important to building reputation, a factor vital to long-term relationships. They described the value of experience for building knowledge and cultural understanding of particular countries, but also in terms that are best represented as 'reputation development'. Many emphasised the importance of related concepts of trust and long-term relationships at both the individual and the institutional levels. Reputation is developed through long-term, repeated interactions characterised by integrity and trust and requires person-to-person interaction (Putnam 1995), which is both vital and difficult. As one interviewee explained:

> The personal relationships, the individual, the ability to build trust, which is what underpins the relationship, to understand what that means in the cultural context, and it can be quite different and it can be very challenging. (Interview 11)

For several interviewees, the reputation development possible through experiences like those outlined above was seen as instrumental to "leverag[ing] a relationship" (Interview 24). Here, reputation development through individual experience becomes a means of extending positive relations back into relevant departments or agencies. As one interviewee stated, "...If, at a personal level, you build a good relationship with [your overseas counterparts] and that person feels comfortable with dealing with the government here, it's likely there will be interest in that investment later on" (Interviewee 24). Interviewees were also asked which particular types of experience best foster reputation development and build long term relations or result in greatest value back to their departments. These key types of experiences are noted in Fig. 10.1 and outlined, below.

Key Types of Experiences

From work placements abroad to leisure travel, in-country experience helps to develop an understanding of cultural dynamics and to improve intercultural communication. Domestic interactions with Asian counterparts can be equally helpful. The main types of experiences suggested in the interviews included:

- Overseas internships or study opportunities;
- Overseas work experience (e.g. being embedded in a 'sister' department or working in a domestic department's overseas office);
- Domestic work experience with visiting Asian counterparts; and
- Domestic intercultural exchanges, such as one-off seminars or programs.

More targeted experience in business or government overseas provides an extra layer of building the networks and reputation applicable to public service work. Interviewees also described how participation in conferences or study tours in Asia helped to extend networks and catalyse relationships. For example, one interviewee explained how it is eminently useful to have someone in the department who is able to telephone Asian counterparts and receive an immediate, cooperative response (Interview 18). Yet as mentioned earlier, a fully realised global capability is found at the nexus between Asia-specific knowledge and experience and more generic skills and attitudes, to which the chapter now looks.

Generic Capabilities

Skills

Skills and attitudes were generally conceptualised by interviewees as 'generic' or generally relevant. As such, skills represent the personal characteristics that differentiate capability—the ability to perform and achieve outcomes—from 'literacy', which is more often equated to book learning or language, as discussed previously. Interestingly, the majority of interviewees stated they believed that skills such as interpersonal relationship-building are not inherent to particular individuals but could be taught through good training programs. These opinions are echoed in the training literature (Rosen et al. 2000) and suggest that even those capabilities more commonly associated with individual personality can be acquired. But, as one interviewee pointed out, attitudes about training and professional development may also need to change in order to support the type of training necessary to develop these generic capabilities:

> I'm not sure that that discussion [about training] is going to yield quite the depth and richness that perhaps it might. It's more likely to be in terms of 'Oh yeah, I need to go along and learn how to do Word 7 or how to do a particular mechanical skill,' as opposed to [a manager] sitting back and saying [to an employee], "Look, you're doing very well, these are areas in your general skillset where you might want to focus'. (Interview 12)

The five generic skills identified in the research: intercultural, interpersonal, relationship building, agility and diplomacy are summarised in the following sections.

Intercultural

Intercultural skills may be classified according to varying degrees of comfort interacting and communicating within different cultures, mindsets and perspectives. This includes the sensitivity not to offend, and general awareness or appreciation of difference. At its most basic level this may mean simply the passive ability not to "stomp all over" others' cultural practices (Interview 17), instead exercising a healthy dose of circumspection that filters into behaviours. As one interviewee explained, intercultural skills can be critical to achieving desired policy outcomes:

> The whole notion that I've been putting forward is that if you're going to reach a satisfactory outcome, you have to understand where the other person is coming from in a broad sense. You have to understand what their motivations are, what they're seeking to achieve, where that interacts and overlays with what you are seeking to do and to achieve. So, you need to actually be able to interpret what they are saying, what it means and what it doesn't mean. Another good example from Japan was a classic book published a number of years ago. Its title was *Never Take 'Yes' for an Answer*. Because what does 'yes' actually mean? It can mean in a Western sense, 'I agree'. In a Japanese context, it's often taken to mean, 'I've heard what you've said, I'm acknowledging what you said. It's not that I'm agreeing with what you say.' And that's an important distinction to understand. So, when you're actually interacting with people, if you are listening to what they are saying, you may be able to understand where they are coming from and hence where you'll be able to achieve an outcome. (Interview 12)

Thus, a deeper level of intercultural skills involves working within: "different expectations, mechanisms of human respect" (Interview 23); having the "sensitivity" to interact in an environment where your native language is not the dominant language (Interview 11); the ability to defy one's own assumptions to identify where people are coming from and then adjust your words and behaviour accordingly (Interviews 9, 12, 26); skills that result from practice interacting or negotiating with Asian counterparts (Interview 13); "incredible comfort" in an "Asian environment" or dealing with Asian business people or diplomats partly through adopting a certain "mindset" (Interview 15); general social awareness and understanding of sociology (Interview 25); and an honest appraisal of one's own biases and viewpoints (Interview 10).

Overall, interview findings suggest that sophisticated intercultural understanding is perceived as being uncommon in the context of Australia's relatively homogenous and monolingual population. Intercultural skills involve the ability to "traverse different worlds in a cohesive way", reconciling behaviour that is appropriate both as a public servant and in engagements with Asian counterparts, as well as identifying government priorities and translating them to outcomes in a different cultural context (Interview 26). One interviewee suggested that this ability may be more common in Europe due to geography (Interview 25). Yet intercultural skills may also be developed not only through intercultural experience, as defined above, but also through personal experience of difference (e.g. cultural, linguistic, religious, sexuality or otherwise). It may be the type of skill developed over a lifetime of conforming without being consumed, of operating within the context of recognised dissonance and contradictions. As one interviewee explained, this requires great awareness and balance:

> When I first went as a student to Japan, the Japanese were not accustomed to Westerners. They are a very exclusive society. A lot of people find that very, very personally threatening. So the reaction was typically one of two—rejection, or alternatively so deep immersion that you actually try to become more Japanese than the Japanese, which is fine at some point in your overall development of that understanding but to be effective, you also have to retain that sense of personal identity and the interests that you actually maintain. I had this classic kind of case usually dismissed under the title 'local-itus'. (Interview 12)

Interpersonal

Interpersonal skills include a broad range of skills and abilities relevant generally to engaging with people. Interviewees described interpersonal skills as involving empathy with the positions of others (Interview 10, 12); listening (Interview 12); adopting and understanding nuances of interaction, including body language (Interview 13); and skilled communication through being able to meet people "where they are at" (interview 8). In line with an extensive field of literature on interpersonal skills (see, Spitzberg and Cupach 2011 for a meta-analysis), the findings suggest that, while broad, interpersonal skills are "the fulcrum on which the levels of social life are maneuvered" (Spitzberg and Cupach 2011, p. 481).

Relationship-Building

Relationship-building skills—those which comprise both developing and managing relationships—were emphasised by many of the individual interviewees and in the group interview. Interviewees noted that a focus on relationship-building skills is critical, given their perception that "a great deal more interaction in Asia is based on trust and personal relationships" (Interview 12) which makes it important to "network" and "maintain international networks" (Interview 15) in business and government. Relationship-building was described as being focused on the long-term, and interviewees consequently discussed how organisations must facilitate interactions that allow the development of "lifelong" partnerships (Interview 16) and relationship maintenance, such as following up on trade missions (Interview 14). One interviewee who had worked extensively on building 'Asia capabilities' throughout departments in his state said that relationship-building skills were the foundation on which successful engagement with non-Western countries must be founded:

> To be able to do whatever you have to do in Asia or whatever part of Asia you have to do it, you're going to need skills, knowledge, personal qualities, mindsets. But you're also going to have to have a network of relationships and more than that, not just a network but you're going to have to have standing and credibility. (Interview 2).

Agility

The interview findings also demonstrate that a general flexibility and ability to adapt to circumstances as they develop and to respond to the unexpected is required. Numerous interviewees employed terms like "adaptability" (Interviews 2, 13, 14, 24, 26), "nimbleness" (Interview 27), "resilience" (Interview 14, 27) and an ability to "operate in a dynamic environment" (all but Interview 1). For the purposes of refining the global capabilities framework, this generic skill is defined as 'agility'. Agility allows public servants to go beyond "just being able to speak the language or know when to offer your hand and shake it or when to bow" (Interview 26) to being able to pick up rapidly on and respond to cultural and emotional cues. Agility supports public servants to "navigate instability" via "an appreciation and understanding of different perspectives and an ability to navigate between them and across them" (Interview 26). Furthermore, as one interviewee explained when discussing urban development planning in partnership with a Chinese firm, agility helps public servants to balance the competing pressures of others' expectations with policy requirements by navigating *through* the relationships they have built:

> We can't necessarily change our planning rules, because we have a community that has expectations, but if we can actually deal with the relationship, then we can actually manage through it. (Interview 17)

Agility is also related to nuance and comfort in ambiguity. Interviewees noted this as particularly important in Asian contexts:

> In the Western world we tend to be very black and white. We like things to be clear cut. We like direct responses. Whereas, in Asia, it's not always like that. (Interview 13)

Similarly, another interviewee stated, "Unless you're open to [the nuance] you won't firstly pick up on the cues and you won't be as effective as you could be" (Interview 14). Agility is therefore also related to the ability to discern among Asian cultures and even to recognise regional and other differences within one country. For instance, while it is important to understand Chinese values, it is a fallacy to imagine the country as a monolith, or even that it may be captured by conceptions of one single value such as collectivism (Interview 25).

Diplomacy

Interviewees stressed the importance of maintaining "a sense of personal identity and interests", in these cases within the context of acting as a representative of Australian government (Interview 12). For many, this meant striking a careful balance between intercultural and interpersonal skills and cultural understanding, while maintaining an 'Australian' position, outlook or identity. For the purposes of the framework, the skill of maintaining a sense of one's self while responding to the interests or requests of others is defined as 'diplomacy'. One interviewee described this balancing act as follows:

> I see ...people engaging for the first time—as a very basic example in Japan—feeling the need to bow down lower and longer and they have to act more Japanese than the Japanese themselves. That's a bit like us when you meet an Asian who says, 'Where are you from?' and you say, 'Australia' and the response is 'G'day mate. Have you had a vegemite sandwich today?' I think we need to be conscious that we still have our own identity. When we negotiate, we have outcomes in our interests that we have to achieve and it's about doing it the right way and not necessarily copying Asia. ...It's about the balance and understanding how it works and being respectful of that. (Interview 13)

Attitudes

Many interviewees suggested that the Asian century may disrupt conventional Australian perspectives, sentiments and mindsets regarding not only 'Asia' but also Australia vis-à-vis Asia. The following attitudes represent those deemed most helpful to ensuring that Australia can thrive in a socio-political world potentially very different to the one we know today. Importantly, the attitudes defined below are viewed as mindsets which will facilitate successful application of the global capabilities framework's skills, knowledge and experience.

Respect

Nearly half of the interviewees referenced an attitude of respect as underpinning successful Asian engagement. Respect may be the basis of any healthy and productive relationship. In relation to Asian nations, interviewees suggested that an attitude of respect requires transcending neo-colonial attitudes that lead us to "look down" on Asia (Interview 9). Here, interviewees argued that Australia's public servants must demonstrate a willingness to "come to the table on equal terms" (Interview 13). Such respect is vital both to effective engagement with Asian counterparts and to opening up numerous possibilities of policy transfer, to learn from others' experience (Interviews 1, 11, 22, 23). As one interviewee summed up:

> We engage from Asia almost from a colonial sense, in a sense that, 'Well it's in your interest to deal with Aussies 'cause we've got such a great system and we can help you and we can teach you.' And that comes across as a little bit arrogant or very arrogant. They have their systems, cultures and processes based on a range of factors. (Interview 13)

In this manner, respect creates an environment in which influence flows two ways.

Curiosity

The importance of general inquisitiveness and the ability to ask genuine questions, listen to and understand others' opinions was noted by ten interviewees. Defined here as 'curiosity', this attitude involves a "willingness to try new things—to think broadly, to think creatively" (Interview 15). Curiosity is being open about different ways of thinking and doing (Interview 22). Broadly, this attitude captures a "general level of curiosity about the world and understanding how the world fits together" (Interview 25). Two interviewees described curiosity as being even more important than any specific knowledge or experience in Asian nations (Interview 25, 20). Curiosity, therefore, reflects the framework's positioning away from 'literacy' and towards generic capabilities which foster strong critical thinking and an inquiring mind. To paraphrase one interviewee, a public servant who is curious may be much more effective at Asian engagement than someone who has developed entrenched, inflexible ideas about the way Asia is or was (Interview 25).

Openness

The attitude of 'openness' encompasses a willingness to recognise and interrogate one's own biases, assumptions and cultural filters. Interviewees described openness as a key aspect of any intercultural engagement. It is related broadly to identifying where assumptions, perspectives and values diverge (Interview 12), in part as the recognition of one's own lenses through which the world is experienced. This awareness of one's own positioning or unconscious biases is a necessary step to transcending or changing those lenses to view the perspectives of others (Interview 20). An attitude of openness which allows for critical self-reflection must be supported at the organisational level, as it requires vulnerability. In the opinion of at least one interviewee, sector-wide support for openness is something that Australia's public sector as a whole could "afford to do some work on" (Interview 20).

Integrity

An attitude of integrity, encompassing a desire to "do right by people" (Interview 27) underpins building the long-term relationships and reputation defined within the generic skills element of the framework. Like the other core attitudes, integrity may prove difficult to teach or measure. Yet it is widely recognised in existing capabilities frameworks at all levels of Australian government and has been acknowledged as a characteristic central to leadership and the sustainability of Australia's public sector (Podger 2004). It is therefore important but unsurprising that integrity (or its synonyms) was positioned by all interviewees (including the group interview) as critical to operating successfully in a global policy environment. Integrity was demonstrated throughout the interviews as an attitude already well-entrenched within the Australian public sector. Its inclusion here may therefore serve to add another facet to its already robust justification.

Humility

Finally, interviewees were quick to note the role of humility in demonstrating respect, supporting openness, creating two-way dialogues and fostering successful engagement throughout Asia. For purposes of the framework, the findings suggest that humility is related to recognising the "strengths of other countries" (Interview 1) or the idea that "we haven't designed the perfect world and that there are other ways of viewing things" (Interview 23). Humility was strongly connected to listening skills (Interviewee 17), a notion which aligns strongly with the management literature on humble inquiry (Schein 2013). Within the global capabilities framework, a humble attitude supports self-reflection. One interviewee described how humility among the public service leadership is particularly important to the future success of building global capabilities throughout the sector:

> To some extent, I think this brings us into the conversation about silos and barriers and ways of information flow to and from and across and that's why we're now thinking about this ... We're trying to move away from having to own all the capability but move the idea of unlocking capability and being able to say, 'Okay, [government], you have certain needs and interests in terms of understanding what's happening in Asia and being able to take opportunity of that. Well, how are you going to get that knowledge?' You've already got people who think in this clever way. You've already got people who are really good at community engagement. You've already got a number of Asian communities who are very well-connected to Asia and already know what's happening in the culture and the economy and they have very high-level interactions. You've got the academic community. You've got the business community. Let's bring all that together and start making those connections. (Interview 2)

In this example, humility allows public sector leaders to identify and engage existing resources, a perspective which taps into existing capabilities as opposed to operating from "a deficit model" (Interview 2).

Opportunities for a Global Capabilities Framework: Application and Future Research

This chapter has introduced a research-derived global capabilities framework for public administrators. It builds on theory and experience from business and management literature to suggest how components of global business leadership and CQ might be applied in a globalised public service environment. The research extrapolates four key elements—knowledge, experience, skills and attitudes—which are central to facilitating successful engagement in a global policy environment. The framework goes on to define five key components for each of these elements, offering a comprehensive 'menu' from which individual administrators, groups or departments might select and build their own capabilities. Importantly, the chapter has suggested that these capabilities, many of which relate to strong interpersonal and intercultural skills, are not necessarily inherent within particular personality types. Instead, these are learnable capabilities that can be developed through good and consistent leadership training, especially of a type that concentrates on habit-formation and relationship building.

The framework can support public administrators' growth and development in these key areas in a number of ways. Returning to the chapter's opening discussion, it is clear that capabilities for a globalised public service must stretch beyond basic 'literacy' to encompass more generic skills, but also culturally specific experiences. In terms of practical implementation, the framework could be employed at several key points within public service careers: through incorporation into public policy studies at university; during the recruitment or graduate in-take process; as a key component of professional development or managerial 'upskilling' programs, including internal training; or via incorporation into statements that define organisational culture or values. For example, global capabilities could contribute an enriching component the leadership frameworks used widely throughout different branches of the Australian public service.

The global capabilities framework is steeped within CQ and global business leadership literature that relies heavily on the needs and experiences of corporate executives. Future research could enrich the framework by exploring whether and how the identified capabilities may differ from or be better refined to suit the unique roles of public administrators. Exploration of public servants' motivations for wanting to work more proactively into global environments could also offer interesting insights to enhance the framework. The framework's early iteration also suffers from a 'Westerner looking outward' approach, like much other public policy scholarship. The words of one interviewee remind us of the importance and value of shifting perspectives and ensuring that tools like the global capabilities framework are informed from multiple, diverse vantage points:

> I think that Asian Capabilities, you can deal with as two ways. For us it's that we need to understand Asia more, but at the same time, how do we position ourselves in those Asian countries and make them understand us more? It can't be one way, because otherwise there will still be misunderstanding, miscommunication. (Interview 24)

Future research could explore global capabilities from non-Western perspectives to interrogate whether and how the generic values, skills, knowledge and experience hold. This would result in a framework better able to support truly global engagement.

The chapter's focus on global capabilities stems from a broader concern about the changing nature of public policy, public administration and policy scholarship. The development of the global capabilities framework also reflects the more theoretical and values-based concerns of this volume. Ultimately, the framework intends to offer a means of improving public servants' understandings of one another and each other's values, positions, roles and principles. Awareness of these concerns, as highlighted through application of the framework, provides an important opportunity to improve relationships and encourage self-reflection.

References

Bazeley, P., & Jackson, K. (2013). *Qualitative data analysis with nvivo*. London: Sage.

Bell, D. (2010). *China's new confucianism: Politics and everyday life in a changing society*. Princeton: Princeton University.

Berke, D., Kossler, M., & Wakefield, M. (2008). *Developing leadership talent*. San Francisco: John Wiley.

Bice, S., & Merriam, A. (2016). Defining Asia capabilities for Australia's Public Service. *Australian Journal of Public Administration*.

Bice, S., & Sullivan, H. (2014). Public policy studies and the Asian century: New orientations, challenges and opportunities. *Governance, 27*(4), 539–544.

Brereton, M., & Temple, M. (1999). The new public service ethos: An ethical environment for governance. *Public Administration, 77*(3), 455–474.

Cheung, A. B. L. (2005). The politics of administrative reforms in Asia: Paradigms and legacies, paths and diversities. *Governance, 18*(2), 257–282.

Cheung, A. B. L. (2013). Can there be an Asian model of public administration? *Public Administration and Development, 33*(4), 249–261.

Corby, S. (2000). Employee relations in the public services: A paradigm shift? *Public Policy and Administration, 15*(3), 60–74.

Denhardt, J., & Denhardt, R. (2015). The new public service revisited. *Public Administration Review, 75*(5), 664–672.

Denhardt, R., & Denhardt, J. (2009). *Public administration: An action orientation*. Belmont: Thomson Higher Education.

Department of Foreign Affairs and Trade. (2012). *Australia in the Asian century: White paper*. Canberra, ACT: Australian Commonwealth Government.

Dickinson, H., & Sullivan, H. (2014). *Imagining the 21st century public service workforce*. Melbourne: The University of Melbourne.

Dickinson, H., Sullivan, H., & Head, G. (2015). The future of the public service workforce: A dialogue. *Australian Journal of Public Administration, 74*(1), 23–32.

Drechsler, W. (2013). Three paradigms of governance and administration: Chinese, Western and Islamic. *Society and Economy, 35*(3), 319–342.

Earley, P. C., & Peterson, R. S. (2004). The elusive cultural chameleon: Cultural intelligence as a new approach to intercultural training for the global manager. *Academy of Management Learning & Education, 3*(1), 100–115.

Earley, P. C., & Mosakowski, E. (2004). Cultural intelligence. *Harvard Business Review, 82*(10), 139–146.

Earley, P. C., & Ang, S. (2003). A theory of cultural intelligence. *Cultural intelligence: Individual interactions across cultures*. Stanford: Stanford Business Books.

Flyvbjerg, B. (2001). *Making social science matter: Why social inquiry fails and how it can succeed again*. Cambridge: Cambridge University.

Grimshaw, D., Vincent, S., & Willmott, H. (2002). Going privately: Partnership and outsourcing in UK public services. *Public Administration, 80*(3), 475–502.

Gulrajani, N., & Moloney, K. (2012). Globalizing public administration: Today's research and tomorrow's agenda. *Public Administration Review, 72*(1), 78–86.

Haque, M. S. (2013). Public administration in a globalized Asia: Intellectual identities, challenges, and prospects. *Public Administration and Development, 33*(4), 262–274.

Haque, M. S. (2007). Theory and practice of public administration in southeast Asia: Traditions, directions, and impacts. *International Journal of Public Administration, 30*(12–14), 1297–1326.

Haque, M. S., & Turner, M. (2013). Knowledge-building in Asian public administration: An introductory overview. *Public Administration and Development, 33*(4), 243–248.

Hebson, G., Grimshaw, D., & Marchington, M. (2003). PPPs and the changing public sector ethos: Case-study evidence from the health and local authority sectors. *Work, Employment & Society, 17*(3), 481–501.

Julsrud, T. E., & Gjerdåcker, A. (2013). Managing obligations and opportunities: Long distance travels and personal network strategies in global organizations. *Research in Transportation Business and Management, 9*(4), 29–40.

Junhee, J., & McLean, G. N. (2015). An integrative framework for global leadership competencies. *Human Resource Development International, 18*(3), 235–258.

Kivland, C., & King, N. (2015). Six reasons why leadership training fails. *Leadership Excellence Essentials, 32*(1), 5–8.

Legard, R., Keegan, J., & Ward, K. (2003). In-depth interviews. In J. Ritchie & J. Lewis (Eds.), *Qualitative research strategies: A guide for social science students and researchers* (pp. 138–169). London: Sage Publications Ltd.

McCall, M. W., & Hollenbeck, G. P. (2002). *Developing global executives: The lessons of international experience.* Boston: Harvard Business.

Mendenhall, M. E. (2012). *Global leadership: Research, practice, and development.* Abingdon: Routledge.

Needham, C. (2008). Realising the potential of co-production: Negotiating improvements in public services. *Social Policy and Society, 7*(02), 221–231.

Needham, C., Mangan, C., & Dickinson, H. (2014). *The 21st century public service workforce: Eight lessons from the literature.* Birmingham: The University of Birmingham.

Newman, J., Barnes, M., Sullivan, H., & Knops, A. (2004). Public participation and collaborative governance. *Journal of Social Policy, 33*(02), 203–223.

Podger, A. S. (2004). Innovation with integrity—The public sector leadership imperative to 2020. *Australian Journal of Public Administration, 63*(1), 11–21.

Putnam, R. D. (1995). *Bowling alone: The collapse and revival of American community.* New York: Simon and Schuster.

Rosen, R., Digh, P., Singer, M., & Phillips, C. (2000). *Global literacies lessons on business leadership and national cultures.* New York: Simon and Schuster.

Schein, E. (2013). *Humble inquiry: The gentle art of asking instead of telling.* San Francisco: Berrett-Koehler Publishers.

Shergold, P. (2013). My hopes for a public service for the future. *Australian Journal of Public Administration, 72,* 7–13.

Spitzberg, B., & Cupach, W. (2011). Interpersonal skills. In M. Knapp & J. Daly (Eds.), *The Sage handbook of interpersonal communication* (pp. 481–526). SAGE: Thousand Oaks.

Svara, J. H. (2001). The myth of the dichotomy: Complementarity of politics and administration in the past and future of public administration. *Public Administration Review, 61*(2), 176–183.

Turner, M. (2002). Choosing items from the menu: New public management in southeast Asia. *International Journal of Public Administration, 25*(12), 1493–1512.

The University of Birmingham. (2011). *When tomorrow comes: The future of local public services*. Birmingham: The University of Birmingham.

United Nations Educational, Scientific and Cultural Organization. (2009). *Investing in cultural diversity and intercultural dialogue*. Retrieved from: http://unesdoc.unesco.org/images/0018/001847/184755e.pdf.

Vesa, S. (2002). Global leader development: An emerging research agendanull. *Career Development International, 7*(4), 218–233.

CHAPTER 11

Hurdles to an Asian Century of Public Administration

Kim Moloney

Modern public administration (PA) scholarship is dominated by Western scholars, theories, and concepts (Gulrajani and Moloney 2012). This influence extends to non-Western states, pervades international organisations, and influences relations among states, citizens, and civil society. It reflects the economic and political power of its two key actors: the United States and Western Europe. In the last five decades, however, Asian economic growth and socioeconomic progress has increased

This chapter was initially prepared for a two-day symposium at The University of Melbourne in which participants explored the question of whether we are witnessing an "Asian Century" in Public Administration and Public Policy. The Symposium basis was a call by then-PM Julia Gillard to create an 'Asia-literate' and 'Asia-capable' Australia. The chapter was later modified for presentation at the 2017 Fred Riggs Symposium at the American Society of Public Administration (ASPA) Conference in Atlanta GA (16–20 March 2017). The chapter benefitted from audience comments and an extensive review by two anonymous reviewers along with this volume's editorial team. Any errors are my own.

K. Moloney (✉)
Murdoch University, Perth, WA, Australia
e-mail: k.moloney@murdoch.edu.au

S. Bice et al. (eds.), *Public Policy in the 'Asian Century'*, International Series on Public Policy, https://doi.org/10.1057/978-1-137-60252-7_11

the power and influence of its states. In an altered global environment, this chapter explores whether there has been a concomitant rise in Asian PA influence. The unfortunate answer is "not quite". This answer is explored across space and time to unravel "how we know what we know", where knowledge is created, and how it is diffused.

The chapter framework is focused on the *structure* of knowledge and its intellectual histories and the *values* espoused in administrative life. This involves asking whether administrative models are largely Western[1] and if the intellectual histories, model choices, and methodological tools are "decolonised". The "not quite" answer indicates which knowledge is prioritised and how training, hiring, and publication opportunities influence knowledge creation. Barriers which limit a full bi-directional influence between Western—and Asia-based administrative scholarship include language, methods, concept relevancy, editorial space limitations, and questions about which scholars (e.g., by gender, ethnicity) dominate the intellectual discourse.

Space, Time and of Whom We Speak

This section has three tasks. The first is to select a geographic boundary to Asia. The second explores the limits of evaluating a century as "Asian" before the end of this century. Each task prefaces the third: an incomplete decolonisation of what is "Asian" public administration. The "Asian" label (and its Western counterpart) requires definition. We cannot know from where our intellectual currents emanate if we do not clarify to whom we are making geographical reference. This is more important than asking any "big" questions of public administration (Behn 1995, p. 26; Kirlin 2001), whether public administration is an art or science (West 2005), or whether New Public Management (NPM) is indeed "new" (Rosenbloom 2001). It is not that each question is unimportant but rather, the questions are often asked in an ahistorical manner and often do not consider geographic location. The structural (and value-based) assumptions behind what is knowledge or a "big question" (in the West) are assumed to exist across time and to be relevant to all regions. This is unlikely to be the case.

Assigning Geographic Boundaries

This geographic exercise begins by defining the West to include Western Europe, the United States of America, Canada, Australia, and New Zealand. It is a narrower categorisation than the OECD's inclusion of Japan and South Korea. This "West" does not refer simply to wealthy and democratic states but the states from which the dominant intellectual currents of twentieth century PA largely originate.

Less clear are the boundaries of Asia. Should it include Australia, as per the former Australian Prime Minister Paul Keating? Perhaps it should include South Asia and the Pacific island states, or extend westward along the path traveled by Marco Polo to Baghdad and the Western Mediterranean. It might also include the Silk Road through Kazakhstan or the sea trade routes running throughout Indonesia, the sub-continent, Madagascar, and East Africa. The inclusive answer is that all are Asia. The narrower answer might include Northeast Asia, South Asia, Southeast, and Southwest Asia—none of which include the South Pacific or Australia and New Zealand. Given word limits, chapter discussion limits "Asia" to China, South Korea, Japan, and to a lesser extent, India. This limitation creates its own bias since each country often dominates "Asian" PA intellectual exchanges. Since global intellectual dominance need not equate to "right" or "appropriate", this observation must also be extended as a cautionary note to each of the four countries discussed here.

This geographic boundary simplifies the chapter task via a narrower scope of countries, cultures, and histories. However, complication also arises since Asia, like the West, lacks a singular administrative history or even identity (Cheung 2005; Painter and Peters 2010). If Asia has "no settled identity" (Ibrahim 1996, p. 186) and there is no "collective actor" called Asia, then claiming an "Asian Century" is nearly impossible (Cox 2012, p. 379). It is to this question of "century" to which attentions now turn.

Assigning a Century Boundary

Answering the "what is a century" question also appears simple. A century begins at Year 0 and stops at the end of Year 99. Using 1900 as a start-point, European PA scholarship has dominated the twentieth century even as its focus changed from domestic and colonial administrative concerns to a literature that incorporates multilevel governance and the European Union. In contrast, early twentieth century scholarship in the United States infrequently travelled across borders and instead, was informed by European ideas. It was not until the second half of the twentieth century that US (and European) PA scholarship would jointly dominate the PA discipline. This chapter goes to press just before the end of the first fifth of the twenty-first century. Just as a student essay cannot be evaluated with just two of its ten pages, caution is required if labeling a century as either Asian or even Western. The folly of such an early characterisation is discussed in the next paragraphs. At the start of the twentieth and twenty-first centuries, US scholarship for the twentieth century, and Asian scholarship for the twenty-first century, did not yet dominate their centuries. As illustrated below, this changed for the United States shortly after the end of WWII. For Asia, this may also happen if some of the hurdles discussed in this chapter are overcome.

If the question of whether the twentieth century would become a century of US public administration had been asked in 1920, the answer would have been "no". It was still too early in 1920 to foresee the United States' later influence. WWI had just ended, the Bolshevik Revolution was only a few years old, the Germans were in flux, and Australia had just begun to internalise Gallipoli. The British, French, Portuguese, Dutch, and Spanish were at or near their height of colonial power. Global administration experiments at the League of Nations and the International Labor Organization were less than a year old. The 1929 stock market crash, escalating tariffs, and the Depression were not on the horizon. In the aftermath of WWI, the US slipped back into its pre-war isolation. Few could have imagined how the "war to end all wars" would somersault within a generation into WWII. Atomic bombs, a Western Europe in disarray, a rising Soviet threat, and the Cold War were unfathomable in 1920.

In 1920, US-based public administration scholarship was dominated by European trends (Heady 2001). The US had just extended women the right to vote. Labor concerns, a new taxation system, progressive debates, meritocracy, and Taylorism were shaping US public administration theory and practice. Concepts that anchor current administrative scholarship were not fully articulated, for example: the politics-administration dichotomy; satisficing; the importance of implementation; the interaction of social justice with public administration; street-level bureaucracies; neoclassical economic influences on development administration; public service motivation, NPM; networks; and collaborative governance, among others. Unlike Western Europe's development (colonial) administration studies (Gulrajani and Moloney 2012), US administrative scholarship infrequently reflected its (neo)colonial forays (e.g., regarding the Philippines). The exportation of a still-developing US administrative model was a generation away.[2]

What was already occurring by 1920, however, was a reframing of perspectives to recognize (what was known about) local values, expectations and responses as uniquely US contributions. Within three decades, this history included the progressive and orthodoxy eras, the *Administrative State*, debates among Waldo, Appleby, and Simon, and the tensions between Friedrich and Finer; each defined and redefined US public administration for generations to come (see Appleby 1946; Finer 1941; Friedrich 1940; Simon 1946; Waldo 1984 (1948)). Shortly after WWII, and in parallel with the increased global importance of the US economy, bi-directional US and Western European administrative interaction was on the rise. This coincided with an increased US interest in the administrative development of post-colonial societies (Gulrajani and Moloney 2012), the Marshall Plan, and a US desire to strengthen security arrangements in Western Europe.

In contrast to the United States' early twentieth century, many parts of Asia in 1920 were either colonised and/or had not yet formalised their modern-day borders. Much of the Asia-focused PA research that gained international (e.g., Western) attention was written not by Asian scholars but by Westerners. The directionality of who created twentieth century administrative knowledge and how it was distributed was largely unidirectional to Asia, from the West.

In the first fifth of the twenty-first century, this chapter asks if Asian PA is bi-directional influence. The answer is "not quite". This answer rings true (and disappointingly so) despite the comparative youth of US administrative life against a millennium of documented administrative writing in India and China. The historical and intellectual importance of the latter has not translated into diffusible "lessons learned" for Asian and non-Asian societies. While the colonial yoke has been legally dismantled, a modern and internationally dominant Asian century of public administration has not arrived. Before illustrating the hurdles that prevent a bidirectional Asian administrative influence, the next paragraphs reference the ongoing decolonisation of the Asian administrative experience.

The (De)colonisation of the Asian Experience

Scholars of Asian PA have published within Western-based academic journals for more than half a century. Publication, however, need not imply that Asian administrative models and concepts have substantively influenced Western scholarship or its practice. Before unpacking this troubling situation, the next paragraphs highlight typical Asian PA scholarship.

Outside of multiple colonial administration studies or post-colonial studies carried out by former colonial powers (see Cooke 2003 for a critical perspective), early Western-written examples include Fred Riggs' book on Thailand (Riggs 1966), his *sala* model[3] (Riggs 1964, 1967), or his editorship of a 19-chapter reflection on development administration in 1969. This edited book, which was largely written with contributions by Western-born administrative scholars, included two chapters on pre-Nixon Communist China (Barnett 1969; Vogel 1969). Other early examples include reflections on India (Appleby 1953; Merriam 1928), as well as Malaysia and Pakistan (Braibanti 1966; Esman 1972).

Among the many Asian PA scholars with substantial scholarly legacies, there are those who focus on Thailand (Bowornwathana 2000; Burns 2013), write on Japan's civil service reforms (Kim et al. 1995), explore Singapore and other ASEAN states (Quah 1980, 2003), and focus early on Indian pubic administration (Ruthnaswamy 1956). Recent examples include work on China by Hon S. Chan or on India by Krishna Tummala (e.g. Chan 2004; Tummala 1999, 2003), as well as edited collections highlighting diverse administrative experiences (Berman et al. 2010; Kim 2009, 2010, 2011; Sabharwal and Berman 2016).

By expanding the time horizon beyond a century, the US' comparatively short administrative history becomes clear. With dynastic origins as early as 1600 BCE, the Chinese administrative state predates Athens by more than 800 years. One of the earliest public administration texts is not Western, but Chinese. *Wan Yan Shu* (published in 1058) addressed Chinese civil service challenges, encouraged public sector reform, and considered human resource management issues (Drechsler 2013). India's fourth century BCE *Arthashastra* text focused on how to govern a (largely autocratic) state. Broadly speaking, most Chinese and Indian *administrative* histories (as opposed to a broader political and economic history) are condensed into text not yet translated or made accessible to readers unfamiliar with Mandarin or Sanskrit. Western unfamiliarity with a discoverable Asian administrative canon extends beyond China and India. The translation of pre-twentieth century Korean and Japanese texts is increasingly discoverable but infrequently distributed across Asia and the world.

Western public administration builds upon several early history documents. One such document is the Athenian Oath, written in the fifth century BCE. The Oath is an honor code and a call to serve the public good. Its creation existed alongside the Athenian decision to pay its civil servants, a radical decision for its time (Gilman 2005). An Asian PA not built upon its earliest works nor shared across languages creates a "missing" history inhibiting the placement of Asia-specific administrative events into a larger global timeline. The outcome is an under-emphasis on what was administratively known in Asia, an overemphasis on the Western experience, and a narrowed discourse. Given that many of the ideas Western scholars ascribe to their own civilisational development may originate from Asia (Turner 2002), any under-emphasis is troubling. In other words, it is not Asian PA that is in its infancy but rather a Western understanding of Asian PA. This includes also an insufficiently deep comparative effort among and between Asian PA scholars on country-specific administrative differences. The existing (but still suppressed) Asian PA tradition sits in flux. The next section explores whether an Asian model exists and how Asian PA scholars interact with Western PA ideas.

Structure and Values: Which Model for Asian PA Research?

The earliest US public administration scholars reflected both European scholarship and early US history (Heady 2001). Asian public administration scholarship also reflects its history, the selective insertion of non-Asian intellectual currents, and the modification of foreign currents to suit its state-driven development practice. But whereas Western PA scholarship may infiltrate Asian PA and its scholarship, there has been minimal infiltration of broadly Asian ideas into Western PA theories, concepts, or practice.

Western Model and Asia

Western PA scholars, aid agencies, and international organisations frequently recommend Western administrative ideas for Asia (Turner et al. 2013). Scholars have explored the applicability of Western ideas to an Asian context (e.g. Kim 2009; Samaratunge et al. 2008; Turner 2002) and/or what happens when Western ideas do not apply to Asian contexts (e.g. Bowornwathana 2000; Kilby 2004; Manning 2001). While some scholars accept that what works in Bangladesh may not work in Bhutan, many scholars infrequently question whether what works in the West *should* apply elsewhere. In addition, Western administrative history often reflects its earlier origins while Western-written scholarship on Asian PA infrequently incorporates dates or administrative histories earlier than colonial reinterpretations of its past. Some academics might suggest that Western models *need not* apply even if their base values do not change, that is, the West's market-based democracies are not just desirable but perhaps also an *End of History* (Fukuyama 1992).

An Asian "Developmental State" Model?

Western characterisation of Asia's public sector describes the region as administering a "developmental state" model (see, Pierre, Chap. 13 of this volume). This model emphasises a state- and export-led growth along with limited democratic commitments and a downplaying of Western prescriptions for transparent and accountable administrative practices (Haque 2007). Using the narrowest Western characterisation of this "Asian" model, the Asian Financial Crisis (AFC) rattled many of its assumptions (Haggard 2000). Subsequent model modifications have occurred as Asian countries democratise or, as in the case of China, publicly tackle corruption and to a lesser extent, financial opacity (Tu 2016; Wang 2014). Despite Western condemnation of Asia's "crony capitalism" and despotism (Philippi 2003; Woo-Cummings 2005), this model persists as a descriptive tool for Western scholars. This includes Korea's state-industrial complex (*chaebol*), its export-ready "New Village" (*saemaul undong*) agricultural modernisation (e.g. Kim 1988; Park 2009) or studies that extol a Chinese *nomenklatura* (Chan, 204).

In the aftermath of the AFC, scholars questioned whether East Asia's "spiritual features" (Philippi 2003, p. 292) influenced the crisis onset. Such features were said to influence public sector institutions and state-government relations and include "loyalty, faithfulness, and obedience to the ruling party as well as adherence to party decisions and policies" (Chen 2010, p. 371). From the Western perspective (including traditional PA and NPM), such values may undermine individualism and encourage corruption. This includes the Weberian assumption that Confucianism is not "conducive to the individual achievement to fuel a capitalistic system" (Rarick 2007, p. 26). Others, such as the late Prime Minister of Singapore (Lee Kuan Yew) believed that that "cronyism and corruption" occurred due to a broad "debasement of Confucian values" and not as an outcome of Confucianism itself (Milner 2000, n.p.).

Certainly the classification of this model as "developmental" is itself contested. Asian administrative practices are amalgams of national and Western practice. The Meiji administrative state (and its restoration), its partial exportation to Korea, and its influence on other Asian states is one such example. Model developments are autonomous and innovative and they reflect the coexistence of local tradition, modernity, and increased regional and global engagements (Cheung 2005; Painter and Peters 2010). Turner et al. (2013) argue that an Asian developmental state "does not simply dominate society but interacts with it, sometimes intimately and at other times aggressively in pursuit of the joint project of socioeconomic transformation" (p. 486). The resulting Asian "model" is less a reflection of a single influence but instead, many.

An Asian "Amalgamation" Model?

Just as there is no single Western model (Raadschelders 2008), there may also be no single Asian administrative model. Instead, its frequently state-driven characteristics are both reflections of its past and its vision for the future. Asia has incorporated and adopted external influences while seeking to redefine its differences from the West. In Korea, for example, the Japanese occupation altered the Korean administrative landscape by its method of linking law with public administration. The 1950s occupation of South Korea by the US furthered encouraged a borrowing of ideas (Kim 2012). This occurred alongside an indigenisation drive that sought to revise Western concepts for the Korean experience. This indigenisation rhetoric was (and is) often pitted against a separate "Koreanisation" effort. In contrast to indigenisation, Koreanisation seeks to understand and study its past, to question Western influence, and to create Korean-specific theories. Counterintuitively, indigenisation and

Koreanisation may over-emphasise border importance while limiting the development of an Asian PA capable of crossing Asian and non-Asian borders (Kim 2012).

Nonetheless, there are key administrative differences between Asia and the West. As noted by one Chinese observer, "authoritarian" in the Western sense "implies that the state controls society through coercion. It assumes that the state and society are separate… [t]his is a western dualist view of state-society relations" (Wu 2008). In contrast, there is no clear politics-administration dichotomy in China (Wu et al. 2011). The "good" Chinese civil servant is loyal to the Communist Party and as such, is political (Chen 2010). This "reform with Chinese characteristics" with a "crossing the river by feeling the stones" shares one goal: economic growth (Aufrecht and Bun 1995; Wu et al. 2011). At the local level, economic growth was paired with "conducting ideological indoctrination and recruiting new party members" (Chan and Gao 2013, p. 367). The resulting administrative reforms were to be non-political in order not to upset the larger political structures (Wu et al. 2011). Others use a Western-derived Weberian model to justify existing practice. The Chinese perceive the creation of a "modern state in the terms defined by Max Weber. That is, China created a centralised, uniform system of bureaucratic administrative that was capable of governing a huge population and territory" (Drechsler, Chap. 2 of this volume; Drechsler, 2013, p. 327 citing Fukuyama 2011, 2012; Jacques, 2011, 2012; Tao, Chap. 4 of this volume).

An Asian reframing of Western trends is also found elsewhere. Under Mao and the Cultural Revolution, administrative reform did not diminish state importance but instead, strengthened the Party and its state (Cheung 2005). The creation of a neoliberal urban class is less a reflection of Chinese direct incorporation of Western values than an output from a Chinese indigenous modernisation or "capitalist restoration" project (Wu 2008, p. 1094). Even the efficiency-first focus of NPM is reframed for Asian states. Rather than such an emphasis leading to the "dispensing with bureaucracy altogether," Asian scholars reframe efficiency as an important value for *retaining* bureaucracy. In this perspective, efficient practices strengthen the state and not, as Western scholars assert, weaken or "hollow out" the state (Cheung 1997).

In the West, scholars focus upon how impartial administrative structures may increase state efficiency. In contrast, Korea's cultural and structural hierarchies may require the opposite. Korean civil servants' "non-substitutability" and individualised jobs means that in a "Confucian understanding of government workers... [they are] defined not by the range of tasks that they have mastered but rather by the underlying general character of their education and the presumption that they are aligned with the public interest" (Im et al. 2013, p. 293). The links among employee non-substitutability, hierarchy, a highly-bureaucratic structure, and a civil service rooted in their duties and a societal meaning of bureaucracy imply that a West-based PA focus on responsibility, motivations, incentives, and performance measurement may have little direct application (Im et al. 2013).

In many Asian states, the "rule of man" refers to the values espoused by an individual's relationship with the state and society. Just like pre-modern China emphasised a "society of acquaintances" under a benevolent and paternalistic state, both ancient and modern civil service exams reflect societal expectations of its bureaucracy. In China, this included requiring applicants to be familiar with the Four Books and Five Classics of Confucianism (Rarick 2007). Similar requirements were emphasised during Korea's five-century *Joseon* dynasty (1392–1897). Latter-day Korean exams "tested both a scholar's learning as well as their ability to apply the principles of the Neo-Confucian philosophy to the practical affairs of government" (Im et al. 2013, p. 287). In addition, the learned civil servant and his importance reinforced a weak monarch who served as both "master and student" of his civil servants (Im et al. 2013, p. 289).[4] In other words, meritocracy or the entrance into civil service life through qualification is not a Western invention (see, Drechsler Chap. 2 of this volume, 2013).

Further indigenisation and assertion of Asian concepts and claims is underway (Frederickson 2002; Kim 2012). One example links Confucianism, family elder relations, and favor exchange (*quanxi*) to ask what is administratively discussed in Asia and how such discussions influence Asian politics and economic development (see, Pierre, Chap. 13 of this volume; Jun and Sherwood 2007). This includes efforts to define an Asian identity that is more nuanced than is often asserted. Ongoing intellectual, ideological, and political debates are working to marry modern states with their pasts, re-conceptualise national identities, and potentially, an Asian identity (Milner 2000).

Limited Bi-Directionality of Asian Models

Asian PA is deepening and broadening its administrative scholarship. It is a field increasingly reflective of its pre-colonial past and its efforts to adopt or partially internalise external influences. This engagement is the opposite of the minimal adoption or even adaptation and internalisation of any Asian administrative ideas into modern Western theory or practice. A key barrier to the incorporation of Asian administration into non-Asian models is a frequent assumption that modernisation equates to Westernisation (see, Drechsler, Chap. 2 of this volume). Unfortunately, this assumption "delegitimize[s] the former in those contexts in which Westernization is at least an ambiguous concept for many" and as such, simply acknowledging that "modernization is not necessarily Westernization, would be a major accomplishment" (Drechsler 2013, p. 322).

Discussions of Asian administration by either Asian or Western scholars infrequently suggest that what is learnable in Asia is potentially transferable to the West. It is highly unlikely that what is learnable in China or Pakistan has no potential policy transferability. Just as medicine has benefitted from the discovery and use of indigenous plants or the Zulu's *indaba* helped climate change negotiators find solutions previously considered unachievable (Zimmer 2015), Asia-to-West policy ideas transfer could offer new pathways. But still-limited Asia-to-West transfer hampers administrative theory developments. The application of selected Asian histories and ideas to Western understandings of administration would symbolise an end to colonisation. The next section explores in greater detail many of the hurdles to bi-directional learning and practice.

Structure and Values: Education, Publication, Language, and Methods

Several hurdles prohibiting deeper exchanges between Asia and the West are inseparable from which administrative histories are deliberated or shared across contexts. This includes from where scholars receive their training, academic hiring practices, publications, language, methods and concept relevancy, and gender and ethnic balances. This section discusses each hurdle and its implications for an Asian Century in PA.

Terminal Degree Location and Hiring Practices

Many of the contemporary Asian-born scholars who publish in top-ranked journals obtained their terminal degree at an American, Canadian, Western European, or Australian universities. Within this cohort, the greatest prestige is often reserved for scholars with a terminal degree from the highest-ranking US/UK public administration, public management or public policy programs. The choice of where to obtain a PhD influences where a scholar is hired, which conference papers are valued, publication preferences, and ultimately, the promotion practices that may harden a perception of what is considered valuable or legitimate administrative knowledge.

If an Asian PA student desires a career at a Western or top Asian university, terminal degrees obtained at Western universities are more likely to lead to academic employment. This bias reflects the location of colonial and neocolonial knowledge hubs, as well as the academic hiring preferences of Asian and Western faculties. Variation may exist for Asian scholars who obtain PhDs from the top four or five Asian universities. Regardless, the general perception exists that terminal degrees obtained in Asia are more likely to lead to employment at a low- or mid-level Asian university than employment either at a top-ranked Asian university or even less likely, a Western university. If the desire is to work in the West or land a job at a top Asian university, West-based PhDs are a near necessity.

Despite an offering of PA courses in many countries, the prevalence of graduate-level Master of Public Administration (MPA) programs remains low. An important exception is South Korea. Korea has the highest number of PA programs as a proportion of its universities (Kim 2012). At the PhD level growth is harder to ascertain. India offers nearly 30 PhD programs in PA and many more at the MPA level. China's first PhD in PA was created in 1998 (Wu et al. 2013).

Specific to the "Social Policy and Administration" category within which Public Administration sits, twenty Asian universities were in the world's Top 100 in 2016–2017. Two universities were Top Ten: University of Tokyo and University of Hong Kong. Four of China's seven top 100 universities in this subject area were not from mainland China but from Hong Kong (QS 2017). More broadly, there is a centering (or perhaps, insufficient de-centering) of knowledge in Asia. In this landscape, only universities in China, Hong Kong, Japan, Singapore, South Korea, and Taiwan were found in the top 100.

Despite two Malaysian universities placing in the bottom half of the "Social Policy and Administration" top 100, universities from other Asian countries are not in the top 100. In a university-wide evaluation, and as noted by Cox (2012), China only has five universities among the top 100 in the world with three of those five based in Hong Kong. This statistic compares unfavorably with the US and the UK who were home to 76 of the top 100 while Asia, as a whole, only had 13. By 2017, the number of Asian universities in the top 100 increased to 19. Four of the eight Chinese universities in the Top 100 were based in Hong Kong (QS 2017).

The University of Hong Kong, University of Tokyo, Seoul National University, Yonsei University, and the National University of Singapore are not just respected Asian universities but also universities with two or more decades of international collaboration. But crucial to an intellectual tradition and its regional or international transmission are graduates capable of securing jobs in countries outside their own. Current knowledge colonisation suggests that Asian students are best served (in terms of employment, publishing capacity, theoretical and methodological training) in their study of Asia *by leaving Asia* to earn a PhD in the West.[5] The intellectual colonisation which results may devalue (or often, infrequently discuss) the Asian experience (Haque 2007). A hiring preference for Western-educated PhDs creates a river of Asian administrative intellectuals leaving Asia, entering Western PhD programs, and in most cases, not returning to Asia (Haque 2013; Jun 2006).

This reality also reflects not just the language utilised in one's terminal degree but also the historic relationship among Asian states, their civil service exams, and the universities that graduate individuals capable of passing such exams. In a cultural environment that attaches prestige to civil servant employment, many Asian-based universities focus less on doctorate-level PA training than ensuring their undergraduate students pass the civil service exam. In 2016, nearly a million Chinese took the civil service exam for the chance at 27,000 jobs (Liu and Wang 2016). In India, nearly a half million test-takers recently sought approximately 1000 federal-level jobs (Agarwal 2016). Similar to China and India, civil service appointments also earn prestige in Korea. In the last 20 years, Korean test-takers numbers more than doubled despite acceptance rates infrequently higher than two percent (Park 2017).

Publication Outlets

No matter whether one utilises a global Thomson-Reuters Journal Citation evaluator or an Australia-specific "Excellence in Research" guide, Asia-driven PA journals infrequently hold an impact factor higher than their global peers. This includes journals with forty or more years of publication experience such as the *Asian Journal of Public Administration*, *Asia Pacific Journal of Public Administration*, *Indian Journal of Public Administration*, and the *Hong Kong Journal of Public Administration*. Nearly twenty years into this century, Asia-based journals are not first-choice locations for a scholar who desires a journal with a high impact factor. Greater reputational, promotion, and career rewards may accrue when scholars publish in a top-ranked US— or UK-based journal. In some Asian universities, such publications may also pay financial rewards such as a congratulatory fund to an Asia-based scholar who publishes in faculty-identified "top" journals.

If Asia's administrative knowledge is neither decolonised nor creating strong bi-directional flows of influence, it is not a leap to suggest that journal editors and reviewers may also show discomfort or an inability to evaluate (value-free) an Asia-dominant perspective. The impact of this implicit bias may push Asia-focused scholars to research what is understood, and not what reflects Asia-driven intellectual histories, theories, and trends. The outcome of journal impact factor pressure and a Western bias may be an altered intellectual agenda and a limiting of theoretical and practice-based developments. Living and working in a non-Western context inevitably poses contradictions between the literature familiar to Western editors and reviewers and the reality in a particular Asian country. Examples include asking whether public service motivation indices (e.g. Perry 1996), as constructed in the US, should apply without modification to another country (see Appendix of Moloney and Chu 2016) or why NPM struggles in developing country contexts (Schick 1998).

Journal location and intellectual preferences are not unrelated to where conferences are held and which abstracts are procured and accepted by conference committees. Excluding recent efforts by top universities to host more administrative conferences, most conferences remain outside the region. With more than 60 percent of the world identifying as Asian and one-third of the globe identifying as Chinese or Indian, this trend will need to reverse if Asia is to claim its (modern) century of PA.

Language, Methods, Concept Relevancy, and Space

Knowledge creation is a difficult enterprise regardless of a scholar's origin, theories, or methods of analysis. However, what is difficult for Western scholars may be *even more difficult* for Asia-based scholars. This is not due to the brilliance (or lack thereof) of one group or the other but that Asian scholars face additional hurdles. One such hurdle is language. Language reveals its importance in three ways. The first relates to the prior argument about where Asia-focused knowledge is created. If the dominant disciplinary journals are written in English and draw upon Western constructs and methodological preferences, then scholars wishing to publish in such journals will require an advanced familiarity with the English language. One method of inserting oneself into such "elite" scholarly circles is attainment of a PhD from an English-language university in the West.

In addition, much of what the English-speaking West knows about Asian administration is written in English. Nearly all top-ranked PA journals use English as their method of communication. One exception is the mid-ranked *International Review of Administration Sciences* that translates its articles into French and Chinese. Certainly English-language academic journals are not the only academic outlet. In one analysis, three Chinese journals produced nearly 2500 Chinese-language articles (Wu et al. 2013), whereas only fifty or so articles were published on Chinese administration within English-language journals between 1999 and 2009 (see, Bice, Chap. 10 of this volume; Walker et al. 2013). The Chinese journals are not unique. There are dozens of local journals published across Asia in a language other than English. But without translation, or an explicit agreement by local-nonlocal co-author teams to share non-English articles, the result is a missed opportunity for English and non-English language scholars to engage in a bi-directional dialogue.

Second, and looking specifically at Chinese-language administrative scholarship, insufficient methodological engagement in Chinese public administration journals "cannot be overstated" (Wu et al. 2013, p. 269). Chinese public administration journals were less likely than their Western peers to include rigorous methods. The authors found an empirical analysis in less than five percent of reviewed Chinese-language articles between 1998 and 2008. Even "more disconcerting" was their finding that 90 percent of published articles contained *no* research methods (Wu et al. 2013, p. 272). Explanations include Chinese-language journals with article word limits as low as 4000 (Wu et al. 2013) or more broadly a problem of conducting survey research in which the "conflation of politics and administration" in Chinese administrative life may challenge academic surveyors (Chen 2013; Su et al. 2013). Questions about Chinese rigor and its insufficient methodological depth may "perpetuate archaic and highly inefficient bureaucratic practices in Chinese institutions" and ultimately, threaten the intellectual engagement between imported Western practices and China's administrative history (Wu et al. 2013, p. 262).

Values are not removed from this discussion. In one interpretation, the "positivist-empiricist research in American public administration… is inappropriate for the inter-subjective and context-based analysis need for understanding the sociocultural milieu of public administration in Asian countries" (Haque 2013, p. 270). Most damning of all is that while other social science disciplines may actively discourage anti-Western biases, in "PA, this is certainly not the case" (Drechsler 2013, p. 323).

In addition, a conflation of politics and administration in some Asian contexts reflects both a systemic choice and a (lack of) robustness in a state's accountability and transparency pressures. Censorship, in particular, will alter what might be questioned and what is knowable. Local or regional Party leaders may be as prominently displayed on a university website as its professoriate. Government limitations of social media discussions (e.g. Communist Party removal of Panama Papers analysis) or even ministerial declarations on what is a "no speak" and thus what is researchable[6] shall limit publication depth and variety.

Another barrier is the relationship between article space and which knowledge is valued. Scholars of under-researched countries often must use 1000 or more words to familiarise their journal audience with public sector context. The relative injustice of this requirement becomes clear if we ask whether Western authors must deliver similar summaries for each of their publications. The implication for an Asia-focused scholar is even less space from which to position and defend an argument. In addition, the effort to politely engage reviewers that an "accepted" Western theory or concept may not, and perhaps should not, apply in their specific case is often more arduous and word-consuming than the application of a likely inapplicable Western concept to Asia. Asia-focused research questions are often more intellectually costly in their design and risk to the scholar. Deviation from Western constructs (and without the space from which to deviate) may raise the rejection risk. It takes significant time to modify Western constructs along with their infrequently-tested cultural assumptions. With few article translations and limited Asian scholar participation within top editorial boards, it is no surprise that "serious challenges" remain (Candler et al. 2010; Gulrajani and Moloney 2012; Haque 2013, p. 271).

Gender and Race

The above discussion was largely written without specific gender or ethnicity identifiers. This is problematic. Simply stated, knowledge creation within public administration is dominated by white men from the West (Feeney 2015). This chapter has not asked whether there is a Black or Chicano century of public administration or if we are in a "female century" of administrative scholarship. Instead, the chapter questions whether we are in a century dominated by an "Asian-ness". Such distinctions are about more than geography. It is about race, gender, and the intersectionality which arises from boxing a region or country into one characterisation. A failure to critically reflect about who researches and teaches Western and Asian administrative life risks overemphasising what is "known" and devaluing voices less frequently heard.

Feeney (2015) observed that few female public administration scholars become journal editors, sit on editorial boards, or serve in associational leadership positions. Potential explanations such as insufficient numbers of female faculty members or female faculty without seniority were dismissed upon her empirical review. While Feeney (2015) does not explore ethnicity or scholarly origin, the perusal of faculty pages at top Asian public administration faculties suggests a strong majority are men. Many of these Asian men (like their female colleagues) will also not hold a majority of the top positions explored by Feeney (2015) even if the dominance of such men within Asia will alter what is knowable.

Explored less frequently than gender are questions about whether Asian PA is dominated by men of a particular ethnic origin, caste (as in India), economic class, or geographic origin. It may be that placement of universities from only a few Asian states in the world's Top 100 may also create questions of whose voice is heard. Just as scholars have explored whether Western university faculty reflect diverse experiences, similar questions must be asked in Asia. The "American century" of PA was and is a century dominated by a particular gender and ethnicity. The discouragement of diverse voices limits knowledge creation and its reflections.

As Asia moves towards (or returns to) an Asian century of PA, consideration of who speaks and from where they originate will become increasingly important.

Conclusion

Asian PA has existed for more than a millennium. But unlike its Western peers, this scholarship has infrequently received the attention it deserves. The present hurdles suggest that we are not yet in a modern Asian century of public administration scholarship. This answer is disappointing. It is uncomfortable to suggest that an administrative history extending over a millennium has not reached its "century" of global influence. Defining the Asian space, clarifying the boundary of time, and understanding its incomplete intellectual decolonisation is a contested terrain. The hurdles faced by Asia-based scholars of PA are largely structural. This includes the location of a scholar's terminal degree and university hiring practices. It also includes value-influenced variables such as language, methods and concept relevancy, journal space, and the gender and ethnic characteristics of Asian faculty. The reasoning behind this chapter's "answer" has as much to do with the West, its neocolonial and parochial histories as its global power over the last several centuries to impose its perspectives upon Asia.

Looking forward, we must be cautious in our model identification and utilised concepts. If the current structures and values have created a largely unidirectional arrow of intellectual engagement, then we have short-circuited the opportunity to engage each other. If the Western scholar asks why Asia is not like the West, and if the answer is because they (Asia) are not yet enough like ourselves (West), then there is a missed opportunity to sufficiently question assumptions, directionality, and the dynamics that limit the reward offered by translating, interpreting, and publishing Asia-driven administrative histories.

To infiltrate and critically engage assumptions and to encourage a global bi-directional and multi-directional engagement among PA scholars, we must expect to be challenged by alternative perspectives, to not assume that modernity equates to Westernisation, and to constantly reassess how knowledge is created, distributed, and rewarded. A reflective and critical administrative historicism will deepen engagement and improve intellectual understanding. It is certainly true that the desire to "constantly question oneself" is "not too high a demand… of the university" and must be honed (Drechsler 2013, p. 338). By being aware of our assumptions and willing to question "how we know what we know", the first step may be taken toward both a global and context-specific PA practice. If done, this will create a space for a modern Asian century of PA to not only rise but to also influence and engage Western administrative theory and practice.

Notes

1. For the purposes of this chapter, "Western" models are assumed to be relatively similar. In reality, however, there is no monolithic "Western" administrative model (refer Raadschelders 2008).
2. It is arguable that PA still has not cast a critical eye on the colonial period (Haque 2007). This limits the West's understanding and interpretation of its past and ultimately, limits knowledge generation and the historical basis upon which we create our theories and frameworks.
3. Based on Riggs' comparative work on the United States and Thailand, he developed an administrative model in which developing country societal views are altered by the arrival of bureaucracy. The prismatic society or *sala* (living room) model describes a mix of formality and informality as the bureaucracy (and state) negotiates its developmental path.
4. This late *Joseon* pattern stood in contrast to China where "imperial governments without limits on their powers" reigned from 1368 to 1912 (Im et al. 2013, p. 289).
5. This need not imply that other options do not exist. With over 4000 accredited Asian universities, it is likely that the majority of PhDs are locally-earned. Nonetheless, a perusal of highly rated Asian PA programs indicates that significant numbers of faculty (with top journal publications credited to their name) earned their terminal degree in the West.
6. The "seven no speaks" in China include "universal values, citizen rights, civil society, judicial independence, freedom of the press, the privileged capitalist class, and past mistakes of the Communist Party" (Anderlini 2015; Clark 2013).

References

Agarwal, V. (2016). Meet the woman who got the top score on India's toughest exam. *Wall Street Journal.* Retrieved from https://blogs.wsj.com/indiarealtime/2016/05/11/meet-the-woman-who-got-top-score-on-indias-toughest-exam/.

Anderlini, J. (2015, January 30). 'Western values' forbidden in Chinese universities. *Financial Times.* Retrieved from http://www.ft.com/cms/s/0/95f3f866-a87e-11e4-bd17-00144feab7de.html#axzz47TcKK6EM.

Appleby, P. (1946). *Big democracy.* New York: Alfred A. Knopf.

Appleby, P. (1953). *Public administration in India: Report of a survey.* Delhi: Manager of Publications.

Aufrecht, S. E., & Bun, L. S. (1995). Reform with Chinese characteristics: The context of Chinese civil service reform. *Public Administration Review, 55*(2), 175–182.

Barnett, A. D. (1969). Mechanisms for party control in the government bureaucracy in China. In F. W. Riggs (Ed.), *Frontiers of development administration* (pp. 415–436). Durham: Duke University Press.

Behn, R. (1995). The big questions of public management. *Public Administration Review, 55*(4), 313–324.

Berman, E. M., Moon, M. J., & Choi, H. (Eds.). (2010). *Public administration in East Asia: Mainland China, Japan, South Korea, Taiwan.* Taiwan: CRC Press.

Bowornwathana, B. (2000). Governance reform in Thailand: Questionable assumptions, uncertain outcomes. *Governance, 13*(3), 393–408.

Braibanti, R. (1966). *Research on the bureaucracy of Pakistan.* Durham: Duke University Press.

Burns, J. P. (2013). Bidhya Bowornwathana. *Asia Pacific Journal of Public Administration, 35*(2), 135–136.

Candler, G. G., Azevêdo, A., & Albernaz, R. O. (2010). Toward global scholarship in public affairs. *Public Administration, 88*(3), 836–850.

Chan, H. B. (2004). Cadre personnel management in China: The Nomenklatura system 1990–1998. *The China Quarterly, 179,* 703–734.

Chan, H. S., & Gao, J. (2013). Can the same key open different locks? Administrative values underlying performance measurement in China. *Public Administration, 91*(2), 366–380.

Chen, X. (2010). State-generated data and contentious politics in China. In A. Carlson, M. E. Gallagher, K. Lieberthal, & M. Manion (Eds.), *Contemporary Chinese politics: New sources, methods, and field strategies* (pp. 15–32). Cambridge: Cambridge University Press.

Cheung, A. B. L. (1997). Understanding public-sector reforms: Global trends and diverse agendas. *International Review of Administrative Science, 63*(4), 435–457.

Cheung, A. B. L. (2005). The politics of administrative reforms in Asia: Paradigms and legacies, paths and diversities. *Governance, 18*(2), 257–282.

Clark, A. (2013, May 22). China bans seven topics in university classrooms including mistakes of communism. *Examiner.* Retrieved from http://www.

examiner.com/article/china-bans-7-topics-university-classrooms-including-mistakes-of-communism.

Cooke, B. (2003). A new continuity with colonial administration: Participation in development management. *Third World Quarterly, 24*(1), 47–61.

Cox, R. W. (2012). Power shifts, economic change and the decline of the west? *International Relations, 26*(4), 369–388.

Drechsler, W. (2013). Three paradigms of governance and administration: Chinese, Western, and Islamic. *Society and Economy, 35*(3), 319–342.

Esman, M. J. (1972). *Administration and development in Malaysia: Institution building and reform in a plural society*. Cornell: Cornell University Press.

Feeney, M. K. (2015). *Power in editorial positions: Where are the women in public administration?* Retrieved from https://ssrn.com/abstract=2611771.

Finer, H. (1941). Administrative responsibility in democratic government. *Public Administration Review, 1*(4), 335–350.

Frederickson, H. G. (2002). Confucius and the moral basis of bureaucracy. *International Review of Administrative Science, 33*(6), 610–628.

Friedrich, C. J. (1940). Public policy and the nature of administrative responsibility. In C. J. Friedrich & E. S. Mason (Eds.), *Public policy: A yearbook of the graduate school of public administration* (pp. 3–24). Cambridge, MA: Harvard University Press.

Fukuyama, F. (1992). *The end of history and the last man*. New York: Free Press.

Gilman, S. C. (2005). *Ethics codes and codes of conduct as tools for promoting an ethical and professional public service: Comparative successes and lessons.* Washington, DC: World Bank.

Gulrajani, N., & Moloney, K. (2012). Globalizing public administration: Today's research and tomorrow's agenda. *Public Administration Review, 72*(1), 78–86.

Haggard, S. (2000). *The political economy of the Asian financial crisis.* Washington, DC: Institute for International Economics.

Haque, M. S. (2007). Theory and practice of public administration in Southeast Asia: Traditions, directions, and impacts. *International Journal of Public Administration, 30*(12–14), 1297–1326.

Haque, M. S. (2013). Public administration in a globalized Asia: Intellectual identities, challenges, and prospects. *Public Administration and Development, 33*, 262–274.

Heady, F. (2001). *Public administration: A comparative perspective* (6th ed.). New York: Marcel Dekker.

Ibrahim, A. (1996). The next 50 years. *Far Eastern Economic Review*, p. 186.

Im, T., Campbell, J. W., & Cha, S. (2013). Revisiting Confucian bureaucracy: Roots of the Korean government's culture and competitiveness. *Public Administration and Development, 33*, 286–296.

Jun, J. S. (2006). Rethinking the theoretical perspective: Beyond the quest for indigenous theory of Korean public administration. *International Review of Administrative Science, 10*(2), 6–15.

Jun, J. S., & Sherwood, F. P. (2007). *The social construction of public administration: Interpretative and critical perspectives.* New York: SUNY Press.

Kilby, P. (2004). Is empowerment possible under a new public management environment? Some lessons from India. *International Public Management Journal, 7*(2), 207–225.

Kim, E. M. (1988). From dominance to symbiosis: State and chaebol in South Korea. *Pacific Focus, 3*(2), 105–121.

Kim, E. M. (Ed.). (2010). *Civil service system and civil service reform in ASEAN member countries and Korea.* Seoul: Daeyoung Moonhwasa Publishing Company.

Kim, E. M. (Ed.). (2011). *Public sector reform in ASEAN member countries and Korea.* Seoul: Daeyoung Moonhwasa Publishing Company.

Kim, E. M. (2012). A historical overview of Korean public administration: Discipline, education, association, international cooperation and beyond indigenization. *International Review of Administrative Science, 78*(2), 217–238.

Kim, H.-K., Muramatsu, M., Pempel, T. J., & Yamamura, K. (Eds.). (1995). *The Japanese civil service and economic development.* Oxford: Clarendon Press.

Kim, P. S. (Ed.). (2009). *Public administration and public governance in ASEAN member countries and Korea.* Seoul: Daeyoung Moonhwasa Publishing Company.

Kim, S. (2009). Revising Perry's measurement scale of public service motivation. *The American Review of Public Administration, 39*(2), 149–163.

Kirlin, J. J. (2001). Big questions for a significant public administration. *Public Administration Review, 61*(2), 140–143.

Liu, C. & Wang, S. (2016). Could you pass China's grueling, 5-hour civil service exam? *CNN.* Retrieved from http://edition.cnn.com/2016/11/28/asia/china-civil-service-exam/.

Manning, N. (2001). The legacy of new public management in developing countries. *International Review of Administrative Science, 67*(2), 297–312.

Merriam, L. (1928). *The problem of Indian administration.* Baltimore: Johns Hopkins University Press.

Milner, A. (2000). What's happened to Asian values? In D. S. G. Goodman & G. Segal (Eds.), *Towards recovery in Pacific Asia* (pp. 55–68). London: Routledge.

Moloney, K., & Chu, H.-Y. (2016). Public service motivation, ethics, and corruption: The Jamaican case. *American Review of Public Administration, 46*(4), 436–458.

Painter, M., & Peters, B. Guy. (2010). Administration traditions in comparative perspective: Families, groups and hybrids. In Martin Painter & B. Guy Peters

(Eds.), *Tradition and public administration* (pp. 19–30). London: Palgrave Macmillan.

Park, S. (2009). Analysis of *Saemaul Undong*: A Korean rural development programme in the 1970s. *Asia-Pacific Development Journal, 16*(2), 113–140.

Park, S. (2017). South Koreans compete for government jobs as economy flounders. *Korea Expose*. Retrieved from https://koreaexpose.com/south-koreans-compete-jobs-economy/.

Perry, J. (1996). Measuring public service motivation: An assessment of construct reliability and validity. *Journal of Public Administration Research and Theory, 6*(1), 5–22.

Philippi, C. (2003). Between 'Washington Consensus' and 'Asian Way': Japanese newspaper authors discussing the East Asian financial and economic crisis of 1997/1998. In*Japanstudien: Misunderstandings in the encounter with Japan* (pp. 281–314). Munich: Iudicium Verlag.

QS. (2017). *QS world university rankings 2016–2017*. Retrieved from https://www.topuniversities.com/university-rankings/world-university-rankings/2016.

Quah, J. S. T. (1980). The public bureaucracy and social change in Singapore. *Hong Kong Journal of Public Administration, 2*(2), 16–37.

Quah, J. S. T. (2003). Causes and consequences of corruption in Southeast Asia: A comparative analysis of Indonesia, the Philippines and Thailand. *Asian Journal of Public Administration, 25*(2), 235–266.

Raadschelders, J. C. N. (2008). Understanding government: Four intellectual traditions in the study of public administration. *Public Administration, 86*(4), 925–949.

Rarick, C. A. (2007). Confucius on management: Understanding Chinese cultural values and managerial practices. *Journal of International Management Studies, 2*(2), 22–28.

Riggs, F. W. (1964). *Administration in developing countries*. Boston: Houghton Mifflin Company.

Riggs, F. W. (1966). *Thailand—The modernization of a bureaucratic polity*. Honolulu: East–West Center Press.

Riggs, F. W. (1967). The 'Sala' model: An ecological approach to the study of comparative administration. In N. Raphaeli (Ed.), *Readings in comparative public administration* (pp. 412–432). Boston: Allyn and Bacon.

Rosenbloom, D. H. (2001). History lessons for reinventers. *Public Administration Review, 61*(2), 161–165.

Ruthnaswamy, M. (1956). *Principles and practice of public administration*. Central Book Depot.

Sabharwal, M., & Berman, E. M. (Eds.). (2016). *Public administration in South Asia: India, Bangladesh, and Pakistan*. Boca Raton: CRC Press.

Samaratunge, R., Alam, Q., & Teicher, J. (2008). The new public management reforms in Asia: A comparison of South and Southeast Asian countries. *International Review of Administrative Science, 74*(1), 25–46.

Schick, A. (1998). Why most developing countries should not try New Zealand reforms. *World Bank Research Observer, 13*(1), 123–131.

Simon, H. A. (1946). Proverbs of administration. *Public Administration Review, 6*(1), 53–67.

Su, T.-T., Walker, R. M., & Xue, L. (2013). Reform and transition in public administration theory and practice in greater China. *Public Administration, 91*(2), 253–260.

Tu, L. (2016). China's banks may be getting creative about hiding their losses. *Bloomberg*. Retrieved from http://www.bloomberg.com/news/articles/2016-02-16/china-banks-seen-hiding-losses-in-opaque-receivables-accounts.

Tummala, K. (1999). Policy of preference: Lessons from India, the United States, and South Africa. *Public Administration Review, 59*(6), 495–508.

Tummala, K. (Ed.). (2003). *Comparative bureaucratic systems*. Lanham: Lexington Books.

Turner, M. (2002). Choosing items from the menu: New public management in Southeast Asia. *International Journal of Public Administration, 25*(12), 1493–1512.

Turner, M., O'Donnell, M., Suh, C.-S., & Kwon, S.-H. (2013). Public sector management and the changing nature of the developmental state in Korea and Malaysia. *The Economic and Labour Relations Review, 24*(4), 481–494.

Vogel, E. F. (1969). Politicized bureaucracy: Communist China. In F. W. Riggs (Ed.), *Frontiers of development administration* (pp. 556–568). Durham: Duke University Press.

Waldo, D. (1984 (1948)). *The administrative state* (2nd ed.). New York: Ronald Press.

Walker, R., Brewer, G. A., & Choi, Y. (2013). Public administration research in East and Southeast Asia: A review of the English language evidence, 1999–2009. *American Review of Public Administration, 44*(2), 131–150.

Wang, Y. (2014). China's shadow banking sector valued at 80% of GDP. *Forbes*. Retrieved from http://www.forbes.com/sites/ywang/2014/05/21/chinas-shadow-banking-valued-at-80-of-gdp/#6005fab239cc.

West, W. F. (2005). Neutral competence and political responsiveness: An uneasy relationship. *The Policy Studies Journal, 33*(2), 147–160.

Woo-Cummings, M. (2005). Back to basics: Ideology, Nationalism, and Asian values in East Asia. In E. Helleiner & A. Pickel (Eds.), *Economic nationalism in a globalizing world* (pp. 91–117). Ithaca: Cornell University Press.

Wu, F. (2008). China's great transformation: Neoliberalization as establishing a market society. *Geoforum, 39*, 1093–1096.

Wu, J., Ma, L., & Yang, Y. (2011). Innovation in the Chinese public sector: Typology and distribution. *Public Administration, 91*(2), 347–365.

Wu, X., He, Y.-L., & Yang, L. (2013). Public administration research in China and Taiwan: An assessment of journal publications 1995–2008. *Public Administration, 91*(2), 261–280.

Zimmer, B. (2015, December 18). The African discussion style 'Indaba' thrived at climate talks. *The Wall Street Journal.* Retrieved from http://www.wsj.com/articles/the-african-discussion-style-indaba-thrived-at-climate-talks-1450456996.

CHAPTER 12

International Policy Coordination and its Impacts

Adrian Kay

The traditional dominance of Western nations in global governance is being increasingly counter-balanced by the rise of Asia, whose nations' growing economic power and distinctive values, principles and strategies of international engagement may unsettle existing understandings of the processes, practices, and prospects for policy-making across borders. As Bice and Sullivan (2014) note, the 'Asian Century' is one amongst many manifestations of the globalisation phenomenon regularly identified. However, far from observing the erosion of national political borders and state capacity as proxies for globalisation, studies of international policy coordination in Asia have consistently observed a strong assertion and recognition of sovereignty at the *nation state-level* as a central and defining feature. In terms of international policy coordination, national sovereignty claims are expressed in norms of non-interference in internal

A. Kay (✉)
Institute of Policy Studies, Universiti Brunei Darussalam,
Bandar Seri Begawan, Brunei Darussalam
e-mail: adrian.kay@ubd.edu.bn

S. Bice et al. (eds.), *Public Policy in the 'Asian Century'*, International Series on Public Policy, https://doi.org/10.1057/978-1-137-60252-7_12

affairs by global governance actors, a typical preference for international agreements that are non-binding and lack legal force as well as declarations that do not commit resources.

As a corollary, the general argument is advanced that such tightly held claims of nation state sovereignty in Asia limit international policy coordination. In dealing with the policy problems of growing economic interdependence and policy spillover effects across borders, assertions of nation state sovereignty are argued, in many policy sectors, to cut into the options available for the effective implementation of international governing arrangements (for example, in health, see Stevenson and Cooper 2009). Ultimately, the argument runs, successful international policy coordination relies on undermining national sovereignty and the development of strong, formal institutions at the international level are necessary.

In case study methods terms, Non-Communicable Diseases (NCD) policy is a typical case of international policy coordination in Asia; health is a policy sector where strong norms of national sovereignty tend to operate, and by hypothesis, these would be expected to act as a barrier to the development of effective governing arrangements for international policy coordination. Case allows us to explore the claim that national sovereignty limits the development of international governance for international policy coordination. It limits opportunities for innovation, proscribes certain options for coordination and precludes the establishment of hard, formal authority at the international level. The need for effective international policy coordination is manifest in the multiple disease patterns associated with globalisation that criss-cross Asia, novel in the speed, intensity and directions of their pathways. Although the emergence of new infectious diseases in Asia are salient in global health agenda, the increasing burden of Non-Communicable Diseases (NCDs) in poor and middle income Asian countries is the dominant epidemiological transition driven by globalisation. This is both a health challenge and development problem in Asia; macroeconomic effects of chronic poor health and preventable early deaths are significant in Asia and at the level of the household, NCDs may act as a barrier to exit from poverty.

The central argument of the chapter is that there is greater capacity for international policy coordination in Asia in health than implied in the claim that national sovereignty obstruct effective international policy coordination to protect public health. The argument is developed first conceptually through an understanding of relationships between formal and informal institutions in the governance arrangements for international policy coordination in Asia. Next the argument is illustrated by the NCD case of international policy coordination in terms of the WHO Framework Convention on Tobacco Control and the ability of Thailand, India, Malaysia and Singapore to develop informally health related interpretations of formal institutions in intellectual property rights for medicines. The conclusion reflects on whether this is a health policy-only case or of more general relevance to thinking about international policy coordination in Asia.

International Policy Coordination: Two Ideal Types

As a starting point for the analysis of governing arrangements for international policy coordination, Ginsburg (2010a, b) posits two ideal types: the *first* is some form of global constitutionalism, following the EU model of establishing supranational sovereignty, whilst the *second* is an emerging Eastphalia model constructed in terms of Westphalian sovereignty. In an Eastphalia model, the commitment to state sovereignty is maintained alongside shallow and weakly institutionalised forms of mutual support and informal cooperation in international policy coordination that will be explored later in the chapter as the 'ASEAN way'.

There is nothing distinctively Asian about the concept of Eastphalia. For example, one could plausibly read UK government preferences towards the EU over the last thirty years up to the Brexit vote of June 2016 as exemplary Eastphalian. However, as Ginsburg (2010a, b) employs the term, it does help to highlight a countertendency to claims of a global constitutionalism driving developments in global governance in which the EU model, at least in ideal form, is the pioneer of establishing formal legal architectures above and beyond states. In the EU, sovereignty is pooled so that formal legal integration has been able to underpin a regional governance arrangements in which the European Court of Justice sits above, and supervenes upon, the policy preferences and actions of the EU member states.

Without doubting the analytical value of imposing a dichotomy between global constitutionalism and Eastphalia for a macroscale consideration of new world orders, for the practical concerns of public policy and international policy coordination these two ideal types already coexist in practice: policy-making across borders in Asia is typically some mix of *formal* institutions of supranational authority and *formal* institutions of nation state sovereignty. This chapter explores how the effects of this mix of formal institutions on international policy coordination is mediated by a set of *informal* institutions. This chapter looks, empirically in terms of NCD policy, at the combination of these two types of formal institutions with coexisting informal institutions and what these may imply for international policy coordination in Asia.

Although elusive and difficult to reign in analytically, the notion of an 'ASEAN style' of international policy coordination is a useful starting point for describing the hybrid of formal and informal institutions that govern international policy coordination in Asia. At a minimum, Fidler (2013) argues it is a preference for non-interference in internal affairs by global governance actors, for weak formal institutions and non-binding coordination solutions. It is a helpful term here by serving as a convenient label to contrast two policy coordination styles: an ASEAN way as opposed to a more formalised global governance system, characterised by trends such as increasing the legalisation of international trade and investment flows. As Fidler (2013), building on Somers Heidhues (2000), argues: the ASEAN way is characterised by consensus building rather than discord; pragmatism rather than higher order principles; and gradualism rather that abrupt change. For our purposes in this chapter, it also includes the preference for elite level policy negotiations conducted through informal networks rather than formal and strongly institutionalised regional organisations.

Once informality is recognised as a central feature in international policy coordination in Asia intertwined with the two types of formal institutions, we can state the core contribution of the chapter: investigating empirically the relationship between informal and formal institutions for international policy coordination in Asia. For example, although the ASEAN Free Trade Agreement (FTA) is weakly institutionalised, lacking an effective dispute resolution mechanism, ASEAN countries also participate regularly in the formal institutions of the WTO dispute settlement process. The ASEAN Regional Forum has developed as the main security structure for the region but as Ginsburg (2010a, p. 865) argues, it is "… hardly institutionalized in the sense of its institutional structure having any independent effect on outcomes". Rather, it is very much a Westphalian conception of discussions and relational, informal policy coordination.

Yet ASEAN countries are also members of formal institutions within the UN system (Friedrichs 2012).

This chapter uses the case of NCD policy to explore the different institutional factors that may shape, constrain and enable the strategies of Asian countries in international policy coordination. Four pivotal relationships between formal and informal institutions are identified to help characterise distinctively Asian features of international policy coordination. The chapter will discuss the role of Asian nations in international coordination of NCD prevention policy. This can be divided a priori into two sub-cases: (a) tobacco. The development the Framework Convention on Tobacco Control (FCTC) has been frequently observed as a case of 'binding' international policy coordination; (b) other commodities. The regulation of the consumption of other commodities which are NCD risk factors, in particular alcohol and ultra-processed food, have conventionally been contrasted as a case of strong national sovereignty claims and relatively ineffective international policy coordination. These are employed in the chapter as illustrative cases of the different ways in which Asian nations might exert their leadership and influence across formal and informal institutions of international policy coordination in the coming decades.

Informal and Formal Institutions: Relationships and Interactions in International Policy Coordination in Asia

The key concept that this chapter seeks to reconsider and recast in terms of policy coordination in Asia is informality in institutional design and practice. The case studies in international health policy reveal different informal institutions, and their relationship to different formal institutions, as key aspects of governing international policy across Asia. Informality in international governance in Asia is most regularly asserted as a set of distinctly Asian norms and values—including mutual respect for state sovereignty—but for the purposes this chapter we can interpret the five principles of peaceful coexistence set out by Fidler (2013) as informal institutions that operate in different ways alongside formal institutions in regional collaboration and international engagement.

Neo-institutional theory stresses the importance of examining institutions, organisations and the actors within them and the ways these interact to shape policy and its practice. In public policy terms, formal institutions refer to official rule-setting and legal obligations with coercive mechanisms acting as the key driving force for action. They count as *formal* in terms of being: codified, official, purposefully designed and third party enforced. From this perspective, behaviour is constrained and regulated formally: organisations act in a certain way because they have to and not necessarily because they want to. Informal institutions describe values and norms that not only define goals or objectives but also designate ways to pursue them. We can call these *informal* on the grounds they are unofficial, uncodified, self-regulated and often emerge rather than being designed. Like formal institutions, they can impose constraints but also, at the same time, empower and enable social action.

New institutionalism allows that formal and informal institutions may be misaligned in certain contexts, which not only produces confusion and conflict, but may also provide conditions that are highly likely to give rise to institutional change. In their summary of new institutionalism, Lowdnes and Roberts (2013) observe a dialectic relationship between the formal and informal aspects of institutions and place analytical importance on agency in the shaping, bending and challenging of institutional practices. An emphasis on the interactions and influences of different institutional norms, culture and actors within a broader context helps gain traction on the balance of informal and formal institutions in international policy coordination.

A starting proposition for the study of international policy coordination is that political-administrative jurisdictions tend to have fixed territorial limits/borders; and these are fixed even as the territorial scale of economic activity has changed both globally but also variety in some cases, at regional and urban and local scales. These changing economic geographies change carry attendant policy problems at those scales which are mismatched with the scales of political-administrative jurisdictions and national sovereignty as the basis of international policy cooridnation.

Recent research has begun to uncover the role of informal governance in international policy-making for such problems (e.g. Stone 2013; Kleine 2014). A precise definition of informal governance in terms of transboundary policy issues remains elusive, however at a minimum we can say it refers to the unwritten rules, strong norms and/or shared expectations within the international system that may modify, complement or substitute for formal institutions such as treaty provisions (Stone 2013). So defined, 'informalism' is everywhere: both within formal international organisations (IOs), as well as operating separately as informal institutions, and in a broad array of international policy networks constituted by state and non-state actors.

Importantly, whilst Stone (2013) argues that the informal may well complement or substitute for the formal, there remains an important possibility that has been neglected by current scholarship: a much more tense and problematic relationship where the formal can upset and even destroy informal institutions with severe and adverse consequences. For example, knowledge-based critiques of formal institutions argue that knowledge is necessarily fragmented and dispersed (and in large part tacit) which means that any attempt at 'command and control' or central planning is likely to be inimical to the informal because the 'all knowing' policy-maker and institutional designer is impossible. Conversely, and again ignored in the international governance literature, the work of Stinchcombe (2001) develops an argument in favour of formalism: when a formal institution is designed to correct and update itself over time in response to feedback, it can be successful in adapting and learning formally about processes which are in essence informal.

This chapter argues that it is in the different interactions between formal and informal interactions that we may explore the claim that national sovereignty undercuts effective international policy coordination. As noted, most institutionalist work in international policy tends to see the formal and informal as substitutable and existing in a coordinate relationship; for example, Stone (2013) describes the growing informality of international governance where non-state actors perform important functions in advocating for, implementing provisions within and reinforcing the legitimacy of formal treaty arrangements. In other literatures, the informal develops in the shadow of the formal, and a symbiotic relationship develops to ensure efficacy and stability of the formal.

Background to Case of International NCD Prevention Policy Coordination in Asia

An important feature of Asia's rise in economic power has been trade liberalisation, the systematic reduction in barriers to cross-border trade and investment. It has facilitated the development of the region's advanced cross-border production networks that underlie its status as a 'global industrial dynamo' (Asian Development Bank 2011). In recent decades, and especially since the Asian financial crisis, trade liberalisation has accelerated in both pace and scope through unilateral structural adjustment, accession to the multilateral (i.e. World Trade Organization) system, and more recently through the proliferation of a 'noodle bowl' of preferential trade agreements (PTAs) at the bilateral and regional levels.

Amongst its many social and economic consequences, trade liberalisation has been identified with some large-scale negative effects on the health of Asian populations by facilitating the spread and growth of the region's tobacco, alcohol and ultra-processed[2] food industries. Consumption of these commodities is rapidly increasing in the region, especially within the industrialising middle-income countries (Baker et al. 2014). Thus, by way of the commodities they produce, advertise and distribute, these industries have been identified as a key driver of the region's rising burden of non-communicable diseases (NCDs), predominantly cardiovascular disease (CVD), cancer, diabetes and chronic respiratory diseases. NCDs are the leading causes of death and disability in Asia, accounting for 17 million or 65% of regional deaths in 2008 (Dans et al. 2011; Baker et al. 2014). Alongside still prevalent rates of infectious diseases, NCDs are generating considerable harms for Asian societies through costs to health systems, workforce productivity losses, and implications for poverty (Baker et al. 2014).

Trade liberalisation allows transnational risk commodity corporations (TRCCs) to move investments, technologies, production capacity, raw materials and final products more easily across borders and thereby drive risk commodity consumption transnationally (Baker et al. 2014). Attracted by their young and growing populations, burgeoning middle-class consumer base, and rapid economic growth rates TRCCs have increasingly targeted developing Asian markets. Although trade remains important, market penetration is primarily achieved through foreign direct investment (FDI) whereby TRCCs establish new affiliates or acquire complete or partial ownership of existing firms. Subsequently, FDI inflows are correlated with higher rates of risk commodity consumption and NCDs globally (Stuckler 2008). Among developing countries East Asia was the recipient of more net FDI inflows than any other region since 1990, equating to 64.5% of the world's total in 2013 (World Bank 2014). Many countries are also home to large state-owned risk commodity enterprises that compete with TRCCs, particularly in the tobacco sectors of China, Thailand and Vietnam (Barraclough and Morrow 2010).

A menu of policy instruments are available to regulate these industries and attenuate risk commodity consumption including raising product prices through taxation, marketing, promotion, and sponsorship restrictions, and product labelling controls (Magnusson and Patterson 2014). However, because trade agreements contain formal institutional rules about how markets are regulated they may constrict 'domestic regulatory space' or the 'freedom, scope, and mechanisms available to governments to adopt, design and implement such regulations in the public health interest' (Baker et al. 2014). The evolving global and regional trade regimes are likely, therefore, to influence risk commodity consumption and associated health risks in Asia.

In order to apprehend more fully different dimensions of the relationship between formal and informal institutions and their consequences for international policy coordination, the next section sets out four distinctive patterns: informal institutions support formal institutions; informal institutions complement formal institutions; informal institutions undermine formal institutions; informal institutions coordinate formal institutions. These are neither a comprehensive set of relationships nor mutually exclusive sets, but instead offered as a means to explore the salient patterns of intersection and interaction between formal and informal institutions operating in international policy coordination. In doing so, we unpack some of the hidden drivers in the chapter's initial argument that national sovereignty claims in Asia tend to undermine international policy coordination such as the existence of negative or positive feedbacks from the informal to the informal; and the relevant consistency issues between formal and institutions and the possibility is that informal institutions may operate at variance with formal institutional arrangements with the potential to undermine them or expand the scope of policy coordination beyond them.

Informal Institutions Supporting Formal Institutions: Prospects for NCD Policy Coordination in Asia

At the multilateral, global governance level Asian nations are members of the two principal institutions governing health and trade respectively—the World Health Organization (WHO) and the World Trade Organization (WTO). Regulations developed by these institutions are likely to be critical to future capacities to address trade in risk commodities and health in Asia. But the participation of Asian countries in other institutions whose functions spillover into health, including the UN General Assembly (UNGASS), Food and Agricultural Organization (FAO), Codex Alimentarius (Codex), World Bank, World Intellectual Property Organization (WIPO), and United Nations Conference on Trade and Development (UNCTAD) is also highly relevant (Smith et al. 2009). The capacity of this system to address trade in risk commodities in Asia is limited for several reasons.

The first is the limited capacity of these institutions to develop, independently and in unison, effective regulations addressing trade in risk commodities. This stems at least partially from the divergent roles and powers of WHO and WTO. Although it has enabling constitutional powers to make legally-binding rules that could in principle regulate risk commodity trade, in practice WHO is a largely technical and normative agency that shapes national health policy through its power to convene national health ministries and to develop technical standards and guidelines. The WTO in contrast institutionalises a set of binding trade rules (i.e. General Agreements on Tariffs and Trade (GATT) and subsequent WTO agreements) supported by enforcement panels, and engages more powerful ministries of finance and trade (Lee et al. 2009; Magnusson 2010). Provisions in GATT/WTO agreements designed to protect health (so-called 'flexibilities') have been interpreted very narrowly to date. Health is therefore subject to trade rules much more so than trade rules are subject to health regulations.

There is, however, *potential* for Asian states to use informal institutions to strengthen policy capacity within the formal institutions of trade governance. Most Asian countries, as former members of the GATT, became members of the WTO upon its establishment in 1995. Others, concerned with the protection of domestic industries from foreign competition, proceeded with a more cautious approach to determining the depth and timing of trade liberalisation, acceding to the WTO considerably later: China in 2001, Cambodia in 2004, Vietnam in 2007 and Laos in 2013 (Baker et al. 2014). Although the GATT/WTO agreements prohibit governments from adopting measures (policies and other regulations) that discriminate between foreign and domestic goods and investments, and between the goods and investments of different countries, trade restrictive measures are permitted if they are non-discriminatory, not used as disguised barriers to trade, and when the content of those measures is consistent with international standards including those developed by the WHO.

In this regard, the 2003 *Framework Convention on Tobacco Control* (FCTC) (adopted under Article 19 of the WHO constitution) is a legally binding treaty that can be used to uphold domestic tobacco legislation in trade disputes. This was exemplified recently in arguments used by Australia to defend its plain packaging legislation in response to WTO dispute arbitration and in a dispute bought by the tobacco company Philip Morris under the Hong Kong–Australia FTA (Commonwealth Government of Australia 2011). In this way, formal institutions can provide a legal mandate for Asian countries to protect domestic regulatory space to address risk commodities in trade disputes. However, developing informal institutions alongside the formal to help provide WHO with financial and political support to develop stronger multilateral risk commodity standards is a key potential opportunity for addressing risk commodities in the region.

For ultra-processed foods and alcohol, however, standards comprise non-binding recommendations (adopted under Article 23), especially the 2004 *Global Strategy on Diet, Physical Activity and Health*, and 2010 *Global Strategy to Reduce the Harmful Use of Alcohol* respectively. The former states that no provisions in the recommendations should be construed as justification for trade restrictive measures, while the latter recognises the important role of trade as a determinant of alcohol consumption. The feasibility of and approaches for strengthening international standards to address ultra-processed foods and alcohol have been explored elsewhere, and may include the development of more selective mechanisms targeting particular products (e.g. soft drinks) or services (e.g. advertising) as well as standards set by other international organisations including Codex Alimentarius on food labelling, health claims and food composition (Magnusson 2007; Barraclough 2009).

The second challenge concerns the *power* of Asian nations to influence the development of international standards. Some, such as Thailand and India played important supportive roles in the development of the FCTC. Their role in strengthening future risk commodity standards is, however, uncertain but likely to be constrained by several factors. Evidence suggests that Asian governments have engaged in global health negotiations in a largely state-centric and individualistic manner rather than through regional configurations (Lee et al. 2013). This reflects the commitment to state sovereignty discussed earlier and related lack of sense of interdependence due to the diverse political and economic positions of the countries that may seek to act collectively in this regard.

At present Asian governments also make relatively small contributions to the financing of multilateral organisations governing health and trade, likely to weaken their capacity to influence the respective agendas. A much improved understanding of the potential for Asian nations is needed in this regard, especially given that their increasing economic and political power is likely to lead to greater influence in global health and trade governance more generally (Lee et al. 2012; Lee et al. 2013).

Many Asian nations are also at a disadvantage in using WTO rules due to existing asymmetries in bargaining power and the resources available to nations to make or defend disputes. Of the 26 WTO trade disputes made against Asian nations pertaining to agriculture, alcohol, tobacco and pharmaceuticals between 1996 and 2013, 21 were made by the United States (US) and European Community (EC) alone and of these 9 were against developing countries. Disputes pertaining to alcohol were most common. To the contrary only 5 claims were made by developing Asian countries against the US and EC (Baker et al. 2014). These difficulties are accentuated when the delegations of the US and EU countries are backed by deep-pocketed TRCC lobbyists and extensive legal teams (Shaffer 2003).

Related to sovereignty and lack of sense of shared interests is that relative lack of programmatic capacity within the multilateral system in Asia. In 2006 the World Health Assembly adopted a resolution on trade and health, calling for engagement with trade policy-makers to 'take advantage of the potential opportunities, and address the potential challenges that trade and trade agreements may have for health'. The WHO *Global Action Plan for the Prevention and Control of Noncommunicable Diseases 2013–2020* (GAPNCD) further recognises the role of WHO in offering technical assistance to developing country governments to mitigate the impact of trade agreements on health. The GAPNCD also calls on the FAO to 'Support ministries of agriculture in aligning agricultural, trade and health policies' and on the WTO to '…support ministries of trade in coordination with other competent government departments (especially those concerned with public health), to address the interface between trade policies and…noncommunicable diseases' (World Health Organization 2013, p. 74). Such assistance may be critical to addressing the proliferation of risk commodity industries in Asia, especially in developing countries with limited institutional capacity.

Some WHO programmes have been established to this end. A programme on globalisation, trade and health was initiated in 2000, 'to strengthen knowledge, develop analytical methods, and produce training materials for supporting member states in addressing trade and health issues'. This led to some collaboration with WTO staff, including the production of a joint report on trade and health, although further commitments and activities have been vague (Lee et al. 2009). More recently this programme was merged into the WHO programme on global health diplomacy, which has produced a number of publications and offers executive training including on trade and health. Health diplomacy is likely to be a key force in achieving health and trade policy coherence for attenuating risk commodities, as it already has for access to medicines under the WTO's TRIPs agreement (Aginam 2010). This includes building leadership capacity within the health community, and skills for advocating public health principles and methods in trade policy-making and implementation (Lee et al. 2009; Magnusson and Patterson 2014). WHO has, in the past, provided critical assistance to Asian governments during risk commodity trade disputes. For example Thailand successfully defended a 1990 GATT dispute, bought by the US Trade Representative on Thailand's tobacco import restrictions, partly due to scientific evidence provided by WHO officials (Drope and Lencucha 2014).

The future of such programmes is uncertain, however. Political pressures from powerful donor countries, particularly from the US and EU countries which are home to some of the largest TRCCs (Lee et al. 2009), alongside increasing industry engagement (tobacco excepted), has led to reluctance from within WHO to tackle issues likely to cause confrontations with powerful industries (Lee et al. 2009; Magnusson and Patterson 2011). WHO is also challenged by significant structural changes in global health governance (GHG) more broadly that weakens its capacity to govern responses to risk commodities. This includes the proliferation of new state and non-state actors in GHG, so-called 'third-way norms' and an expanded role for economic actors through public-private partnerships, philanthrocapitalism, and the financing / disciplinary power of international financial organisations. At present many of these actors, particularly the most powerful, give little priority to financing or supporting the prevention or control of NCDs (Sridhar and Batniji 2008). More broadly, these contemporary changes in GHG significantly constrain the capacity of WHO and its regional offices in Asia (SEARO and WPRO), to enhance responses to risk commodities at the health-trade nexus.

Informal Institutions Complementing Formal Institutions: Trade Rules and NCD Prevention Policy

Notwithstanding the US withdrawal from the Trans-Pacific Partnership (TPP), the proliferation of bilateral and regional preferential trade agreements (PTAs) in Asia, alongside various investment provisions and treaties, is the salient feature international economic policy coordination (United Nations Conference on Trade and Development 2012). Trade negotiations within the multilateral system have stalled since the failed Doha Development Round in the mid-2000s and PTAs have provided an alternative institutional mechanism for high-income countries to achieve accelerated trade liberalisation. Initial agreements may also trigger a domino effect as other countries initiate further PTAs to retain trade competitiveness (World Trade Organization 2011).

Countries involved in PTA negotiations must comply with relevant WTO rules governing such agreements. This includes an 'enabling clause', permitting developing countries to protect certain sectors from liberalisation and foreign competition. However, compared with the formal institutions of the international trading system, increasing regionalism creates significant challenges for regulating in the interests of public health. First, such PTAs are becoming increasingly 'deep' with commitments and concessions that go beyond those required by the WTO system (WTO-plus), but also those outside of it (WTO-X) (Friel et al. 2013; Baker et al. 2014). These are not so much concerned with facilitating trade but with removing 'behind-the-border' regulations that represent threats to global intra—and inter-firm supply chains. Four types of WTO-X provisions are most significant in recent PTAs: competition policy, intellectual property rights, investment liberalisation and the movement of capital. These are the same issues ruled off the agenda by developing countries during the multilateral Doha Development Round, but are now common in PTAs led by developed countries, including the Trans Pacific Partnership currently under negotiation and involving a number of Asian countries (Friel et al. 2013).

Further, while the multilateral system does provide aforementioned flexibilities on public health grounds these can be excluded from or highly restricted within PTAs. In the WTO system trade disputes are also made by one government against another, whereas the investor-state dispute settlement (ISDS) provisions in many PTAs enable corporate investors to enact proceedings directly against governments to recuperate losses resulting from the adoption of domestic regulations (including health regulations). Finally, PTA negotiations are usually 'closed door', therefore lacking the greater transparency of multilateral negotiations and the checks-and-balances that come from closer scrutiny by civil society (Friel et al. 2013; Baker et al. 2014). These observations underpin the importance of Asian governments acting unilaterally and collectively to build informal institutions to protect regulatory space in such agreements.

Informal Institutions Undermining Formal Institutions: The Challenge of Policy Coherence in NCD Prevention

Growing economic integration in Asia brings the need for regional-level trade and health policy coherence. Yet in Asia, relative to the process of European integration, there has been an evolution of a hybrid mixture of formal and informal institutional arrangements that govern health and trade relations, reflecting the region's economic, social and political diversity. In economic terms, for example, there is a 55-fold difference in Gross National Income (GNI) per capita (Atlas method) between Japan and Cambodia (World Bank 2014). Politically the region accommodates Marxist-Leninist Communism in Laos and Vietnam, unitary authoritarian parliamentary systems in Singapore and Indonesia, and the world's largest parliamentary democracy in India. Unlike in the EU and North America, regional economic hegemony is also contested. This is evident in the two competing opportunities towards further regional economic integration, the first led by China, the Regional Comprehensive Economic Partnership (RCEP) involving the ASEAN + 6 countries, the second involving the United States, the Free Trade Agreement of the Asia Pacific (FTAAP) to which the TPP is a pre-cursor (Lewis 2013).

This institutional diversity in Asia creates particular challenges for collective action to address trade in risk commodities. Regional institutions governing trade include the Asia Pacific Economic Cooperation forum (APEC), the East Asia Summit (EAS), and the Association of South East Asian Nations (ASEAN). Regional institutions governing health include ASEAN, and the offices of the World Health Organization (SEARO and WPRO) as well as bilateral agreements for health (Lee et al. 2012; Fidler 2013). The effectiveness of these institutional arrangements in global and regional health governance has been variable. During negotiations of the FCTC for example, ASEAN and WHO regional offices served as important platforms for consolidating a regional position. These same organisations however, have been particularly ineffective at generating regional consensus in other areas including negotiations of the International Health Regulations and pandemic influenza response (Lee et al. 2012).

For historical reasons, WHO has divided East Asia into two regions, a significant challenge for building cohesion and co-ordination (Lamy and Phua 2012). Although WPRO is developing an evidence base to inform regional trade and health policies in the Pacific, neither SEARO nor WPRO appear to have engaged with the same topics in regards to Asia. Although ASEAN has played, at times, an important role in facilitating regional cooperation for health its role been relatively minor, and ASEAN health ASEAN Post-2015 Health Development Agenda exhibits the charactersitics described by Fidler (2013): the predominance of national sovereignty over collective action, a culture of consensus-building rather than open conflict, and highly politicised decision-making processes. For example, it remains problematic in the ASEAN Health cooperation that is that one of it key constituent members, Indonesia, is yet to ratify the FCTC.

Despite the primacy they give to trade liberalisation, ASEAN and APEC have recently demonstrated increased commitment to addressing regional health issues, in particular infectious disease threats (Lamy and Phua 2012). The ASEAN Health Ministers Meeting is held biennially, yet it has confined its work largely to infectious disease control and disaster preparedness, with agreements to date focused largely on sanitary and phyto-sanitary measures. However, in a joint statement in 2012, ASEAN + 3 Health Ministers recognised the region's growing NCD burden and affirmed their commitment to implementing the UN General Assembly's *Political Declaration on the Prevention and Control of Non-communicable Diseases* (Association of Southeast Asian Nations 2012). Actions to address NCDs have fallen under the ASEAN Strategic Framework on Health Development (2010–2015) with working groups established for regional tobacco control, but not ultra-processed foods or alcohol (Association of Southeast Asian Nations 2012).

The literature has yet to apprehend fully the potential for ASEAN and other regional bodies to constitute an effective platform for generating regional positions or informal institutions to address trade and risk commodities. Lamy and Phua (2012) have argued that increased cooperation on social issues through ASEAN, including health, is likely to strengthen its 'soft power' as a regional and global actor. However, weak financial commitments and human resource capacities may limit an ASEAN-led response. Such capacity could be buttressed by expanded technical collaboration between WHO and ASEAN, by achieving greater financial and technical commitments from China, Korea and Japan through the ASEAN + 3 framework, and through stronger engagement with regional non-government organisations and epistemic communities working to address risk commodities (Lamy and Phua 2012).

Coordinating Formal and Informal Institutions: Tobacco Control as an Exception

In assessing the capacity of norms as informal institutions to contribute to health and trade policy coherence in Asia there are several relevant considerations. Health actors often view trade as a threat to population health, taking a 'harm-minimisation' approach, with little consideration for trade objectives. Trade actors, conversely, tend to view health as a barrier to trade with the objectives of reducing barriers to cross-border commercial flows and economic growth (Smith et al. 2009). Trade and health debates usually pivot, therefore, around norms of 'anti-trade' and 'open-trade'. For example, between an international tobacco control norm on the one hand and open tobacco trade on the other (Drope and Lencucha 2014).

Asian nations have differed considerably in how they have balanced the above norms as they relate to addressing risk commodities. For example, during the FCTC negotiations, Japan and China took steps to weaken the binding nature of adopted measures, making assertions of 'protecting sovereignty'. In contrast Thailand and India demonstrated considerable leadership in building regional consensus towards a strong tobacco control treaty, alongside their adoption of 'enabling' legislation at the national level. Thai delegates explicitly emphasised the need to achieve a strong treaty with provisions that take priority over trade rules (Lee et al. 2012).

These observations tend to suggest that norm divergences serve to misalign informal institutions and thereby threaten the potential to undermine any collective action to coordinate policy on risk commodity control by Asian nations. Conversely, state sovereignty has also been invoked in the public health interest: by India, Malaysia and Thailand to challenge intellectual property rules governing access to essential medicines, and by Indonesia to challenge perceived inequities in rules governing access to vaccines (Lee et al. 2012; Kamradt-Scott et al. 2013). Although these are different issues strong assertions of sovereignty may have, therefore, potential utility when it comes to protecting domestic policy space for risk commodity control. Overcoming anti-trade vs. open-trade debates is also another path forward. Such debates often ignore the potential for trade agreements to promote health. The liberalisation of the tobacco sector, for example, could potentially result in the dismantling of powerful state-owned enterprises SOEs thereby removing the conflict of interest arising from the state as both producer and regulator (although admittedly to be replaced by TRCCs) (McGrady 2011).

The Future: Emerging Asian Varieties of International Policy Coordination

The chapter has explored the argument that assertions of national sovereignty and the primacy of formal national level political institutions in policy-making tends generally to undermine international policy coordination in Asia. The NCD prevention policy case presents some suggestions that there is greater international policy coordination capacity in Asia than this argument implies. In addition to challenging the scholarly utility of an ideal type dichotomy in international policy coordination of the EU and Eastphalian models in which the latter is seen as an immature and weaker version of the former, this case study casts light on the importance of informal institutions and their intersection and articulation with formal institutions in international policy coordination. This latter insight is developed conceptually in the chapter through sketching some possible simple relationships between formal and informal institutions.

For example, increasing participation in international trade agreements requires countries to strengthen their domestic policy capacity; to evaluate the costs and benefits of entering into trade agreements; to ensure compliance with their international obligations when they do; and to ensure adequate protections for domestic regulatory space (Walls et al. 2015; Baker et al. 2014). This is a significant challenge especially for poorer countries that may struggle to develop the required scientific and legal expertise, as well as formal institutional capacity.

However, networks of informal institutions operation across Asia, such as technical support and mutual capacity-building, are important in supporting the functioning of formal institutions.

Options identified by the WHO for attenuating risk commodity consumption include raising product prices through taxation, restrictions on product marketing, promotion, and sponsorship, and product labelling controls (Magnusson and Patterson 2014). This necessitates informal institutions to establish collaboration between health and trade policymakers to protect policy space in future trade agreements (Thow and McGrady 2014). By reducing tariff revenues and imposing significant costs associated with compliance and negotiation, trade agreements may also reduce the resources available to governments used to fund policies and programmes to address risk commodities. Consumption taxes are a key strategy for off-setting such losses, and can therefore be adopted for both revenue-raising as well as public health reasons.

In public health policy terms, Asia is also home to exemplary countries that have sought to advance public health through staunch assertions of national sovereignty through unilateral, and uncoordinated, regulation their domestic markets. Thailand, for example, has one of the most comprehensive tobacco control regimes globally (Chantornvong and McCargo 2001). It has implemented a hypothecated 2% tax on alcohol and tobacco to fund its Thai Health Promotion Foundation (Casswell and Thamarangsi 2009). The re-regulation of risk commodity markets policy option is a key consideration for governments that have already liberalised the relevant sectors; this requires the development of informal institutions around formal institutions of trade agreements. For example, Thailand is a world leader in establishing novel informal institutional designs for public health with trade agreements. Its Trade in Health and Social Services committee, for example, brings together officials from ministries of industry, public health, food and agriculture, as well as various professional groups to investigate how trade agreements effect health, to advocate for the inclusion of health in trade negotiations, and to coordinate action between concerned agencies (Smith et al. 2009).

Although the health sector was selected for investigation as a typical case of international policy coordination challenges, it is moot whether the details of the NCD prevention policy explored here is generalisable directly to other policy sectors. However, it is hoped that the sketch of basic and potential intersections and articulations between formal and informal will help public policy scholars begin to apprehend the variegated patterns, processes and practices of international policy coordination in Asia across different sectors.

References

Aginam, O. (2010). Health or trade—A critique of contemporary approaches to global health diplomacy. *Asian Journal of WTO & International Health Law and Policy, 5*(2), 355–380.

Asian Development Bank. (2011). *Asia 2050: Realizing the Asian century*. New Delhi: Thousand Oaks.

Association of Southeast Asian Nations. (2012a). *Joint statement: 5th ASEAN plus three health ministers meeting*. Phuket: ASEAN Secretariat.

Association of Southeast Asian Nations. (2012b). *ASEAN secretariat: ASEAN cooperation on health development*. Jakarta: ASEAN Secretariat.

Baker, P., Kay, A., & Walls, H. (2014). Trade and investment liberalization and Asia's noncommunicable disease epidemic: A synthesis of data and existing literature. *Globalization and Health, 10*(1), 66–84.

Barraclough, S. (2009). Chronic diseases and global health governance: The contrasting cases of food and tobacco. In A. Kay & O. D. Williams (Eds.), *Global health governance: Crisis, institutions, and political economy* (pp. 102–121). Basingstoke: Palgrave Macmillan.

Barraclough, S., & Morrow, M. (2010). The political economy of tobacco and poverty alleviation in Southeast Asia: Contradictions in the role of the state. *Global Health Promotion, 17*(1), 40–50.

Bice, S., & Sullivan, H. (2014). Public policy studies and the "Asian Century": New orientations, challenges, and opportunities. *Governance, 27*(4), 539–544.

Casswell, S., & Thamarangsi, T. (2009). Reducing harm from alcohol: Call to action. *The Lancet, 373*(9682), 2247–2257.

Chantornvong, S., & McCargo, D. (2001). Political economy of tobacco control in Thailand. *Tobacco Control, 10*(1), 48–54.

Commonwealth Government of Australia. (2011). *Phillip Morris Asia limited claimant and the commonwealth of Australia respondent: Australia's response to the notice of arbitration*. Canberra.

Dans, A., Ng, N., Varghese, C., Tai, E. S., Firestone, R., & Bonita, R. (2011). The rise of chronic non-communicable diseases in southeast Asia: Time for action. *The Lancet, 6736*, 1–10.

Drope, J., & Lencucha, R. (2014). Evolving norms at the intersection of health and trade. *Journal of Health Politics, Policy and Law, 39*(3), 591–631.

Fidler, D. (2013). Asia and global health governance: Power, principles and practice. In K. Lee, T. Pang, & Y. Tan (Eds.), *Asia's role in governing global health* (pp. 198–214). London: Routledge.

Friel, S., Gleeson, D., Thow, A.-M., Labonte, R., Stuckler, D., Kay, A., et al. (2013). A new generation of trade policy: Potential risks to diet-related health from the trans pacific partnership agreement. *Globalization and Health, 9*(1), 46.

Friedrichs, J. (2012). East Asian regional security. *Asian Survey, 52*(4), 754–776.

Ginsburg, T. (2010a). Eastphalia and Asian regionalism. *University of California at Davis Law Review, 44,* 859–877.

Ginsburg, T. (2010b). Eastphalia as a return to Westphalia. *Indiana Journal of Global Legal Studies, 27,* 34–35.

Kamradt-Scott, A., Lee K., & Xu, J. (2013). The international health regulations: Asia's contribution to a global health governance framework. In K. Lee, T. Pang, & Y. Tan (Eds.), *Asia's role in governing global health* (pp. 83–98). London: Routledge.

Kleine, M. (2014). Informal governance in the European union. *Journal of European Public Policy, 21*(2), 303–314.

Lamy, M., & Phua, K. H. (2012). Southeast Asian cooperation in health: A comparative perspective on regional health governance in ASEAN and the EU. *Asia Europe Journal, 10*(4), 233–250.

Lee, K., Kamradt-Scott, A., Yoon, S., & Xu, J. (2012). Asian contributions to three instruments of global health governance. *Global Policy, 3*(3), 348–361.

Lee, K., Pang, T., & Tan, Y. (Eds.). (2013). *Asia's role in governing global health.* New York: Routledge.

Lee, K., Sridhar, D., & Patel, M. (2009). Bridging the divide: Global governance of trade and health. *The Lancet, 373,* 416–422.

Lewis, M. K. (2013). TPP and the RCEP (ASEAN6) as potential paths toward deeper Asian economic integration. *The Asian Journal of WTO & International Health Law and Policy, 8*(3), 359–370.

Lowdnes, V., & Roberts, M. (2013). *Why Institutions matter, the new Institutionalism in political sciences.* Basingstoke: Palgrave.

Magnusson, R. S. (2007). Non-communicable diseases and global health governance: Enhancing global processes to improve health development. *Globalization and Health, 3*(1), 2.

Magnusson, R. S. (2010). Global health governance and the challenge of chronic, non-communicable disease. *The Journal of Law, Medicine & Ethics, 38*(3), 490–507.

Magnusson, R., & Patterson, D. (2011). Role of law in global response to non-communicable diseases. *The Lancet, 378*(9794), 859–860.

Magnusson, R. S., & Patterson, D. (2014). The role of law and governance reform in the global response to non-communicable diseases. *Globalization and Health, 10*(1), 44.

McGrady, B. (2011). *Trade and public health: The WTO, tobacco, alcohol, and diet.* Cambridge: Cambridge University.

Shaffer, G. (2003). *Defending interests: Public private partnerships in WTO litigation*. Washington, D.C. Brookings Institution Press.
Smith, R. D., Lee, K., & Drager, N. (2009). Trade and health: An agenda for action. *The Lancet, 373*, 768–773.
Sridhar, D., & Batniji, R. (2008). Misfinancing global health: A case for transparency in disbursements and decision making. *The Lancet, 372*(9644), 1185–1191.
Stevenson, M., & Cooper, A. (2009). Overcoming constraints of state sovereignty: Global health governance in Asia. *Third World Quarterly, 30*(7), 1379–1394.
Stinchcombe, A. (2001). *When formality works*. Chicago: The University of Chicago.
Stone, R. (2013). Informal governance in international organizations: Introduction to the special issue. *The Review of International Organizations, 8*(2), 121–136.
Stuckler, D. (2008). Population causes and consequences of leading chronic diseases: A comparative analysis of prevailing explanations. *The Milbank Quarterly, 86*(2), 273–326.
Thow, A. M., & McGrady, B. (2014). Protecting policy space for public health nutrition in an era of international investment agreements. *Bulletin of the World Health Organization, 92*(2), 139–145.
United Nations Conference on Trade and Development. (2012). *World investment report 2012: Towards a new generation of investment policies*. Geneva. Retrieved from http://unctad.org/en/pages/PublicationWebflyer.aspx?publicationid=171.
Walls, H., Smith, R., & Drahos, P. (2015). Improving regulatory capacity to manage risks associated with trade agreements. *Globalization and Health, 11*(1), 14.
World Bank. (2014). World development indicators. Retrieved from http://data.worldbank.org/data-catalog/world-development-indicators.
World Health Organization. (2013). *Global action plan for the prevention and control of non-communicable diseases*. Geneva. Retrieved from http://apps.who.int/iris/bitstream/10665/94384/1/9789241506236_eng.pdf.
World Trade Organization. (2011). *World trade report 2011*. Geneva. Retrieved from https://www.wto.org/english/res_e/booksp_e/anrep_e/world_trade_report11_e.pdf.

CHAPTER 13

Beyond the East-West Dichotomy: Economic Development Policies in Asia and Europe

Jon Pierre

Endemic (adj.),.
Regularly found among particular people or in a certain area.
Functional (adj.),.
The way in which something works or operate.
Oxford Dictionary.

The "Asian Century": Territoriality, Culture, or Functionality?

This chapter explores the issue of whether the institutional and political features that we tend to associate with the notion of the "Asian century" are endemic to Asia as a political and economic cultural region or

J. Pierre (✉)
University of Melbourne, Melbourne, Australia
e-mail: jon.pierre@unimelb.edu.au

J. Pierre
Melbourne School of Government, The University of Gothenburg, Gothenburg, Sweden

S. Bice et al. (eds.), *Public Policy in the 'Asian Century'*, International Series on Public Policy, https://doi.org/10.1057/978-1-137-60252-7_13

whether they are tied to particular models of economic governance and stages of economic development. The governance arrangements and state-society interactions which the Anglo-American literature sees as central to the notion of the Asian century (see, Drechsler, Chap. 2 of this volume) are, we suggest, functional, culturally embedded responses to challenges associated with economic development centered on a manufacturing industrial sector. This embeddedness will manifest itself in a particular model of policymaking and governance.

Designating centuries to different regions of the world suggests not only that there exists a continuous process of changing gravities of ideas, economic leadership or military supremacy (Massey 1995); it also implies that seemingly lagging regions could catch up by emulating the development strategies pursued by leading regions. This would, however, be missing an important point. Economic governance arrangements could be seen as models of mutual role expectations between state and market. The nature of state-society exchanges in economic governance depends, as Peter Hall (1986) points out, just as much on the configuration of the market and society as on the configuration of the state itself. Unless economic governance is a case of strict state-centric *dirigisme*, government needs to implement a governance arrangement that allows it to articulate collective interests in the market and to perform a coordinating role without interfering with the allocative efficiency of the market. Thus, ideas about economic governance are more deeply socially embedded and therefore more difficult to move from one national or regional context to another. In other words, ideas travel less lightly than is sometimes understood.

Furthermore, we need to remind ourselves that economic governance is to a large extent a self-regulating process. It is interesting to note that in the typology of a total of 23 economic governance mechanisms in the United States, outlined by Campbell et al. (1991, p. 14), none is executed by government institutions. As we will discuss below, political presence in the market—particularly assigning a leading or coordinating role of the economy to government—is a contested policy position. Since the Asian Century model accords government such a role, it becomes all the more important to investigate whether in fact this model is typical to the Asian region or whether it is a functional response to collective action and coordination problems in the economy.

As far as economic governance is concerned, the proposition that the Asian Century is more a matter of functionality and societal embeddedness than a coordinating mechanism typical to Asian economies raises questions about the prospect of similar processes of learning and diffusion of policy practices as we move towards a post-industrial economy. Furthermore, it gives us an opportunity to study the capacity of the political, social and economic underpinnings of the Asian Century to accommodate the transformation that this development will entail.

Thus, we are looking at two overarching research questions about the degree to which policy making arrangements can travel in time and space. First, what are the key features of the Asian Century model and is there any point in other countries trying to emulate an Asian model of economic governance? Secondly, how will the development towards a post-industrial economy—already well underway in some Asian countries—challenge the entrenched model of economic governance? A slightly different way of putting these two questions would be to ask how well an Asian model of economic governance travels in space (i.e. to other national or regional contexts) and time (i.e. from providing governance to an industrial economy to a post-industrial economy). The chapter will be devoted to a discussion on these two sets of issues.

The chapter also explores the argument that the developmental state model, described by Chalmers Johnson (1982) as state-led market-conforming development sustained by extensive societal consultation on policy is functional only at specific stages of economic development. To that effect, we compare the local government policy agenda in Japan with those in Sweden and the United States, a sample selected in a most-different systems design (for an elaborated discussion see Pierre 2013). If there is merit to the proposition that the Asian Century model of policymaking is geared primarily to economic development issues, differences in the Japanese, Swedish and American policy agenda at the local level would be good predictors of the degree to which ideas about policymaking and public service design should be able to be adopted outside the region within which they first emerged.

The chapter proceeds as follows. We first give a broad overview of economic governance in the Asian region, using Japan as a main example of Asian Century governance as manifested in different versions of the developmental state model (Fields 2012). We then look more closely at the policy details and governance arrangements that sustain that model. The third section asks whether the emergence of a post-industrial economy in the Asian region poses a challenge to the developmental state, given its emphasis on big industry and overseas market penetration. The chapter closes by discussing the capacity of the Asian Century model of governance to travel in space, as well as in time.

Economic Governance in the Asian Century

There have been several "Asian Centuries"—we need only think of the historical times when Europeans opened up trade paths with China in order to bring technological innovations back to Europe—just as there are different *types* of Asian centuries indicating economic, cultural, political or military hegemony exercised by countries in the Asian region. There has been an extensive debate on whether we are headed towards a new Asian Century (Bice and Sullivan 2014; Krugman 1994).

The literature on the twentieth century as the "American Century" draws primarily on outcomes in political, cultural, military and economic terms as evidence of the predominance of US values (Eckes and Zeiler 2003; Spulber 1995). In contrast, the early debate about the Asian Century has been more concerned with process and the degree to which Asian countries share a common approach to policymaking and state-society interaction and whether that approach would also work in other cultural and economic contexts. The strategy has been to depart from a successful outcome, for instance in terms of economic development, and uncover the specific features of the policy processes or their social underpinnings that led to the successful outcome.

The Asian Century discourse immediately identifies the notion of the developmental state as central to this construct (Johnson 1982; Okimoto 1988; Pempel and Muramatsu 1995; Woo-Cumings 1999). Different versions of the developmental state model have only been associated with Asian countries, primarily Japan but also to some extent to Taiwan, Singapore, Malaysia and Korea (Fields 2012). The model accords the state, i.e. executive government and the bureaucracy, a leading and coordinating role in the economy while at the same time subscribing to the basic features of market capitalism.

The governance logic of the developmental state hinges on its capacity to fend off overseas competition and pressures for domestic regulatory reform. Thus, it is to a significant degree a pre-globalisation model of economic governance as it emerged mainly in the postwar period before global free trade agreements defined the terms of international trade. Equally important, domestic perceptions of the overseas world and the cultural factors that define those perceptions play a fundamental role in shaping the intellectual frame of policymakers, societal partners and the public towards other countries and the values they represent.

The distinction between inward and outward globalisation, which is commonly made in Japan, substantiates a tension in Japanese culture between *sakoku* ("secluded nation") and *kokusaika* ("internationalisation"), leading some observers to suggest that *kokusaika* "has been a mere coerced Westernization" (Itoh 1998, p. 13; also, see Stronach 1995). Itoh (1998) notes that while Japan has excelled in outward *kokusaika*, primarily in economic terms, it has largely failed to elevate its political significance in world affairs to a level corresponding with its economic standing in global affairs. Also, Vinh (2004) points out that Japan has not succeeded in inward *kokusaika*; the Japanese society has yet to embrace overseas cultures and values.

These deeply entrenched normative structures underpin and shape governance, both in terms of the goals of governance and the degree to which those norms can accommodate political projects that do not conform to what society expects from government (see March and Olsen 1989). Fundamental to the developmental state model is the political perception that there is a very close linkage between economic growth, on the one hand, and national security and autonomy on the other. This means that economic development and global competitiveness are seen as overarching policy objectives and that, by extension, the policymaking and executive institutions in the economic development policy sector enjoy a privileged and prestigious position. This circumstance helps to explain, for instance, the prominence of the Japanese Ministry of International Trade and Industry (MITI, later METI) during the 1960s and 1970s (Pierre and Park 1997) and its subsequent decline when other policy areas such as environmental protection became more prominent on the political agenda.

In this respect, the defining feature of the developmental state model is the centrality of the state in the governance of a capitalist economy. Through the bureaucracy the state coordinates the development of the domestic market. This coordinating role covers the full range of approaches to solving collective action problems among nominally competing businesses, so that for instance, "excessive competition" in emerging sectors of the economy is minimised and that research and development facilities are shared (see Brahm 1995).

Another critical role of the bureaucracy is to protect domestic businesses from overseas competition. This soon becomes a delicate problem in the international trade policy community since economic growth through export revenues is predicated on free trade and the success of corporations in overseas markets. Schaede and Grimes' (2003) notion of "permeable insulation" highlights the (largely pre-WTO) strategy of selectively allowing limited imports, while at the same time helping the domestic industry to make inroads into overseas markets.

Schaede and Grimes also implicitly suggest that "permeable insulation" was exercised only in the Japanese political economy context. However, a similar strategy was implemented also with regard to overseas attempts to influence the domestic regulatory framework in the developmental state. In the case of Japan but also Korea, the US devoted years of sustained efforts to attempting to break up the regulation of domestic markets, with very limited results (see, Pierre 2013). It was not until the US could harness IMF-coordinated multinational pressure on Japan to open up its domestic markets that regulatory reform was introduced on a broader scale. There is some irony here, as the problem was not primarily one of excessive regulation. Indeed, the governance of the financial system was severely *under*-regulated, a circumstance which, as Amyx (2004) points out, greatly impaired the capacity of the system to address the crisis swiftly and forcefully.

The IMF's support of Japan and Korea to alleviate the financial crises during the 1990s became a useful vehicle to promote US trade interests in Japan when bilateral negotiations proved fruitless. As the then US deputy treasurer Lawrence Summers commented in February, 1998: "In some ways the IMF has done more in these past few months to liberalize these [East Asian] economies and open their markets to United States goods and services than has been achieved in rounds of trade negotiations in the region. And it has done so in serving our critical, short-term and long-term interest…" (Summers 1998; Philippi 2003, p. 288).

In the development state model the bureaucracy achieves domestic economic coordination less by relying on command and control instruments and more by defining "visions". These visions set long-term trade targets for the major industrial conglomerates, the Japanese *keiretsu* (previously *zaibatsu*; see Aoki and Lennerfors 2013) or the Korean *chaebol*. Although subtle, the visions were quite efficient in providing direction for the industry. As Chalmers Johnson (1982) notes, private industry was well aware that there was an iron fist in a velvet glove and did not raise any to objections to MITI's visions. Also, some observers have described the relationship between the bureaucracy and the industrial conglomerates in Confucian terms, with the state as the *père de la famille* and the corporations his sons. Either way (or both), the leading and coordinating role of the bureaucracy in the vast economic development project was not challenged or questioned.

The contrast between the developmental state model and the governance arrangement we find in Anglo-American political economies is striking (Campbell et al. 1991; Hall 1986; Hall and Soskice 2001). The defining features of the developmental state model are largely absent in the Anglo-American countries. The likelihood of any significant changes towards Asian institutional arrangements in these respects is therefore extremely low.

Meanwhile, policymaking and administration in central and northern Europe shares many of the defining Asian features of societal consultation. In the smaller, industrialised democracies in Europe we see both a higher degree of state centrality and also institutionalised systems of societal consultation and even involvement of societal actors in policymaking and implementation (Katzenstein 1984, 1985, 1987; Schmitter 1974). As Peter Katzenstein (1985, p. 24) argues, the economic development strategies of these countries "differ profoundly from the liberal and statist principles that inform the political choices and structures of the large industrial states". While state centrality is the outcome of long historical trajectories that do not lend themselves to short-term political manipulation (Dyson 1980), corporatism and other governance arrangements can be altered on shorter notice. The choice to facilitate such governance may be explained by the political economy of these smaller, industrialised and trade-dependent political economies. We will elaborate this point below.

Katzenstein (1985) also makes the important argument that corporatism is a powerful economic governance arrangement for social compensation and accommodation in response to changes in the global economy. As "price takers" rather than "price makers", these countries "live with change by compensating for it. In so doing, the small European states have cultivated a strategy that both responds to and reinforces their domestic structures" (Katzenstein 1985, p. 24). This observation speaks directly to the current issue of why some developmental states like Japan, despite their institutional strengths and legitimacy, have chosen to rely on extensive deliberation and consultation with key societal actors. Positioning an industrial economy in a global market requires strong networks in the domestic political economy to enhance the capacity of the system as a whole to adapt to, or anticipate, or even drive, change.

We will now look more closely at what appears to be the policy and institutional defining features of the Asian Century model. In this analysis we will draw on the developmental state model, recognising that the validity of the model varies significantly across the Asian region. We will then proceed to discuss the extent to which the model is susceptible to diffusion to other regions of the world.

Asian Century as a Policy Construct

As is the case with most institutionalised models of policymaking, an Asian Century model of economic governance is sensitive to changes in its political, economic or societal underpinnings. This might appear paradoxical given that the very purpose of economic governance is to drive and coordinate development. However, political institutions and agents are often contested phenomena in the market—albeit it less so in Asia than in other regions—which means that the legitimacy of such presence requires continuous reproduction. In order to better understand the internal and external logics of this governance model we will briefly discuss the key aspects of the developmental state.

Primacy of Economic Development

A significant, if not key, component of the Asian Century model is the conviction that autonomy is not possible without a strong economy. The sense of urgency that weak economic growth and growing international debt impose on all governments seems to be particularly strong in Asian societies. While this perspective may have deep cultural roots, it gained more contemporary currency during the financially turbulent 1990s in several Asian countries. For instance, Japan's increasing sensitivity towards international financial institutions has largely been dictated by the failing performance of its economy.

Economic development, as already pointed out, is overwhelmingly a matter of managing structural changes in the economy. Countries or regions that swiftly manage the transition from one type of economy (e.g. an industry-based economy) to a more knowledge-and-research based economy, without demanding massive public spending and in a socially and environmentally sustainable way, will enjoy sustained economic growth. Conversely, countries that allow market mechanisms to run their course will experience a more sluggish economy, with shorter periods of high economic growth but also deeper recessions and significant social and environmental ramifications. Thus, the capacity to managing change—either in a proactive, *dirigiste* manner or a *laissez-faire* policy style—is the canary bird in the coal mine; when it fails there is reason to expect a long-term impact on society.

An Asian Century model of economic governance is based on a conviction that the state can and should play a critical role in coordinating market behavior and accommodating domestic interests for the social costs incurred by economic change. This perspective also holds that the state, by its presence in the market, can in fact deliver what Weaver (1985) refers to as an "accelerationist" industrial policy and thus bring about economic modernisation more quickly than the market itself would have been able to accomplish.

This is not to suggest that the developmental state model of economic development is devoid of social or environmental problems or issues related to social cohesion. Essentially all the Asian developmental states have experienced severe problems created or exacerbated by the almost unilateral political focus on economic growth, including environmental problems and problems of social exclusion and decreasing cohesion in growing industrial cities.

State-Centrism

A high degree of state-centric governance is a necessary but not sufficient condition for the emergence of a developmental state. France, for instance, is often portrayed as the epitome of a state-centric society (but see Cole 2008), yet very few would argue that France is a developmental state. In the Asian century governance model the state is expected to lead and coordinate market behavior without distorting the basic allocative mechanisms of the market, as such interventions would be detrimental to the global competitiveness of domestic corporations. The cultural and normative aspects of state-centrism allow the state to govern the economy with only very light-touch instruments (Johnson 1982; Okimoto 1988). For instance, Malcolm Trevor shows how the Japanese Ministry of Posts and Telecommunications uses "guidance" (MITI used the label "visions"; Johnson 1982) to communicate its objectives to market actors who followed that guidance carefully since "those on the receiving end of guidance knew that inside the velvet glove there is a mailed fist" (Trevor, 200, p. 153).

Time

The Asian Century model of economic governance shows little understanding for Western shortsightedness, its obsession with the quarterly dividend or its focus on immediate results. In a perspective which is not very different from the West European "Rhineland" model of a capitalist economy (Albert 1993; Hall and Soskice 2001), Asian economic planning takes a more long-term view than US or UK institutions and corporations (Okimoto 1988; Pempel and Muramatsu 1995). This is to some extent the result of differences in ownership and the role of the stock market between the two regions.

These differences cause problems when an Anglo-American corporate model is introduced in Asia, as happened when Japanese corporations were acquired by US businesses. But the different approaches to economic planning also yield different outcomes in terms of adaptive capacity. A senior METI bureaucrat suggested in an interview with the author in 2006 that "the *laissez-faire* style of the Washington consensus is not efficient in Asia. Asian culture is very different compared to the Anglo-American culture. The pace of change is slower in the *laissez-faire* systems compared to countries typical to the Asian culture. The political-economic culture of the Asian countries gives them a better adaptive capacity" (quoted in Pierre 2013).

Accommodation of Interests

The paradox of the developmental state is that although government and the bureaucracy enjoy strong support for their economic development strategy and indeed their presence in the economy, government insists on extensive deliberation across society, albeit mainly with strategic partners in the market (Peters and Pierre 2017). This paradoxical pattern is also common in European countries like the Scandinavian countries, Germany, Austria and Switzerland, as we noted earlier. The argument we outline here is that the paradox in both regions is explained mainly by the demand for adaptive capacity in highly export-dependent economies. Anglo-American models of economic governance, where organised interests are more marginalised in the policy-making process, are more inclined to let the market run its course and to allow for Schumpeterian "creative destruction", i.e. to see the closedown of uncompetitive businesses and industries as part of a process of economic renewal (see, for instance, Campbell et al. 1991; Hall 1986; Hall and Soskice 2001).

The accommodation of societal interests and corporatist-style policy making (see Pempel and Tsunekawa 1979) and implementation are closely related aspects of a larger strategy to boost the adaptive capacity of the economic system, i.e. to increase its capacity to design and execute policies to continuously modernise the economy and ensure that its output is internationally competitive. While some U.S. observers associate corporatism with rigidity and economic decline (Olsons 1982), the European perspective emphasises corporatism as integral to adaptive and transformative capacity (Katzenstein 1984, 1985). For instance, by deliberating about policy with corporate leaders, utilising their expertise on industrial and economic development and ensuring their compliance with that policy prior to formal decision-making, government ensures smooth implementation of those policies (Lundqvist 1980). Indeed, in terms of regulatory reform there is clear evidence that these "coordinated market economies" outperform the Anglo-American "liberal market economies" (Pierre 2015).

In sum, the developmental state model has proven highly successful in catapulting industrial economies into high-speed, internationally competitive economies. As a model of economic governance it represents a functional response to a major nation-state challenge of boosting the country's economic growth. It is also a culturally deeply embedded governance arrangement. There are many similarities between the Asian Century model of economic governance and the European economic development strategy, such as state centricity, a long-term perspective on economic development and a strong inclination to include key societal actors in the process of governance. The main difference is that European countries did not display the same unilateral focus on economic development as an overarching policy objective; neither did the bureaucracies tasked with economic development issues enjoy a privileged position in government.

Thus, if we argue that the Asian Century is defined in part by the economic success of Asian economies in global markets, then the developmental state model of economic governance is a functional governance arrangement in a growing industrial economy. The fact that the developmental state model is, empirically speaking, largely found in the Asian region also suggests that there are factors in addition to functionality that underpin the emergence of a developmental state. This could be social and cultural norms and values of collective action as opposed to individual initiative or holistic perceptions of society and social groups.

The other major question we should address is to what extent the developmental state also provides effective governance in a post-industrial economy. One significant consequence of continuing globalisation is the "delocalisation" of capital ownership. Coming back to the Confucian analogy about the state as the father and the industrial conglomerates as his sons and daughters, globalisation could be illustrated by the children leaving home. As many parents will testify, this may be conducive to domestic peace and harmony while at the same time provoking growing uncertainty and concern about what the children are now up to. Once the *keiretsu* or *chaebol* become global rather than national corporations, they might be less inclined to follow the "visions" issued by domestic ministries of economic development.

Towards Post-Industrialism?

The delocalisation of capital ownership is sometimes said to be a component of the transformation from an industrial to a post-industrial economy. In terms of governance, the post-industrial economy poses a bigger challenge to government than did the industrial economy. The post-industrial economy is more fragmented than industrial society, with a larger number of smaller businesses and fewer big industries or conglomerates.

Given the need for proximity to customers the service-sector based economy could be assumed to be more firmly localised than industrial corporations who could relocate (or threaten to relocate) to economically more attractive environments if government imposed increased taxes or regulations on them. However, service-sector corporations, too, soon became more international than domestic economic players, as we see for instance in the financial management, insurance, higher education and telecom sectors. The areas of the service sector that remain local are businesses that rely on face-to-face contact with their customers like retail shops, restaurants, and legal services. These developments have made economic governance far more complex than was previously the case, where governance required a limited number of bilateral interactions. The myriad of small businesses that is typical to the post-industrial economy coupled with delocalised big corporations in financial management is in many ways an urban economic development governance nightmare because of the very large number of interactions that local economic development officials must maintain.

The emergence of the post-industrial society has also driven changes in the developmental state so that in some national contexts we can now see the contours of a post-developmental state. Some of the defining features of the developmental state remain in this model of governance while others are more muted. For instance, privatisation of state-owned companies and service providers has been implemented in Japan. Furthermore, post-developmental state Asian countries, such as Cambodia, and even the still somewhat secluded Myanmar (see, Farrelly and Win, Chap. 5 of this volume), have improved their inward globalisation and opened up to the rest of the world. Economic strength remains closely linked to national autonomy and security, thus countries that generated a debt during the financial crisis have for the most part paid off that debt.

Are there similarities or convergences among Asia, Europe and the United States in terms of policy challenges? If the adoption of overseas ideas is less a matter of fad and fashion and more a process of inserting ideas, concepts and models that have proven able to address similar problems as those facing your own nation, what are the key challenges facing contemporary countries, and what is the potential for learning?

In the local public sector, that is to say local authorities, the gradual shift towards a post-industrial economy should be felt mainly in terms of a shifting agenda, from primarily economic issues towards service areas such as the environment, child care, care of the elderly, and immigration. To what extent do we see that happening in the Asian region? A study conducted in 2006 surveyed city managers in Japan, Sweden and the United States to indicate what they see as the most significant challenges facing their respective cities (Pierre 2013). Table 13.1 presents their responses to a set of such challenges.

Judging by what the city managers define as the most salient problems facing their cities, the urban policy agenda at this time was a "grab bag" of challenges, some of which are typical to post-industrial politics and some of which are typical to the industrial society. Japan scores high on demographic challenges and local environmental issues but also in regard to classic industrial issues like a weak local tax base, declining local industries and efficiency problems in local service delivery.

Table 13.1 Challenges to local governments in Japan, Sweden and the United States

Percentage of city managers who identified various challenges as a "major problem"(2006) (percentages)

	Japan	*Sweden*	*United States*
Protecting the local environment	47.9	4.5	33.3
A weaker local tax base	84.0	47.1	26.7
Citizens' service expectations	49.7	49.5	51.2
Increasing unemployment	27.5	44.8	8.4
Increasing number of elderly people	80.7	53.8	20.5
Declining local industries	55.1	17.6	18.1
Ethnic diversity, immigration	4.3	6.2	20.0
Weak political leadership	6.0	21.1	14.0
Inefficiencies in service production	32.9	7.2	9.0
Increasing wages for city employees	31.5	11.9	28.5
Size of local authority is too small	10.9	27.9	6.8
N	487	206	664

Note The survey item was "Which are the main challenges and problems confronting the city today?" The response alternatives were "major problem", "minor problem", "not a problem" and "irrelevant". Adapted from Pierre (2013)

It should be noted that Japan is to some extent an outlier in international comparisons on these matters. It accepts extremely few immigrants; fertility is very low by most international standards; and life expectancy is high, posing a significant burden on the public sector. Nevertheless, it appears as if in 2006 the emergent, post-industrial issues had not replaced the industrial-economy issues but were rather layered upon them. In addition, many of the perhaps most obvious post-industrial issues—those that relate to gender, identity, mobility, the environment, and safety and security just to name a few—are not part of the local government jurisdiction in many countries but are addressed primarily by central government.

All of that having been said, it would appear as if the developmental state model of economic governance is not ideally designed to tackle the core issues of post-industrial society. It is specifically geared to promote economic development in an industrial economy characterised by few but large industrial conglomerates. Secondly, post-industrial politics is less about economic development compared to an industrial era. Certainly, economic growth remains high on the agenda but this does not enjoy the same prominence as in times past. This also applies to the institutions charged with coordinating economic development. In Japan, MITI's *primus inter pares* position among the ministries during the high-growth era evaporated when other issues, primarily environmental protection, gained more political attention and MITI to some extent became part of the problem rather than the solution (Pierre and Park 1997).

The data in Table 13.1 does not suggest that there are significant opportunities for learning among the three jurisdictions from which the data is extracted. To some extent this is due to differences in the jurisdiction and tasks which cities are given in the three countries. However, when there is convergence in terms of responsibility there has indeed been exchange of knowledge and concepts. For instance, Japan and Sweden are both facing a major increase in the percentage of elderly and have been engaged in extensive exchange of ideas and models for providing service to that cohort (for example, during a visit to a service facility in Sweden by the Japanese Emperor Akihito in 2000).

Policy Diffusion: Japan's Export and Import of Policymaking and Institutional Arrangements

The notion of the Asian Century implies, to some at least, the idea that given the increasing economic and political gravity towards Asia there would also be a diffusion of policy and policymaking arrangements from Asia to the Western world. In a spirit of policy learning, countries outside Asia should adopt the policy and institutional features of the Asian development state model in order to boost their economic development. A somewhat less encompassing view on inter-regional learning suggests that even if Western governments see little benefit in adopting policy strategies from the Asian region, such exchanges could still offer opportunities for evaluating their own policy strategies and for reflecting on what the Asian Century means in terms of policymaking and governance and the challenges and opportunities that this transformation brings (Bice and Sullivan 2014).

In the 1970s and 1980s aspiring corporate leaders in Europe and the United States would read the Japanese *samurai* literature to demystify the psyche of their competitors and learn "how they do it". There was also a debate about the virtues of a national industrial policy which some US observers believed gave Japan a competitive edge over the US where such policies are not generally held in high esteem (Graham 1992; Nester 1997).

In more recent discussions the main issues derived from the Asian Century concept revolve around the ascendance of China in economic and military terms (Bice and Sullivan 2014). It would appear as if the West has very little to learn from Asian countries in terms of policy processes or societal consultation. The "West" is, however, just as heterogeneous as "Asia" and as we discussed earlier there are many similarities between Europe and the Asian developmental states in terms of their economic governance.

If the United States and Asian countries like China and Japan in many respects represent opposite ends of the governance spectrum, the prospects for learning and exchange of ideas between Europe and Asia seems more likely. Indeed, the diffusion of ideas, institutional roles and development strategies between these regions has a long history. Some of the institutional features underpinning the "Japanese miracle" in the 1960s and 1970s were replicas of European models of administrative and economic organisation brought to Japan during the Meiji restoration in the 1860s (Johnson 1982; Okimoto 1988).

Indeed, as Hoshino (1996) argues, emulating Western administrative practices and organisations was a key element of modernisation as a form of adaptation to Japan's changing international environment. Ito Hirubumi, one of the Meiji oligarchs, for example, was strongly influenced by the Prussian model of military and bureaucratic organisation, "which he saw as a route to Western rationality and modernity but also as an alternative to Anglo-Saxon liberalism" (Woo-Cummings 2005, p. 100). Hirubumi played a key role in making the Prussian-style of bureaucracy "the absolute, unassailable base and center of political power in the state system" (ibid; Woo-Cummings 1995).

Moreover, key features of macro-economic and financial governance such as Keynesian ideas emerged more or less simultaneously in different parts of the world as functional responses to economic downturn (Westney 1987). Again, this pattern raises the question of whether there was a diffusion of ideas or whether policy was mainly a functional response to similar problems. The functionality argument is sustained by the significant differences in the embeddedness of the economy in domestic or regional culture and mutual expectations between state and market in terms of coordination, risk management, accommodation and regulation. Such cultural embeddedness of economic governance has been the focus of extensive recent comparative research (see, for instance, Albert 1993; Hall and Soskice 2001; Pierre 2015).

The diffusion of Asian Century norms, policy objectives and organisational arrangements would suggest that these arrangements should travel fairly easily across national and jurisdictional boundaries, but their relevance was greater in the industrial era than it is today. Also, cultural embeddedness would suggest that diffusion is difficult to achieve. All of this begs the question of whether there are policy models related to a post-industrial society that countries seek to adopt from successful regions, and, if so, what are the key components of those models?

Conclusion

There are three broad conclusions that we can draw from the preceding analysis. First, in terms of governing the economy, Europe and Japan have had a rather similar journey through the postwar years, rebuilding and modernising a vast industrial sector. These projects have been conducted in political, economic and social terrains that are not terribly different from each other. Both contexts accord a leading role to the state; both tend to take the long-term view when it comes to economic growth; and both acknowledge that managing change is fundamental to economic development and therefore requires the involvement of key strategic partners in their governance. The two regions differ in the degree of state centrality and also in the degree to which they associate national autonomy with economic prosperity. This pattern would suggest that the functionality explanation is more important than culture, i.e. similarities in challenges lead to similarities in responses, regardless of cultural differences.

Secondly, given the cultural embeddedness of economic governance, the prospects of policy diffusion would appear limited. In a policy area where trust and expectations are as important as regulation or legislation, the likelihood of successfully introducing new governance arrangements would appear small. Such reform would require extensive deliberation and adaptation. Incidentally, this observation speaks volumes about the global diffusion of market-based public management models which have had quite mixed success (see, e.g. Manning 2001; Schick 1998).

A final observation is that while different versions of the developmental state model—the leading economic governance model in postwar

Asia—were a vehicle facilitating unsurpassed economic growth, the model's social and economic underpinnings were such that it is less likely to be equally efficient in governing post-industrial economies. The model emerged prior to economic globalisation and drew on peak-level involvement by organised interests, primarily from the corporate side. With the Japanese *keiretsu* significantly weakened, or at least less visible (but see Aoki and Lennerfors 2013; Matous and Yasuyuki 2015), the bureaucracy would face a far more complex situation if it tried to reinstall its authority and expect submission from all major players in the Japanese economy.

These findings do not make the current growth of the significance of the Asian region any less interesting or important to Western policymakers and public servants. If nothing else, Asia is emerging as the region of considerable gravity in all major respects and other regions have little choice but to engage with it. How and with what outcomes that engagement evolves will obviously differ.

References

Albert, M. (1993). *Capitalism against capitalism*. London: Whurr.

Amyx, J. A. (2004). *Japan's financial crisis: Institutional rigidity and reluctant change*. Princeton, NJ: Princeton University.

Aoki, K., & Lennerfors, T. L. (2013). Whither Japanese *Keiretsu*? The transformation of vertical *keiretsu* in Toyota, Nissan and Honda 1991–2011. *Asia Pacific Business Review, 19,* 70–84.

Bice, S., & Sullivan, H. (2014). Public policy studies in the 'Asian Century': New orientations, challenges, and opportunities. *Governance: An International Journal of Policy, Administration, and Institutions, 27*(4), 539–544.

Brahm, R. (1995). National targeting policies, high-technology industries, and excessive competition. *Strategic Management Journal, 16*(S1), 71–91.

Campbell, J., Hollingsworth, J. R., & Lindberg, L. N. (Eds.). (1991). *Governance of the American economy*. Cambridge: Cambridge University.

Cole, A. (2008). *Governing and governance in France*. Cambridge: Cambridge University.

Dyson, K. H. F. (1980). *The state tradition in Western Europe*. Oxford: Oxford University.

Eckes, Jr., A. E., & Zeiler, T. W. (2003). *Globalization and the American Century*. Cambridge: Cambridge University.

Fields, K. J. (2012). Not of a piece: Developmental states, industrial policy, and evolving patterns of capitalism in Japan, Korea and Taiwan. In A. Walter & X. Zhang (Eds.), *East Asian capitalism: Diversity, continuity, and change* (pp. 46–67). Oxford: Oxford University.

Graham, O. L. (1992). *Losing time: The industrial policy debate*. Cambridge, MA: Harvard University.

Hall, P. A. (1986). *Governing the economy: The politics of state intervention in Britain and France*. Oxford: Oxford University Press.

Hall, P. A., & Soskice, D. (Eds.). (2001). *Varieties of capitalism: The institutional foundations of comparative advantage*. Oxford: Oxford University Press.

Hoshino, S. (1996). Japanese local government in an era of global economic interdependency. In J. S. Jung & D. S. Wright (Eds.), *Globalization and decentralization: Institutional contexts, policy issues, and intergovernmental relations in Japan and the United States* (pp. 359–373). Washington, DC: Georgetown University.

Itoh, M. (1998). *Globalization of Japan: Japanese* Sakoku *Mentality and U.S. Efforts to Open Japan*. New York: St. Martin's.

Johnson, C. A. (1982). *MITI and the Japanese miracle*. Stanford: Stanford University Press.

Katzenstein, P. J. (1984). *Corporatism and change*. Ithaca, NY: Cornell University Press.

Katzenstein, P. J. (1985). *Small states in world markets: Industrial policy in Europe*. Ithaca, NY: Cornell University Press.

Katzenstein, P. J. (1987). *Policy and politics in West Germany: The growth of a semi-sovereign state*. Philadelphia, PA: Temple University Press.

Krugman, P. (1994). The myth of Asia's miracle. *Foreign Affairs, 73*(6), 62–78.

Lundqvist, L. J. (1980). *The hare and the tortoise: Clean air politics in the United States and Sweden*. Ann Arbor, MI: University of Michigan.

Manning, N. (2001). The legacy of the new public management in developing countries. *International Review of Administrative Sciences, 67*, 296–310.

March, J. G., & Olsen, J. P. (1989). *Rediscovering institutions: The organizational basis of politics*. New York: Free Press.

Massey, D. B. (1995). *Spatial divisions of labor: Social structures and the geography of production* (2nd ed.). New York: Routledge.

Matous, P., & Yasuyuki, T. (2015). Dissolve the *Keiretsu*, or die: A longitudinal study of disintermediation in the Japanese automobile manufacturing supply networks. Tokyo: University of Tokyo, The Research Institute of Economy, Trade and Industry. RIETI Discussion Paper Series 15-E-039.

Nester, W. R. (1997). *American industrial policy: Free or managed markets?*. New York: St. Martin's.

Okimoto, D. I. (1988). *Between MITI and the Market*. Stanford: Stanford University Press.

Olson, M. (1982). *The rise and decline of nations: Economic growth, stagflation, and social Rrgidities*. New Haven, CT: Yale University.

Pempel, T. J., & Muramatsu, M. (1995). The Japanese bureaucracy and economic development. In H.-K. Kim, M. Muramatsu, T. J. Pempel and

K. Yamamura (Eds.), *The Japanese civil service and economic development: Catalysts of change* (pp. 19–76). Oxford: Clarendon Press.

Pempel, T. J., & Tsunekawa, K. (1979). Corporatism without labor? The Japanese anomaly. In P. Schmitter & G. Lehmbruch (Eds.), *Trends towards corporatist intermediation* (pp. 231–270). Beverly Hills: Sage.

Peters, B. G., & Pierre, J. (2017). *Comparative governance: Rediscovering the functional dimension of governance*. Cambridge: Cambridge University.

Philippi, C. (2003). Between 'Washington Consensus' and 'Asian Way': Japanese newspaper authors discussing the East Asian financial and economic crisis of 1997/1998. *Japanstudien 15: Missverständnisse in der Begegnung mit Japan* (pp. 281–314). Munich: Iudicum Verlag.

Pierre, J. (2013). *Globalization and governance*. Cheltenham: Edward Elgar.

Pierre, J. (2015). Varieties of capitalism and varieties of globalization: Comparing patterns of market deregulation. *Journal of European Public Policy, 22*, 908–926.

Pierre, J., & Park, S.-C. (1997). The dynamics of abstract and Manifest Institutional Change: MITI and the Japanese 'Economic Miracle' Reconsidered. *Governance, 10*(1997), 351–376.

Schaede, U., & Grimes, W. W. (2003). Introduction: The emergence of permeable insulation. In U. Schaede & W. W. Grimes (Eds.), *Japan's managed globalization: Adapting to the twenty-first century* (pp. 3–16). Armonk, NY: M. E. Sharpe.

Schick, A. (1998). Why most developing countries should not try New Zealand reforms. *The World Bank Research Observer, 13*, 123–131.

Schmitter, P. C. (1974). Still the century of corporatism? *Review of Politics, 36*, 85–131.

Summers, L. H. (1998, February 23). American farmers: Their stake in Asia. Office of public affairs, US Treasury Department, Washington, DC.

Spulber, N. (1995). *The American economy: The struggle for supremacy in the 21st century*. Cambridge: Cambridge University.

Stronach, B. (1995). *Beyond the rising sun: Nationalism in contemporary Japan*. Westport, CT: Praeger.

Vinh, S. (2004). Ryotaro Shiba (1932–1996) and the call for Meiji values in a global age. In M. Nakamura (Ed.), *Changing Japanese business, economy and society: Globalization of post-bubble Japan* (pp. 17–39). Palgrave: Basingstoke.

Weaver, R. K. (1985). *The politics of industrial change*. Washington, D.C: The Brookings Institution Press.

Westney, D. E. (1987). *Imitation and innovation: The transfer of western organizational patterns to Meiji Japan*. Cambridge: Cambridge University.

Woo-Cumings, M. (1995). Developmental bureaucracy in comparative perspective: The evolution of the Korean civil service. In H.-G. Kim, M. Muramatsu, T. J. Pempel, & K. Yamamura (Eds.), *The Japanese civil service and economic development* (pp. 431–458). New York: Clarendon Press.

Woo-Cumings, M. (Ed.). (1999). *The developmental state*. Ithaca, NY: Cornell University Press.

Woo-Cumings, M. (2005). Back to basics: Ideology, nationalism, and Asian values in East Asia. In E. Helleiner & A. Prickel (Eds.), *Economic nationalism in a globalizing world* (pp. 91–117). Ithaca: Cornell University Press.

CHAPTER 14

Conclusion: Five Emergent Themes for Public Policy in the Asian Century

Sara Bice, Avery Poole and Helen Sullivan

The Asian Century holds the potential to generate a paradigm shift in how we understand public policy, administration and governance, equivalent to the impacts of neo-liberalism and the New Public Management (NPM) of the late twentieth century. This book began with the premise that the definition, practice and implementation of public policy and administration is undergoing transformational change in the Asian Century. Globalisation is at the heart of these changes. The temporal and spatial compression of our contemporary world means that policy issues that historically may have been bounded by geography, culture or national sovereignty are today felt more widely by a greater number of

S. Bice (✉) · A. Poole
Melbourne School of Government, The University of Melbourne, Melbourne, Australia
e-mail: sara.bice@unimelb.edu.au

A. Poole
e-mail: adpoole@unimelb.edu.au

H. Sullivan
Crawford School of Public Policy, Australian National University, Canberra, Australia
e-mail: helen.sullivan@anu.edu.au

S. Bice et al. (eds.), *Public Policy in the 'Asian Century'*, International Series on Public Policy, https://doi.org/10.1057/978-1-137-60252-7_14

people. 'Wicked problems' that require policy attention at a global scale are perhaps the most obvious of these issues. But this volume has also demonstrated that even those concerns that, on the surface, appear to be contained within particular borders are representative of global questions and global lessons.

The futures that this book imagines for public policy in the Asian Century require an openness of perspective, a willingness to acknowledge the values and histories that sit behind diverse countries' approaches to public policy, and an embrace of collaboration and knowledge exchange. To this end, this chapter attempts to draw together the central threads of this volume, to acknowledge its limitations and to set out five emergent themes that we believe are imminent in the Asian Century and ripe for exploration by future research.

A Word on Limitations

This volume is ambitious in its scope and intentions and is necessarily limited in its capacity to address the range and complexity of issues raised by the Asian Century. Our contributors were purposefully drawn from a variety of disciplinary backgrounds in an attempt to provide readers with a diversity of style and opinion. In the preceding pages, we have heard from world-leading political scientists, policy scholars, governance specialists, demographers, economists, social scientists, public administration experts, scientists and health policy experts. The volume has aimed to pose different perspectives and open different dialogues on critical policy challenges. But even with this focus, it was still limited in its capacity to engage policy studies from a non-Western approach. Language barriers and access to non-Western policy scholarship were critical hurdles in this regard, and, as Kim Moloney reminds us in Chap. 11, it is clear that there is much work to be done before public policy studies are able to progress from purely comparative approaches or a 'West-to-rest' positioning. The volume was also necessarily limited in the number of topics and country case studies it could present. While the chapters presented here have been carefully selected to showcase the potential of public policy studies in the Asian Century, a variety of potential topics and cases were necessarily excluded. Future work could include such interesting and varied topics as international policy responses to climate change; implications of China's renunciation of the One Child Policy; the role of ASEAN in regional governance and democratic rhetoric in a largely non-democratic region; or the implications of rising Western nationalism for globalised approaches to public administration, among many others.

Despite these limitations the carefully curated contents of this volume provide a platform for an informed dialogue to encourage thinking about public policy in the Asian Century. In the remainder of this chapter we reflect on the various contributions and derive a framework of emergent themes to shape future conversations and research.

Five Emergent Themes for Public Policy in the Asian Century

Policy is Embedded in Histories, Cultures and Values

The contributions in this volume highlight and embrace the role of histories, cultures and values in shaping the conceptualisation, performance and evaluation of public policy. Public administration is commonly portrayed as staid, bureaucratic and unemotional. In its idealised version, it is the most apolitical of politicised tasks. The works in this volume remind us of this paradox. Policy is political. And shared histories, culture and collective values necessarily influence public administration, even when they are not overtly acknowledged.

Conceptual work like that of Wolfgang Drechsler (Chap. 2) and Shamsul Haque (Chap. 3) reveal the tendencies to approach understandings of what public policy is and what it can do from inherently Western perspectives. Here, scholars and policymakers unconsciously position themselves from the West looking out, and the dialogue that results tends towards one of telling, not sharing. Future policy studies could benefit from more intentional engagement with the history, cultural values and philosophies that inform policymaking and administrative practice. But such engagements will also need to be sensitive to the diverse values present even within cohesive national systems of public administration. As Jill Tao's (Chap. 4) work suggests, even where strong and historically embedded cultural values have clearly informed policy directions and administrative practice, internal tensions may exist. In China and South Korea, policymakers grapple with the philosophical expectations and historical experiences of Confucianism. In China, this context informs an attempt to reconcile a desire to return to more traditional domestic values. In Korea, it brings into focus the discrepancies between the values on which public administrators are schooled and those that shape their daily work.

Transnational Governance will Play an Increasing and Increasingly Important Role

The volume demonstrates the increasing role and importance of transnational governance. Whether this comes in the form of international policy cooperation on issues like health (Kay, Chap. 12) or through knowledge-sharing to advance science and technological innovations (Jensen and Palmer, Chap. 6), governance approaches that are shared across borders will be essential. Increased policy collaboration, however, does not necessarily signal an end to competitiveness, nor does transnational governance mean that countries will cede autonomy or the distinctiveness of their administrations (Pierre, Chap. 13). Instead, the increased transnational governance of the Asian Century will likely generate a deliberative space in which diverse but collective responses to multinational challenges are formed. These responses will be guided by transnational governance principles that allow for the flexibility and ingenuity of local responses.

Individual Policy Cases Hold Intrinsic Value

The contributions to Part II of this volume demonstrate that individual policy case studies hold intrinsic value. While our scholarly tendency is to undertake comparative analysis wherever the 'other' is concerned, the value of understanding others' experiences on their own merit is shown by cases like those of Myanmar's first Hluttaw (Farrelly and Win, Chap. 5), China's understanding of urban development (Lee, Anderson and Wang, Chap. 8), and the role of traditional cultures in how NPM models have been integrated into Thailand's public administration (Fotaki and Jingjit, Chap. 7). Reflection on the cases presented in Part II encourages us to ask how we might better value individual cases and identify broader lessons while avoiding or limiting the types of comparisons that encourage a Western-centric outlook. What new opportunities for novel understandings and policy scholarship become possible when we simply consider how and why others approach policy challenges as they do? To what extent do we lean upon comparative analyses as a means of keeping ourselves within our own comfort zones?

Policy Work will be More Tightly Linked to Innovation and National Progress

As the nature of public administration shifts in response to an increasingly globalised environment (Bice, Chap. 10), the linkages forged through transnational policy work will fuel innovation and national progress in developing and advanced economies. Public administration reform will continue to be a priority for many developing economies (Turner, Chap. 9), as they seek to leverage the successes seen in other states while also carving out individualised approaches to support their evolving administrations (Fotaki, Chap. 7).

The combined work of this volume shows that a shift from traditional West-to-the-rest policy transfer approaches to more deliberative models that support policy co-creation and exchange will be critical to the next generation of public policy. These shifts will require strong commitment to relationship-building, awareness of unconscious biases and strong transnational governance structures necessary to support complex policy development and decision-making. More deliberate and systematic collaboration across the places and spaces of public policy is necessary if policymakers are to be able to meet successfully the challenges posed in the Asian Century.

The Role of the Public Service will be Transformed

Part III's focus on the future of public policy and administration in the Asian Century reveals that considerable changes are underway in terms of organisational environments, reform policies and public service roles. These changes are driven by both reactive and proactive forces. On the one hand, cases like those in Chap. 7 (Fotaki and Jingjit) and Chap. 9 (Turner) suggest adoption of alternative models and public service reform in direct response to modernisation efforts that are conflated with Westernisation.

On the other hand, the need for public administrators to respond effectively to complex, global policy environments is encouraging the development of new skills, knowledge, experiences and attitudes (Bice, Chap. 10). While commonalities and divergences between countries will continue strongly to influence institutional structures and organisational environments, the demands of policymaking in the Asian Century will also place renewed emphasis on the similarities among administrative environments, especially the ways in which policymakers might leverage these similarities for shared policy solutions.

Global Policy and Administration During a Rise in Nationalism

The Asian Century so far is proving to be a period of great transformation and deep contradiction. At no time in history have individual countries been more tightly interconnected by a need to respond cooperatively to wicked policy problems. At the same time, a rise in populist leadership and a return to nationalism in countries as diverse as the United States, the Philippines, Austria, Indonesia, Denmark and the UK signal an ideological rejection of globalisation. Despite a growing insularity, these countries and others will continue to face crucial policy challenges and opportunities that reflect their global interconnectedness and demand collaborative responses. What can considerations of public policy in the Asian Century contribute during this time of polemical politics? How can attention to divergent histories, cultures and values espoused in this volume be used as a means of encouraging interaction, rather than closing off the 'other'?

A return to nationalist thinking raises key challenges linked to the potential futures imagined in this book. Firstly, an expanding and changing role of the public administration will never negate the importance of a strong core policy and administrative function for individual states. But a concentration on strength at home does not have to come at the expense of relationships abroad. The work of this book demonstrates that policy and administrative systems require investment—in time, resources, intellectual and human capital—beyond domestic borders, if they are to respond to the demands and opportunities outlined in the book.

Secondly, these concerns are directly linked to the issue of how a 'core function' for public policy and administration is defined. And this takes us full circle to the concerns that opened this book: that of the taken-for-granted aspects of policymaking, public administration and governance. If we accept that integrity is a major challenge for all governmental systems, for a range of different reasons, then we need to hold a deep understanding of exactly what it means to make and do public policy. We must be able to consider the role of the public service in promoting that core task. This is a situation that is regularly characterised in the

West as 'speaking truth to power'. But is a similar dictum appropriate in contexts where the relationship between the political and the bureaucratic is not so dichotomous? This is where politics and administration butt up against each other in different ways depending on the system, with potentially devastating consequences.

Thirdly, a global community of public policy and administration scholars have a vital role to play through teaching and research to support robust institutions and capable actors. But a global community will only have meaning if it is genuinely embracing of the range of public policy and administration being practiced. This means that we must pay closer attention to the experiences of individual countries, to the histories, values and philosophies that support them, without necessarily applying comparative lenses as a first point of order. Otherwise, there is a risk that the political closing of borders will be matched by a similar closing of scholarly and training borders, especially as 'Asian' universities grow more powerful and regional interactions strengthen.

If this volume achieves nothing else, it is our hope that the ideas contained within will prompt policy scholars, public administrators and others to reflect upon the importance of understanding diverse contexts. As populism and nationalism threaten the cosmopolitan advances of recent decades, those who design, lead and implement public policy have a critical role to play in pursuing policy solutions that take a longer-term view and incorporate our international interconnectedness. Current government climates place extraordinary pressures upon policymakers. These individuals have historically tread a fine balance between ensuring the functionality of the nations for which they are responsible, while also operating within highly politicised realms. When does encouraging global awareness or international collaboration become a political act? When is silence in the face of a repressive regime equally political? And who ultimately bears responsibility for whether and how public administrations respond to the challenges and changes set out in the early Asian Century?

Public policy and public administrators have an important role to play in continuing a globalised openness. The contributions in this volume demonstrate clearly the value and necessity of public policy that is designed and implemented in light of global contexts. Public administrators must continue to expand their relationships and capacities to look beyond their domestic situations. And governance institutions and structures must continue to evolve in a way that is inclusive and capable of responding to the wicked problems that show little interest in the formality of national borders.

Index

S. Bice et al. (eds.), *Public Policy in the 'Asian Century'*, International Series on Public Policy, https://doi.org/10.1057/978-1-137-60252-7

Political

Printed by Printforce, the Netherlands